FROM A CLEAR BLUE SKY

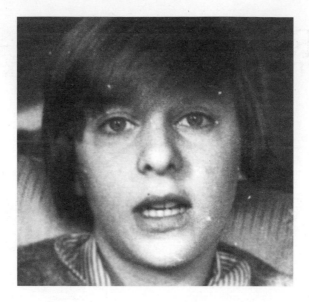

Nicholas, photographed at home, before we
set off for Ireland, August 1979.

From a Clear Blue Sky

Timothy Knatchbull

HUTCHINSON
London

Published by Hutchinson 2009

2 4 6 8 10 9 7 5 3

First published in Great Britain in 2009 by
Hutchinson
Random House, 20 Vauxhall Bridge Road,
London SW1V 2SA

www.rbooks.co.uk

Addresses for companies within The Random House Group Limited
can be found at: www.randomhouse.co.uk/offices.htm

The Random House Group Limited Reg. No. 954009

A CIP catalogue record for this book
is available from the British Library

ISBN 9780091931469 (Hardback)
ISBN 9780091931476 (Trade paperback)

The Random House Group Limited supports The Forest Stewardship Council (FSC), the leading
international forest certification organisation.
All our titles that are printed on Greenpeace-approved FSC-certified paper
carry the FSC logo. Our paper procurement policy can be found at
www.rbooks.co.uk/environment

Mixed Sources
Product group from well-managed
forests and other controlled sources
www.fsc.org Cert no. TT-COC-2139
© 1996 Forest Stewardship Council

FSC

Typeset in Goudy by Palimpsest Book Production Limited,
Grangemouth, Stirlingshire

Printed and bound in Great Britain by
CPI Mackays, Chatham ME5 8TD

For Isabella
to whom I owe everything.

The great events of world history are at bottom profoundly unimportant. In the last analysis the essential thing is the life of the individual. This alone makes history, here alone do the great transformations first take place, and the whole future, the whole history of the world ultimately spring as a gigantic summation from these hidden sources in individuals. In our most private and most subjective lives we are not only the passive witnesses of our age, and its sufferers, but also its makers.

C. G. Jung

CONTENTS

PREFACE

We all have a car crash in our lives. To date I have had one; it happened to be a bomb. I was a boy at the time, on a small boat in Ireland. Three of my family and a friend died in the explosion. One of the dead was my identical twin brother Nicholas. My parents and I were the only survivors.

Over a period of months I pieced together a daily routine without my twin. I was pleased to demonstrate to my parents that I was able to cope, but later I found that the bomb had left me with a legacy of mental and emotional wounds which refused to go away. I kept these to myself. After more than twenty years I finally decided to try to heal myself. By then I had come to two conclusions: first, I could not do this alone; second, I needed to return to the place of the murders and confront painful truths from which I had been shielded as a boy.

With a series of visits spanning a year I pitched myself back into an intensely frightening episode in my life. It was at times a horrible and painful process but through it I entered a new stage of healing. My symptoms started to fade and I found a sense of inner peace that I had lost the day Nicholas was killed. It was not simply his death which so devastated me. It was the suddenness of it; the violence of it; and my own inability subsequently to discover what had happened to him, or to make any sense of it, or to grieve for him.

By returning to Ireland and piecing together the story, I reconnected to feelings which I had briefly felt but which I had not been able to resolve as a child. This allowed me to undergo a vital process which had escaped me as a boy: the letting go of my continued emotional attachment to Nicholas. Put simply, I said goodbye.

Before setting out on the journey, I was frightened. My fear was that by returning and seeking the truth I might do more harm than good. Had I learned from someone else who had trodden a similar path I would perhaps have started my own journey earlier and found a more direct route. This has motivated me to share my story with others who have suffered trauma or grief. The book is an account of the path I took. I hope it will encourage others to find their own.

My story is a description not a prescription. I do not pretend to offer answers but I hope 'the validity of the questions raised will be evident'.[1] Where I cause harm or upset by what I have written or left unwritten, or by mistakes honestly made, I apologise.

There will no doubt be more difficulties for me to face in future; hopefully I will do so better prepared as a result of the journey and the subsequent healing which I describe in these pages. It is the healing that counts, and in this I think there are elements that are universal.

The bomb exploded in Ireland during the Troubles which killed over 3,500 people. By 2001 the killing had stopped and the political climate had changed enough for me to contemplate returning. I knew that by doing this I might arouse strong feelings in the area where the attack happened. Some would be pleased to see me back; some no doubt would resent me; for others I would simply be a reminder of a painful episode which had faded with the years. I therefore proceeded cautiously, and more often than not I found a warm welcome.

The bomb was the work of the Irish Republican Army, the island's predominant paramilitary force. It is therefore inevitable that the IRA features heavily in the story, rather than other paramilitaries, the British Army or any of the other forces involved in the violence in Ireland. I recognise that as a picture of the Troubles, my account will be highly incomplete; but I did not return to Ireland to analyse the Troubles. I went to engage in a human process, not a political one. I went to understand my twin's death. Gaining a basic understanding of the IRA was one of a series of necessary steps towards that.

Following the attack, the years rolled by and I became increasingly interested in the idea of moving on and putting the attack behind me. To do this I felt the need to forgive but I found myself with more questions than answers. Was I capable of forgiving? Whom should I forgive? What had they done? And how? And why? There was precious little information available so I decided to look for the answers myself. By revisiting Ireland I slowly became better informed, and as I re-evaluated my experiences I eventually found the path to being able to forgive.

Some people have been amazed at my desire to revisit the bombing or think in these terms. Some have questioned my motives or found my interest in the details mawkish. To them I can say only that no offence is intended. Some have worried I would open up old wounds. I have found the opposite to be true. Countless times I have been told by those who have agreed to meet and help me that old wounds have healed through the process. Some have mistaken my endeavour as a plea for sympathy. Nothing could be further from the truth. I am deeply aware of my own good fortune in escaping the sort of prolonged misery that many have had to endure.

I welcome the new order in Northern Irish politics and I salute the achievements of its leaders in creating an increasingly peaceful province despite the evidence that implicates at least some of them in the murders of yesteryear. The future of Ireland depends on 'a measured and sane approach to its bloody past'[2] and I hope the line I have taken in this book passes that test. Needless to say, the views I express are mine and mine alone.

While researching this book I came across this definition: 'Happiness is a matter of one's most ordinary, everyday mode of consciousness being busy and lively and unconcerned with self.'[3] To this I add a caveat: to deny self is unhealthy; to be unconcerned with self is the key. I am now as never before at liberty to be unconcerned with self, and therefore to be of use to others. What more could anyone want?

Timothy Knatchbull
June 2009

PART ONE

FAMILY
1964–1979

PROLOGUE

On the morning of Monday 27 August 1979, Paul Maxwell asked me the time. He laughed when I told him it was eleven thirty-nine and forty seconds. We were as carefree as skylarks, out together in my grandfather's small fishing boat off County Sligo on the west coast of Ireland. My identical twin brother Nick was a few feet away, tinkering with something in the cabin. We were fourteen, Paul was fifteen.

The sun was warm, and the sea flat and calm. We were enjoying ourselves like countless other families that morning. My grandfather was at the helm, looking very content. He was never happier than when mucking about in a boat. In this respect he was unremarkable; what was less normal was his life story. At his christening, Queen Victoria had been his godmother. He had joined the Royal Navy as a small boy and had retired having been the head of all British armed forces, a Supreme Allied Commander in the Second World War, and the last Viceroy of India. Now in old age he was still internationally famous. His name was Earl Mountbatten of Burma; to us he was Grandpapa.

A few paces away in the stern sat his daughter, my mother, her feet up in front of her. In her lap she had her little dachshund, Twiga. Not far from her in the middle of the boat was my father and to her left his mother, who now said, 'Isn't this a beautiful day?'

A few minutes later Paul, Nick and my grandfather lay dead in the water. A bomb had detonated under their feet. The wooden boat had disintegrated into matchwood which now littered the surface, and a few big chunks which went straight to the seabed. My grandmother was pulled into a nearby boat but died the next morning in the Intensive Care Unit of Sligo Hospital. She was eighty-three. I lay in the bed beside hers with wounds from head to toe. Surgical tubes led into my body. Opposite, my mother was connected to a machine that breathed for her; she was not expected to live. Her face was unrecognisable, held together by one hundred and seventeen stitches, twenty in each eye. In a nearby ward lay my father, his legs twisted and broken and multiple wounds all over his body. Between the three survivors, we had three functioning eyes and no working eardrums. The bodies of Paul, Nick and my grandfather were pulled out of the sea that day. Twiga's corpse was recovered the day after.

The bomb had been hidden on the boat early that morning by two members of the Irish Republican Army. By killing my grandfather they hoped to draw attention to the long struggle for an end to British rule in Northern Ireland. They got plenty of attention.

The world mourned. Every newspaper headlined the news of his assassination. Letters in their tens of thousands poured in upon the survivors. In Rangoon, Burma a book was opened in the Embassy for people to sign in tribute; for four days people queued before it, the line often stretching far out into the garden. In New Delhi, every shop and office was closed, a week's state mourning was declared. The rulers of the great nations hastened to express their sympathy.[1]

Paul was buried in Enniskillen in Northern Ireland; my grandfather's funeral was held in London; Nick shared one with our grandmother in Kent. Meanwhile, my parents and I lay helplessly in our hospital beds in Ireland. The kind nurses put my parents' beds together and wheeled mine opposite theirs. At night they held hands. It was the first time I saw my father cry.

When our injuries permitted, we returned to our home in England

and a mass of supportive letters. Many of the writers were unknown to us. We replied to those who gave addresses.

> Stephen Street, Sligo.
> January 22nd 1980.

Dear Timothy

This is just a short note to let you know that we all in Sligo appreciate that your loss in the tragedy in Sligo was very special.

I hope that your injuries are now healing well and that time is taking the sharpness from the pain of the great loss of your brother.

There is now a great responsibility on you to help your parents through this terrible year and also since you have been close to the tragedy to be an example to the civilized community and to the oncoming generations.

Soon in the future when all this trouble will be over I hope you can enjoy this lovely part of the world which God put here for us all to enjoy.

Again Timothy my deepest sympathy and try and understand and forgive Ireland for your terrible loss.

Yours very sincerely,

Dr Desmond Moran

Coroner for Sligo Borough & North County Sligo

Having read the letter I withdrew into a room at the back of my parents' London home. I wanted to read it again without interruption and think. It was the first time someone had expressed what was already in me: the wish to return to Ireland.

On the day we had left Ireland I told my family that I was going to return. They told me that would never happen. I repeated myself but they were firm. In the circumstances they were right. The security services had already visited my father in hospital and told him that we would always remain possible targets as survivors of an attack that had received so much publicity.

Twenty-four years later, I did what I had always wanted. I spent a year travelling back and forth to Ireland, staying for up to ten days at a time. I wanted to discover what had happened, and understand it;

and forgive. I wanted to meet old friends and say the goodbyes I had missed. I wanted to stop hearing the sound of the bomb as I went around my daily business. I got everything I went for and much more. This book is that story.

I

TWINS

The heart of a human foetus starts to beat three weeks after conception. Mine started beating in the middle of March 1964. A few millimetres away another heart was beating alongside mine. It belonged to my identical twin. Our hearts beat in loose synchronicity over seven hundred million times until he was killed, aged fourteen.

His names were Nicholas Timothy and he was born at 3:40 on a cloudy Wednesday afternoon in November at King's College Hospital in Camberwell, London. Twenty minutes later, I was born, to be named Timothy Nicholas.

In simple terms, identical twins are produced when a fertilised egg splits and develops into two embryos. Essentially one human divides at an early stage and emerges from the womb as two genetically identical clones. It is not just that they look the same; to all intents and purposes, they are the same. Even DNA analysis will not reliably tell them apart. It has therefore always surprised me that Nick was half a pound heavier than me and remained so for the rest of his life. We never paid any attention to diet and rarely looked at the bathroom scales but whenever we did, there were always eight ounces more of him than me. For such apparently identical children, it was equally surprising that we had feet of different sizes. More precisely, we had three feet one size, while my left foot was half a size bigger. This frustrated my mother whenever it came to buying shoes.

Our parents lived in a large eighteenth-century house on the edge of Mersham, a small village in Kent. From our first day at home we were put in a shared bedroom and dressed in similar clothes. To differentiate us my mother put a small gold bracelet on Nick's left wrist. We were the youngest of seven children. My eldest brothers, Norton and Michael-John, aged seventeen and fourteen, were away at boarding school. Joanna and Amanda, then nine and seven, went to school in nearby Ashford. Philip was less than three years older than us and leader of our little triumvirate. He was more immersed in our twinhood than anyone else. Sometimes the closeness was too much. One day Nick lay down with a headache and someone asked what was wrong with him. 'Too much Phi,' he replied.

My father John had grown up in Mersham before going away to boarding school and then serving in the Second World War as an infantry soldier. His father had died suddenly in 1939 in India, and his only brother had been murdered by a Nazi soldier while a prisoner of war. When my father returned to Kent after the war, he had inherited the family's farming estate, and he settled there to build it up slowly from years of neglect. He also took himself to London and entered the film industry as a production assistant, rising to become one of the most successful producers of his generation, as well as a respected businessman. Because of his work my parents kept a London house. My mother joined him there at least one or two days a week, while she worked for charities such as the Red Cross and the National Society for the Prevention of Cruelty to Children. She was also a magistrate in Kent and this took a great deal of her time. We therefore had not only the love and attention of our parents and siblings but also a doting family nanny, Helen Bowden. 'Nanny' joined our family shortly after Norton was born. She lived with us and looked after all seven children in turn, retiring only when Nick and I went to boarding school. By then she was eighty-one.

One day when we were toddlers, Nick's gold bracelet broke, fell off his wrist and was lost. I realised everyone was going to be confused about which twin was which and I felt a flash of fear as I wondered if they would ever sort us out. The bracelet was never replaced because by then our family and friends had started to tell us apart by looking for a mole on the left side of my neck, underneath my chin. It seemed like an indelible proof of my identity but, like any such device, its potential for misuse made it a double-edged sword.

Our identical appearance confused everyone including us. To identify ourselves in photographs we had to ask Philip. As toddlers, mirrors sometimes confused us. Once I walked into one because I thought I saw Nick on the other side. Later I saw him but was cautious; I moved one of my arms and it was only when my image did not move that I decided it was safe to go to him.

Our bedroom was immediately above our parents' and for the first few years we shared it with Nanny. On the very rare occasions Nanny was away, my mother would sleep with us. Once she was away as well so my father slept with us. Nick and I thought this was great fun because he was obviously an amateur at managing the potty and we felt at a considerable advantage over him.

Our home was called Newhouse and we were never bored there. We bicycled round and round the driveway, often racing until one or other flew off and ran screaming to Nanny with skinned knees. In summer we each kept a small patch in the kitchen garden. The crop which gave me most pleasure was my radishes; I would pick and wash them and keep them safe until my father came home from work. They would then be served on the dinner table. I would already have had my supper in the nursery, and after my bath would rush downstairs and stay close to my father at his end of the dining-room table, proudly sharing the radishes. Their taste was hot enough to bring colour to my cheeks but I loved them because he loved them. When he told me I had 'green fingers' I later checked them for greenness.

At school, pupils, teachers and parents alike were amazed by our similarity. By now we shared our genes, names, clothes, habits and hobbies. We did not share our toys, his were his and mine were mine; and we were very different characters. In some respects we were opposites. He was neat, I was messy. He was focused, I was easily distracted. He was perfectionist, I was slap-dash. He would lie awake at night if he had something on his mind, I would fall asleep. He liked to organise, I liked to perform. When our brother Michael-John, known as Joe, introduced us to *Monty Python* at the age of six we both loved it, but it was me who used to perform long recitals of it for family and friends.

Occasionally we fought and then it was often Nick who got the upper hand. But the fights were quickly forgotten. Our twinhood provided us with fun when we wanted it; constant companionship and total empathy. We made it central to our lives and became each other's closest friend, protector and partner. If one of us were in difficulty, the other would immediately help. Likewise we shared any worries. In the summer holidays of 1972, when we were seven years old, Nick often lay awake and talked of his concerns about the school year ahead. He was apprehensive about learning joined-up handwriting, especially as we would be under a strict new teacher, Miss Barwise. I wanted to go to sleep but instead I lay awake and listened to his worries. In some ways we were married to each other, and in our early years we never doubted that our relationship was for life.

At the age of nine we joined our brother Philip as boarders at the Dragon School in Oxford. Just before we were due to start our second term, Nick caught German measles so he was kept back while I returned with Philip. It was one of the very few times we were ever separated. As an end-of-holidays treat my mother took Philip and me to visit our father at the film studios where he was making *Murder on the Orient Express*. We visited the set, met the stars and had lunch with my parents, but our hearts were heavy because we were aware that in the evening we would be on the school train. Perhaps I concealed my feelings better than Philip for my mother wrote: 'Phi got paler and quieter in usual pre-school form, poor lamb.'[1]

At school next morning I tore open an envelope during our morning break.

TOP PRIVET
  Do not look
  23/4/74
  Dear Timmy and Phi and . . .
  I hope you aren't feeling to home sick.
  The time now is eleven o'clock and time for eleven'sy', try not to be to bad while I am away and I will soon join you at school with mummy.
  I wonder if this term is going to go fast? and I also wonder if you are eating biscuits all over my beautiful letter. I hope you had a nice time at the studios yesterday, with dad.

. . . Please show this letter to Phi as soon as possible please.
With ton's of love from
Nick'y?
xoxoxoxo

The next day a similar letter arrived saying he was still sick and would
be staying away a third day. Later he wrote to our grandfather about
his experience: 'I had a lovely time but I was a bit lonely without Phi
and Timmy.'[2] When my mother drove Nick back to school she noted
that I was 'delighted to see him'[3] and we all went for tea together at a
local hotel. I kept the two letters he sent me. They turned out to be
the only ones I would ever receive from him because after that we were
hardly ever separated. We spent individual days away from each other
but even these amounted to no more than a handful in the remaining
five years of his life.

We took every advantage of being identical. When we signed up in
a doubles snooker competition at school, we played well through the
early rounds but at a later stage I started missing shots. I looked at Nick
and without a word he knew what was in my mind. From that point
on he stepped in and took all my shots. We still lost the match. Another
day I wanted to skip a football match so Nick turned up in my place.
No one spotted the substitution.

We felt the world was our oyster, and when it suited us it was going
to be a very confused oyster. Our parents' London house was run by a
kind and conscientious housekeeper, Scotty, and despite her no-nonsense
attitude and parsimonious character, Nick and I liked her very much.
She indulged us every morning with chocolate biscuits but our mother
had ruled that we were to be given only one each. One morning Nick
was preoccupied with some task and I slipped away and claimed my
ration. I left, hid the biscuit and returned seconds later to duplicate the
request. Assuming I was Nick, Scotty gave me another. A minute later
I appeared a third time; Scotty told me to clear off. I protested my inno-
cence. She was scandalised by Nick's apparent duplicity and gave me
two further biscuits. I scarpered before Nick arrived and caught her
wrath.

At the end of the holidays my mother would normally put us on the
school train back to Oxford. She hated the goodbyes as much as we

did and we would watch her stand forlornly on the platform waving a hanky until she was a dot in the distance. Very occasionally her work meant she could not take us to the station and she would then break the news to us that it would be our father's mother, Doreen Brabourne, who would see us off instead. Although we were fond of our grandmother, she was no replacement for our mother at such a tender time. I discovered this when still a small boy. Holding back tears, I kissed my mother goodbye and climbed into the back of my grandmother's chauffeur-driven car where she was sitting bolt upright. As we pulled away down the street, Nick and I craned our necks and waved. Our grandmother commanded, 'Don't look back, boys.' She was not someone we could easily disobey and I was torn between watching my still-waving mother and submitting to the authority and firmness in my grandmother's voice. I waved as long as I reasonably could and then turned and faced ahead so my grandmother could not see my brimming eyes. The steely inflexibility in her came from somewhere I could not fathom. When in 1933 she had said goodbye to her own small boys and sailed to India in the service of the Empire, she knew she would see little of them again until they were men. Her long life had been marked by painful separations and loss, and these appeared to have inured her to pain. She seemed as hard as nails but underneath, as I would discover in 1979, she wanted nothing more than to protect her children and grandchildren.

Our Brabourne grandmother lived in Knightsbridge just around the corner from my parents' London home. We often visited her and she regularly accompanied us to museums, restaurants, theatres and cinemas. One night we went with her to see the Second World War epic *A Bridge Too Far*. All evening we had been on best behaviour but when we arrived at the cinema late, Nick uncharacteristically forgot his manners and darted into the auditorium ahead of her. Her spindly hand grabbed his collar and without for a moment losing her poise she hitched him back into place behind her and swept majestically past.

Our grandmother joined us now and again at our home in Kent. The longest and best times we spent with her were the Christmas and summer holidays hosted by our Mountbatten grandfather, who unfailingly included her. They were very different characters. She was an instinctively shy and private person, physically fragile, socially reserved and unconcerned with the past. Their commonalities were also many: physically attractive; vain;

mentally strong; fiercely loyal to their causes, their staff and their family. They endured long removal from their children for their public service; were bad with money; had their spouses as their greatest partners in life and saw them die young. Both were the children of Marquesses, both had family murdered in the upheavals of the twentieth century, both sat on the Viceregal thrones of India. The first half of their lives led them on parallel but separate tracks, their children brought them together, their grandchildren made them friends; but it was their deaths together in Sligo that would finally link them.

Given our facsimile experience of life, it is perhaps unsurprising that Nick and I often had very similar thoughts. We frequently started the same sentence with the same words at the same time. We were often asked if we were telepathic. Once, as small boys, we were at home on our own on two different floors when suddenly I felt frightened for no apparent reason. I ran down the corridor, around the corner and onto the staircase. Here I collided with Nick at the very centre of two symmetrical paths which we had simultaneously run. Neither of us could explain what had prompted this and, bemused, we went back to what we had been doing.

Many people could tell us apart if they had us both to look at, but if one of us walked into a room without our twin we would often be asked, 'Which one of you am I talking to?' Aged fourteen, the number of people who could identify us in isolation was probably in single figures.

Part of the joy of being twins was intellectual. It gave us the sensation of amounting to more than the sum of our parts. It was as if we could tap into each other's knowledge and processing power. The year before he was killed, Nick and I had studied astronomy at the Dragon School under an eccentric academic from Oxford University. We had thrived on subjects such as red giants, white dwarfs, black holes, the speed of light, antimatter and the tantalising possibility of time travel. Six months later we sat up late one night with Amanda and described our interest in the topic. She soon made us feel as if all she had ever wanted was a class in astronomy from a pair of fourteen-year-olds. Nick and I flew into overdrive. Each of us in turn explored the frontier of our own understanding and then passed the intellectual ball to the other. The receiving twin would carry on intuitively. The seams in our shared intellectual tapestry appeared faultless. To be so completely on the wavelength of another human was more than fun, it was a gift. I was to realise this only once I had lost it.

At the Dragon School we gently competed with one another in an unspoken way. This helped our academic performance and after three years we were placed in the top stream, and the following year we sat three days of scholarship exams for Gordonstoun School. Our results were within 1 per cent of each other and the school was unable to decide how to award the scholarships on offer. When we travelled to Scotland to be interviewed we made a vivid impression on the headmaster, John Kempe. 'I asked Nicholas the first question and he talked so much that I didn't think Timothy would get a look-in. Needless to say he did, and he was given a chance, and there was a kind of competitive exuberance which was refreshing.'[4] Unable to identify the stronger candidate, he awarded us the top scholarship jointly. We were over the moon as well as privately relieved that neither of us had been knocked into second place.

We knew a bit about Gordonstoun from Norton, Joe and Amanda who had already passed through the school, as had quite a few cousins. It was a ten-hour train journey from London into the far North of Scotland and was famously Spartan. Somewhere in its ethos seemed to linger the notion that *Chilliness was next to Godliness*. A school rule mandated that every warm shower was to be immediately followed by a cold one. We slept in poorly heated dormitories of up to thirty boys. Occasionally the mug of water I took to bed froze. We were woken by a ship's bell at which signal we would have to change into shorts and take a bare-breasted run. When the run was cancelled by snow, ice, rain or the complete absence of daylight, we would cheer.

At first the school was rather daunting but it was reassuring to be placed in the same class as another boy from the Dragon School, Simon Jones. It was also a great help to have Philip, now in his penultimate year at the school. We talked to him for guidance and support and on one occasion he was my protector. 'Robbie', a boy in the year above me, used to push and trip me as I walked into assembly each morning, to laughter from his cohort. When I admitted this to Philip it reminded him of his first days at the school when older boys had bullied him. Without my knowledge, he and several of his mates walked into 'Robbie's' boarding house one evening and gave him a good hiding, to the approval of other boys in his dormitory. He later apologised and stopped bullying me.

By the summer of 1979 we were enjoying the school. Neither of us was a star on the sports pitch so we took up cross-country running. At the end of our runs, feeling sick and dizzy, we would walk around with blinding headaches having obstinately refused to let the other win. As a result we built up our pace and stamina and were surprised to find we could out-run almost all of our classmates. The same dynamic occurred in the classroom where we occupied neighbouring desks and usually scored top grades.

Gordonstoun was not all cross-country runs and cold showers. I adored working with clay in long, tranquil pottery classes which were punctuated by the irreverent wit of our teacher. It was one of a number of gentle counterpoints in a school which otherwise might have been overbearingly rugged. Another was fishing. On Saturday evenings in the summer term, Simon Jones, Nick and I went fishing on a loch a few miles away. On still evenings we were captivated by the beauty of the loch and its mirror-like surface, disturbed occasionally by the splashing of a trout.

We missed our parents and treasured the detailed weekly letters they each wrote. They visited us once a term, and as our father was a governor of the school this gave him the chance to see us for an extra evening or lunch. Twice during the school year we had a half-term break to go home. These visits and the school holidays were like beacons by which we navigated our year, continually counting down to the time when we would travel home.

The 1979 school year finished in July and our school reports arrived. Our housemaster, Peter Larkman, wrote on Nick's:

Academically Nick has had another good term and whoever actually comes top in the most subjects is less important than the fact that the average percentage which he had achieved in all his exams is very high.

On my report, in contrast, he noted:

I was interested to see the competitive streak which he displayed in relation to the Physics exam result! It obviously mattered who came top . . .[5]

The recently appointed headmaster, Michael Mavor, wrote:

This is all most encouraging. Though the fact that they have been seen apart around the school makes identification more difficult for all of us I am glad that it is happening. This will not prevent them from competing against each other in the classroom![6]

Attached was a list of exam results and as usual it made our parents chuckle. In Latin we both scored 86 per cent. In Physics I scored 86 per cent and Nick got 84.

2

FAMILY

When Nick and I started school we experienced enormous curiosity about our identical appearances. We also encountered interest in our royal connection which was through our grandfather, Louis Mountbatten, known as Dickie. A great-grandson of Queen Victoria, he had grown up immersed in the royal families of Europe. His aunt married the last Tsar of Russia; one sister married the King of Sweden and another married Prince Andrew of Greece. His nephew Prince Philip married our own Queen. By the 1970s there was hardly a European monarch who did not look to 'Uncle Dickie' as the 'shop steward of European royalty'. Prince Charles regarded him as his 'honorary grandfather'. My mother thought of him as the perfect father and he regarded her in a similar vein. On New Year's Eve 1953 he wrote to her:

> It is close on midnight. Most people are out at parties . . . but I have just finished work and my mind, as always, turns to you . . . Of course, the miracle of our relationship is that you make me feel truly unselfish and wanting only your happiness. Why else should I have done so much to induce you to marry John when you were wavering? [1]

My father, John Knatchbull, had met my mother in Ceylon during the final stages of the Second World War. She was a Women's Royal

17

Naval Service signals officer in the headquarters of my grandfather, the Supreme Allied Commander in south-east Asia. He fell for her immediately and managed to have himself posted to my grandfather's staff. Their relationship soon took off but she declined his repeated proposals of marriage. Months later, in England, she accepted, only to break off the engagement forty-eight hours later. Next morning when his mother saw her battle-hardened son sitting at the breakfast table with tears running into his porridge she realised how deeply in love he was. He continued to pursue my mother and three days later she finally relented. They were married in October 1946.

My parents made our grandfather a central part of their lives and we spent so much time at his house Broadlands, in Hampshire, that it felt like our second home. Nick and I were four weeks old when we decamped there with the rest of the family for Christmas 1964. Since my grandmother Edwina's death four years earlier, my grandfather had made a point of filling Broadlands as often and as much as he could. He had two children: my mother Patricia and my aunt Pamela who was married to David Hicks, an up-and-coming interior designer. Their daughter Edwina, the same age as Philip, their son Ashley, a year older than Nick and me, and daughter India, two years younger than us, rounded out our intensely close family.

We charged around Broadlands as if it was ours. The grand rooms of the first two storeys gave way on the top floor to labyrinthine corridors leading to cosy rooms. Here each grandchild had a favourite bedroom which over the years became his or her own. Tucked away from view in each room was an inconspicuous hatch. At an early age we discovered we could squeeze through these into a network of central-heating conduits which allowed us to move unseen from room to room. Having mastered this, we tried something more daring and climbed out of the dormer windows into a roof gully to make our way around the outside of the building. Unfortunately, although we had used the heating conduits for years without detection, on the roof we were soon spotted. Seriously worried, our parents decided they would hand us over to the ultimate figure of authority, our grandfather. We sat in subdued silence while he spoke. We would have been resistant to general threats or admonishments; instead he exploited our love for our mothers. He firmly but congenially explained that we were being thoughtless because what we had done caused our mothers so much worry. Feeling he understood us and shared our love for our mothers, we marched out and never again set foot on the roof. It was a master-class in managing the junior ranks.

Broadlands seemed like an adventure playground, and the room which held my fascination more than any other was the cinema. Here, after tea, Nick and I sat in rare silence to watch films such as *Dumbo* and *Bambi* from Nanny's knee and my mother's lap. We would steal back to the nicotine-hung air the following morning to help our grandfather's electrician, Ron Heath, rewind the previous evening's film and load it into canisters nearly as large as we were.

Our grandfather loved to play with our toys. He and my father had bought a Lionel toy train set in New York in the 1950s and set it up in the cellar at Mersham. It comprised three sets of interconnecting tracks and a large array of electric points. My grandfather would take the controls and post children around the table to operate the points. Under his command it ran much better. He got excited when the trains ran well, frustrated when they did not, and cross if a member of the team was negligent and let the side down. It was mildly disconcerting to have him holler at you for not doing something quickly enough, but exhilarating to find a grown man who shared our passion. He was not childish but he had retained the ability to be childlike and we enjoyed his company enormously.

When he admired a model steam engine I had been given, I asked him to help me run it. We met in the scullery next day and while I filled the boiler and lit the burner, my grandfather explained the principles of steam power. After a while he paced the room impatiently and asked me if I had filled the tank with hot water. When he discovered I had used cold, he scolded me as if I were a ship's engineer whose incompetence could cost lives. I shrugged it off, knowing that his temper would pass, while making a mental note never to make the same mistake.

I loved his sense of humour. He shared simple jokes, word play, puns, ditties and nonsensical poems of the type popular in his own childhood. Sometimes he made them up for us, apparently on the spot. 'Nick'las, Nick'las, don't be so ridic'las,' he said while grabbing and tickling Nick, aged five. Turning to me, he said, 'Timothy Titus, please don't bite us', whereupon he lunged, gnashing his teeth and sending grandchildren into flight.

When he asked us if we knew the Lord's Prayer we gravely confirmed that we did. 'Do you know the bus drivers' version?' he asked.

> Our Father which art in Hendon
> Harrow be thy name
> Thy Kingston come, Thy Wimbledon,
> In Erith as it is in Hendon.
> Give us this day our Leatherhead
> And forgive us our bypasses
> As we forgive those who bypass against us.
> Lead us not into Thames Ditton
> But deliver us from Ewell
> For thine is the Kingston, the Purley and Crawley
> For Esher and Esher,
> Crouch End.

Aged seven, I started a stamp collection which I showed to my grandfather at Christmas. He approved. Realising he would be a good ally, I wrote to him later:

Dear Grandpapa
    I hop you are well. Thank you for the nice Christmas. If you have any stamps. could you send them to me. for my stamps book.
    Love from Timmy.

A couple of months later he replied from the royal yacht *Britannia*:

Dear Timmy
    You wrote and asked me for stamps. Here are some from Burma – rather rare because so few people go to Burma and rather

interesting for the family because I am 'Mountbatten of Burma' and my Burmese title is 'Agga Maha Thiri Thadhamma'.*

   Love from

   Grandpapa[2]

In the coming weeks he wrote to me repeatedly, enclosing more stamps from different parts of Asia.

   In the Maldives.

   My Dear Timmy,

    . . . I was walking with the Queen (in uniform) through the streets of the tiny capital, Male, when I caught sight of these sets of stamps. I persuaded her to stop while we went in and bought the stamps for you. I had no money so the Foreign Minister of the Maldives paid for the stamps. I shall look forward to seeing you in the Bahamas at Easter.

   Much love

   Grandpapa[3]

Our grandfather was often travelling but he was never far from mind. If a glass was knocked and starting to make a ringing sound, we were warned as children that we should place our hand on it immediately, for if it was left to fade into silence, somewhere in the world a sailor would perish. After Amanda warned, 'Grandpapa is a sailor so it could be him,' I always tried to stop any glass I heard ringing.

Of all the adventures we had with him, some of the best were at his holiday home in the West of Ireland, Classiebawn Castle. Here we discovered a whole new world. We learned of leprechauns and rode on wild beaches dotted with ghostly reminders of the Spanish Armada. We grew to love donkeys and thatch, stews and sand dunes, shamrocks and fuchsia, pollack and lobster, Yeats and fiddles. My grandfather's relationship with Classiebawn was love at first sight. In 1941 he wrote to his wife Edwina: 'You never told me how stupendously magnificent

* Literally 'Honourable, full of elegance and justice'.

the surrounding scenery was. No place has ever thrilled me more and I can't wait to move in.'[4] This was during some of the most difficult days of the Second World War when he was a destroyer captain, docked in Londonderry for repairs. My grandmother had to wait two more years for her first visit since childhood to the estate she had inherited, which had been mothballed since the First World War.

> For twenty years the only occupants had been mice and spiders. Edwina wandered through the house, across creaking floors, into deserted rooms. When evening came she went down into the village, and in the morning she turned back to England. Twenty-four hours and five changes of transport later, she was in London. Her excursion might have been a dream.[5]

With the end of the war in 1945 came a slow return to normality, and the following year my parents and grandparents visited Classiebawn. They stayed in Mrs Hannon's Hotel in the nearby village of Mullaghmore and made plans for the castle's renovation. The next year, while my grandparents transferred power in India, Ron Heath installed power in Classiebawn, and when they returned in 1948 Edwina wrote: 'A lot of work has been done, repairs, light installed, bath, cooker etc . . . the place quite transformed'.[6] But it was still far from ready and again they stayed in the village, accompanied by my parents and aunt Pamela. Edwina did not mind that the inn had 'one bath with only cold running water' but what came out of the taps did not appeal to my grandfather and he 'declared that he would wash elsewhere'.[7]

For my grandmother, Classiebawn was a refuge. She had led much of her life on public view and had learned to think carefully before doing or saying anything. This made her miserable. She wrote of feeling 'almost suffocated' and 'low and discouraged, like an animal in a trap'. At Classiebawn she forgot all this as she 'shrimped off the rocks and sat about in shorts sunbathing'.[8] Her spirits were lifted by the 'beach of white sand' and the 'multi-emerald coloured seas and countryside with its white-washed thatched cottages', and she described her long walks along empty beaches, over rolling dunes and down lanes banked by wild fuchsia as 'a solace'.[9]

After four years of restoration, the castle was at last ready for use in 1950. In time, money and effort it had cost her dearly but she did not resent this.* 'I felt I should make a tremendous effort', she wrote. Perhaps she had been struck by the family motto which her great-great-uncle had inscribed above the front door when he completed the castle: *Tuum Est*, meaning *It is your duty*. But to whom was she feeling dutiful? Her forebears who built it? The local people, who had so little when she had so much? Her tenants and neighbours who were looking forward to better and more peaceful times? Or perhaps the oncoming generations who might not otherwise experience the happiness and freedom she had found there?

My father's mother, Doreen, was another link to Ireland. Her father, the Marquess of Sligo, was from an Anglo-Irish family with an estate at Westport, County Mayo, eighty miles south of Classiebawn. My grandmother, known as Dodo, her two sisters and brother spent their summer months in this small bustling sea port. When she was in her teens she witnessed a rising tide of violence which became known then, as in the later part of the century, as the Troubles. By 1919 the country was gripped in a War of Independence and Anglo-Irish families found themselves the target of house burnings, kidnappings and murder. One Sunday morning the estate manager was shot dead through the open window of his Westport home as he sat reading. Every element of the British establishment in Ireland was vulnerable to attack, and in 1921 her father's fishing lodge, Aasleagh, was burned down.

In December that year the British agreed to a peace whereby Ireland's thirty-two counties were partitioned. Six northern counties remained within the United Kingdom while the others, including County Mayo, became the Irish Free State. Such revolutionary turmoil must have deeply shaken my grandmother, but by 1919 she had made a new start

---

* My grandmother's wealth had been eroded by high spending, punitive taxes and the economic chaos of war. She furnished and decorated the castle using cast-offs from her former, much grander homes. She wrote: 'our drawing room carpet is one I questioned years ago being good enough for our old Servants' Hall in London and I am overcome now at its excellent quality! How times change!' Source: Janet Morgan, *Edwina Mountbatten: A Life of Her Own*, (London: HarperCollins), 1991, p. 453.

in life, marrying my grandfather, Michael Knatchbull, and moving to the tranquillity of Kent. A lifelong friend wrote: 'I have never met a more perfect marriage; they were as one in every aspect of it.'[10]

Micky Knatchbull was a Member of Parliament until his father died and he inherited his title, Lord Brabourne, and his seat in the House of Lords. Recognising his talent, the government sent him to India as governor of Bombay, one of the most important jobs in the country. He was thirty-eight. After three years he was promoted and sent to the largest city after London in the British Empire: Calcutta. From here he governed the troubled state of Bengal which contained a population far greater than England's. Having acted as Viceroy for nearly six months, he was tipped to be Viceroy in his own right when catastrophe struck. For some months he had been having stomach pains. A top surgeon was brought in and one Saturday morning in February 1939 his bedroom was converted into a makeshift operating theatre. Shortly before he was anaesthetised he received a telegram from the King wishing him luck, but his luck had run out. The doctors found his stomach riddled with cancer. They sewed him up and he was dead within five days. Initially my grandmother was stunned. Soon she wrote: 'Began to realise what it meant never to see my adored Micky again in this world.'[11] It was the darkest period of her life. 'It's like living in an eternal nightmare,' she despaired.

One of her closest friends later recorded:

Doreen came home a ghost. Her friends feared she would never recover and she never did. But she was a very brave woman and there were Micky's sons to live for. So she lived, to face alone yet more tragedy and bereavement, for forty years of widow-hood. Her loneliness was intensified by losing the kind of life he and she had loved to share. It is no crime to rejoice in public life. And she lost India. Very, very few of the rulers we sent out to that country have loved, served and understood her as Micky and Doreen Brabourne did. She lived on with a fractured heart but unfailing courage, hidden under a facade of restless glitter. To the end of her days she found it painful to dwell upon Indian affairs, Indian books, Indian anything . . .[12]

A ray of happiness entered her life from an unexpected quarter in 1973. Ever since his childhood my father had continued to visit Aasleagh, the fishing lodge in County Mayo which his grandparents had rebuilt after it was burned in the Troubles. When in 1973 he opened a fishing magazine and saw it advertised for sale, he swung into action. By then he had made enough money to buy the lodge, its river, the Erriff, and its lough, Tawnyard. In the following years he restored them as one of Ireland's foremost salmon and sea trout fisheries. In her final years my grandmother found herself as a guest of her son, in the lodge built by her father. She must have felt history turning back on itself, but she could not have foreseen how the Troubles which she had escaped as a girl were going to catch up with her in old age.

Whether at Broadlands or Classiebawn, our Mountbatten grandfather was always a great storyteller. Like most children, we enjoyed tales of kings and queens, murder and intrigue, romance and exile, wars and battleships. In this respect he came into his own for he told us such stories from his own experience and fed us tantalising snippets of information on postcards from wherever he was. Our mother would expand on them for us. Sometimes it bored us, mostly it was fascinating, occasionally grim. 'This is the southern end of the Nicholas Palace in the Kremlin where I first lived as a baby in 1901 when my Uncle Serge was governor of Moscow,' he wrote to Nick in a postcard from Moscow in 1975. From my mother we learned how, as he left home one afternoon, a political extremist had thrown a bomb into Grand Duke Serge's carriage. Hearing the explosion, his wife Ella rushed out to find that he had been blown into so many pieces that she could only identify him by the ring on a finger.*

Our grandfather sent me a postcard the same day showing 'the North End of the Nicholas Palace when I lived in the Kremlin in

* Devoutly religious, Ella had established an order of nuns. Drawing on her faith and Christian duty of forgiveness she visited her husband's killer in prison. He was later executed. Her end was as violent as her husband's. After the revolution she and several companions were thrown down a mineshaft followed by hand grenades.

1908 when my Uncle Nicky was Tsar'. He had been devoted to his first cousins, the Tsar's children. They holidayed together and as the years passed he developed something of a crush on Marie, who was a year older. When she was nineteen, she and the rest of the family were taken one night into a cellar and shot. Their bodies were covered in acid and buried where the Bolsheviks hoped they would never be found.*

At home our grandfather would sometimes talk of their horrible deaths but we had no wish to satisfy our curiosities if it meant asking him too much about one of the unhappiest episodes of his life. One occasion stuck in my mind, however. In 1978 BBC television showed a dramatised account of the fall of the Russian royals called *Nicholas and Alexandra*. We watched it as a family, my grandfather in the chair nearest the television. At one point it showed the young princesses in their nightclothes unexpectedly coming face to face with one of the soldiers holding them prisoner. Suddenly Tatiana opened her nightdress to reveal her body to the man. He stared and after a pause walked backwards out of the room, closing the door behind him. Tatiana was shown falling into the arms of her sister Olga, sobbing, 'I'm twenty-one and I'm pretty, everyone says I'm pretty. And that's the only man who's ever seen me . . .' As she was soothed by Olga she added, 'Do you know what's funny? I wanted to ask him in. Just once. I wanted somebody.' Very quietly my grandfather murmured, 'I don't believe that', as if he was defending the honour of his much-loved, much-wronged cousin. He said the words with a sadness I very rarely heard in his voice, and a gentleness, as if to himself, and I felt deeply for him.

As teenagers, Nick and I sat in our room at Broadlands one afternoon and talked about what the deaths must have meant for our grandfather, himself a teenager at the time. We were awakening to the reality of political violence and what it had done to successive generations of our

---

* The remains of the Tsar, Tsarina and three of their children were uncovered in 1991 and buried in the family crypt in St Petersburg in 1998. To prove their identities the Russian authorities asked for a DNA sample from their cousins in the British royal family. Prince Philip provided a sample and was later among the congregation when the bodies were finally interred. The remains of the two other children, Marie and Alexei, were discovered in 2007.

family. It never occurred to us that within months our family would again find itself in a bloodbath, causing an American newspaper to claim: 'No single family in recorded history, including the Borgias and the Cosa Nostra families of Sicily, Chicago and New York, was more susceptible to violent death among its members than the family of Queen Victoria and her descendants.'13

Over breakfast one day in April 1977, my parents let us in on a secret they had been keeping for months: our grandfather was to be ambushed by the television programme *This is Your Life*. Later that month he was duly brought to a venue under the pretence that the whole family was getting together to celebrate my aunt's birthday. He arrived unsuspecting and started to kiss his children and grandchildren hello. When the programme's presenter Eamonn Andrews tried to get his attention, he seemed uninterested and went on greeting the family. Eventually Andrews managed to get my grandfather's attention and in front of a suddenly revealed TV camera declared, 'Earl Mountbatten of Burma, this is your life!', thrusting the programme's famous big red book into his hands. 'What do you mean?' asked my grandfather, looking perplexed. Suddenly it seemed the programme might not be as familiar to him as to the 22 million viewers who tuned in to watch that night. Then, looking around and realising our duplicity, he added, 'Well, I'll be b—' A curtain was pulled back, and as he was led into a studio an electrifying cheer went up. It was from his old shipmates, many now in their seventies or eighties, from the wartime destroyer HMS *Kelly*. He stood and rocked back and forth. I had never seen him more surprised or more moved. His eyes watered as he smiled, waved and pointed, picking out faces from the dozens of veterans from every part of the British Isles, now bobbing up and down in front of him like young men, their medals going askew. In that moment I realised what an extraordinary bond existed between him and his former *Kelly* comrades.

It was after the *Kelly* was torpedoed off the coast of Holland and seemed likely to sink at short notice that he had first come to national prominence. He ordered most of the crew to be evacuated while he and a small complement fought to keep her afloat for the ninety-one hours it took to reach their base. They came under repeated air attack and were in constant danger of capsize. Their safe homecoming became a national story and Churchill minuted: 'surely this gallant young officer is worth a Distinguished Service Order'.*

Our grandfather tried to steer us, even in small matters. One day at school we opened an envelope from him. Inside was a typed letter to which he had added a small note in his handwriting, headed: 'Please destroy this after you have read it.' He had noticed that one of us, he could not remember which, signed letters to our parents 'With all my love' whereas the other signed 'With lots of love'. I took his point and after that often adopted Nick's more affectionate wording.

In 1979 Nick wrote from Gordonstoun:

Dearest Grandpapa
    This is to wish you a very happy birthday today and hope you're very well. I also hope you got the photos which you asked for . . .
    . . . I'm looking forward to seeing you in the holidays . . . We must bring over 'Computer Battleships' to show and play it with you since you haven't seen it since we got it, have you? It really is great fun and we all played with it endlessly last holidays!
    Looking forward to seeing you before long,
    Very much love,
    Nicky[14]

My grandfather replied:

My dear Nicky,
    I must say I am delighted with the photographs you sent me and they are all very good, except the two you took without my co-operation!

---

* The recommendation was turned down but 'the interest taken in his career by Winston Churchill was to prove to be worth a dozen D.S.O.s. The Prime Minster believed that this dashing and courageous young officer was being unfairly held down by stick-in-the-mud admirals who had no idea how to fight a contemporary war.' Philip Ziegler, *Mountbatten: The Official Biography*, (London: Collins), 1985, p. 133.

I hear that you and Timothy are doing extremely well at Gordonstoun, as I was sure you would, and I am delighted to hear it.

I shall look forward to seeing you both in Ireland in August . . .

Much Love

Grandpapa[15]

Nick and I were longing to be back at Classiebawn with him. But it was to be the holiday that would change everything.

3

CLASSIEBAWN

Classiebawn is not a true castle but a turreted Victorian manor house. It stands in a commanding position above the Sligo coastline, near the village of Mullaghmore. The local climate is tempered by the Gulf Stream, which ensures the coastal waters are well stocked and the air temperature is unusually mild for such northerly climes.

During my grandmother Edwina's childhood, the family used it primarily as a shooting lodge. It was lit by candles and oil lamps and had just one bath. Water from a well was carried a quarter of a mile uphill by donkey. The sandy beaches on which the children played rolled into dunes and fields. Seal colonies lived nearby and birdlife abounded. The Gaelic language and culture were still strong, relative informality was the norm, and the tempo of life was gentle.

As a five-year-old, Edwina had led her younger sister Mary by the hand and 'played on the beach and looked for shrimps in the pools',[1] just as Nick and I were to do sixty years later. She rode in her grandmother's small pony trap through the quiet, stone-walled lanes to the hamlets and villages dotted around the estate; but she would have been unaware of the hatred reserved for her family by many of the local population, part of a seven-hundred-year tradition of resistance to the British in Ireland.

The First World War had presented the Irish with a real chance to get rid of British rule. Aware that Britain could not fight on every front, armed groups heightened the attacks that had sporadically taken place for generations. One of the foremost groups was the Irish Republican Army, who fought a ruthless underground campaign. On Easter Monday 1916, an attempt was made to seize power in Dublin. The Easter Rising was soon quashed by the British, who then set about swiftly executing its leaders. Fourteen-year-old Edwina stayed at Classiebawn as usual that summer but the Troubles ensured it was her last childhood visit. Her father, sensing the turning tide, returned that winter, closed it up, stored the furniture and never set foot in the place again.

By the time Nick and I came to Classiebawn as toddlers in August 1966, we were joining a routine which had become a well-established tradition for the rest of the family. On our first visit, an old-fashioned pram big enough for us both was waiting, borrowed from the shooting tenant on the estate, Richard Wood-Martin and his wife Elizabeth. Every year our family spent the month of August in Ireland, and soon I grew to feel almost as at home there as my parents and grandparents evidently did.

'I simply cannot imagine what all our summer holidays would be like without you at Classiebawn as the focal meeting point,' my mother wrote to my grandfather after one such visit. 'Certainly nowhere else could so many of us enjoy a traditional Victorian-type family holiday, in a modern setting, or rather a timeless one.'[2] My mother was right to steer away from the word 'modern', for many of the trappings of modernity were yet to make themselves felt in the area. Televisions were scarce and our telephone number was easy to remember: Cliffoney 6. Kathleen Clancy, the operator, knew who was saying what to whom, and Myles Doyle, the postmaster, was privy to the contents of any telegrams. As the community was tight-knit and neighbours ran into each other in church, at the pub, in the harbour, and at the shops, everyone's secrets were safe with everyone.

My grandfather kept half a dozen horses and ponies which were cared for by the stockman, Michael Connolly. Michael took us for long trips in the same pony cart our grandmother had used as a little girl. When older, we accompanied our grandfather for long rides through the woods before galloping home along the empty beach.

Our old black and white television set could receive only two channels and these were very faint. For entertainment we therefore played a lot of board games such as Dover Patrol, Monopoly and Risk, and spent hours at jigsaws and card games such as Canasta. One day, rooting around in the attic, we came across a gadget used many years before to send telegraph signals by Morse code. We interrupted our grandfather at work in his study and he demonstrated it, his 75-year-old fingers tapping out code with lightning speed. I was impressed.

At times my grandfather could be very stern. One day when I was about seven, he learned that I had pressed the bell in the dining room and then hidden underneath the table, repeating the mischief each time Peter Nicholson, the butler, arrived and found the room empty. My grandfather summoned me to the library where he gave me a severe dressing-down. I left chastened. Peter, however, never seemed to mind our naughtiness. In the corner of the library was an unused door to the back passage, now walled up on the far side. Peter told us that Irish fairies, leprechauns, lived behind that door and he seemed content when we stuffed cornflakes into the keyhole for them. We were very fond of him and he led a happy team. In the words of boatman Michael Kelly, 'no one working at the castle had any complaints, other than Molly Kennedy, the cook, who had a constant moan about everyone'.[3]

The neighbouring estate, Lissadell, had belonged to the Gore-Booth family for generations, and my grandfather had persuaded Gabrielle Gore-Booth to manage Classiebawn alongside her own family's affairs. Over the years she became a family friend. Sometimes she stayed at the castle and organised the evening's entertainment. A bagpiper would enter the dining room and usher everyone into the hall where Peter Nicholson's cousin, Peter Mullaney, would be playing the fiddle and Gabrielle would lead everyone in Irish dances. My grandfather would tap his feet to the sound of the music before getting up and dancing 'an old time waltz'.[4] Unlike Lissadell, Classiebawn did not have a piano, which meant we were spared the sound of Gabrielle singing and her alarming habit of going lower and lower until whoever was accompanying her was forced into making 'a deft switch of key'.[5]

When I was eight, Gabrielle died of cancer. It was the first time someone I knew had died and I was perplexed that most of the adults did not want to talk about it. My mother, however, allowed me to ask as many questions as I wanted and this made me feel better. But I missed Gabrielle's infectious, high-pitched laugh and wondered how she could be at Classiebawn happy and healthy one year, and gone the next.

Classiebawn offered many sources of adventure but I was clear which was my favourite:

Dear Grandpapa,
　　I hope you are very well. Thank you for having me at Clasibawn.
　　The thing I most liked was the boat, but it was sad we didn't catch a shark.
　　With lots of love from
　　Timmy.
　　PS It was very sad not to have Miss Gore-Booth this year. It was great fun prawning and catching so many.[6]

Shadow V had been built before I was born. After a decade of summer holidays at Classiebawn, my grandparents had decided they needed a small fishing boat to add to the range of activities on offer. Ireland still had an artisan culture and for the necessary boat-building skills they had to look no further than the nearby hamlet of Moneygold. During the winter of 1959, brothers John and Thomas McCann and their father, Johnnie, used Classiebawn timber to create a clinker-built cabin cruiser that owed its features to a combination of traditional Irish designs and my grandfather's inventiveness.* She was twenty-eight feet in length and powered by a thirty horsepower diesel engine. At different stages of his life my grandfather had owned a series of boats called *Shadow*, and this was the fifth to carry the name. He took enormous interest in her design and construction, and in the new year of 1960 he wrote to a friend in the village: 'Edwina and I hope to come over the Easter weekend to see the boat and the [castle] alterations . . . and back for the summer holidays at the end of July.'[7]

---

* Among his specifications for the cabin were large portholes with glass an inch thick. There were eight in all, weighing twenty-seven pounds each. The Mullaghmore boat-builder Rodney Lomax, who later maintained her, told me he thought this madness as they were more suited to an ocean-going ship. Their weight and position several feet above the waterline significantly impeded her agility and stability. It seems no one chose to voice this opinion to England's senior naval officer and the portholes were duly installed.

One night soon after, he was woken by a phone call from Borneo. The line was poor and at first all he could understand was that it concerned his wife who was in the middle of an official visit there. He asked the caller to put her on the line. Then slowly the fog of his sleepy mind lifted and he realised what he was being told: she was dead. She had gone to bed the evening before feeling exhausted and had died without warning during the night. She was fifty-eight. He later described her as 'that beautiful, unique wonderful girl Edwina Ashley who was more than a wife to me, she was a partner in every sense of the word'.[8]

As well as facing the terrible loss of his spouse of nearly forty years, he also had to plan for life without her money. Death duties were going to take 80 per cent of her wealth, then 7.5 per cent went to each of their daughters, and my grandfather was left with 5 per cent plus his own comparatively small amount of money. Looking for economies everywhere, he decided to sell Classiebawn.

His decision was short-lived. After visiting in early 1960 he wrote: 'I found that this would cause such distress among the inhabitants of our local village that I ought to try as an alternative to let the place.'[9] Subsequently he began to spend more time, not less, at the castle he had inherited. My family's summer holidays became centred on the place and revealed in him a passion for Classiebawn and Ireland that was if anything even greater than my grandmother's.

By the time the family returned that summer, my grandfather's final boat had emerged from the McCanns' small workshop and been floated for the first time with Tom Duffy as her skipper, a local man from an old Mullaghmore fishing family. Painted green and white, with a radio mast on her cabin roof and a thick rope running around her as a fender, she was unlike any other boat in Mullaghmore harbour.

Shadow V not only took us fishing but also allowed us to travel back thousands of years in time, or so it seemed. Directly out to sea lay the deserted island of Inishmurray. Measuring just two miles by half a mile, it had been abandoned in 1948, after habitation for nearly four thousand years. Our day trips would often entail taking a well-stocked picnic hamper, checking our lobster pots, trawling for mackerel and then opening up the throttle for the forty-minute trip to the island. We consumed hot Bovril and cheese crackers while the diesel engine rattled and whined and behind us Classiebawn gazed sternly down. After scrambling ashore with the hamper, we played among the empty houses and ancient remains while our grandfather told us the island's history in stories which captivated our imagination. On the way home he would take us to the rocky outcrop of Bowmore, where a colony of seals would let us come very close before lazily rolling into the clear water and gliding away.

On foggy days we relied on the local knowledge of Thady Duffy who had fished the waters around Mullaghmore for decades and could pick out a few yards of fog-shrouded coastline and know where he was. Thady had been the boatman himself for three or four years but his health was failing, and from 1967 he took a back seat and helped train younger men to operate the boat. First was Liam Carey, the sixteen-year-old son of Classiebawn's gatekeeper Michael Carey. Later Liam handed his *Shadow* V summer job to his school friend Michael Kelly.

Michael Kelly landed himself in trouble one day when he overslept and arrived in the harbour to find the tide had gone out and *Shadow* V lay stranded with the family sitting around waiting forlornly. Normally he got on 'excellently' with my grandfather but on this occasion my grandfather was furious. When Michael said, 'I'm sorry, sir, but I had to go to Mass', my grandfather did not say another word.

By the mid-1970s Classiebawn was eating into my grandfather's savings. In 1975 he admitted to the British Ambassador: 'quite frankly . . . I just cannot afford to keep the Castle on at the present rate'[10] and writing to the Irish Prime Minister, Liam Cosgrave, he offered to make it available rent-free for 'the President, you, your Ministers or official visitors to Ireland, for a period to be mutually agreed'. The offer was 'a genuine token of friendship'[11] but there were catches. He wanted the state to pay for its 'normal upkeep, such as rates, maintenance, etc'. The Prime Minister declined but said he greatly appreciated the 'generous gesture and the friendly feelings towards Ireland'.[12]

Word of my grandfather's financial worries must have spread locally. Through a Sligo auctioneer, Sean Meehan, my grandfather heard that a wealthy man with local roots was interested in the castle. Ambitious, workaholic and with a shrewd sense for business, Hugh Tunney had turned himself into a high-profile millionaire through the export of Irish beef. Aged forty-eight and separated from the mother of his four children, he owned Dublin's prestigious Gresham Hotel, where he now stayed in the penthouse with his companion, Caroline Devine. He also kept a house in Clones, County Monaghan. He was amazed when, soon after first hearing that Classiebawn might be available, he was invited to dinner at my grandfather's London home in Belgravia. At this stage he had not even seen inside the castle.

The eldest of ten children from Trillick, County Tyrone, Hugh Tunney had worked as a youngster in his father's butcher's business in Bundoran. He told my grandfather that as a boy he had often looked up at Classiebawn on the skyline, but he had never imagined that he might one day live there.* These two men from startlingly different backgrounds and with very little in common got on surprisingly well, and in January 1976 Hugh signed a twenty-one-year lease of the castle. This allowed the family to go on using it and *Shadow V* for the month of August while for the remainder of the year he picked up the running costs and paid an annual rent of £3,000.

It was an unusual arrangement which pleased both parties but not everyone warmed to the new tenant, a man who had carved out success in a ruthlessly competitive environment. Some wondered whether my grandfather was well advised to let out his property to such a man, let alone befriend him. Charlie Browne, my grandfather's lawyer at the Sligo firm of Argue and Phibbs, said that 'having fished for sharks for many years he hoped we would now land a Tunney and that he would not turn into a shark'.[13] Typically dismissive of conservative opinion, my grandfather did not show any doubt about this odd but engaging man and welcomed him as a family guest for one night at the end of each family holiday. He was relieved to have found someone who shared his passion for the castle and had the means to pay for it. Hugh Tunney was polite and solicitous but he did not lose his business head. The costs of renovations, according to the expensive designs of my uncle David Hicks, were higher than expected and he pushed for better terms.

---

* My grandfather loved romantic tales such as these. One of his own stories told how he had stood to attention on the parade ground of the Royal Naval College in Dartmouth aged fourteen, with tears streaming down his face after his German-born father had been forced to resign as Britain's First Sea Lord early in the First World War, and swearing that one day he would avenge the injustice by himself becoming First Sea Lord.

In late 1978 his lease was extended from twenty-one to thirty years, while the annual rent dropped to £2,000.

My grandfather was hugely relieved to have found a way of securing Classiebawn's future. He was happier there 'than anywhere else on earth'[14] and I felt the same. Before each holiday there I was filled with an intense excitement, and when the time came to leave Classiebawn I felt like crying. My cousin Ashley invariably had tears running down his face. We sensed that we were leaving a place where normal life was suspended and dreams were played out, impossible to be regained in another time, another place.

4

EDGE OF TROUBLES

Despite the activities on offer at Classiebawn, as children we begged our mothers to let us go to the funfair in Bundoran. Occasionally they relented and sent us off with our elder siblings and some extra pocket money. We spent hours running from one attraction to another, our faces stained pink with candyfloss and our ears ringing with the cacophony of the carousels and din of the dodgems. At the end of one such trip the family squeezed into two cars and drove away leaving me behind. I have no recollection of it; perhaps I was enjoying myself too much to have noticed. What is more surprising is that at the time we were meant to be under the watchful eye of the Irish police service, An Garda Síochána. Since 1970 the Irish government had been providing my grandfather with security, and after he wrote to their ambassador in London pointing out that there had been a recent kidnapping in Bundoran,[1] the Gardai had decided that we should only go to the funfair if they accompanied us. Despite this, our experience confirmed how relaxed they were.

Security had become an issue after Northern Ireland had been plunged into crisis in 1969, when Catholics in several cities rioted against the Protestant-dominated government.* As Catholic and

* Catholics were woefully neglected by both the Assembly in Belfast and Parliament in London. The Home Secretary spent only half a day in Northern Ireland between

Protestant paramilitary groups sprang up, British troops were deployed on the streets and the situation descended into something that seemed warlike.* The IRA had not run a paramilitary campaign since 1962 and when their leadership and that of their political arm, Sinn Féin, appeared unprepared, a splinter group emerged calling itself the Provisional IRA. The 'Provos' believed that a sustained guerrilla campaign would prove so costly to the British in economic and human terms that they would withdraw as they had done from the southern counties in 1921. When assassinations and kidnappings proliferated, my grandfather was among the prominent figures given Garda protection. Eight men were allocated to the task, with two on duty at any one time. Some were in uniform, some were plain-clothes detectives from Special Branch.

Perhaps the arrival of the detectives fired the imagination of my cousin Ashley. He soon devised a club which became the principal means of play for the youngest six grandchildren. He called it the NDSU, the National Detective Spy Unit, and produced sophisticated-looking identity cards, stationery, codebooks and a flag. When this was raised above the castle one day, it had the unfortunate effect of drawing a complaint from the real detectives outside who thought we were lampooning them. We swiftly explained this was not the case and all was well.

One day our NDSU games brought us face to face with a local nationalist. We had taken up a defensive position on the drive and positioned a command post behind a convenient clump of grass. Ashley, aged ten, explained the procedure. He would stop all traffic and ask for identification. Edwina and I would talk to the occupants while Nick and India inspected each vehicle.

The postman was duly stopped, interrogated and allowed through. Paddy Joe Gallagher, Molly Kennedy's son, soon followed, with a delivery

---

1964 and 1969. The plight of Catholic workers speaks volumes: in 1911, 20 per cent had been in unskilled occupations. By 1971 the figure had risen to 25 per cent.

* Operation Banner became the longest campaign ever waged by the British Army, lasting thirty-eight years and involving 300,000 personnel. 99.75 per cent of them returned alive; 763 were killed by paramilitaries.

of bread and groceries. A family party including our grandfather returning from the harbour came next and was quickly waved through. The Garda car behind was subject to a fuller investigation including a search of the luggage compartment for weapons. After lunch, trade was much slower, and at our command post, time dragged. Then a red van turned into the drive and we moved into position. It sped up the drive towards us and Ashley stepped forward with his hand in the air. When the van stopped an angry young man put his head out of the window and barked that he wanted to see 'Mister Mountbatten'. Taken aback and struggling to maintain our composure, we told him that our grandfather was out in the boat, which was a lie. He turned around and roared away leaving us feeling very pleased with ourselves but also a bit worried: who was the man and why was he so cross?

We later mentioned this to one of my sisters, and after tea we were all unexpectedly called into the drawing room. Our grandfather was sitting with a detective we had not seen before. We felt subdued but the policeman reassured us we had not done anything wrong and asked what we could remember of the angry man. His face fell when Ashley produced a notebook and delivered a well-recorded account of everything that had happened, including the man's description and the number plate of his van. Our mood lightened when we noticed tiny twitches at the corner of our grandfather's mouth; he was finding it hard not to smile. We were praised and thanked, and later the Gardai paid the man a visit. I imagine the worst of which he could have been accused was driving 'while he had drink taken', as it was often described in the area.

For my grandfather such incidents were no more than dim reminders of the hostility which in 1917 had been violent enough to drive away Edwina's family, who had left the estate in the hands of their trusted game-keepers Jules and Walter Bracken. Under the care of the Brackens the castle survived the Troubles, unlike many other houses belonging to Anglo-Irish families. Later it transpired that the IRA had planned to destroy it but it was saved by the intervention of local members.[2] Instead the IRA secretly billeted men in it and at one point held hostages there to secure the release of condemned IRA prisoners. 'If the Brackens noticed anything unusual, and they must have, they said nothing',[3] a local historian wrote later.

My grandparents must have seen the political climate of the 1970s as relatively tame compared to the violence which had afflicted Ireland in their youth. As children we were only dimly aware of the violence in Northern Ireland but it was much on my grandfather's mind. The numbers killed by the IRA rose from two in 1969 to eighteen in 1970 and eighty-six in 1971.[4] That year the number of Gardai at Classiebawn was increased to twelve and my grandfather abandoned a visit to see friends across the border. 'I am being very sensible, and taking care,' he wrote to Northern Ireland's governor. 'Here it is absolutely quiet and friendliness all round and it is difficult to believe that you are having these horrors just across the border.'[5]

Before returning in 1972 he corresponded with the Cabinet Office in London and only on their 'very firm advice' did he decide to go ahead with the holiday. Then he heard a rumour he did not like and, perhaps mindful of divided loyalties among Classiebawn staff in earlier times, decided to check it out. Writing to officials in London about Liam Carey who lived in the Classiebawn gatehouse and had been 'a very great friend of the family all his life', my grandfather said 'Liam . . . used to play with my grandchildren and come out in our boat and for three years was paid as a boatman . . . He then got involved with an Irish girl who . . . is related to a senior member of the Provisional IRA . . . What do we do about this?'[6] A reply stated that the Irish authorities had been asked to look into it and 'would not advise you to put off your visit . . .'[7] When British Embassy staff in Dublin made enquiries of their own, the message passed to my grandfather was: 'If you do not go to Classiebawn for your holiday in August, the locals (for example the Horse Show Team) would be upset and disappointed.' The letter closed with the feeling of the diplomat who had made the enquiries and had himself recently holidayed in the area: 'Even if Carey shows any disposition to be troublesome, he would simply not be allowed to embarrass you.'[8]

My grandfather took further soundings from the Irish Ambassador Donal O'Sullivan and the Home Secretary William Whitelaw, both of whom 'strongly recommended' him to go.[9] 'I shall have a very good holiday because my mind is entirely at rest now,' he wrote to his long-time friend Solly Zuckerman, chief scientific adviser to the government, while at the same time inviting him and his wife Joan to Classiebawn, where 'we are on very good terms with the locals, so there is nothing for you to worry about'.[10] The relationship with the locals may have been very good but clearly this was not universal, as the Zuckermans were to discover during their stay. At breakfast one day, news arrived that someone had sabotaged *Shadow V*. My mother wrote in her diary: 'Sad to hear *Shadow V* has 3 small and inefficient holes bored in her in night and so somewhat wet inside. One co-resident apologised for village . . . Some hot head.'[11] When my grandfather and Norton went down to the harbour they found the damage was minimal, and next day we used her for a trip to Inishmurray.

That year, 1972, turned out to be the bloodiest year of the Troubles, but at Classiebawn as in most of the Republic all was quiet. The following year saw the number killed by the IRA fall by nearly half.* However, in 1974 concerns mounted again, partly due to a well-publicised kidnapping in the Irish Republic. In June and July that year, my grandfather had a flow of correspondence with Metropolitan Police Commissioner Sir Robert Mark, who summarised the Garda's position as: 'Do let him come as usual and we will look after him.' While he had 'no doubt' that they would honour the undertaking, Robert Mark pointed out:

> Whether a posse of Garda would be sufficient to deter a small group of determined and unscrupulous men you are probably better able to assess than I. The official view must, of course, be that if you do decide to go all reasonable precautions will be taken and it is unlikely that anything will happen. But speaking personally I would prefer that you did not take the risk or, as some might say, offer the challenge.[12]

When my grandfather wrote back seeking reassurance about the safety of my parents, who were about to make a visit of their own, the Commissioner passed on a strong recommendation from the Garda that the visit should proceed. He even quoted their words: 'We cannot show

---

* Although the number of shootings and bombings by all paramilitaries peaked in 1973, the number of people killed by the IRA that year fell to 125, down from 235 in the previous year. Source: obituary of Sir Peter Leng, *The Times*, London, 18 February 2009.

the white flag to the IRA and although we do not think there is any real danger we feel obliged to assure you that as many men as are needed will be applied to the task of looking after Lord and Lady Brabourne if this is what is required to ensure that the visit takes place.'[13]

My grandfather was still not satisfied. The British Ambassador in Dublin had telegrammed that he was not 'altogether free from anxiety'[14] and when the Foreign Office 'entirely endorsed'[15] the ambassador's assessment my grandfather spoke to the Prime Minister, Harold Wilson. After a 'long conversation'[16] he sadly decided to cut his holiday by almost half.

He replanned his itinerary so that he would accompany my mother on an official engagement in Canada and then fly with her to Ireland. He therefore sent his car ahead to await their arrival in Dublin. He realised that this would be 'an ideal moment to put a bomb in the car'[17] so asked the police to look after it in the meantime. If he hoped to slip into Ireland unnoticed he was disappointed. Dublin's *Evening Press* headlined his arrival and quoted him as saying that while the Irish government had assured tourists that the country was safe, he wanted 'no publicity' given to his arrival and that the length of his visit was 'a state secret'.[18]

He had proceeded with the holiday on the basis that if there was any change in the security situation which made the Irish authorities uncomfortable, he would 'jump into a car'[19] and fly home from Dublin. This possibility must have entered his mind when a tip-off was received after he had arrived that a breakaway group of the Provisional IRA were planning a major kidnap. This leaked into the press, which reported 'signs of increased security'[20] at Classiebawn and stated that soldiers and a helicopter from the Irish Army's nearby Finner Camp had been deployed. As children we never learned any of this but one afternoon we encountered the elevated security while stalking each other with toy guns in the sand dunes. Suddenly a helicopter descended from the sky and dropped into a low hover just behind where I was crawling through long grass. As it slowly approached from behind, its terrific downdraught blew the vegetation flat and I turned around and stared. After a few seconds the machine flew away as suddenly as it had arrived, leaving me perplexed.

Another year rolled by, and in June 1975 my grandfather turned seventy-five. He had now been retired from the Navy for ten years and was spending most of his time on charitable work. The number of bombing and shooting incidents had dropped by 20 per cent and the security assessment for his Irish holiday that year was much more straight-forward. Writing to Britain's ambassador in Dublin, he passed on his arrival and departure times and added that he had promised to let the Irish prime minister know the next time he visited Ireland 'as he said that he wanted to be sure I had proper security. I do not think it neces-sary to worry him personally but I presume you are taking any steps that the Irish may regard as necessary for security. I would be grateful to know what they are likely to be this time.'[21]

One aspect of security which seems to have particularly caught my grandfather's attention that year was *Shadow V*. He raised the matter with Aideen Gore-Booth, who had succeeded her sister as his manager at Classiebawn. She suggested: 'If you agree to this, we could tell the sergeant [John Hennessy] to keep an eye on her.'[22] From the day of his arrival two guards were posted in a car to watch *Shadow V* at night. Fifteen days later, on Monday 18 August, this was suddenly stopped. Who stopped it and why is not clear. All Sergeant Hennessy knew was that the decision was passed down from the Garda superintendent in Sligo.[23]

By the second half of the 1970s my grandfather's summertime corre-spondence with the police in London and the ambassador in Dublin was a well-established routine. In 1976 he started both letters with: 'I am writing my annual letter . . .'[24] The one-paragraph reply from the Metropolitan Police Commissioner simply confirmed 'the neces-sary arrangements' were going to be made with the Garda.* In his letter to the ambassador my grandfather added: 'You might care to point out to the Prime Minister that I am keeping my promise to him to come over in full strength every August for our holiday in Classiebawn Castle.'[25]

---

* The Metropolitan Police were more forthcoming to the Garda, revealing that along with fifty-six others, my grandfather's name had been on 'target' lists discovered in a 1974 raid on an IRA safe house in Southampton, ten miles from Broadlands. There is no evidence this information was passed to my grandfather, and if it had been, it would have been against normal policy. Source: Metropolitan Police Special Branch.

London had just sent Christopher Ewart-Biggs to Dublin as the new ambassador, a rising star from a new generation of diplomats. His son Robin was at school with Nick, Ashley and me, and the ambassador invited us all to breakfast at their Dublin home. Ten days before we were due to meet, I was shocked by newspaper pictures of the remains of his armour-plated car which had been blown up by the IRA, killing him and a colleague and seriously wounding two others. It was the closest I had come to terrorism and my thoughts often turned to Robin.

Getting to Aasleagh that year, we were surprised to see 'an enormous aerial'[26] on the roof of the house. Apparently the Gardai protection detail wanted to stay in continual radio contact with their local headquarters, following the recent discovery of an IRA munitions store and camp in the woods near Tawnyard where we fished. 'Security is stricter', my mother noted in her diary, but our routine did not change.

Year after year our Classiebawn visits continued, and the Gardai seemed to get only more relaxed and more friendly. Prime among these was a detective called Jim Kelly. In August 1977 Nick wrote in his diary: 'Had a bath then saw Jim Kelly at 10.00pm in the kitchen. He let us see his machine gun; v. interesting.' I too was grimly fascinated as I handled the weapon and Jim described how he was trained to enter a building and, aiming low, use short bursts to 'clear' rooms. Never had 'clearing rooms' sounded so interesting.

The only drama of our 1978 holiday occurred on the very first afternoon. Fionn McArthur, a recent school-leaver from Sligo, was looking after *Shadow V* that summer. As he walked into the harbour he noticed the boat seemed to be low in the water. On reaching her he found water up to the seats. As he struggled to stop her sinking he grabbed the radio and 'screamed up to the castle for help'. We arrived soon afterwards and helped bale her out. Fionn was shaken out of his 'seaside mode' by the arrival of the guards and particularly when local Garda sergeant John Hennessy took him to one side and suggested he 'check the boat over with more care'[27] in future.

In my mother's diary the episode warranted no more than: 'Slept and woke to find "bung" had been loosened in Shadow V (sabotage?) but much baling and changing of oil got her out later.'[28] Next day the Gardai told us they thought it was 'probably accidental'. My grandfather's record of the incident included: 'Saw Inspector Noonan . . . who said "no sabotage".'[29] If my grandfather was unconvinced by this, perhaps his mind was going back to 1965 when *Shadow V* had sunk in the harbour. On that occasion his Sligo lawyer Charlie Browne took statements from her skipper, Tom Duffy, as well as Mullaghmore boat-builder Rodney Lomax who maintained her. Charlie Browne reported:

> When I interviewed Lomax at Mullaghmore Harbour he expressed his grave doubt about the damage being accidental. It certainly seems strange that within 1½ months the boat should suffer damage in the same place, at the same time, and in the same circumstances . . . In view of that, on the way back I interviewed the Sergeant at Cliffoney Garda Barracks. As is usual in such cases the Sergeant was not at all keen on investigating a criminal injury matter but stated he would go down and see Rodney Lomax.[30]

As the same sergeant, John Hennessy, was still in place in 1978, my grandfather may have taken the 'no sabotage' verdict with a pinch of salt. After all, holes had been bored in *Shadow V* in 1972, an unquestionably criminal act, but no investigation had been forthcoming then.

When we left Classiebawn in 1978 we got the distinct impression that the Gardai were more relaxed than ever. My grandfather went ahead accompanied by Gardai for a meeting in Dublin. When the time came for us to leave we found the rest of the Gardai had already disappeared. While this felt liberating, it also seemed odd. After so many summers when they had been eye-catchingly present, now they seemed conspicuous by their absence. My mother noted in her diary: 'for once, no police escort'.

It was Friday 3 August 1979 when Philip, Nick and I helped our parents pack the family Peugeot in London for our annual trip to Classiebawn. After lunch my grandfather arrived, and by the time we set off at 3:30pm, a mass of thick storm clouds had rolled over London. The streets were eerily dark. Shops and offices switched on their lights, and street lamps flickered automatically into life. Then an exceptionally violent thunderstorm unleashed itself. As lightning and thunder set in, the roads were lit up by headlights. I was thrilled by the spectacle and pleased to have a distraction from the long journey ahead through north London and across nine counties of England to Liverpool where we would catch the ferry to Dublin. In her cabin that night my mother wrote in her diary how she hated leaving in summer weather 'knowing it will be nearly autumn on return'.

Unbeknown to us, a novel was published that week in New York. The central character was a fictitious lord who was a cousin of the Queen and 'loved Ireland and its people and spent a lot of time there'.* The story described an IRA plot to blow him up in his boat. When its author had talks with a British publisher, he was asked to alter some of the details because the target sounded 'too much like Lord Mountbatten'.[31]

Three weeks before we arrived at Classiebawn, the police in Northern Ireland arrested two IRA suspects on Lough Ross in a cabin cruiser loaded with radio-control equipment. They had no reason to make any connection to Mullaghmore. The arrests were made ten miles from the County Monaghan home of one of the IRA's top bomb-makers, Thomas McMahon, but again this would not have set any alarm bells ringing in connection to my grandfather's safety.

As we steamed across the Irish Sea we were enormously excited. We had met up with our cousins Ashley, Edwina and India and their mother, Pamela. Also on board was our brother Norton who had recently undergone jaw surgery and was coming to Classiebawn for a week's convalescence.

As usual, my grandfather had planned the trip meticulously. In early July he sent 'the usual routine letters'[32] about security. One was to the new head of Scotland Yard, Sir David McNee who replied: 'Please be

---

* *The November Man* was the first novel of former Chicago journalist Bill Granger who had twice visited Northern Ireland in the early 1970s. It was republished in the US by Ballantine Books in October 1979 as a mass market paperback, and in the UK by New English Library of London in 1981. Granger later wrote a series of *November Man* novels.

assured that all the necessary arrangements will be made as in previous years for your visit to Classiebawn Castle.'[33] Telephone calls and letters between Scotland Yard and my grandfather's private secretary, John Barratt, followed.

The security situation in Ireland did not appear to have changed much in the previous year but the Garda protection detail had grown again. In 1979, twenty-eight men were provided to mount a day-and-night guard at Classiebawn with a further twelve at Aasleagh, my parents' fishing lodge in County Galway.

A combination of factors seems to have satisfied the authorities that my grandfather's security was adequate. They were aware that even in the most turbulent period of the Troubles he had been untouched. In the intervening years there had been a reduction of almost three-quarters in IRA killings.* Furthermore the IRA had rarely mounted an operation in the rural west of Ireland. Additionally my grandfather was now of increasing frailty and fading influence. It seemed that although he continued to be a possible target, any danger was diminishing.

As well as writing to Scotland Yard, my grandfather wrote to the ambassador in Dublin, Robin Haydon. The ambassador replied that he was 'so glad' that we were all going to Classiebawn again and invited us all to breakfast; a member of his staff would meet us at the docks in Dublin. He promised 'to let the Garda, Department of Foreign Affairs and the [Irish Prime Minister's] office know your plans as usual' and asked for more details of the family group, cars 'and so on'. Most of these questions were routine and were handled by my grandfather's private secretary but they included one rather odd inquiry. The embassy was concerned to know if 'Ted', a chef from Dublin, would be at the castle that month as he had been in August of the year before.[34] The answer was no. We duly arrived in Ireland and breakfasted with the ambassador. Later my grandfather wrote to thank him and his wife and received a chatty and relaxed letter in reply.

We arrived at Classiebawn in time for a late lunch and, after a meeting with the Gardai, made our first trip in *Shadow V* with a fifteen-

---

* Killings by the IRA had dropped from a high of 235 in 1972 to a plateau of about half that from 1973 until 1976. In 1977 the number halved again to 68 and in the most recent year, 1978, it had held at 60.

year-old schoolboy who had joined us for the month to look after the boat. Paul Maxwell lived in Enniskillen but had been coming to Mullaghmore since the age of four when his parents had bought a holiday cottage there. He had been recommended to Aideen Gore-Booth by Rodney Lomax and had jumped at the chance to earn some holiday money. At sea we soon found *Shadow V*'s condition had deteriorated. The cooling system was leaking and unless water was added every quarter of an hour it overheated. We checked our lobster pots and came home with one lobster for the dinner table where we were joined by Aideen Gore-Booth. She had persuaded Freda Rooney, the catering manager at Sligo Grammar School, to cook at Classiebawn for the month. To help around the house, Mrs Rooney had brought her twelve-year-old daughter Sheela and three friends aged sixteen, Siobhán Burgess, Libby O'Connor and Grace Ryan. Also helping out for the month of August was sixteen-year-old John O'Grady whose parents, now dead, had lived and worked in the castle. Like Paul Maxwell, he walked in from Mullaghmore at eight o'clock each morning and the two boys soon became good friends.

The cast of characters at Classiebawn had changed a little but there were plenty of familiar faces. As normal the Gardai spent their days in two cars parked outside the castle and at night they came in and used the kitchen as a base. Peter Nicholson the butler and Michael Connolly who looked after the horses never seemed to change; nor did our activities. On the second day a pre-lunch fishing trip by my grandfather, mother and India yielded a pleasing catch of a hundred prawns while Nick and I went to Bundoran to play golf with our father. In the following days we took our dogs for long walks and picked wild flowers, our favourite being honeysuckle. We often went riding through the woods and dunes. One evening we all stayed up late watching a Marx Brothers comedy on television. It was deeply peaceful. The roads were quiet, even the poorly fitting sash windows which used to rattle and screech as the Atlantic wind beat against them were now quiet, thanks to Hugh Tunney's expensive renovations.

In the second week of August, Norton, Philip, Nick and I left Classiebawn with our parents for Aasleagh and a fishing holiday with our close friends Jamie and Sylvia Crathorne and David and Susie

Dugdale.* Before long I was over the moon when I caught my first salmon and then a short while later David, my godfather, also caught one, his first for twenty years.

Norton had already stayed longer than he had intended and soon decided to return to London. As he said goodbye to my mother at Shannon Airport he had 'the most appalling premonition'[35] that something was about to go terribly wrong and that life would never be the same. Unable to explain what he was feeling, he silently boarded the plane. When my mother returned to Aasleagh after a five-hour round trip in pouring rain her only diary comment was 'poor Gardai'.

A few days later when my parents had a meeting with the local Garda superintendent, my mother noted: 'Maybe we can reduce some of the 12 Gardai next year.'[36] Friends visiting us quickly noticed how casual the Gardai were and asked us if they served any real purpose. My father replied that there were two he felt he could especially rely on: Mick and Bert, both Special Branch detectives whom we liked. Mick adored his golf and often accompanied us to the local courses. Bert was a keen fisherman and liked to walk along the riverbank when we went fishing. In contrast his non-fishing colleagues used to sit in their cars to avoid the area's infamous 'midgies'. One evening my father hooked a sea trout and Bert helped him land it. As he leaned down, his handgun fell out of its shoulder holster and splashed into the river. A Garda team came the next day to fish for it.

One day as my father and I were sorting out our fishing equipment, my mother passed us on the way to deliver a salmon to Joe, a local builder who had helped to modernise the lodge. My father explained that Joe's family and ours had been friends for generations and that Joe's father had been a strong supporter of the old IRA in the early part of

---

* Jamie and Sylvia had become Lord and Lady Crathorne in 1977, a title inherited from Jamie and David's father, Tom Dugdale MP. A leading politician from the 1930s, until the 1950s, he was created the 1st Lord Crathorne in 1959. He was a close friend of my great-grandfather, Lord Sligo (Ulick) and visited the family in the Westport area from the early years of the twentieth century until he died in 1977. My father was a boy when Tom met and mentored him, teaching him to fish and shoot. The friendship between the families endured over the following generations and we continued to share our Irish holidays.

the century and had been rightly proud of it. Suddenly my father looked at me. 'Don't confuse that with the *Provisional* IRA. They are very different sorts of people,' he said. I nodded but did not fully understand. My father turned back to the task in hand and was quiet after that. It seemed he had touched on something uncomfortable.

Late one evening I took our dog Twiga into the garden and stood waiting patiently as she wandered across the lawn. Suddenly I felt I was being watched. I stared into the bushes and around the garden in the near dark. Two Garda cars were parked near the house as usual but the Gardai were nowhere to be seen and I suddenly felt frightened. I anxiously called Twiga back and hurried inside. Among family and friends again, I could not imagine what had overcome me and I kept the experience to myself.

At Aasleagh that week my mother's mind unexpectedly turned to her own mortality and she spent 'hours'[37] one morning going through lists of her jewellery and deciding who should inherit each heirloom, something she had not done for sixteen years. On that occasion the trigger had been a series of heart attacks suffered by my father.

Next day she drove a hundred miles to Limerick to collect my grandmother, who was coming to stay at Aasleagh and then return with us to Classiebawn.

A hundred miles away, our relations were enjoying the normal Classiebawn routine, punctuated by moments that were later to stick in their minds. One day Edwina was in her bedroom revising for school exams.

> I heard these thumping footsteps trudging up the stairs and I knew it could only be Grandpapa. He absolutely hated being left alone anywhere. He came into my room and he was completely exhausted after the long climb so he lay down on my bed and stayed there for an hour or so, and we had a long cosy conversation about everything: love, school, boyfriends, mine and Amanda's, who he was rather worried about at the time because one of them had long hair. We just about covered everything.[38]

At 10:30am on Friday 24 August, Garda Patrick Davey was off duty and driving to his hometown of Bundoran when he was overtaken by a yellow Ford Cortina. He recognised the front passenger as 'Flynn', a known IRA man originally from Carrickmore in County Tyrone. He was now working in Bundoran for local IRA boss 'Conor'. Five days earlier Garda Davey had arrested 'Flynn' in Bundoran for being drunk and disorderly. Now he had two men with him in the car. A little later Garda Davey passed the car which was empty and parked by the road, within a mile of the turn for Mullaghmore and Classiebawn. It was not near any houses and he became suspicious. He noted its registration CIT 717, and a short while later called into the Garda station at Ballyshannon. The car came from Carrick-on-Shannon, nearly fifty miles away in County Leitrim. A call to the car tax office there did not reveal anything suspicious and the matter was dropped.

My family and I drove up from Aasleagh to Classiebawn for the final week of the holiday, reunited with my grandfather, Hicks cousins and my aunt Pamela. Mindful of how exhausting a family holiday can be, my mother registered no surprise that she found 'Daddy more rested; Pammy rather overtired'.[39] The weather had been bad for two weeks but our first day back, Sunday 26 August, was perfect and we spent the morning on *Shadow V*. After lunch my grandfather assembled everyone outside for a group photograph. Later my father took Nick and me to Bundoran to play golf. Nick kept the score and our father proudly photographed our progress. We had taken up the game that year and he now called us 'Nicklaus' (after golfer Jack) and 'Timlaus'. At one point Nick and I raged at each other when we realised one of us had left our shared bag of clubs several hundred yards back. I refused to go back and so did he. My father watched, amused. I saw we were getting nowhere and suddenly dropped my club and sprinted back. As I ran I heard my father laughing which caused Nick and me to break into laughter as well.

That afternoon my mother had driven down to the harbour with my grandfather and India. Also in the village was a doctor from Dublin, Alan Browne, who for many years had owned a home in Mullaghmore and had with him a newly arrived English friend, Dr Terence Dudeney and his family. Soon after arriving in the village, Alan Browne had driven them to the harbour where he spotted in his rear-view mirror my grandfather's car followed by the Garda. The Dudeneys were 'intrigued' and watched as my mother, grandfather and cousin paddled around the harbour catching prawns. They finished at four o'clock and were making their way back up to the castle when they ran into Paul Maxwell on his way to *Shadow V*. My grandfather chatted to him and Kevin Murray, a radio engineer who had come out from Sligo to investigate why *Shadow V*'s radio was not working. By five o'clock Kevin Murray had finished and as he left, taking the radio with him for tests, Paul locked up the cabin as usual and Kevin went up to the castle to report his findings to my grandfather.

Hugh Tunney arrived at 5pm to spend the night with us, our annual opportunity to agree a plan for the management of the estate in the year ahead. In these discussions my grandfather generally deferred to my father. On the subject of *Shadow V*, however, my grandfather led the way. In a long meeting starting at 6pm with Hugh Tunney, Aideen Gore-Booth, Rodney Lomax and, briefly, Kevin Murray, my grandfather gathered each person's view of *Shadow V*. She had been in use for nearly twenty years and was no longer economic to maintain. Hugh Tunney felt she was unsafe and was relieved when my father joined the meeting and backed up his suggestion that in future years a modern boat should be chartered when needed. My grandfather then sadly agreed that when the holiday finished in five days' time, *Shadow V*'s life would be at an end.

At dinner my grandfather talked about a recent newspaper interview in which he referred to his plans for his funeral. Telling Hugh Tunney he hoped it would be a very happy day, he was clearly in an upbeat mood. Aideen Gore-Booth was also at the dinner. She had written to my grandfather the year before: 'It is a wonderful thing for this wretched country that you still come and that you and Mr Tunney have, as it were, in a sense amalgamated. I find Mr Tunney a good man in every way and he so often talks of you all in such a nice manner.'[40] But for some reason she could not fathom, Aideen felt 'dreadfully depressed'[41] that night and could not shake the mood off when she drove home to Lissadell.

Mullaghmore was alive with people that evening, the number swelled by an influx of visitors from Northern Ireland where the August bank holiday was due the next day. At nine o'clock Sergeant John Hennessy saw *Shadow V* at her berth in the harbour alongside Rodney Lomax's boat, and half an hour later so did Inspector Noonan from Sligo. The sun had set at 8.45pm throwing a glorious red into the sky which slowly faded into night. A new moon hung low on the horizon for a little over an hour but by half past ten that too had set, leaving an inky black night. The harbour in Mullaghmore was plunged into an unusual darkness causing Alan Browne to question why the newly installed harbour lighting was not working.*

Away from Mullaghmore, the attention of regulars at a local pub was drawn by the odd behaviour of some men who walked in late that evening. They seemed elated, as if they had won the lottery, but when asked what they were celebrating they could not say. Two witnesses later described their sense of unease, particularly as the men were from outside the area.

The tide was dropping, and with low water not due until the early hours the beach became the venue for a barbecue. Both the village hotels, the Beach and the Pier Head, had bar extensions until 2am. In Bundoran Garda Davey was on patrol when at half past midnight he saw a sober-looking 'Flynn' walking through the west end of town. This was the man who had aroused his suspicions two days earlier near Mullaghmore. He was now with another local IRA man.

From the age of twelve, I had been addicted to reading at least one newspaper a day. One afternoon at school I cut out an article and left it in Nick's locker for him to read. Later, in private, we discussed it. It said that the chance of a pair of twins celebrating their one hundredth birthday was one in a million. We tried to calculate how many birthdays we could reasonably expect to share. We were not prone to such thoughts but occasionally we touched on our mortality. When we did, we usually ended by talking in silly voices as we spoke a dialogue we had heard in a children's cartoon. Two mice, Nixie and Tixie, are being chased. One says in a high-pitched staccato voice, with an American accent from the deep south, 'Hurry, Tixie, *hurry*, Tixie! Hurry, hurry,

---

* A holidaymaker in a caravan reported having heard that the lights in the harbour went out 'for no apparent reason' that night. The witness, from County Tyrone, gave a Garda statement on 28 August 1979 but was reluctant to go into more detail.

hurry!' The other replies, 'I'm a-hurryin', Nixie, I'm *a-hurryin*.' The performance took us no more than a few seconds. Its theme was our own Armageddon: to find ourselves caught in a disaster and be exhorting each other to outpace whatever was engulfing us. Our fear was that one twin would survive and the other would not. We played out the routine many times but only in private because we felt it would be incomprehensible to anyone else. It allowed us to refer to our nightmare obliquely and in a comic tone. Over the years it became shorthand for a topic which we avoided.

One day during that final Classiebawn stay, Nick and I were talking in our bedroom when the conversation unexpectedly arrived at the question of how one of us would feel if the other died. I looked into his eyes and was lost for words; so was he.

5

BOMB

Dawn broke on Monday 27 August 1979 to reveal a flat, calm sea and a clear blue sky in which the only clouds to be seen were distant white puffs. An enormous high pressure system had moved in from the Atlantic thirty-six hours before, bringing with it sunny conditions and a mild seventeen degrees. The strong breeze had dropped to the gentlest of draughts and the ocean rollers were gone. The sea looked like a millpond.

Twenty-four-year-old Kevin Henry had been up early that morning. He was a detective attached to the Garda's Special Branch and was one of the men allocated to guard my grandfather at Classiebawn. He dressed as usual in plain clothes. Underneath his jacket he carried a Webley .38 handgun.

At six o'clock that morning he quietly drove up the half-mile drive to the castle in an unmarked Ford Escort and parked on the grass verge thirty yards from the front door. He was joined by Garda Kevin Mullins in uniform. They chatted for a few minutes to four colleagues, three of them armed, who were going off duty.

At a quarter past eight a yellow Ford Cortina, registration CIT 717, was driving away from the area through the small town of Boyle, a little over forty miles away. It was the same car that IRA volunteer 'Flynn' had been driving the previous Friday morning, and which had aroused

Garda Davey's suspicions when he saw it parked two miles from Classiebawn.

I had spent that night as usual in the Lower Tower Room with Nick. By 8:30 I was up and dressed, a few minutes ahead of Nick. I went across the first-floor landing to the South Room, where my parents slept. Normally at about this time I would hear a 'thump, thump' coming from my grandfather's room opposite, where he would be doing his exercises, learned from the Canadian Air Force many years before. A short while later he would emerge in his string vest and go next door to the bathroom he shared with my parents.

My father was listening to the news on a small bedside radio that hissed and crackled as it picked up the BBC transmitting from the other side of the border in Northern Ireland. I kissed him good morning. I went around to my mother on the other side of the bed. I loved this room; it was bright and cosy. Today the sunshine was pouring in from the east-facing window from which I could make out the harbour wall in Mullaghmore. To the south the lines in the face of Benbulben were throwing shadows across it, making Sligo's most famous mountain look especially dramatic.

My mother was finishing her diary for the day before, her handwriting a mass of curls and difficult to read.

Sunday August 26th 1979. Absolutely glorious day; first in two weeks. Dodo and I went out with Daddy, John, Amanda, twins & Edwina in Shadow V, not at all easy for Dodo and Daddy to clamber down ladder at bow at low tide or over boats moored alongside. We picked up lobster pots and got two lobsters and two crabs. Edwina always loves the boat. After lunch Pammy (organising meals for this week rather unwillingly as I did the first week), Daddy and I had an enjoyable time prawning. Tied small bucket round him as India, who usually holds it, and Amanda and Edwina went riding. [John] and twins golfing. Phi and Ashley to amusements in Mullaghmore. Dodo slept in deckchair. Aideen came to dinner and Hugh Tunney, our tenant came for night . . .

The eiderdown quilt moved. Underneath was my mother's dog, Twiga. Knowing that I would take her out, 'Twee' now emerged, tail wagging, and sat in my lap. The room smelled gently of the honeysuckle by my mother's bedside. She had picked it from the wild and grassy Roskeeragh Point which jutted out into the Atlantic like a finger pointing towards America. It reminded her of her mother Edwina, who had loved to pick the same fragrant flowers here.

My father turned on his electric shaver and I took Twiga downstairs, out through the front door and into the sunshine. She raced towards the Garda car, barking. Embarrassed, I waved at the Gardai and called her back, turning right along the drive that wound tightly behind the house. Passing into the shade on the western side of the house, goose-bumps rose on my T-shirted arms and I wished I was wearing a sweater. I hurried on, hoping Twiga would follow and not do her usual rooting around in the long grass and gorse bushes, looking for rabbits. I kept my eyes peeled in case I saw a mushroom I could pick for breakfast. Out to sea the morning sun was catching the smoothed edges of Inishmurray, now a pancake floating on oil.

At a quarter to nine the yellow Ford Cortina was a further twenty miles from the Mullaghmore area, parked in the village of Lisheen near Strokestown. Two men transferred from it into a red Ford Escort with a black roof, registered LZO 915, and drove off.

Before leaving the dinner table the previous night, my grandfather had as usual called everyone to order, bellowing 'Hotel business!' theatrically through cupped hands. He liked life to be thoroughly well organised. Peter stood by and took notes on a clipboard while my grandfather took orders from around the table. It was agreed breakfast would be at nine o'clock. My aunt asked for breakfast in bed, and Hugh Tunney asked for a wake-up call at eight with a cup of tea. Peter did not have to ask my grandfather for his requirements, they were always the same: a wake-up call at 7:55 so he could be ready for the eight o'clock news. When Peter woke him that morning he wanted to know what the weather was like. Peter told him how beautifully the day had started and then led his Labrador, Kimberley, downstairs and outside. Earlier in the stay my grandfather had told Peter that the weather had been the worst in the thirty years he had been coming. As a result, he had managed far fewer trips in *Shadow V* than normal. He had his usual bath and went downstairs in his boat clothes by 8:55am.

Paul Maxwell was in the pantry, having woken at eight o'clock and walked in from the village where he was staying with his parents John and Mary. Before leaving home he had checked the money he had earned looking after *Shadow V*, in case his sisters Donna and Lisa had borrowed some from the miniature lobster pot in which he kept it. In less than fifteen minutes he had reached the castle and was now chatting to John O'Grady. Paul was in a blue shirt and some ripped jeans which had been sewn up by his mother. She had been angry with him for not taking better care of his clothes. She was not the only one. As Paul and John were talking in the pantry, my grandfather came in and reminded Paul to take a rag out on the boat so he did not have to use his jumper to remove the hot lid from the oil tank. He said he would be leaving for the boat at a quarter past ten and asked him to go and get it ready.

Peter had called on Hugh Tunney with tea at just after eight to find him awake, sitting on the edge of his bed and reciting a Rosary Novena, a Catholic prayer. 'I have made it a habit in my lifetime and still adhere to it strictly,' he explained years later.[1] When Hugh came down at exactly nine o'clock, my grandfather was the only person already in the dining room. Freda Rooney had gone home with her daughter Sheela the evening before to prepare her son for a golfing outing. She was due back at 5pm and for dinner she planned to cook a salmon which Nick had caught at Aasleagh. In the kitchen sixteen-year-old Grace Ryan was trying to maintain Mrs Rooney's high standards but it was not easy. Peter soon returned with my grandfather's poached egg which he had sent back, the yolk surrounded by water.[2]

By the time I arrived in the dining room it was heaving with family. As I walked past the table towards the sideboard, my grandfather was coming the other way. He was wearing a sweatshirt given to him recently by the survivors of HMS *Kelly*. In 1941 their wartime experiences together culminated at the Battle of Crete.

At 0800 hours on the morning of 23 May, 24 Junkers dive bombers appeared in the sky above his ship. 'Christ, look at that lot,' Mountbatten is said to have said, quite calmly. Within thirty seconds of being hit, with guns firing and the captain standing firm on the bridge, *Kelly* was capsizing. 'I felt I ought to be last to leave the ship,' Mountbatten wrote to his daughter, Patricia, soon after, 'and I left it a bit late because the bridge turned over on top of me and I was trapped in the boiling, seething cauldron underneath. I luckily had my tin hat on, which helped to make me heavy enough to push my way down past the bridge screen, but it was unpleasant having to force oneself deeper under water to get clear.' He managed it, he 'suddenly shot out of the water like a cork released' and, with his 1st Lieutenant, set about swimming desperately through the oily water around the wreckage rescuing wounded men and dragging them to the safety of a raft. As the ship finally went down, he called for three cheers for the *Kelly* and, bobbing up and down in the treacherous water, led his surviving crew in an extraordinary chorus of *Roll out the Barrel!* It was the heroic stuff of which movies are made.[3]*

The sweatshirt he was wearing as he approached me was dark blue and had on its front the crest of the HMS *Kelly* Reunion Association and the ship's motto: *Keep On*. From the *Kelly*'s bridge he had led the Fifth Destroyer Flotilla and across the top of the sweatshirt was the nickname he had given it: *The Fighting Fifth*. He stopped and with one hand lifted my chin. He saw my mole and now knew which twin he was greeting. Leaning down he kissed me and said, 'Morning, Timmy.' I replied,

* 'In July 1941, back in England, Mountbatten went to the pictures with Noël Coward. "Dicky told whole story of the sinking of *Kelly*," Coward noted in his diary. "Absolutely heart-breaking and so magnificent." In 1942, Coward turned the story into a fine propaganda film, *In Which We Serve*, and Mountbatten – who was involved at every stage, although officially the film was based "on no Royal Navy destroyer in particular" – took the King and Queen and their daughters along to Elstree Studios to watch some of the filming. Coward admired Mountbatten inordinately ("I would do anything in the world for him") and Mountbatten was suitably appreciative of Coward's cinematic skills. He saw the film at least fifteen times." Gyles Brandreth, *Philip and Elizabeth*, (London: Century), 2004, p. 154.

'Morning, Fighting Fifth.' All my life, family and friends had looked for that mole, proof as it was of my identity. That was the last time.

Another former *Fighting Fifth* captain, retired Vice Admiral Sir Geoffrey Robson had awoken that morning at his fishing lodge in the West of Scotland.* At about 8:30 he had come down to breakfast and told his wife that he had woken during the night having dreamt that he was organising 'Dickie's funeral' and that he had gone back to sleep again. 'Strange thing, when I woke up I had dreamt it all over again.' His wife reminded him that he had dreamt about his sister just before her death in a landslide in South America and encouraged him to contact my grandfather. He replied, 'He's somewhere in Ireland, I don't know how to get in touch.'[4]

At breakfast my grandfather talked to Philip about the school assignments he had been sent home with that summer. He said, 'Phi, you haven't been doing enough work so I am banning you from coming out on *Shadow V* this morning.' Upset, Philip later climbed the castle's staircase and went to the very top of the turret where he arrived at a bolted door. The bolts slid open easily because Peter used this door each morning to get to the flagpole where he would raise my grandfather's standard. Here Philip found the solitude he was looking for as he stared out over the Bay of Donegal and the Atlantic Ocean.

By 9:30 Michael Connolly had driven Paul to McGloin's Garage in nearby Bunduff to get some diesel for *Shadow V*. The attendant, John McGovern, filled the two containers they had brought with them, and Michael and Paul loaded them into the back of the car and drove to Mullaghmore harbour.

---

* As Captain of HMS *Kandahar*, Geoffrey Robson saw a great deal of action alongside my grandfather, who was designated as *Captain (D)*. In May 1940 his ship and the *Kelly* had pursued a U-boat off the Dutch coast. '*Kelly* began to signal . . . with a bright Aldis light . . . "How are the muskets? Let battle commence?" . . . Retribution swiftly followed. A torpedo hit *Kelly* on the starboard side under the bridge, blasting a fifty-foot hole in the side . . . enveloping the ship in a cloud of smoke and steam which rose several hundred feet in the air. David Milford Haven, Mountbatten's nephew, was on the bridge of *Kandahar* . . . "Kelly has gone" he said in horror . . . "Is Captain (D) alive?" signaled Robson. "Yes. You are not in command of the flotilla yet!" replied Mountbatten triumphantly.' Philip Ziegler, *Mountbatten: The Official Biography*, (London: Collins), 1985, p. 130.

Eighty-six miles away in Granard, a small market town in County Longford, Garda James Lohan was setting up a regular roadside checkpoint under the Road Traffic Act to check the tax and insurance of passing cars. Having come on duty at eight o'clock that morning, he had set out alone from the Garda barracks a little later by car and had made a general patrol. He parked in the main street shortly before 9:45 and, stepping into the road, started waving down occasional vehicles.

Approximately the third car he stopped was a red Ford Escort, LZO 915, with a black roof, heading north. It had two men in it, neither of whom he recognised. As he walked around to the driver's window he saw that the car was in a very poor condition. The driver said he had been to O'Hara's scrapyard in Longford looking for a petrol tank for a Hillman Hunter. Given it was now not much past a quarter to ten and most businesses were only just opening, Lohan thought it was unlikely that the man could have already been to Longford, over seventeen miles away, completed his business and reached this checkpoint. He asked where and when the man had started his trip. The driver said Kilnaleck at 8:30. To Lohan this seemed incredible; Kilnaleck was nearly thirty miles from Longford. The driver, who had given his name as Patrick Rehill, now seemed extremely nervous. Lohan asked him to pull over to let traffic pass. In doing so, perhaps from nerves, he reversed into a car behind.

When Garda Lohan asked the driver if he knew the registration number of the car he was driving he could not remember it. At Lohan's request the driver got out with the car keys to open the boot but he was by now shaking so much he had trouble putting the key in the lock. Lohan knew something was very wrong, and he himself started to shake. From his patrol car he radioed to the Garda barracks. Station Orderly John Geraghty, known as Gerry, answered the call and put him straight on to their boss, Superintendent Patrick O'Donnell, who happened to be standing beside him. According to Lohan, some officers would have told him to 'eff off',[5] but O'Donnell agreed to come straight out. Within minutes he appeared in his own car, with Gerry Geraghty alongside him, and said he wanted the two men brought into the station. Lohan asked the men, 'Would you come to the station to clarify your name and address, it should only take two seconds?'[6] They quickly agreed. The passenger, who had by now given his name as

Thomas McMahon, got into Lohan's car and Geraghty transferred into the red Escort alongside the driver. As they headed for the station Thomas McMahon said to Garda Lohan, 'What kind of an idiot is your man when he didn't know the number of his car?'[7] Later he said, 'Maybe there's no reason for me to come into the station.' Garda Lohan replied, 'You had better, it will only take a few minutes.'[8]

From the roof of Classiebawn, Philip was looking down at Nick who was practising his golf swing. His shots were dropping nicely into a grassy area next to the castle. Then one went much further and crashed into some ancient weather-beaten trees. When Philip yelled down, 'You idiot!', Nick spun around and looked up. 'It doesn't matter,' he shouted, 'I'll find it later,' and he carried on.

The tide was dropping. High water had been at about 8:30 and the longer we left it, the more difficult it would be to get *Shadow* V back into harbour. My grandfather was therefore keen to get the boating trip going by 10:15. After breakfast he had vacated his study, known as the Morning Room, for my father to continue his detailed talk with Hugh Tunney. In a house heaving with family it was one of the few places where they could talk in peace. The broad terms of the agenda had been agreed the previous afternoon. My grandfather was now more than grateful that he did not have to deal with the tedious details and waited as patiently as he could for the meeting to finish. Noticing Edwina, he said teasingly, 'What are you doing, hanging about like an envelope waiting to be stamped?' He settled down on a chair and picked up a nearby book, a biography of Adolf Hitler. It was part of Ashley's coursework at school and soon he came looking for it, only to find that my grandfather refused to give it up, saying he needed to read it till it was time to go to the boat. As he sat reading, Amanda walked past and headed for the door of the Morning Room. The long delay was getting to him and the last thing he wanted was for another inter-ruption to the meeting. 'Don't go in there, you bloody fool!' he boomed. Amanda backed off but she knew not to take his words to heart. He adored her and he would no doubt later apologise for his unwarranted grump.

*　　*　　*

By half past ten, Superintendent O'Donnell in Granard was trying to establish what to do with the two men sitting in the Public Office of his Garda station. He had called colleagues in nearby Cavan town who checked the names and soon told him he was dealing with two senior IRA men. As they were not under arrest they were technically free to leave, but James Lohan and Gerry Geraghty were taking it in turns to stay with them and keep them in the station. However, they were not trained to deal with 'subversives', as the Garda officially labelled the IRA, and they were far from sure how to proceed. The Superintendent asked Garda Lohan to walk to Sergeant Fanning's home a few hundred yards up the road. On his doorstep, in his string vest, Vincent Fanning explained that he would be down to the Garda station in fifteen minutes. He told Lohan in the meantime, 'If they want to use the toilet, don't let them wash their hands.' He knew the Garda's newly formed forensic team in Dublin would want to take swabs for traces of explosives.

Hearing that Amanda was going to Grange to fuel my parents' car, Ashley suddenly decided to join her. He did not tell his mother that his real reason for going was to buy cigarettes. As they drove away from the castle, they stopped and Ashley called out to Nick not to leave for the boat without him. Nick reassured him and then swung at his golf ball, apparently aiming right for the car. Amanda screamed and covered her head only to hear Nick's laugh. He had deliberately missed the ball which lay harmlessly at his feet.

At the castle Peter took the post through to my grandfather who was now in the drawing room with my aunt. My father was next door in the Morning Room with Hugh Tunney; aware how late it was getting, he suggested to Hugh that they should continue their discussion on board Shadow V. When Hugh declined, saying that sadly he had to get back to his business, they brought their meeting to an end. My grandfather was pleased that they could at last leave for the boat. When Peter saw him putting on his fishing coat in the hall, he told him that Paul had been in the boat for about an hour already. 'He said "Thank you",' Peter later recalled, 'and that was the last I saw of him.' Turning to India, my grandfather asked her to look after his dog, Kimberley. He hated leaving him behind even for short periods.

From the front door of the castle my grandfather walked over to the Garda, explained he was now ready to leave for the harbour, and asked if one of them would mind taking a few snaps with his camera. He was a notoriously poor cameraman but adored compiling his albums and was determined to get a good record of the day's activities. Kevin Henry came to the front door and took photographs as my grandfather directed him with gusto. Amused, my father snapped a picture of him in full flow and with Hugh Tunney and my mother at his side.

It was now about a quarter past eleven and in Mullaghmore John Maxwell drove to the shops to buy *The Irish Times*. On the far side of the harbour he saw his son Paul alone on *Shadow V*, getting her ready for sea. 'He happened to look over at the same time and I waved at him. He waved back.'[9]

Amanda and Ashley were hurrying back from Grange in my parents' car so that Ashley could join in the boating party. As they were chatting, Ashley put a sweet in his mouth, lowered the window and threw out the wrapper. When Amanda objected and pulled over, they had a blazing row. Amanda refused to carry on until Ashley had walked back and retrieved the litter. This delayed them still further. Refusing to wait a moment longer for them, my grandfather was now in need of a car. His own was in the garage for repairs so my father borrowed the keys to my aunt's car. My father wanted to get some farewell shots of *Shadow V*, and knowing the conditions could never be bettered he had taken his camera with him. With Nick, my mother and grandmother in the back, my grandfather in the front passenger seat and my father at the wheel, we set off in my aunt's white Ford Granada Estate. I sat on my father's lap and, until we got to the public road at the lodge, steered the car, quietly fuming at the indignity of it. Normally I would be allowed to drive the car myself and swap into the passenger seat at the end of the drive. Today we were late, the car was full to bursting point and my father would not budge. When we got to the gates I slid off his lap and sat very uncomfortably between him and my grandfather, the handbrake underneath me.

We drove into the village, turned into the harbour and proceeded carefully along the harbour wall. *Shadow V* was on the outside of *Celtic Dawn*, Rodney Lomax's black fishing boat. Because the tide was low, we had to climb down a metal ladder attached vertically to the wall. This was no problem for Nick and me but we were frightened as we helped our 83-year-old grandmother and 79-year-old grandfather down the greasy, salty ladder. The two guards who had tailed us from the castle also helped them down and across Rodney's boat into ours.

Despite the pressure to get going before the tide got too low, my father stayed back on the quay while my grandfather stood at the helm and had the boat pushed out a few feet for a photograph. He wanted her recorded in her final days. My father later wrote: 'After taking this photograph I climbed down into the boat, put the camera in the cabin and threw my coat on top of it.'[10]

In Granard, Thomas McMahon and his accomplice did not say anything that betrayed their actions earlier that morning. They had climbed aboard *Shadow V* and hidden five pounds of gelignite under the deck close to where we were all standing. It was probably in a plastic tube seventeen inches long and about three inches wide. Gelignite, also known as dynamite, gives off a powerful smell of almonds. When Thomas McMahon prepared the explosives he would have done so in a well-ventilated place to prevent getting a blinding headache. The bomb would have been wrapped in plastic which would have reduced the smell. Any remaining odour would have been masked by the salty, fishy air of the harbour, mixed with the fumes from *Shadow V*'s cranky old diesel engine. It had a large gearbox operated by a handle at its rear. My grandfather called, 'Astern!' and whoever had been posted on gear duty, probably Nick or me, pulled the lever backwards. Normally my grandfather nursed the engine and restricted the engine speed to 2,000 RPM with a careful eye on the tachometer. Today he did not seem to care. He put the throttle wide open and then, having boiled up the water beneath him, cut the power and called, 'Ahead!', before opening the throttle again, now applying opposite lock to the steering. *Shadow V* wheeled around under his strenuous inputs. My father said, 'You are having fun today, aren't you?' He paid no attention.

My father's account continues: 'We left the harbour at about 11.35 a.m. Dickie remained at the helm, which was the first time that he had done so this year. Usually, he allowed the children of various ages to steer the boat in and out of the harbour.' Members of an IRA Active Service Unit now kept a careful eye on us and our two friendly Gardai who went to our car, removed the keys from the ignition and locked it. Next the Gardai got into their patrol car and with Kevin Henry at the wheel drove alongside us on the coast road.

My mother was sitting with her legs stretched out and her back resting against the stern, on the left side of the boat, with Twiga on her lap, and an old copy of the *New Statesman* which she had not yet had time to read. August was a great month for catching up. My grandmother was sitting on the right side of the boat and, like my mother, had her legs stretched out in front of her. My father recorded: 'When the boat left the harbour I went to sit in Dickie's fishing seat, just above and behind the engine, where he always sat unless he was steering the boat. I thought that he would soon stop steering the boat and hand over to one of the twins.'

I was having similar thoughts on the deck just outside the cabin, hovering close to the helm in case my grandfather decided he no longer wanted to steer. Nick was close by, perhaps with the same thought in mind. When Paul asked if I had a watch on, time seemed strangely irrelevant in such perfect conditions. I playfully examined my black plastic Casio watch and announced, 'Eleven thirty-nine and forty seconds.' As I did so, my grandfather was using full power and we were cutting through the water at about fifteen or twenty miles per hour. He obviously intended on staying at the helm so I decided to get up on the cabin roof as an extra pair of eyes. From there I would have the best vantage point in the boat, and in today's smooth sea I would not get bounced about as was sometimes the risk. Carefully placing my feet on the edge of the boat and taking a good hold of the wooden handrail on top of the cabin, I pulled myself forward, clinging to its outside, and then pulled myself up onto the roof and dropped into an old car tyre lying there. In harbour this dangled vertically down the side of the boat as a makeshift fender; when at sea it was stored horizontally on the roof and it was now my seat.

There were many boats out and quite a few lobster pots. With my grandfather at the helm I felt a duty to be extra-vigilant and help his septuagenarian eyes pick up the small buoys and faint lines in the water that betrayed the presence of the lobster pots. I knew from experience that if we ran over one, we would most likely foul our propeller, stall our engine and possibly cut the rope, meaning the loss of the pot. I raised my arm and pointed saying, 'Buoy twenty yards ahead and slightly to port.' No response. A short while later I saw another one and pointed it out. Again, no acknowledgement; he was in another world.

It seemed anyone who had a boat was on the water that morning. Dick and Elizabeth Wood-Martin, in whose borrowed pram Nick and I had passed a good deal of time as infants, were out in their boat. It was seventeen feet long, with a small forward cabin and an eight horse-power outboard engine. Their fifteen-year-old son Michael had been on the quay as we left harbour. He had decided not to go out with his parents that morning, leaving it to them to check the lobster pots, which we saw then doing as we passed them. Church of Ireland minister Canon Thomas Wood, chaplain at Sligo General Hospital, was out with his son fishing for mackerel and pollack and later recalled my grand-father waving at him.*

Another of the boats we passed was a thirteen-foot Avon dinghy. On board were the owner Charles Pierce, a long-standing visitor to the area, his wife Kathryn, and her brother-in-law William Wilkinson. He later recalled:

> We were fishing for mackerel roughly about a hundred or a hundred and fifty yards off the shore when Charles said to me, 'Did you ever see Lord Mountbatten before?' 'Well,' I says, 'I have seen him on the television and read about him.' 'So,' he says, 'there he is just coming out from the harbour.' So, of course, I was very interested to see Lord Mountbatten in the flesh. As the boat came along I could see him standing up. I could see his white wavy hair coming along and I noticed other people in the boat.[11]

On the cliff top about two hundred yards away, the Gardai had parked close to a caravan opposite our lobster pots. They were looking down

---

* Canon T. P. S. Wood was a colourful character. He told of the disparaging looks he got in a bank when he asked if he could change his wife of fifty for two of twenty-five.

on the boat as it approached the shore at a slight angle, closing in on the buoys and still moving. As my grandfather slowed the boat, my grandmother turned to my mother and said, 'Isn't this a beautiful day?' We were now as far from the harbour as we were going that day. My father's account reads:

> Just before we reached the place where the lobster pots [were], I moved from the [fishing] seat and sat down on the bench running along the starboard between my mother and Dickie and facing the engine. Just as I saw the first buoy Dickie speeded up the engine and I turned round so that my legs were still left on the inside of the boat, and my body was looking out over the starboard side trying to spot the buoy.

On the roof, my head was turned in the direction of the buoys off to my right. My bottom was tucked inside the old tyre. My body was facing the bow of the boat; my arms were tucked up around my knees in front of me.

William Wilkinson again:

> As the boat approached us I had lost a wee bit of interest in the fishing as I wanted to focus my eyes on this man, for nosiness shall we say, because I had never seen him before. As the boat got closer I was given a nice clear view of him because he wasn't much further than maybe about thirty yards. The boat passed and I said, 'This boat is moving towards the shore or rocks.' Charlie replied, 'He is probably going over to lift lobster pots.' When it was about sixty yards away, I still had it under observation when all of a sudden there was just this 'boom'.

According to Garda Mullins, at 11:46, 'Suddenly I heard an enormous bang. I saw the boat go up in pieces in the air. There was a lot of smoke and in a second the boat had disappeared. All I could see were very small pieces of wood floating on the water.'[12]

My father later wrote:

My first memory is of a crack, rather than a bang, and then I regained consciousness under the water, being swirled round and round and head over heels. I did not stop to wonder what had happened. I just knew an absolute disaster had occurred. I tried to fight myself up to the surface and eventually reached a piece of wood which I put my arms around and this was also being tossed around by the force of the explosion in the water.[13]

My mother wrote in her diary:

I only remember terrific explosion (and thinking it was the engine which had been playing up) and immediately being submerged and going down and down in sea with water rushing in ears. Frightened I would not get up before drowning (forgot it was shallow) or get caught beneath hull. Remembered Darling Daddy's story of Kelly sinking. Put my hands over nose and mouth to stop swallowing water and made a note to tell him I had if I got up. Remembered Dodo could swim but worried she would get bad chill. It finally got lighter and I surfaced hitting a piece of wood and not minding facial injuries I later thought caused by it! Mentally relieved to hear Darling John's agonised voice shouting 'Help my wife' or 'Where's my wife?' quite close. Vaguely aware of other voices before mercifully losing consciousness.[14]

My grandfather was at the helm three or four feet behind me and slightly to my right. The gelignite under the deck must have been between us because as we rose into the air we went in different directions. I remember a sensation, as if I had been hit with a club, and a tearing sound. I do not remember my journey through the air or hitting the water but before the debris finished raining down, I was unconscious and about a hundred feet from my grandfather.

Eighty-six miles away in Granard, the Gardai had no idea what had just happened outside Mullaghmore but they were convinced they had stopped two IRA men involved in a serious crime and they now decided to act. Within five minutes of the explosion Garda James Lohan stepped up to Thomas McMahon and said, 'I am arresting you under section thirty of the Offences against the State Act 1939.* You are not obliged to say anything unless you wish to do so but anything you say will be taken down in writing and may be given in evidence.' McMahon made no reaction. Next Lohan went to the man who had been driving him. The Gardai were soon to find out that his real name was Francis McGirl. As Lohan used the same words, his right hand on the prisoner's shoulder, McGirl sat and grinned.[15]

* The charge used for people suspected of membership of the IRA and other organisations banned by Irish law.

PART TWO

THE SOUND OF THE BOMB
1979–2002

6

RESCUE

At Classiebawn, Philip was sitting with Amanda, Edwina and India in deckchairs outside the castle. He was turning a page of *Little Dorrit* by Charles Dickens when they heard a loud bang and they all looked at each other. Philip thought it must have been a bomb but he did not say so. He put his book down and walked inside the castle where everything seemed normal. Crossing the hall he found Peter Nicholson near the door of the library. Looking for any explanation other than the one in his mind, he asked Peter, 'Did you just slam a door?'

Downstairs Siobhán Burgess had just walked out of the kitchen to fetch some supplies when she thought she heard a bang. 'I figured I had forgotten to put water on the potatoes and that this resulted in the bang. I checked, however, and the potatoes were all right.'[1]

Charlie Pierce's boat had been so close to the explosion that pieces of *Shadow V* had landed in it. He reacted much faster than his two companions, instantly telling them to 'pull in the lines, quickly, pull the lines'.[2] He had spent thirteen years in the merchant navy and had seen emergencies at sea before. Kathy had been sitting in the bow of the boat with her back turned to *Shadow V* when the bomb went off, whereas Billy Wilkinson had been looking directly at it, and remembers 'Kathryn said, "Be careful, Charlie, be careful." Charles didn't listen to Kathryn, we rushed straight over in only fifteen seconds and I could see heads

75

in the water and I could hear screams. The boat wasn't there, the debris was floating on the sea.'

The explosion vaporised at least some of the diesel in a pair of five-gallon drums which we kept on board in reserve.* In Charlie's words, 'it hung in the air like a swarm of bees, like a fine veiled cloud you wouldn't notice'. In terms of people in the water, 'Lord Mountbatten was the most obvious. He was floating higher and seemed upright in the water. He was wearing a dark blue jacket, I'm not sure if there was some slight buoyancy in it.' Through the 'clear, flat, calm' sea my grandfather's badly damaged legs were easily visible; and from his injuries Charlie quickly formed the impression that he had been standing 'on top of the bomb'[3] and was now dead.

'No matter who we'd seen, we just grabbed,' Billy Wilkinson told me:

We just grabbed and it was your Gran. Between Kathryn and myself we were able to drag her into the boat. She had high hysterics: 'Where am I? Where am I? What has happened? What has happened?' Now we didn't ask her if she was comfortable, we just dragged her and left her and then we seen a sturdily built man and that was your father and got him and we did likewise into the boat, not asking him was he comfortable. We were not interested, our job was to rescue and finally it must have been your mother. She had facial and body injuries and was not speaking. So we pulled those three people into the boat, a ten-foot dinghy with six people. There was no room for anybody else, the water was lapping just over the side of it.

The next person Billy caught hold of was my grandfather.

Charles told me, 'Billy, there's no room in the dinghy but hold him at the side.' So I grabbed out with my arms and I was holding

---

* Shadow V's fuel tank was in the stern behind and under my mother and grandmother, as far from the bomb as anywhere on board. Perhaps this helped prevent it from exploding, or rupturing and catching fire. After the explosion, diesel fuel spread over the surface of the sea and formed a large oil slick. When Garda divers raised Shadow V's stern from the seabed they found diesel oil still in the tank. Source: Detective Inspector Pat Jordan, day five (morning) of the trial of Thomas McMahon and Francis McGirl, question 118.

Lord Mountbatten and I kept his head over water. I thought to myself, 'I'll hold on tight till some other folks come near'. And as I was holding on tight to him I could hear Charles saying, 'There's someone coming in a boat towards us, hold on', which I did. I didn't want to let his body go. I felt that Lord Mountbatten had died.

Soon after coming to the surface, my mother had passed out, and when the Pierce boat arrived she was face down in the water. 'It was incredibly close timing,'[4] said Kathy. My father's account states: 'When I got to the surface I was shouting for my wife and I then grabbed a piece of timber that was swirling in the water.'[5] By the time he was found:

I was lying under the surface with my nose and mouth just above the surface. My next memory is catching hold of a string or rope which was attached to a small inflatable rubber dinghy. I must have passed out again as I can remember nothing further until lying on the bottom of the dinghy with my feet and legs over the side. I opened my eyes with great difficulty and dragged my two legs over the side, which caused me great pain and I realised that I had broken legs at least. In fact, I was relieved to see my feet, as my boots and socks had all blown off. I looked round and found my mother lying next to me and a girl in jeans with her arms round Dickie who was still in the water beside the dinghy. I could see the right-hand side of Dickie's face and there were no marks. However, I had a terrible feeling that he might be dead.[6]

Charlie Pierce recollected, 'The thing I most remember about it, surprisingly, is in a most extraordinary way, your father was very compassionate; he asked several times about your mother.' My father's written account says:

I shouted to the girl and asked if they had seen my wife and that we must pick her up. She turned to me and said there was nothing further they could do as the dinghy was full and at that moment I felt a movement under me and looked down and found I was lying on top of Patricia. She was in a terrible condition and I could not believe how awful her face looked with the injuries and blood. I held her head in my hands and shouted to her to ask if she could hear me. She replied by groaning and this told me at least that she was alive.

Her face was full of wood splinters.

The 'girl' my father described was Kathy who later explained, 'We were in the bare minimum, just shorts and T-shirts. We had no towels or anything on the boat; I don't think we even had a rag. Your grandmother was the least injured. I tried to put my arm around her to keep her warm and she wouldn't let me touch her. She was quite cross.' Charlie's memory was that she said something like 'Do you realise you are hurting me?' as her arm was broken in two places, and 'she seemed to be the most alert. Your father was in a great state of shock and I don't think he could appreciate or assimilate what had happened.'

Next on the scene was Charlie's uncle, Jim Morrison, who lived in Enniskillen and owned a caravan near Mullaghmore. He was familiar with *Shadow V*, having been in her some years before to help lift lobster pots. With him in his thirteen-foot aluminium boat *Pearly Miss* was his thirteen-year-old son Glen and a twelve-year-old family friend. Glen was a close friend of Paul. They were no more than four hundred yards away when the bomb went off, and as they arrived they were met with the sight of the Pierces' 'jam packed'[7] boat, and Kathy supporting my grandfather in the water. Charlie called out, 'Could someone take Lord Mountbatten, we can't move?' Jim came alongside but mindful of the children in his boat Charlie told him, 'Don't lift Mountbatten into your boat.'[8]

A third boat now arrived, belonging to Edward Dawson, a businessman from County Fermanagh, Northern Ireland. This was the fourth summer he, his wife and their daughter had spent in Mullaghmore in their caravan. That morning he had launched his fourteen-foot rubber Zodiac in preparation for a diving trip with a friend who was due to arrive later. Edward was alone in the boat and had been out at sea for about ten minutes checking its engine when he heard a loud bang. At first he thought it might have come from further out in the bay but he could not see anything there. Looking back a few hundred yards towards the shore he could see smoke and a commotion around a small boat. Thinking its fuel tank or engine might have blown up, Edward motored over. Getting closer, he slowed down.

There was a lot of debris, pieces of wood maybe a foot long, maybe some larger, and I was conscious of sailing through this in an inflatable boat. The propeller fouled and the boat stalled. I remember pulling these pieces of green wood from the propeller and got it going again. I realised something very serious had happened and there were people in the water, and that it was Billy Wilkinson and Charlie Pierce in the other boat. Some people had been lifted into their boat which seemed to be leaning over and taking a lot of water. An older man with white hair was being held up against the boat and he was then brought around to the side of mine. Charlie Pierce said to me, 'Do you know who this is? This is Mountbatten.' Then the whole thing hit me, what had actually happened. I was looking for a boat but the boat had disintegrated and all that remained were bits of wood and splinters. It was decided I would get Lord Mountbatten into my boat and get him as quickly as I possibly could back to Mullaghmore.'[9]

Jim Morrison climbed into Edward's boat and helped lift my grandfather in. 'It was very upsetting and gruesome. My daughter remembers me returning home that night and told me my face was grey and I looked an old man. I was forty-nine.'

Seeing the injuries, Edward was 'terribly shocked. I suppose one reacts with adrenalin and a whole mixture of emotions. When I knew what had happened, even at that stage, I was shaken a bit but I was terribly angry.' Grabbing the bag he had prepared for his diving trip that afternoon, he curled a towel on the deck and rested my grandfather's head on it, covering the rest of his body with two wet suits. Not being sure that he was dead, he left his face uncovered and headed for Mullaghmore.

By now the Pierces' boat had left for the harbour. Glen Morrison remembers Edward looking 'very shocked, pale and upset'. Getting back into his own boat, Jim agreed to escort him back to the village, steering his boat alongside.

*   *   *

At the moment of detonation Dick and Elizabeth Wood-Martin were following *Shadow V*. They had just checked their first lobster pot close to Thumb Rock. They found one lobster, re-baited the pot and lowered it again. They had three more to check and were now a hundred yards behind. Dick was steering in *Shadow V*'s direction when 'she just exploded. There was a puff of smoke and a large bang and a shower of little bits of timber. Then the boat was gone.'[10] Elizabeth looked round and saw 'a portion of the boat dropping and one piece landed about ten to fifteen yards from our boat'.[11] The explosion did not strike Dick as terribly loud which he later found strange because 'people much further away reported a bang so loud it shook their windows. I didn't have much time to think about anything. I said something like, "My God they've blown him up." I opened the throttle quickly and that probably drowned the engine because it started to misfire.'[12]

As they moved further out to sea and towards the 'pool of oil and floating timber'[13] Dick and Elizabeth saw boats converging towards it. Then they saw something in the water about thirty yards to the left of that area. Elizabeth remembers, 'We thought it was a football in the distance and we headed for this. The engine on our boat was not behaving properly and we seemed to get slower.' Getting closer they could see it was the head of someone who was, in Dick's words, 'buried in the water and bobbing up and disappearing slightly and coming up again'. It was me. 'You were trying to swim but you weren't moving anywhere and I don't think your mouth and nose ever broke the surface.'

Elizabeth felt I was 'unconscious but doing it automatically. It's a good thing you had a good head of hair because that's how I caught you. But I couldn't pull you out because the weight was too much.' Dick joined her, and as they were dragging me into their boat Elizabeth wondered how damaged my body was going to be. 'My great fear was we've got a head, we've shoulders, we've got a body; have we got any legs? I was shaking.'

Dick remembers:

You had a massive black eye on one side of the face and the other eye was just staring ahead as if it had lost its sight. I had the impression you were not seeing anything. You had little bits blown out of your skin, little incisions as if you had just plucked them. You had a very neat hole blown out of the seat of your trousers. I remember it clearly. We looked around, saw the other survivors were being looked after and headed for the harbour. The engine wasn't running properly, it was sick. It had happened once or twice before but not to that extent.

Dick estimated that I was in the water for less than a minute.[14]

A couple of hundred yards away on the cliff top, Garda Mullins was remonstrating with John Maxwell who had arrived in his car. He had been sitting in the sun outside his cottage nearly half a mile away, reading the sports pages of *The Irish Times* when he heard 'a very loud bang. I knew it was a bomb because I had been close to bombs before in Enniskillen and knew the kind of resonance they had.' The sound came from where he knew *Shadow V* was meant to be and he felt 'it's got to be the boat'. His wife Mary was inside the cottage and he told her to stay there with the youngest of their three children, Lisa. He jumped into his car and drove 'like mad' over the brow of the hill and down to the headland.

There was a Garda car and a guard standing there and all I could see were bits of wood floating about in concentric circles, moving around from a kind of bubbling in the centre. There were boats all over the place but they seemed to be heading towards the harbour. I was in a complete panic and I said to the guard, 'Look, my son's in that boat and I am going to go out there, swim out and see if I can find his body.' He dissuaded me and said, 'Go round to the harbour because you may find him there.[15]

Elizabeth's recollection was: 'After we had hauled you in, at first you just lay there. Then as we struggled to come in you seemed to regain a certain amount of consciousness.'[16] According to Dick, I started to make a noise, not shouting but more like barking, as if trying to clear something from my throat. 'My initial reaction was how anyone could survive at all from the explosion. You were disorientated and moving around, you wouldn't lie down. I wanted to get you down to the bottom of the boat and you kept moving your feet.'[17] Elizabeth thought I was trying to 'clamber out. I said to Dick, "I can't hold him back" so at that stage we changed over completely and I steered the boat and Dick shouted in a very severe voice, "Will you lie down!"'

Those were the first words I remember. I had no idea what was going on, only that I was being spoken to by an unknown, frightened Irishman and that something was very badly wrong. Lying down I felt as if I had shrunk into an inner core and I knew I had to hold on and concentrate. It seems ridiculous but I momentarily thought about Gordonstoun and the preparation I had already received there for joining a rescue service later in my school career. I knew I had to stay calm and that I was too weak to help myself. I understood that the people around me would help if I could just tell them what was wrong, but I could not work out what was wrong with me. In my reduced mental state, I did not even realise I was blind. I was desperately cold and shivering violently. I tried to say 'I'm cold' but the words did not seem to come out. Instead all I could hear was a tiny sound like a click in my throat and I thought, 'I'm much worse than I realised' and now desperately wanted to make myself heard. 'I'm cold,' I tried again, harder. The result still seemed inaudible. I tried again with more effort. A man's voice which sounded angry snapped back, 'Yes, we know, we know, we're doing everything we can.' I realised that he had heard me each time and I felt ashamed. As Dick concentrated on controlling the boat, he heard me say, 'I'm sorry, very stupid of me.' In the midday sun he felt 'roasting hot' but hearing that I was cold, he and Elizabeth covered me in two towels, which were all they had. He later recalled, 'I tried to offer an explanation as to what had happened and told a far-fetched story that your engine had exploded.' I do not remember that or anything else for the next few minutes. With their engine spluttering, the Wood-Martins made slow progress back towards the harbour about a mile away.

On the cliff top were William and Elizabeth Duffy who for the last three years had owned and run a restaurant and guest house in Mullaghmore: Ceol-Na-Mara, Gaelic for 'Music of the Sea'. They had just driven around the village to gauge the number of people they could expect for meals in their restaurant. They were planning for a busy day, including sending some lobsters up to Classiebawn. For the evening they had booked a well-known folk group, Makem and Clancy.* On the headland, William and Elizabeth now arrived to find a guard in a dreadful state looking out to sea through binoculars. He was 'hardly able to talk'.[18]

Shortly afterwards a car arrived and 'a girl and a boy got out'. This was Philip and Amanda. In Mullaghmore they had passed holidaymakers walking hand-in-hand and eating ice cream and had started to relax. Reaching the harbour and seeing our car parked on the quay, they were relieved and agreed to drive around the headland until they were able to see the boat. Half a mile further they came to a junction near the house of our local doctor, Evelyn Flanagan. Just beyond the junction, standing beside the road was a small group of people staring out at what looked like rubbish spread on the sea. One of them was a uniformed guard. Amanda and Philip got out and asked what they were looking at. A man who had been working in the fields said, 'Lord Mountbatten's boat has blown up.' Amanda looked at the guard and the others and her first nonsensical reaction was that they had been involved in an attack and that a bomb had been thrown from the cliff top. Recognising them, someone said, 'Oh no, you ought not to be here.' Concerned, the group moved towards them; Dr Flanagan, whom we liked very much, reached out and put her arms around Amanda who pulled back in hysterics saying, 'Let go of me.' Philip later recalled that Amanda 'went wild'.[19] He had a sensation that they were about to be kidnapped. Saying 'Get away', they ran to the car and drove as fast as they could towards Classiebawn. They felt sure of only one thing: no one on the boat could have survived. However, desperate to say something positive, as she gripped the wheel of the speeding car, Amanda told Philip that people often survived bombs. Then ahead of them they saw the cattle-grid at the entrance to Classiebawn. Instantly they had the same fear: that it was booby-trapped. They shouted as they drove towards it, asking each other what to do. Amanda stamped on the accelerator, and as they raced towards the grid Philip struggled to raise himself out of his seat. As they flew over it, he lifted himself up and partially through the

* Tommy Makem and Liam Clancy and the highly successful group Clannad were performing at the Astoria in Bundoran.

window in an attempt to distance himself from the explosion they expected from below.

At Classiebawn my aunt was in the drawing room talking with Hugh Tunney. When Philip and Amanda walked in, Amanda hoped to draw her into the hall and explain privately what had happened. Philip came straight to the point and told her the boat had blown up. Calmly my aunt walked into the hall with them where they poured out their experience.* Hugh Tunney immediately joined them and produced a box of pills which he fumbled, showering them onto the carpet. Scooping them up, Amanda realised they were tranquilisers. With every other adult in the family dead, wounded or absent, my aunt suddenly found herself at the helm. Icy calm, but obviously in shock, she said in a reassuring tone, 'Don't be so silly. Let's all have lots of tea and then go and find out what's happened.'[20]

The boats carrying the dead and wounded were making for the harbour. In Charlie Pierce's boat, Billy later recalled that those in their care 'didn't know where they were. They asked if they were on land. "Don't be worried, you will be OK. We are with you, we are looking after you,"' he told them. The grossly overladen dingy had taken on a lot of water and its twenty-eight horsepower engine was not capable of lifting the boat so that it could skim the water's surface as normal. Instead it was wallowing slowly along. 'We had no mobile phone, VHF radio or anything like that, this is going back to the bad old days,' Charlie was later to recall.

He did not know that Detective Garda Kevin Henry had already radioed for help, as had the captain of a nearby boat, one of the Maxwells' neighbours, William 'Gus' Mulligan. A retired Commander in the Irish Army, he had been hired for a fishing trip by a couple living in the area, Robert and Christiane Graf. They were Swiss and working in Bundoran for a German travel agency. As they were getting ready to leave harbour, they had invited three German tourists to join them, including Manfred Ottow and his thirteen-year-old son Gregor. Gus had pointed out *Shadow V* leaving harbour. Manfred later told Gardai,

---

* Hugh Tunney's 2004 recollection was of Philip saying, 'Why did they do this?' and my aunt replying, 'They had their reasons.'

'My son saw kids and they said "Hello".'[21] A short while later they too were out at sea, trawling for mackerel from Thumb Rock and about four hundred yards behind *Shadow V*, which Gus Mulligan estimated to be at a rocky spot known as Urchin's Island. According to an account written by Gus Mulligan:

At that point Shadow V become enveloped in a cloud of smoke – grey and brown in colour – followed by a sharp, loud explosion (there was a smack about it) . . . When the smoke cleared (rather quickly) there was a scattering of debris elongated over the water. The debris seemed to shoot out towards the opposite direction in which the boat was travelling.'[22]

Gus grabbed his marine radio and spoke to his wife, who phoned Sergeant John Hennessy at his station in Cliffoney. Switching to Channel 16, the marine emergency frequency, Gus then radioed for all boats in the area to come and help. Within minutes, Gus and his companions arrived on the scene. Robert took a photograph 'as if by instinct', before putting down his camera thinking, 'My God, what am I doing?' A few feet away they saw Twiga, 'drifting by, deep in the water, dead'. Then they saw a body in the water and Gus realised it was Paul. Finding him lifeless, he moved on looking for survivors before returning to Paul. At first he was too deep to reach but after a short while he floated closer to the surface and Gus and Robert, sending young Gregor down into the cabin, managed to drag his body into the boat. 'He looked as if he had been killed instantly; he was in one piece but he had many holes . . . It was just a nightmare,'[23] Robert remembers. They covered Paul with a blanket and Christiane went down into the cabin to comfort Gregor, sheltering him there while the search continued.

In the tiny boat carrying my parents and grandmother, which Charlie Pierce described as 'not much wider than a settee', Kathy's feeling was one of:

vulnerability. The water was everywhere, coming right up and swishing back. We were just going so slowly, that was the problem. Knowing that we were taking all these people on board and we had nothing, not even a towel to put round your grandmother, not a thing to put round your mother's head, didn't have enough room to spread them out, didn't have any first aid experience . . . the whole thing was just so horrible. That's why I just started praying. I said the Lord's Prayer. I don't think that I said much more. I couldn't think of much more to say; just reaching out.

Brian Best and Richard Wallace were on holiday from Northern Ireland. Brian was a registrar at the Royal Victoria Hospital in Belfast, Richard held a similar position at Erne Hospital in Enniskillen. Both were surgeons in their late twenties with over four years' experience of emergencies including bombs. They were out in the bay about to do some water-skiing behind an inflatable boat which belonged to Brian's future father-in-law, John Craig, who had taken us in his boat many times in previous years. When the doctors heard the explosion and saw a plume of smoke, Brian said it sounded like quarrying. They made their way back to the harbour where somebody shouted down from the harbour wall, 'They've blown up Lord Louis's boat.'[24] Two friends got out of the boat taking skiing equipment. Heading out, Brian and Richard soon saw the Pierces waving at them frantically from their boat.

Kathy told me, 'They took charge of the situation. We had found the strength to cope and once the doctors came all the strength was gone.' Richard Wallace remembers the 'glazed look on their faces . . . They didn't know whether to move on or stay where they were. I think they were scared they would do harm if they moved on.' The doctors started redistributing the injured. First they asked my father to come into their boat. Brian remembers him being 'very calm . . . He shifted himself with no murmur of any sound that he was badly injured.'[25] Under his trousers his right leg was broken in two places, the left with one break and shrapnel wounds. Brian had no idea of this; when he found out months later he was astonished. 'He is a man that I have amazing admiration for,' he later told me.

Richard boarded the other boat and helped lift my mother across. The doctors knew that without someone to keep her windpipe open, she could die before they reached the harbour. Unable to do this from his position at the outboard engine, Brian put her in my father's lap and showed him how to support her head while holding the jaw forward.

As my father held her, he feared she was dying and called to her repeatedly. At one point she groaned and said, 'Yes.'[26]

Charlie Pierce's dingy was still seriously overloaded. Billy and Kathy therefore got into Edward Dawson's boat with my grandfather's body, while Richard Wallace stayed with Charlie to look after my grandmother as they all set off for the harbour. Richard remembers that her right arm was badly broken; when she lifted it 'the middle of her forearm bent as if it was her elbow. I said to her, "Don't move that, you'll hurt yourself" and I tried to get her arm in by her side so that she could splint it against her body, and she said, "Oh, don't worry about me, I don't matter." She was sitting with her back up against the side and I just sat there and she leaned against me.' To him she seemed:

> compos mentis and reasonably well. She didn't say that she had any pain and I got the impression that she probably did have, but she certainly wasn't going to complain about it. I could not get her to keep this arm still and she kept lifting it up to draw attention: 'Tell me how are the boys? Do you know who has been hurt?' She kept on asking . . . and when I said that I couldn't tell her she would then ask again. She was being exceedingly stoical and I got the impression that she just cared about the other people. I wasn't all that worried medically. How wrong I was.

Peter McHugh, son of the owners of the Pier Head Hotel, had been sitting on a bench by the pier when he heard 'a loud bang'[27] coming from the direction of the coast road. After running up to the road beside the hotel, he had stood waiting. 'After about a minute a Garda came in a car and asked me where I would get a lifeboat as Lord Mountbatten's boat had exploded.' Peter replied that it was over seventy miles away in Arranmore and took him instead to Rodney Lomax's nearby boatyard but found it empty. They returned to the harbour where they ran into John Maxwell and together they quickly persuaded a friend, Sylvia Mallin from Ballymoney, to take them out in his speedboat, together with his friends Peter Loughran from Castleknock, County Dublin, and Michael Hampsey from Dungannon. Together the five men rushed out to look for Paul. They soon passed Brian Best with my parents in his boat. Peter McHugh reasoned with John that there was little point going further because his son must have already been picked up. John insisted. On reaching the scene of the explosion they found what Michael Hampsey described as 'a mass of debris floating on the water'. He told how Peter McHugh had to restrain John from jumping into the water. 'He was shouting, we were all shouting. It was pandemonium.'[28] They saw, amongst others, Sean Meehan, the Bundoran auctioneer, who told Peter McHugh that Paul's body was in Gus Mulligan's boat. John was beside himself and was calling out as they turned back for the harbour. At the helm of his boat, Gus Mulligan could hear John's shouts of anguish.

Five boats were now carrying us towards the harbour, Paul in Gus Mulligan's boat, my grandfather in Edward Dawson's, my grandmother in Charlie Pierce's with Richard Wallace, my parents with Brian Best, and, bringing up the rear, I was in the Wood-Martins' boat which was making the slowest progress of all. As Dick's engine was spluttering and misfiring he was thinking to himself, 'Of all the times when it would happen, it happens now.'

As Brian came ashore on the strip of sand in the harbour, a throng of people came forward to help. He later told me:

Instantly there was a nurse from Enniskillen. Peter McHugh from the Pier Head Hotel came down with a door and used it as a stretcher to get your mother up to the hotel. Then there was a male nurse who also identified himself. He just said, 'Can I help?' I said, 'Help lift.' Peter came back down and used the same door to get your father up.

As there was no obvious place to put him, someone reversed a van onto the quay and opened its rear doors. My father's account states:

I was placed in the back of a small van, lying across someone's knees who held me in their arms. I remember asking Dr Wallace, who came to see me, where Patricia and my mother were and he said that they were being looked after and I saw them lying near the hotel, lying on what I thought were stretchers but were actually doors, and that he had covered them with blankets. I also asked after Nicky and Paul but there was no reply.

Soon Edward Dawson reached the harbour with my grandfather's body. His later recollection was of 'an awful lot of people there, probably a hundred or so', horrified at what was unfolding in front of them.

> I had concern that within the gathering crowd there may well have been someone who knew something about this terrible atrocity. It was just the way my mind was working at that time. I got quite upset . . . [29]

Tilting up his engine he steered onto the harbour beach.

Moments later Richard Wallace arrived in Charlie Pierce's boat with my grandmother, who was carried up the beach and to the front of the Pier Head Hotel. Richard went with her. He recalls:

> The people in the hotel were exceedingly helpful. Anything you asked for, it turned up. We asked for splints. People suddenly appeared with this brand-new broom and they asked 'Will this do? What length?' and they just started breaking it up. A nurse asked what could she do and I asked her to make a bandage from strips of a sheet but she couldn't tear it and a chap suddenly appeared and he tore the sheet and then she just rolled it up.

Richard applied the homemade splints to my grandmother's arm and later my father's leg. This simple piece of first aid helps raise the blood pressure of someone with a fracture. Normally it is not life-saving but in my father's case it might have been more helpful than the two doctors realised. He had suffered serious heart disease in his thirties, and nine years earlier had undergone bypass surgery.

Meanwhile Edward Dawson covered my grandfather and ran up shouting, 'Is there a doctor, is there a nurse?' He did not know if my grandfather was still alive but it seemed 'human nature' to do all he could. Finding the two doctors he said, 'I think I have Lord Mountbatten in my boat.' Richard Wallace accompanied him and Edward stood back. In a very short time Richard said, 'He's dead.' While Richard went to fetch Brian, Edward wondered if he could keep my grandfather's body hidden from view by leaving it in the boat, putting the boat on the trailer and taking it to the castle.

When the Wood-Martins ran their boat onto the same beach, people stepped forward and, lifting the entire wooden deck from the bottom of the boat, carried me up to the Pier Head Hotel, supervised by Brian Best. Hearing there was a survivor, Rodney Lomax came in to find 'a very frightened little boy, bruised but alive'. He realised I was one of the twins but could not tell which. Years later he told me, 'You looked a mess. I knew you were alive but it looked like you might have been dead pretty soon.'[30] He knelt beside me and I asked him where I was and where the others were. He recalled:

> I remember people were thundering up and down the stairs, pulling blankets and sheets off the beds . . . Somebody called me and I said, 'I'm going out there.' As I got up, you said, 'Don't go.' You were looking for somebody to talk to. The other people around you were total strangers to you, total strangers to me too. I said, 'I'm sorry I have to go.'

I do not remember this or anything else that happened in the hotel. Outside, his wife Trudy came across people in the road 'just standing there with tears pouring down their faces'.[31] Hotel proprietor Theresa McHugh said, 'If anybody wants a drink, you go the bar and take whatever you want.'

Hugh Tunney was on the steps of Classiebawn as Kevin Henry arrived by car. His first words were, 'Have you any brandy in the house?', and Hugh told him he did. The detective then said, 'Look, there's been an accident. Make any excuse you like . . . but don't let [the family] near a phone.'[32] Having fortified himself with brandy and borrowed a pair of binoculars, he then returned to the harbour. Hugh relayed his instructions to Peter, who walked into the kitchen and turned off the radio at the plug, which froze the hands on its clock. Grace Ryan wrote in her diary:

> It was 12:14 when Peter came down to the kitchen (as I remember he stopped the clock at that time) to tell us that the boat had been blown up – of course none of us believed him but the guard came rushing in and met Mr Tunney at the door and they looked very worried so we knew that something was going on . . . At this stage we all moved up to Peter's pantry and now we knew it was

true but we didn't know any details yet. Mr Tunney told us to act normally because the family hadn't been told yet. I went back to the kitchen to finish peeling potatoes.[33]

John Maxwell was now running around the increasingly busy harbour looking for Paul. 'Families with their buckets and spades were coming from all parts for the day not knowing about the tragedy. I was looking for his body thinking, "I shouldn't be doing this on such a lovely day" . . . A man then came to me and said, "Paul is in the Pier Head Hotel, they just brought him in . . ."' He was led inside the hotel where he saw a boy lying in a corridor. At first sight the hair made him think it was Paul. Then he realised it was me. 'That was a kind of devastating blow. I left from the hotel and then it really hit me that Paul must be dead because he wasn't anywhere with the living. And somebody said there was a body in Gus Mulligan's boat.' He rushed to the end of the harbour.

Rachel Johnson, a close friend of Paul's elder sister Donna, was on the quayside looking down into Gus Mulligan's boat where Paul was lying dead, his body partially covered by something resembling an oilskin. She noticed that the jeans she had recently lent him had been blown off. What came into her mind was his promise that he would return them in time for a gig that night. Now she saw John 'roaring like an animal and trying to jump into the boat but people stopped him'.[34]

John later told me, 'I suddenly got in a tremendous rage. I just completely lost it.' His memory was of shouting that the attackers were 'cowards' and that they were killing one of their own. The words which stuck in Brian Best's mind were: 'I'm a fucking Irishman, these bastards.' Edward Dawson described John going 'berserk, walking up and down the quay, sort of screaming'. Brian waded across to Gus Mulligan's boat and climbed in. 'Paul's body was covered with a blanket, I looked under the blanket to see what he looked like and his back was where the injuries had come. His face was fine and I said, "Bring John down."' John remembers:

Gus brought me down and I found Paul in the back of the boat. His head was in a bucket with mackerel which is something that has stayed with me ever since. Gus had been fishing and the bucket must have rolled over. I picked him up and he was very limp but his back was very warm and I recognised him because of the mole. I thought, 'He can't be dead' because he was so warm. You expect dead bodies to be cold.

According to Brian, 'People were saying, "Is that everybody?" The guards did not know. I asked how many were missing; nobody knew. I went into the van and asked your father to tell me who was on the boat. He named each one and I counted them and that was when I realised we were missing one.' It was Nick. Richard Wallace recalls people 'going around the hotel. We thought somebody could have been brought in there, walking wounded. But there was nobody.' Someone suggested that boats should go back out and look for Nick. One of those boats carried Alan Browne and his guest Terry Dudeney. The two men, both doctors, had been on Mullaghmore beach with their families when they had heard the explosion. Alan Browne immediately linked it to my grandfather, saying, 'Oh my God, it's what we've feared. We had better go over and see what we can do.'[35] When they reached the scene of the explosion, the only casualty they saw was Twiga, and they returned empty-handed. Arriving back at the harbour they heard a survivor was in the Pier Head Hotel. Alan Browne went inside to investigate and saw me lying on the floor completely alone. He noted that one of my eyes had 'popped' and I was 'about a quarter conscious'. He went home taking his 'numb and shaken' friend with him.[36]

There were very few telephones in Mullaghmore in 1979, and of those only three were working that day, one of them a payphone. Unable to contact Sligo Garda station by radio, Kevin Henry had gone to the phone box but been told by a large woman who was squeezed inside that he would have to wait. When she prolonged her call he forced the door open, threw his arms around her and heaved her out in mid-sentence. Another of the telephones was in the Pier Head Hotel. Desperate to be taken away, Rachel Johnson walked into the hotel to call her family in Enniskillen. She knew she could not set foot in this 'posh' hotel unless she had shoes on so she was 'stunned' to find the owner, Mrs McHugh, tearing up sheets, and 'one of the twins' lying on the floor wrapped in a sheet, with just head and arm exposed. I do not remember it but apparently she had to lean over me to make her phone call, transfixed by the sight of my bloodless 'marble white' arm with a deep cut in it. On the other end of the line her mother refused to believe her story until Rachel held out the receiver to capture the mayhem around her. Her father quickly left to pick her up.*

Elizabeth Duffy had arrived in the village from the headland to fetch the distressed guard a whisky. Peter McHugh spotted her and, knowing she had been a nurse, asked her to stay as they needed all the help they could get. Elizabeth looked at someone with a badly damaged face lying on a stretcher outside the hotel. It was my mother. Elizabeth later described removing the pearls from around my grandmother's neck. 'When I was kneeling I could feel this thing digging into her and I thought, "What is that?" It was part of the boat lodged in her thigh.' One of the two doctors called Elizabeth over to the van where my father was sitting up and asked for help in cutting off my father's trouser legs. 'I remember holding the trousers as they were cut. His legs were in some mess . . . We thought they would have to amputate, no question about it. I just remember him being full of strength, psychologically.'

On the rocky shoreline not far from *Shadow V* at the moment of the explosion was a nurse who was holidaying in Mullaghmore with her husband. Realising what she and her sister-in-law had witnessed, the women collected the four children they had taken down to the shore and drove back to the village in time to find survivors being brought up to the Pier Head Hotel. She saw me being carried into the hotel and my mother and grandmother lying outside. She later said that when she first saw my mother she did not realise she was a woman until she saw her clothes. Speaking to a man at my mother's side she discovered he was a doctor and immediately offered to help, joining in with Elizabeth Duffy. They put a splint on my mother's left leg and a short while later, at about 12:20pm, the first ambulance arrived. The driver John Kennedy and his helper Cecil Barber had been dispatched from Sligo General Hospital fifteen miles away to go to someone 'who had fallen off a wall at Mullaghmore'.[37] En route this was changed to 'an accident at the pier'. When they arrived they had to fight their

---

* For twenty-five years, until she was contacted during the research of this book, Rachel Johnson wondered whether the twin she had seen had lived or died.

way through the crowds as there was no ambulance lane or Garda supervision of the scene. The ambulance crew saw my father in a van on the quay, me in the Pier Head Hotel and my mother and grandmother outside the door of the hotel. On the doctor's recommendation, they lifted first my mother and then my grandmother into the ambulance. As she was about to leave, my grandmother asked how 'Lord Louis' was. Jim Morrison was with her. 'I said he was all right, "He is down there", meaning in the harbour.' The doctor climbed in and put an oxygen mask on my mother and asked the nurse to accompany her to hospital. Then someone handed her my mother's small wet handbag which she took with them. She sat beside my mother, Cecil Barber sat beside my grandmother, and the ambulance left for Sligo. At one point my mother said, 'Oh my chest, I cannot breathe' and throughout the journey my grandmother asked how my mother was doing.

Peter McHugh's girlfriend at the time, Grainne McInerney from Ballyshannon, later his wife, had stayed the night in the Pier Head Hotel. She had qualified as a nurse in April that year and was now training at Altnagelvin Hospital in Derry. She had just got out of bed and was planning on some waterskiing with Peter and their friends when she heard the explosion and went to the front door. 'The next thing, I saw a car drive through the village from around the point. It was speeding faster than sound. Then all hell broke loose.'[38] One of the doctors asked Grainne to get scissors and splints and help with my grandmother's right arm. My grandmother always took enormous care about her appearance, and as Grainne worked on her arm she asked if her face was all right. Then someone asked Grainne to go and see me in the Pier Head Hotel. Checking my pulse she became worried and asked one of the doctors to come. When I told them how cold I was, all they could do was rearrange the blankets around me.[39]

At about this time at the Garda station in Granard, Thomas McMahon was also complaining that he was cold. The Gardai told him he could put his anorak on and gave him a meal. He was unshaven and his companion Francis McGirl was smoking 'very heavily'.[40] Both men appeared very tired and were yawning.

* * *

At 12:25pm, just as a Sligo fire engine arrived in Mullaghmore, Jim Morrison joined John Maxwell in Gus Mulligan's boat and started to wrap Paul's body in a blanket. Meanwhile, the only other ambulance on duty at Sligo Hospital arrived in Mullaghmore. Its driver was Terry Baker, a former English policeman who had settled in Sligo some years earlier. He and his colleague Frank McGowan were close to Classiebawn, heading for Mullaghmore, when they were stopped by their colleague John Kennedy in the first ambulance. Terry Baker thought they were going to be told they were not needed. Instead, he recalled many years later, 'John said, "Be careful down there, there's a bomb." I said, "We were told it's a car off the pier." "No," he said, "there's a bomb after going off and just be careful, you don't know what's down there."'[41] It was well known that the IRA would sometimes use a second bomb to strike at rescuers. This would be demonstrated that afternoon near Warrenpoint in Northern Ireland when a roadside bomb killed six paratroopers as they were driving along the shore of Carlingford Lough. Twenty-one minutes later a second bomb killed twelve more soldiers as they arrived by helicopter.*

At around half past twelve, Garda Sergeant Paddy Ward of Sligo approached Richard Wallace to discuss my grandfather. It seemed to the doctor that the 'poor guard was in an awful state – he didn't know what to do and he felt a little bit out of his depth at the time'. He had arrived at 12:35pm and they went down to Edward Dawson's boat to go through the formality of Dr Wallace pronouncing my grandfather dead, and for the sergeant, who had known my grandfather for ten years, to confirm his identity. A decision was made to take the covered body to an area at the back of the Pier Head Hotel which Brian remembers acting as a 'temporary morgue'. Richard Wallace was one of the six men to carry the makeshift stretcher. He told me:

* The bombs killed more British soldiers than any other attack of the Troubles. They were detonated by radio control from the other side of the Lough which formed the border with the Irish Republic. No one was ever prosecuted. The surviving soldiers believed they were being fired on and trained heavy gunfire across the water, only to kill holidaymaker William Hudson, whose father worked at Buckingham Palace. William, aged 29, had been standing with his cousin watching events unfold.

I can remember, as we carried him up the beach, the whirring and clicking of an automatic motorised camera. Nobody had motorised cameras then except serious camera buffs and reporters; and I remember thinking at the time that it was wrong that somebody should have taken pictures. It irritated me. Afterwards it struck me: How was a reporter there already with a camera?

Next morning the photographs were published around the world.

Brian had been feeling emotionally detached until now. Then at the shoreline from which my grandfather's body had just been carried, he looked down and felt 'a huge surge of anger. There was a little pool in the sand and his blood had run into it making it bright red. In it there's a toddler of about eighteen months, playing in the bloodstained water.'

Soon Terry Baker and Frank McGowan had loaded me into their ambulance. My only memory of being in Mullaghmore is lying in that ambulance and seeing my father being carried towards me on a stretcher, his face totally haggard. 'Hello, Dad,' I said, smiling broadly, thinking I must do everything I could to lift his spirits and not betray how awful he looked. I propped myself up using my arms but I remember nothing more. My father later told me I fainted instantly. Someone asked Elizabeth Duffy to travel with us in the ambulance and she sat between us. Quoted the day after the attack, she said:

> The lad was in deep shock and I suspect he had had internal injuries. Both asked about Lord Mountbatten and I decided that it was no point lying to them so I told them that he was dead. Lord Brabourne, who showed tremendous courage, remembering what incredible pain he must have been in, just clenched his hands tightly and said nothing. But he leaned across the little space between his son and himself and cradled Timothy's head in his arms.[42]

In later life Elizabeth Duffy told me, 'The ambulance journey was just horrendous. Everybody was in total shock, just wanting to get to the hospital.' Frank drove the ambulance, leaving Terry in the back to help if needed. Elizabeth sat holding up my father's left hand as he lay in a half-reclining position. The top joint of his little finger was attached only by skin. Terry remembers my father asking, 'Where is my son?'

Terry answered, 'He's here, next to you.' When my father repeated the question Terry thought perhaps he could not hear. He asked Elizabeth to move so that my father could see me. 'I said to you, "Will you speak to your father?" and you spoke to him. I think you actually put your hand across to him, and he grabbed hold of your hand. You said, "I'm here, Dad, I'm OK" or something like that. And he spoke to you and then he said to me, "But I have another son."' Elizabeth told me, 'He whispered, "Has he been killed?"' Elizabeth remembers me asking for Nick. 'I have a feeling you were under the impression that your brother was in another ambulance.'

My father's account states: 'On my way to the hospital in the ambulance, I realised that Patricia was in a very serious condition and I was extremely worried, during my few lucid periods, as to whether the treatment would be good enough for a crisis of this sort.' The road to Sligo was a winding single carriageway but Terry estimated we reached eighty to eighty-five miles per hour. 'We hit bumps and used to take off.' I have no recollection of the twenty minutes it took to reach the hospital. We arrived at 12:55pm, fifteen minutes behind my mother and grandmother.

In Mullaghmore a third ambulance arrived, driven by Thady Kennedy from the Shiel Hospital in Ballyshannon on the far side of Bundoran. He saw my grandfather's body at the Pier Head Hotel and carried it into the ambulance. In Gus Mulligan's boat, a group of helpers had been preparing to carry Paul up the steep, slippery stone steps to the quayside. Intervening, Brian said, 'No, we can't hurt him, we'll take him over the side.' With John watching, Brian, Jim Morrison and two firemen carefully lifted Paul over the side and laid him onto a stretcher being held alongside by Peter McHugh, Peter Loughran, Jim's son Glen and two others. They carried him up the beach and into the waiting ambulance which soon set off for the hospital, accompanied by Sergeant Paddy Ward.

Thirteen-year-old holidaymaker Gregor Ottow was shivering with his father Manfred who had wrapped him in blankets after they had reached the harbour in Gus Mulligan's boat. Soon they were reunited with Gregor's mother. She had first realised something was wrong when she and her six-year-old daughter walked off Mullaghmore beach towards the harbour and saw an elderly couple sitting on a wall with their feet dangling and tears coming down their face. The couple were 'incredibly sad'[43] and spoke to them but it seemed to be in Gaelic and the only word they could understand was 'Mountbatten'. The reaction in Gregor took time to come out. By evening he was pale, shaking and in tears.[44] When the family later returned to the village they were struck by 'an apparent division in its inhabitants: half of them pleased and the other half on the other side.'[45]

In the harbour Robert and Christiane Graf spoke to John Hennessy before heading for home and the peace of their garden. As they drove to Bundoran on what should have been a glorious Monday afternoon, the radio played 'I Don't like Mondays'.* Robert hated the song from that moment, telling me twenty-five years later, 'Every time I hear that sound it makes me remember . . .'

* The song by The Boomtown Rats was Number 2 in the charts that week.

7

HAVE A NICE DAY

At 1:38pm a teletype machine in the Foreign Office in London printed a message from the ambassador in Dublin.

TELEGRAM NUMBER 213 OF 27 AUGUST
EXPLOSION ON LORD MOUNTBATTEN'S BOAT
1. AT 1305 WE WERE INFORMED BY THE GARDA THAT THERE HAD BEEN AN EXPLOSION ON LORD MOUNT-BATTEN'S BOAT IN SLIGO. LORD MOUNTBATTEN IS MISSING. THE BOATMAN AND TIMOTHY KNATCHBULL ONE OF LORD BRABOURNE'S SONS ARE BOTH DEAD AND THEIR BODIES HAVE BEEN RECOVERED. LORD AND LADY BRABOURNE HAVE BEEN RESCUED. THEY ARE INJURED. WE ASSUME YOU WILL CONTACT THE PALACE.
HAYDON.

News of the attack was beginning to spread. At about 12:45, forty minutes after Amanda and Philip had burst in, my aunt Pamela had answered the phone at Classiebawn to Bob Pullin who had been hired by my grandfather to manage the opening of Broadlands to the public. He had spoken to my grandfather the evening before. Now he had about three thousand people in the grounds queuing for an hour and a half to get through the front door. He was phoning because the Press Association had just called saying they had heard from a Garda source that my grandfather had been blown up. 'This isn't true, is it?' Bob asked my aunt. 'Yes,' she replied, 'we heard a few minutes ago.'*

As the ambassador was sending his telegram, BBC television interrupted their coverage of the bank holiday sports fixtures. A friend later wrote to us: 'The news room took over to make the horrifying announcement. Frank Bough, who was presenting *Grandstand*, remarked, to his eternal credit, "How can one watch sport after hearing that!" or words to that effect. He clearly wanted to go home and cry.'[1] My eldest brother Norton had been out jogging in Fulham and, getting home, had turned on the television. He was sitting on the sofa with his fiancée Penny Eastwood when the newsflash came; stunned, they just held each other. After a short while the phone rang. John Barratt, my grandfather's private secretary, had also heard the news and now agreed to help get them to Ireland as fast as possible, and to track down my brother Joe. He lived in the house opposite but he had gone away for the bank holiday weekend and Norton had no way of reaching him.

At Classiebawn, my cousin Ashley had been in the library watching a *Laurel and Hardy* film on television. He was joined by his sisters Edwina and India. Edwina had seen Amanda return in tears from Mullaghmore. Then India had seen Kevin Henry rushing back to the castle. As he was about to drive off with a pair of binoculars, she asked, 'What's happened?' 'Nothing,' he replied. 'Just want to see the beautiful day.'[2] Ashley did what he could to keep his sisters calm. After about half an hour their mother came in, sat on the sofa and told them that *Shadow V* had been blown up and that our grandfather had died. India 'screamed with hysterics'[3] and ran out of the house. Huddled in a secluded spot she sat repeating over and over to herself, 'Monday August 27th 1979.'[4] Worried she might have gone to the nearby cliffs, my aunt led a search party comprising Amanda, Philip and, from the kitchen, Grace, Siobhán and Libby, but it was one of the Gardai who later found her. Philip and

* The news started to break at 12:55pm, the first report being by the BBC in Northern Ireland. 'A report is coming in of a boat owned by Lord Mountbatten having been blown up in County Sligo. Lord Mountbatten has a home in the area. No other details are available.' Source: BBC Northern Ireland TV news transcript.

Amanda went up to the Middle Tower Room, still believing everyone on the boat must be dead. My aunt came to offer them some pills to help them stay calm. As they lay down and held each other, they heard sirens in the distance.

Scotland Yard had first heard of the attack at 12:15pm when a detective chief superintendent in Garda headquarters telephoned to say 'a loud explosion'[5] had been heard from the boat and he was waiting for confirmation from Gardai who were going to the scene.* When a superintendent, Philip McMahon, arrived at Classiebawn from the harbour, he spoke with my aunt. Philip and Amanda had by now spent some time on the roof of the castle with Ashley, listening to a radio and drinking tea. Returning downstairs, the two of them met a detective. Standing outside the library he said he could now give some information: their grandfather and Paul were dead, and 'one of the twins' was missing. 'Which twin?' Philip asked. With an awful look in his eyes the man fell silent, looked down and drew away, leaving Philip not just devastated but furious that he had not identified the twin.[6]

Grace Ryan's diary:

During the afternoon Amanda and Philip walked around the place arm in arm. At one stage Amanda came in to ask us to please tell her if her Mother was dead because Philip thought that he had heard it on the news. We tried to reassure them that she wasn't but Philip believed all that day that she was dead . . .

Having heard that steps were in motion to bring Norton and Penny from London and to trace Joe on his golfing weekend, Amanda and Philip now tried to contact Joanna, who was working for a film production company in New York. They tried calling London to get her number

---

* Police in London were struggling to get reliable information. In addition to Paul Maxwell's death, the Garda incorrectly listed 'a further boatman' on the 'seriously injured' list. The police offered to send two top-ranking officers to Ireland, a Commander and a Chief Superintendent. This was 'gratefully turned down' that evening but when Scotland Yard persisted it was agreed that a Detective Superintendent would 'fly to Dublin tomorrow and will stay there as long as he is able to render assistance'. Source: Metropolitan Police Special Branch memorandum, 27 August 1979.

but incoming calls were tying up the line. One of the calls was from my father's long-standing friend and film producing partner Richard Goodwin, who asked Amanda if there was anything he could do. When she explained about the need for a phone number for Joanna he said, 'Leave it with me.' Relieved, Amanda assumed he would ring back with the number; he did much more. He tracked her down to a New York office and broke the news himself.

Joanna went straight back to her apartment and through an operator managed to get a call through to Classiebawn.

Amanda was really good; typical Amanda. Obviously I must have been in quite a state. I think I said, 'Is Mum still alive?' And Amanda being Amanda, she said, 'Yes, she's fine . . . she's going to be fine.' I think she didn't want me to sit on an overnight flight worrying. I didn't believe a word of what she said but I was very glad she said it. I didn't stop to talk about what was happening at her end because it was all a bit of a rush. There were phone calls I had to make; and I had to pack . . . In the middle of packing I laid down with the suitcases on the bed and I said out aloud, 'Please God, I can't believe I'm saying this because I don't believe in you but: Please God, don't let Mum die.'[7]

Desperate for a flight, she started calling the airlines. 'Being in America, every call ended with "Have a nice day". I thought, "For God's sake!"' At the airport, waiting for her flight, she was taken aback to see a pair of twins, then another, then a third pair and a fourth. It seemed she was seeing more twins than she had in the whole of the preceding year. On the flight, passengers around her were reading *The New York Post*. 'I remember having to very deliberately avert my eyes. I kept seeing these headlines and I really didn't want to read anything about it. I didn't want any more information.'

A Garda car brought Elizabeth Duffy to Classiebawn from the hospital. She had accompanied my father and me in the ambulance and had then agreed to a request by one of the doctors to visit the family. She told my aunt all she knew: that my grandfather and Paul were dead; that my grandmother was undergoing surgery but there was grave concern over whether she would survive the anaesthetic; that I was in a critical state and being prepared for an emergency operation in the second of the two theatres; that my mother was critical in the Intensive Care Unit; and that my father was severely injured and in the male surgical ward. He too would require surgery when a theatre became available. She later recalled of my aunt: 'I'll never forget her face. I think the pain she was going through behind that dignified face must have been horrendous, absolutely horrendous.' The meeting lasted just a few minutes and she returned to her home in Mullaghmore. 'I was just sitting looking out. It was as if I was afraid. It was despair, fear, everything, it was so awful. I had a red T-shirt on and from holding your father's hand and your grandmother, it was absolutely soaking with blood. William said, "Will you take that off!"' Later she found herself wondering what had become of my father, had he made it to the operating theatre, and if so had he survived? She had no way of finding out. 'But my main concern was for you, as a child,' she told me.

My aunt Pamela decided that she could not go to the hospital until she had some news of Nick. Meanwhile Classiebawn became busier as people arrived from all directions to offer help. Alan Browne was an old friend of Aideen Gore-Booth and she phoned him to ask if he would go up to the castle and do whatever he could to assist. There he found Amanda was a 'rock', calming and supporting everyone around her.

The phone was ringing off the hook. Calling from his home in Northern Ireland, long-standing friend James Abercorn found the family were terrified that my father's already weakened heart would fail at any minute. He immediately offered to involve Professor Frank Pantridge, one of Northern Ireland's top heart doctors. The castle's only phone was in a noisy passage outside the library. Philip picked it up at one moment to find Prince Charles on the line. They had a heartfelt exchange with the Prince offering to help in any way he could. Philip longed to get everyone safely back to England, a prospect which Charles helped him understand would only be possible when the wounded had been stabilised.

Later Amanda was trying to reach our 87-year-old Nanny in England when an Australian reporter called and became cross with Amanda for refusing an interview. 'How can you be so inconsiderate after I've spent three hours trying to get through?' he said. Amanda eventually snapped, 'Well it's my bloody family,' and slammed down the phone.

Outside Hillsborough in County Down, Professor Frank Pantridge was at home when a car 'screamed up' to his door and a policeman asked him to get in for a trip to Sligo. 'Why?' he asked, indicating that he might not want to go. The officer did not know what it was about but the message had come from the Chief Constable. The Chief was not available but his deputy explained the instructions had come from the Queen at Balmoral. 'Then he said that Lord Mountbatten had been blown up.'[8]

Grace Ryan wrote in her diary:

By around four pm the whole castle had been surrounded by Irish soldiers and the full report was coming in. Lord Mountbatten and Paul were dead, Timmy, Lord Brabourne and Lady Brabourne and the Dowager Lady Brabourne were critically ill and Nicky was missing . . . Kevin Henry, the guard on duty, came in later and he just sat down and cried.[9]

My aunt had refused to leave for the hospital until she could account for Nick. Now she had news and it was what she had dreaded. Nick had been found in the sea close to where *Shadow V* had exploded, and he was dead. Wearing dark glasses she left for the hospital in a Garda car driven by Kevin Henry. They drove in what the detective described as 'near silence and sadness and disbelief'. Suddenly 'she bowed her head and she cried her eyes out, really cried her eyes out. And about two miles further on . . . she took out a tissue, wiped her eyes, wiped her nose, cleared her throat, took a deep breath, sat up, put the glasses back on and said, "Perhaps it does one good to have a good cry at times."'[10]

Photographers, television crews and reporters started to arrive from Ireland, the UK and later from around the world. 'BBC TV was the first to arrive but none of the family wanted to see them at all,' continues Grace's diary. 'That evening we all watched the news together and a picture of Nicky came on the screen. It nearly killed Philip. We were so sorry for them all.'

As Gardai, sightseers and press continued to arrive in Mullaghmore,

Paul Maxwell's parents decided to return home to Enniskillen. A large number of friends came to help them pack. After they drove out of Mullaghmore, the family came across Garda road blocks 'all over the place'. At the border in Belleek they queued for half an hour. Eventually they reached the front and a guard asked for identification. When John said, 'Look, my son has just been killed',[11] he waved them through.

Norton and Penny took a 4:30pm shuttle from London Heathrow to Belfast's Aldergrove Airport. Climbing into a British Army helicopter they were soon joined by Frank Pantridge who was struck by how 'distraught' Norton was. They 'hedge hopped' to the border at Belleek and landed in a field strewn with cow pats, much to the annoyance of the Professor who did not want to walk into Sligo's Intensive Care Unit 'covered in dung'.[12] James Abercorn was waiting in Belleek to brief them, having spent the afternoon at Classiebawn and then Sligo Hospital. Norton and Penny were driven to a narrow bridge which they crossed on foot to Garda detectives waiting on the other side. To Norton it all seemed like a scene from the Cold War. A short while later they were in an Irish Army helicopter on their way to Sligo. Frank Pantridge and James Abercorn stayed in Belleek to call Belfast for two more specialists, one for eyes and one for lungs. Frank Pantridge then crossed the border and was soon at Finner Military Camp, where he was strapped into a two-seat helicopter bound for Sligo Hospital. As they bounced along he wondered what reception he would get there, as 'an interloper'.

8

HOSPITAL

At Sligo General Hospital, Dr Denis Boland was passed a radio message that said ambulances were on their way from Mullaghmore bringing eight serious casualties. He phoned around the hospital to prepare beds and alert the Intensive Care Unit and two operating theatres. In one a routine operation was underway. When the anaesthetist, Tony Heenan, heard someone say that a boat had been blown up in Mullaghmore he asked the surgeon, Thurlock Swan, 'How many motor boats are there in Mullaghmore?' 'I don't know,' he replied. Tony Heenan then stood up and said, 'That's the Mountbattens . . .' Realising he was going to be at the centre of a major event, his first feeling was, 'Christ, this is outside my experience', but then he said to himself, 'No it isn't, they are people just like anybody else. They are born and they die,' and with that he decided even before the ambulances came in, 'I was going to do what I did with everybody else.'[1]

In Mullaghmore, my mother had heard some of the sounds going on around her, including shouts of 'Stretcher!'[2] Later she heard the siren of her ambulance, and as she and my grandmother arrived at 12:40pm they were met by Denis Boland, who noted that my mother was in a 'very shocked condition with no memory of the explosion. She had multiple injuries to her face, eyes and ears. She had obvious fractures [of two bones] of left leg' and was given injections and a drip and sent

106

to the X-ray department and then the Intensive Care Unit. My grandmother was 'very deeply shocked and very confused and had no memory
of the accident. Difficulty was encountered getting a drip into her veins
– so an on-the-spot cut down on . . . vein of left ankle was done and a
canula inserted. Blood pressure was 50/0. She was having difficulty in
breathing due to chest injuries – especially on left side.'[3] She was given
injections and a drip before being X-rayed and transferred to the Intensive
Care Unit where she received blood transfusions. Both my mother and
grandmother were classed as 'critical'.

My father and I arrived in the second ambulance at 12:55pm. I have
no recollection of this or the next few hours but my father's account
says:

When we arrived at the hospital, I was wheeled in and found
myself on the other side of a curtain to my mother, who I spoke
to briefly, so she knew that I was alive and beside her. I had seen
her clearly in the dinghy with me and there was no damage at all
to her face and her hair seemed to be entirely in place, as always!
She had a broken wrist or arm which was giving her considerable
pain and she told me that she was feeling 'uncomfortable'. That
was the last time I spoke to her.

Dr Boland found my father 'very shocked. He was conscious but
with no memory of the explosion and was mentally confused'. He was
given two injections, one of penicillin and another for tetanus, and
had a drip put into his arm. As well as serious leg injuries, the left side
of his face was 'severely peppered with numerous lacerations and woody
splinter foreign bodies'. His left finger was broken and the tendons
severed. 'Instructions were given to cut off the signet ring which was
causing swelling and obstruction . . .' He was sent to the X-ray department and then to a private room in the male surgical department. He
plainly needed surgery but the doctors felt he would survive in the
meantime whereas my grandmother, mother and I might not.

Denis Boland's report continues:

Timothy Knatchbull was in a shocked stuporosed condition and
had no memory of the explosion. Right side of the face, right side

of chest and right side of abdomen were all peppered by wooden splinters with green paint on them. The right eyelid was particularly swollen. Abdominal pain and tenderness with distension of the abdomen were marked.

I was given injections and a drip and waited in Casualty to follow my mother and grandmother to the X-ray department and then Intensive Care. Meanwhile Sister Mary Gantley arrived in Casualty and walked into the cubicle in which I was lying. I greeted her with 'Me, Sister?' Before she had time to reply I said, 'No, she Sister, me Doctor, you Mr Bertenshaw.' Confused, she was about to speak when I said 'Dr Walters?' and answered my own question with, 'Me, nurse . . . you Mr Bertenshaw, she Sister, you Doctor.' Suddenly Mary recognised my words and realised I was reciting a well-known *Monty Python* sketch, in the clipped tones of John Cleese and his fellow comedians.

She spent the next three-quarters of an hour looking after me, holding my hand and telling me that I had had an accident and was in hospital. For much of the time I seemed hardly to see her. When I started talking disjointedly she reminded me where I was and kept on reminding me. When a nurse approached with a needle and syringe, I reverted to my John Cleese voice, and invoking another *Monty Python* catch-phrase said, 'I see, I see, I get the picture.' Then, dropping my voice and turning to her, I added, 'Sorry, Sister, I do this to keep myself cheerful.'[4]

The X-ray department rushed their images to the doctors. When Tony Heenan saw what the blast had done to my grandmother's lungs he knew she was 'going nowhere' and that no matter what he did 'she was not going to make it'. But when he looked at my mother's chest X-rays he said, 'I'm putting her on the ventilator because if I don't we won't have her in a week,' and he did that immediately. He had five years' experience in Northern Ireland. My father's account states: 'Without that experience, he would not have reacted so quickly to Patricia's condition and it is likely that when her heart did fail about three hours after arrival, she would not have survived if she had not already been put on the lung machine.'[5] This involved sedating and paralysing my mother and inserting a tube down her windpipe which controlled the air going in and out of her damaged lungs. Mary Lowry was one of the Intensive Care nurses and she later explained:

> It was total nursing care. You had to do everything from just lifting her arms to do exercises, putting her arms down by her sides, even keeping her eyes moist. Even though we were talking to her continuously, there was no way of knowing just how much she was understanding. It must have been one of the most awful experiences . . . [She] must have gone through hell.[6]

Speaking three decades later, Tony Heenan told me:

> I remember saying to myself about your grandmother, 'We'll jockey her along and if she improves a little bit I'll put her on a ventilator too but really I think it's cruelty.' Today she would be stuck on a ventilator for a week and she'd get bedsores, and she'd get this, that and the other; and she'd be dead in the bed and nobody would turn the ventilator off. I could be in terrible trouble in today's world but I decided that no matter what I did with her, she was not going to make it.

In my case the doctors were in a quandary. My belly had become rigid, a process they called 'guarding' and which they thought indicated internal injuries, possibly a ruptured spleen, but when the X-rays arrived there was nothing to confirm this. They were aware that their decisions would be scrutinised later. It was a situation which 'terrified' Tony Heenan: 'I have a lively imagination and I had visions of being destroyed professionally and made a laughing stock by the English press. The only way I could come to grips with it was saying, "What would you do now if it was somebody else?" I remember asking that question and the answer was, "I would have to open him and take a look."' They operated at 3pm, checking my internal organs while eye specialist Dr Adrian O'Connell examined my right eye which had swollen and shut. They cleaned the wounds to my face, arms, legs, buttocks and back and stitched my right arm, upper lip, and right thigh. They took splinters out of my left arm and inserted a drain, and returned me to Intensive Care with two pints of blood and a bladder catheter.

At 4pm the doctors put my grandmother to sleep and removed numerous wooden splinters, stitched her wounds, and treated her broken right forearm and put it in a plaster splint before returning her to Intensive Care, also with two pints of blood and a bladder catheter. My mother had left Intensive Care and was now on the floor above, where Adrian O'Connell had started the long and painstaking process of stitching her face and eyes.*

My first memory of hospital is waking up feeling very drugged and finding nurses moving quickly and quietly around the room, checking on me frequently. I found their presence reassuring but I just wanted to close my eyes and sleep, desperate to shut out the nightmare I sensed was going on around me. My aunt arrived at the hospital at about 5pm, and found me 'barely conscious'. Almost the first thing she was asked on arriving at the hospital was to identify her father:

> It was such a horrific idea, I think largely because I knew he must have been badly damaged. Anyway we were walking along the corridor and I thought, 'Oh my God, can I do this?' Luckily I see James Abercorn arriving and I say, 'Oh James, can you identify my Papa for them?' I will remain devoted to James all my life, he arrived at the nick of time.[7]

Soon I was woken by the sound of a helicopter landing. Sunlight was streaming through a window on my right and lighting up a curtain half-drawn around my bed. The helicopter seemed to have landed not far from the window and soon took off again, only to be followed by others. I was woken each time and thought to myself, 'How stupid to build a heliport beside a hospital.' The helicopters were in fact using a small car park at the hospital entrance. Norton and Penny arrived on one of them at about 6.30pm and when Norton walked into Intensive Care I was very pleased and surprised to see him. He stayed just long

---

* My father later wrote: 'He was a brilliant surgeon . . . and it was undoubtedly due to his skill and care that Patricia's eyesight was saved.'

enough to say hello and for me to ask him in an amazed tone, 'What are *you* doing here?' He smiled broadly as he walked away, and I fell asleep very reassured to know he was around. Down the corridor at the door of the operating theatre, he and Penny said hello to my father.[8] 'Numerous foreign bodies' had been removed from his face before it was stitched. An object in the left side of his face which was visible by X-ray could not be found. Metal was taken out of his left leg along with several wooden splinters. His right leg wounds were cleaned and the leg put in plaster. His left little finger, which was almost amputated, was sewn back 'in the hope of its survival',[9] and the tip of his left ring finger was stitched and his hand put on a plaster splint for support. At 7.10pm he returned to his room where he was promptly sick.

By the time Frank Pantridge had landed at the hospital, Tony Heenan had been working flat-out since midday 'doing the whole lot' and was now in the ophthalmic theatre on the second floor, 'a small poky place' where Adrian O'Connell was operating on my mother's eyes. Then:

> it all came tumbling down on top of me when a knock came to the door and the Sister was outside. Sister Darcy had trained at Moorfields [in London] and was very English, very Englified.* Somebody else would have walked in but she was correct and knocked. She drew herself up to her full height and said, 'The Queen has sent her representative from Belfast to see you.' I said, 'Jesus, don't bother me.' 'Oh, yes,' she said, 'he's downstairs.' So it dawned on me then that here I was up to my ears in something.

He went downstairs, met Frank Pantridge, said he was welcome to see the patients and told him he would be finished 'when he was finished'. He then returned to my mother's operation. Frank Pantridge was later joined by two more specialists from Belfast. The Professor told James Abercorn that Tony Heenan was 'A1-plus'[10] and one of the leading

---

* Sister Una Darcy had worked many years before at Maidstone in Kent. On days off she used to visit Mersham to walk in the parkland around our ancestral home, Mersham-le-Hatch.

doctors outside the Dublin area. 'The injured,' he told him, 'are in the best hands possible.'*

As my uncle David Hicks descended by helicopter towards Classiebawn that evening, he looked at the setting sun and reflected it had been 'the last day in the life of the last great figure of the British Empire . . . As I walked up to the castle Ashley, India and Edwina surged towards me. I hugged them with all my might.'[11] From inside the castle, Hugh Tunney watched as my uncle then took my aunt into his arms, a rare display of physical affection for either of them. 'Poor Pammy – calm and brave and relieved to see me but full of plans. "I'm off now to the hospital – give the children dinner",' my uncle recalled. At the hospital, my mother was now out of the operating theatre and my aunt went to see her. When she was led to a bed containing someone buried under a collection of tubes and wires, she was not sure who she was looking at. Then she looked down. 'Patricia has these lovely long hands and I knew it was her hand. Otherwise from the face you couldn't recognise her at all.' The doctors told her that my mother had a 'fifty-fifty chance of pulling through – but she *will* be blind'. My aunt found visiting my father just as difficult but in a very different way. He immediately asked about Nick. She was unsure whether the truth might be too much for his heart to take:

> I asked the doctors, 'What do I say?' and they said, 'You have to tell him,' and I told him, 'I'm afraid Nicky is dead.' The next time I saw him he asked the same question, 'What about Nick?' I told him five times over those days but his brain could not accept it. 'Have they found Nick? Is he all right?' It was awful. He said, 'I was wounded in the war and could be positive about it and get better but this I cannot face.' I had to be rather tough and say, 'There is no question of putting your face to the wall, if you do that and die on Patricia she will die too, so you've got to stay alive to keep her alive.'

* In his autobiography Frank Pantridge wrote: 'miraculously, Mountbatten's daughter survived. I encountered her again, by now Countess Mountbatten, at the Imperial War Museum in March 1986 . . . Her eyes had completely recovered. She saw me for the first time. She told me that when she returned to London . . . her chest X-ray was said to resemble that of a cadaver. Despite that her lungs had returned to normal.' Source: J. Frank Pantridge, *An Unquiet Life*, (Hillsborough, Northern Ireland: Pantridge Foundation), 1995, p. 77.

In an upstairs office of Granard Garda Station, Thomas McMahon was sitting quietly talking with his wife Rose. They held hands throughout their meeting until he said goodnight and went back to his cell at 11pm.[12]

Norton and Penny were still at the hospital and by late evening the Belfast doctors had seen the survivors and assembled in the hospital's board room, sitting on one side of the table with Norton and Penny facing them. 'Pantridge was the kind of person who couldn't sit down, he had to be jumping around,' his colleague Stewart Johnston later recalled. 'He said, "There are four survivors. Dowager Lady Brabourne will be dead by morning," and there was an intake of breath from the other side of the table.'[13]

The Sligo Gardai were now keen to return those of the family still at the hospital to Classiebawn; and the Belfast doctors to a helicopter waiting at the border. Frank Pantridge said, 'I'm not going into that helicopter till I get a large whisky.'[14] Tony Heenan looked at him and said, 'My house and nowhere else.'* They talked there until 1am when my uncle, David Hicks, telephoned to invite the Professor to spend the night at Classiebawn. He declined, explaining he had to get back to his patients in Belfast. Reaching home in the early hours of the morning after a high-altitude, moonlit helicopter flight, he dived into a hot bath. 'The telephone rang. It was Balmoral Castle. The Queen wanted information about the injured in Sligo.'[15]

At Classiebawn the family had moved into the library to watch my grandfather's obituary which the BBC broadcast at 10.20pm. Grace Ryan wrote in her diary:

It was really beautiful. I didn't get to see it all as the phone kept ringing, someone trying to get through from Sydney, Australia. Later that evening Peter came back to the castle and he was really in a bad state. The dining room didn't finish until 1.30am and

---

* As they left the hospital, David Capper, BBC's Ireland correspondent, banged on the car window. Frank Pantridge wound down his window and said, 'Capper, if you don't move that microphone from beneath my nose forthwith I'll stick it so far up your arse you'll never walk again. Driver, forward!' Source: Stewart Johnston, interviewed by the author, 31 March 2004.

Peter stayed on after. We went to bed. Libby slept with me but we couldn't sleep. The soldiers were walking around outside all the time and we could hear their radios really loudly.[16]

That evening, the airwaves were saturated with coverage of the attack, and BBC Radio transmitted a programme in which my grandfather said, 'I am very, very lucky with my grandchildren. They've all been nicely brought up, are intelligent, loving, loyal, and seem to have every quality I admire. The happiest times of my life have been spent with the family together, and the thought about death that saddens me is that I shall miss them all very much.'[17]

That night my aunt did something she had never done before and asked India to sleep in her bed beside her. As her mother lay awake, India stared at the patterned canopy strung over the four-poster bed. Her eleven-year-old mind was already deeply disturbed. Now she was mystified as to why her mother had brought her to this bed. Was it, she wondered, because the IRA were coming to get the rest of the family as they lay sleeping? As she fell asleep she thought of her last words to her grandfather that morning, promising him that she would look after his dog while he was gone. But there had been nothing she could do to console the Labrador, and later he retreated alone to his master's room where he sat 'howling'.[18]

In London my brother Joe walked into his home just before midnight, having returned from his golfing trip. His phone was ringing and when he picked it up he heard John Barratt saying, 'Thank goodness, we've been trying to get hold of you.' 'Why?' said Joe, to which the reply came, 'Oh my God, haven't you heard?' He explained the whole story and Joe then said, 'I'm sorry, John, you are going to have to tell me all that again.' He had not been able to take in a word of it. At the end of the call, Joe walked through the house to get as far away as possible from the phone and the news it had just delivered. Sitting in his kitchen he then heard the doorbell. The friend who had minutes earlier dropped him off after their golfing weekend had returned to be with him.

As the sun came up on Tuesday morning, 28 August, Joanna was in an airliner high above the Atlantic. Looking out she thought, 'Is Mum still alive to see another day?' At Classiebawn, Libby and Grace had hardly slept: 'We must have fallen asleep for a bit but were awake again at 6am. There were lots of reporters outside, even ones from Sydney and New York.'[19] As Philip came down from his bedroom he passed a small window on the staircase. 'Norton, you'd better come and look,' he called out. Norton was in the bath and jumped out so quickly that Philip heard water spilling onto the linoleum floor. Moments later Norton was on the doorstep, a towel wrapped around his waist, and whatever he said had the desired effect. Perhaps realising the distress they were causing, and that Norton was not going to tolerate their intrusion a second longer, the mass of photographers and reporters bolted like rabbits. Not a single photograph was taken. Upstairs Philip was overcome by a mixture of relief and gratitude, and when he told us later we all felt a wave of pride and love for our eldest brother. No one doubted he was our fiercest and most devoted defender.

During the morning, the telephone never stopped. Among the callers was the Queen, who had a long conversation with the family. In the hospital Tony Heenan was caring for my grandmother and asking her some questions. She did not like being called by her first name and she seemed to be tiring of the conversation but he pressed on anyway. Straightening herself up, she fixed him in the eye and said, 'Oh do shut up!' Tony Heenan later recalled, 'It was the way she said it. That kind of broke the ice. Here were these people, the same as anyone, the same feelings . . . the same language.' At 8.57am her heart stopped and when resuscitation failed she was pronounced dead. Two paces away in the neighbouring bed I was unaware that she had even been there. Just down the corridor, another doctor mentioned to my father that 'the old lady' had died and asked if he had known her. 'She was my mother,' he replied. 'He could have bitten his own tongue out and never stopped apologising,' my father later told me.

My mother's first recollection starts at 9am the next morning. She was able to hear what was going on around her but was effectively locked inside her own head because she could not move, speak or blink. Aware of this, the nurses told her what was happening and why. They knew the drugs would also affect her memory so they regularly repeated their reassurances and explanations. When she later updated her diary she wrote:

Mercifully unconscious most of the time, with delusions of two teams of nurses, 'Goodies' who do right things to me, and 'Baddies' who come and undo them and put horrid experimental things in eyes. Feel I must later report this to Dr Heenan. Also (although often reassured all well) frightened by inability to even twitch eyelids despite frantic efforts and that they will think me dead and switch off machine. Also terribly worried by noise of expiration of machine which I thought was one of my boys saying 'Mum, Mum, Mum'.[20]

In Mullaghmore the last body was brought ashore that day 'quite unmarked'.[21] My mother later recorded in her diary that it was 'my little long-haired miniature Dachshund (5 ½ lbs. and 7 years), Twiga, found by a vet. So stunned by everything I only feel pleased Nicky has taken her with him – he loved her so.' Initially Twiga's body was taken to Cliffoney Garda Station where it lay beside a pile of wood collected from the scene of the explosion, alongside 'other grim pieces of evidence ... the broken tip of a fishing rod; parts of a green plastic cushion; scraps of foam rubber from a seat; one blue sneaker with the side blown away'.[22] When my aunt was told, her immediate response was: 'It's essential that we have her back.' In later life she said, 'I remember Amanda and I doing Twiga's little funeral. I can't remember who made a box for her but Amanda and I went down and chose the place. I think Peter [Nicholson] and Michael [Connolly] helped; I think that I found some little flowers.' They buried her in the lee of the wood under Classiebawn's southern flank.

In London, Joe was meeting Joanna off her flight from New York. 'We just looked at each other and burst into tears,' he said later.[23] Avoiding the news stands, they settled into seats on a flight bound for Dublin only to be confronted by newspapers on all sides showing photographs from Mullaghmore, one featuring a dead body. In Dublin an army pilot squeezed them into the back of his single engine Cessna and flew them across Ireland to Finner Camp. As they approached Classiebawn by helicopter, Joe asked the pilot to fly over the bay where wreckage from *Shadow V* was still visible. 'It was a dark overcast day and the sea looked incredibly black. I have never forgotten the feeling of flying over the area where our family had been flailing in the water,' he described years later.

Seeing Classiebawn, a place of happiness throughout her life, Joanna sadly thought, 'Well, that's buggered this place for ever.'[24] Joanna was particularly focused on reaching Amanda. They had a special bond, placed by age in the middle of the family and surrounded by five brothers. Joanna never discussed it with Amanda but it seemed somehow natural to her that they were 'taking care of the men-folk' as well as stepping into a mothering role towards me.

Arriving together at the hospital, the family saw what Joe described as:

a sea of people lining either side of the entrance. It felt like several hundred yards of people two or three deep with fencing either side; and having to run the gauntlet of the press, hearing these cameras whirring, the pops of flash photography and voices . . . I couldn't look, I was expecting a bullet in the head any minute. I just completely focused on getting into that door and shutting out that completely alien world. I have never felt more naked, more exposed. I was really frightened.

In the hospital they saw my father, who dissolved into tears on their arrival. He was still asking about Nick and suffering afresh each time someone told him he was dead, saying through his tears, 'Poor little Nicky.'[25] When it came time to go into the Intensive Care Unit, Norton said, 'Joe, I don't think you ought to see Mum.' He explained that her lungs were being moved by a machine and 'You'll find it very distressing.' Years later Joe told me, 'I went in. Sure enough this thing was keeping her alive but it was making a noise . . . All the emotion overcame me then and I just wanted to get out . . . I wasn't ready for that noise.' To Joanna my mother 'looked like a piece of raw steak'. Mary Lowry saw Amanda, accompanied by Joanna, running in tears from the bedside. She went after them but felt awful as she did not have any tissues to offer, only paper fetched from the toilet.

A few feet away, a nurse put her head through the curtains surrounding my bed and announced cheerfully, 'You've got visitors.' As she stepped back, in came Joe, Joanna, Amanda and Philip who all kissed me hello. They studied my black eye and joked, 'What did the other guy look like?' Philip was plainly disturbed. While the others sat down and cheerfully chatted with me, he paced quietly back and forth behind them, unnerved that my one good eye kept following him while my head and body remained motionless. I was pleased to see them and when I asked what had happened they told me something vague about a problem on the boat. I had little appetite for information other than to ask about the others. 'How is Mum? And Dad?' 'Fine,' came the reply. 'And Grandpapa? Granny? Paul?' 'They are in the hospital,' they said. 'And Nick?' 'Yes,' they replied, 'he's in the hospital as well.' None of them had wanted to lie, so they were relieved when Tony Heenan pointed out that this was technically true, as Paul, Nick and our grandparents were in the hospital morgue. Remembering my father had planned to take us on a fishing trip to County Mayo the next day, I told my siblings that I definitely wanted to go. They told me that was fine but I was suspicious there was something they were not telling me. 'Promise me you won't go fishing without me,' I said firmly. I was soon too weak to continue and they left.

Concussion, anaesthesia and sedation made it impossible for me to think clearly or work out what was going on. My recollection of my experiences that day and in the following days was later jumbled for the same reason, and only became clearer years later when short bursts of memory were pieced together with the help of medical records and those around me.

Years later India wrote:

On the Tuesday mum took me with her to the hospital. I can't remember how we got there or who took us, but when we arrived the world's press was lying in wait. A throbbing crowd of flash-bulbs exploded in our faces as we were pushed towards the hospital entrance, people screaming and waving, angry people shouting, police holding them back. I was eleven years old and I had never heard of a political assassination before. I was taken from mum and left in a room, whilst she went upstairs . . . I sat alone in the room, scribbling on the bottom of my Kicker shoes; they had a green spot on one sole, and a red one on the other. Green for go, red for stop. 'Stop, stop, stop' was all I wanted to yell.[26]

Also in the room for a time was London undertaker Christopher Kenyon who had worked through the night to prepare the bodies for travel back to England. He recalls:

We chatted; I asked her name and I told her that I was Christopher and that I was there to help the family. We were reading something like *Country Life* together. It was very hot and stuffy in that room and I found her little head just go *plonk* on my shoulder. I felt very protective and sad so I put my arm round her shoulder and I think I dozed off as well; I was so desperately tired. She was still asleep when Norton and Penelope came back into the room.[27]

When my uncle David Hicks visited me he later noted: 'Brave but a terrible sight.' I slept most of that day, waking now and again to ask the nurses to turn me onto my other side. Waiting to go back to sleep, I listened to the voices coming from the bed beyond the curtain surrounding mine. In their soft lilting Irish accents the nurses were talking to someone called Patricia. They spoke slowly and carefully, telling her what they were doing and reassuring her. I pictured a little Irish girl with red hair and freckles and felt very sorry for her. Only when I was out of Intensive Care did I learn this was my mother.

That night I was sore and restless and asked to be turned time and again. I could not sleep and started to get anxious. When I complained about the bright lights, the nurses switched most of them off. The remaining fluorescent light made a faint hum but to me it sounded deafening and I felt confused and miserable, as if in a nightmare. I asked repeatedly for another injection. The nurses gently told me I would have to wait. When at last the time came for my next jab, I immediately fell asleep, carefree, pain-free and grateful.

Standing at my bedside next morning, Joanna read aloud the card on an arrangement of flowers, declaring it came from 'General Ne Win and the Government of the Burmese Socialist Programme Party'. We burst into laughter. The arrival of my brothers and sisters fundamentally altered my state of mind, making me feel safe and secure. Their infectious humour was soon noticed by the nurses. Mary Lowry used to smoke with her colleagues in a small office. 'You had to have your head down because there was a glass panel at the top and you wouldn't dare let anybody see you, it was most unpopular.' Noticing what was going on, Joe walked up. 'He was looking up over the glass with a big grin on his face. Some of us thought he was gorgeous – so friendly. He always smiled. I thought, "Oh my God, you don't need this."'

My father spent part of that morning in an operating theatre having bomb debris removed from his ears. Afterwards he was seen by Dr Brian O'Connor, father of teenager Libby O'Connor who was working that month at Classiebawn. In the early hours of the day before, he had helped in Nick's post-mortem examination. He did not tell my father but what was going through his mind was 'the sight of his poor wee broken body, so frail . . . dreadful to the nth degree'.[28]

That day my uncle took my cousins home from Classiebawn for the last time. India later wrote: 'Part of my childhood had been raped. Edwina, Ashley and I were helicoptered out by the British Army . . . But I had Grandpapa's dog with me so that was OK and I remember trying to put the headphones over his ears instead of my own and a soldier gently replacing them.'[29]

The IRA detonated a bomb in a public park in Belgium that day.* When Mary Lowry arrived for a series of night shifts in Intensive Care starting that night, she found that the hospital was 'hushed' and a tight security cordon had been thrown around it. Flowers were arriving, 'masses and masses and masses' of them according to Mary who watched them being scanned for explosives.[†]

By Wednesday afternoon my mother's condition had improved enough for her to breathe on her own for three hours. Mary Lowry and the other nurses were careful to keep talking to her. 'I remember telling her a joke one day . . . And she coughed as if to say, "Oh God, take that crazy woman away from me."' In the bed opposite I was making good progress and was no longer considered in danger. At 5.30pm the nurses

---

* The bomb in Brussels, Belgium, was placed under a bandstand where a British Army band were due to play. It wounded two bandsmen and eight spectators, exploding just too early to kill the other twenty musicians, most of whom were still on the coach which had brought them.

† The Garda were twitchy. A painkilling injection gave me hallucinations. When I said I could see something coming through the ceiling, a detective rushed in, hand on gun.

removed the unused ventilator which had been beside my bed. That night I became very distressed and climbed out of bed, trailing behind me the intravenous drip which led into my arm. The nurses rushed to restrain me. Mary Lowry later remembered that I was making no sense, talking about needing 'a uniform for Charles and chocolate for Mildred'; I seemed to be having a nightmare but my eyes were open. I then tried to get under the bed. She and her colleagues did their best to control me but I was 'very difficult to reason with' and started to eff and blind at them. Eventually they contacted Tony Heenan and at 4am he authorised them to sedate me.

When I woke on Thursday morning, 30 August, the nurses found me 'alert and rational'. I said, 'Good morning,' and when Mary Lowry asked me how I had slept I told her, 'Wonderfully, thank you.' She and her colleague looked at each other as they worked on me. 'Do you not remember the night, then?' 'No,' I replied and they smiled at each other. When I asked what had happened they would not tell me. I had already come to be very fond of them, and laughed and teased them to let me in on the secret but all I got was smiles.

As she left the ward that morning, Mary passed my father's room in the neighbouring male surgical department. My mother's life was still hanging in the balance and he had no idea if she had survived the night. On Tuesday morning he had learned that his mother had died and he dreaded hearing the same about his wife. Thinking he was 'probably out of his mind with worry', Mary decided to stop and tell him how my mother and I had fared during the night. The armed guard outside his door did not stop her. Her thoughtfulness and the news she brought made a huge impact on my father. Unable to sleep, he waited through the following nights for her to come again. He later told me how tense he was each morning when she opened the door; and the relief when she brought the news that my mother, the great sustaining force in his life, had lived through another night. 'She went far beyond her duty,' he told me. 'She used to be a little bit worried and didn't stay long because she didn't think she really should.'[30] He gave her a letter to read to my mother, which he had written the day before:

My very own darling,

How I long to be able to come and see you but I am afraid it won't be possible for a few days more. I get continuous reports about you and the intensive care nurses are really sweet and come and see me. My own nurse went to see you this morning and she said you nodded so you got my message. I am really longing to see you again before too long. You know how precious you are to me and I think about you all my waking hours. I do hope you are feeling better and that you will improve rapidly every day from now on. I know you are fairly used to my bad writing but this is the worst you have ever had as I am lying on my side whilst writing. This is due to my having a very sore bottom!

I can't wait to see your sweet face again fairly soon. In the meantime I continue to adore you and once again I realise how incredibly lucky I have been to have married and lived with you for 34 years.

All my love, my darling one,

Johnny.

Mary Lowry 'felt awful reading this letter, so private really, but somebody had to'. She noticed the effect on my mother, still paralysed by the drugs. 'Two tears appeared and that was it. Two tears.' She thought, 'I wish I had somebody to write me a letter like that.' When word reached Tony Heenan, he starting calling my parents 'The Love Birds'. He quickly realised that the day they were reunited would be the day their recovery would take off. When the family asked him when that might be, his reply was: 'One day at a time.' He repeated this so often in so many different scenarios that the phrase became a mantra to us all.

Mary Lowry's visits to my father were a landmark in his recovery and continued when my mother was off the critical list. She found out he was a film producer. 'I remember one morning going over the corridor and straightening my uniform and the guard said, "Where are you going?" I said, "To get a part in a film." Your father was listening and he heard me saying this; I was mortified. "You've got the part," he called out.' Years later my father told me, 'She made all the difference to my life; all the difference. She was the nearest thing to an angel, if there is such a thing.' He added, 'All the time she was talking to me, she was moving her hands and sort of praying and crossing herself. She was a very calming influence. It was one of those very odd things that happened . . . terribly moving.'*

That Thursday morning, the bodies of my grandfather, grandmother and Nick left the hospital for England. Downstairs four government ministers and the mayor joined clergy and hospital staff to see the coffins leave. Upstairs I was not even aware they were dead. There were only a handful of televisions in the hospital and staff and patients crowded around these to watch the scene as it was broadcast. A TV set had been put in my father's room and soon nurses and doctors came in to watch. It was the Sister who noticed my father beginning to crack. He told me, 'It was the first time I had seen the coffins and I was appalled and shocked. Suddenly she got up and led everybody out.'

As the coffins were driven through the streets of Sligo, past Classiebawn and on to Finner Camp, Gardai saluted and onlookers crossed themselves. When press organisations, with the exception of the Irish state broadcaster RTE, were barred they protested 'vocally'. The Minister for Defence relented and they 'surged in'[31] to be met by the sight of three Royal Navy Sea King helicopters with their engines running and rotors turning, ready for an immediate take-off if they came under attack.[†] As Christopher Kenyon buckled up in the leading helicopter, the crew told him they would be flying fast and low. Norton, Penny and Joe followed half an hour later in another helicopter to see the coffins carried into a Royal Air Force Hercules in a ceremony led by the Irish Prime Minister, or Taoiseach, Jack Lynch. The RAF plane landed at Southampton Airport near Broadlands. While the bodies of Nick and my grandmother went to Kenyon's mortuary in Westbourne Grove, London, Prince Philip and Prince Charles accompanied my grandfather's coffin to the hall of his home.

Knowing I had no idea of the day's proceedings, my father wrote:

* Perhaps what was 'odd' about it for my father was that he was not a religious man, in fact he was a firm non-believer yet he found her apparent faith comforting.
† The crews' caution would have been heightened by the experience of colleagues from the same squadron two days earlier, when they had flown to the scene of the Warrenpoint bombing. After landing, a secondary bomb damaged the helicopter. The crew survived.

My darling Tim,

This will be a difficult letter for you to read as I am lying on my side! I hear very good reports of you & I do hope you are really feeling better. Wasn't it lovely to see Norton, Joe, Joanna, Amanda & Phi & Penny too. It was very nice for me to be in the same ambulance that you were in – I wonder if you remember the journey? I do not know how long it will be before I will be able to see you but I am greatly looking forward to it. I hear Mum is on the other side of the room which must be nice for both of you!

I am really longing to see you again soon and in the meantime this letter brings masses of love.

Dad

That evening I said goodbye to the nurses in Intensive Care, who promised to come and see me in the Eye department. I chatted merrily to two hospital porters as they wheeled me from the curtained claustrophobia of Intensive Care and down the 1940s corridor into the modern extension of the hospital. I arrived on the second floor by lift and felt cheered by its bright walls and many windows. At 6:30pm I was wheeled into a single room, with flowers by the bed, and an intercom to the nursing station. They lifted me from the gurney into my new bed and I studied the views over the east of the town to the hills in the distance. I was feeling upbeat. When some of my family visited we chatted happily and I asked about Nick. Again they reassured me that he was elsewhere in the hospital and I was content to leave it at that. Joanna left and went to see my father. I was due to see him the next day and he told her, 'I can't face Tim unless he knows about Nicky . . . Will you tell him?'

Joanna walked into my room with my aunt. I assumed they had a little time to spare before they left for the night. I carried on talking and asking questions. Joanna sat in an upright chair to my left, her arms resting on its sides, and my aunt settled into the other corner of the room. When Joanna looked at me and said she had something to say, I realised she was in a serious mood. Speaking quietly and clearly she said that the explosion had not been an accident, it had been a bomb. 'When you were brought to the hospital, some of you were conscious, some were not. You woke up. Nicky never did.' There was a pause. Lying in my bed with my head propped up on the pillow, I did not move, I could not collapse. Until that moment I had had no inkling of the truth. I stared at her and as I saw her begin to cry, I did the same. My vision blurred and the only noise I could hear was my crying and my breath coming in spasms.

Joanna and my aunt held and cuddled me, which soon reduced my crying. After I calmed down we talked further. Soon a nurse came in to get me ready for the night and it was time for them to leave. I re-assured them that I was all right and they should go back to the others who were waiting to return to Classiebawn. After they left I was pleased because I wanted to cry my eyes out but not in front of them. Each time my tears faded I would start to try to think. I could manage a short bout of quiet concentration and then the air would leave my lungs very slowly and I would hide my face in case the nurses or policeman outside my door could see me crying.

I tried to sort my confused and racing thoughts. I felt utter sadness for Nick and fear for myself, that I would not know how to lead my life without him. There was an underlying flaw to the story of Nick's death because it went against a basic truth of our twinhood: physically Nick was more robust than me so if one of us were going to die it would be me, not him. I had a sensation that the wrong twin was dead. I also had a flash of another emotion: relief. I was alive and it felt good, very good. I was somewhat shocked by this, it seemed selfish and greedy. How could I be feeling this when I had just learned Nick was dead? But the truth was I had my life, my limbs, my hearing and one perfect eye. I had an active, normal life ahead of me and I felt an irrepressible flash of luck. I did not tell a soul about this. It was a confusing impulse that occasionally streaked through me, as unpredictably as the awful feelings of loneliness, grief and fear. Physically, mentally and emotion-ally exhausted, I lay and realised I would never again hear Nick say 'Goodnight' and 'God bless' to me from the next-door bed. I was on my own.

The nurses gave me some pills and recorded: 'Visited by relatives and informed of brother's death – very upset and weepy at report time. Mogadon. To sleep 1015pm. Slept soundly all night.'

*   *   *

Next morning, Friday, my family were back with news and stories from Classiebawn and messages from friends and family. One from Buckingham Palace said: 'It is impossible to find the words to express the numb horror I feel . . . at this appalling moment. All I can do is send you my love and boundless sympathy. Your affectionate and devoted godfather Charles.'³²

As I lay in bed watching, a nurse showed the family a white plastic bag in my cupboard. It contained the clothes which I had been wearing on arrival in Casualty. Also there was my watch, a Casio F-100 with a state-of-the-art digital display which my parents had given me for Christmas; I strapped it back on happily, amazed it still worked. Also in the bag were my white Dunlop tennis shoes with smart green edges which I had inherited from Philip, now soggy and torn. Like my unwashed hair, they ponged of diesel oil, and Joanna asked the nurse to throw them and the clothes away. I did not care in the slightest but I was surprised because I thought my mother would have wanted them washed in case they were salvageable. It was a sign that mothering decisions were now going to be made by my sisters, at least for the foreseeable future. I was longing to be reunited with my parents, but Tony Heenan told me that it was still out of the question in my mother's case but that all going well I would soon be with my father.

In Dublin, Thomas McMahon and Francis McGirl waved and smiled at friends in the Special Criminal Court, having just been charged with my grandfather's murder.* My father later told me, 'I lay in that hospital bed and thought about it and decided the only thing I could do was cut [them] out of my life.'³³

Soon Tony Heenan arranged for my father to be brought up to the second floor and placed in an empty four-bed ward not far from my room. Downstairs the nurses removed the tube from my mother's windpipe and took her off the ventilator and drugs which had paralysed her. My mother wrote three weeks later:

---

* The day before, the court had released the men on a technicality. As they walked away they were accompanied by Gardai who re-arrested them on the street and charged them with being members of the IRA. They were remanded in custody overnight.

I had worked out Dodo must be dead, and Daddy too, and could hear talk of Tim, also in intensive care, and Pammy told me poor John had two broken legs but ALRIGHT (which kept me alive) but no talk of Nicky. Unable to speak – tubes everywhere – but made writing signs and given paper and pen and somehow managed to write 'I think Daddy dead – Dodo dead – and Nick.'[34]

My aunt was at her bedside. Shocked, she decided to play for time. Using her short-sightedness as an excuse she said, 'I can't quite read this, darling. I'm going to take it over to the window for some light.' The medical staff's advice was that if my mother had asked, she should now be told the truth. My aunt returned to her bedside and told her that she was right: Nicky was dead. 'The worst moment in my life,' my mother later wrote in her diary. She decided she did not have the strength even to think about it; she would deal with it once she had a bit more life in her. 'Perhaps Dodo and Daddy – who went out like the blazing comet he was – have been spared a sad old age – but for Nick to be dead at 14 on the threshold of life – before he had even fallen in love – that is true irreparable heartbreak for us all,' she wrote in her diary. 'Cannot even cry for my poor father, who I adored, yet – as misery over Nick too great and all consuming.'* It was still assumed she would be blind and no one was sure how much hearing she would regain. She raised everyone's hopes when she whispered, 'What's that noise like a little canary?'[35] It was wind causing the venetian blinds in the nearby window to buzz.

The Irish government's handling of the attack had been labelled 'a diplomatic disaster'.[36] The Taoiseach Jack Lynch had continued a holiday in Portugal as his country and the world looked on in horror. He was widely believed to be sympathetic to the IRA movement, but under mounting criticism had ordered the biggest round-up of IRA supporters ever attempted. Two hundred sympathisers were interrogated over two

---

* Written four weeks after the attack. She added 'How can I write about these unbelievable horrors but not for lack of J's and my frequent tears and despair in our hearts at this most cruel of losses . . . I feel I must try and record this tragedy factually for the future.'

days. With his wife Máirín, he visited Classiebawn where they sat in the drawing room with the family and formally expressed the condolences of the Irish government. Later they made small talk over tea in the dining room. One of the household staff, deeply distressed by the attack, had 'drink taken' and was rolling around the room alarmingly. At one point Joanna gently collected him and discreetly shoved him in the right direction. The family all prayed he would get through the meal without landing a scalding teapot in the Taoiseach's lap, a disaster which he skilfully avoided.

The hospital was now swarming with soldiers and security who barred entry to anyone except officials. Some of the staff seemed somewhat in awe of their prime minister but not everyone felt like this. His wife was collared by the chaplain Canon Wood who said, 'Where were you? We needed you. Why weren't you here?'[37] Jack Lynch gave an impromptu press call on the steps of the hospital, describing his reaction to the attack as 'Horror, disgust and great sadness – and, being abroad at the time, one of shame as well, I must confess'.[38]

Later that afternoon Tony Heenan told me I could go by wheelchair to see my father. I could not stop smiling as I was wheeled down the corridor and turned the corner to see him in his bed. Although haggard, he looked much better than when I had last seen him in the ambulance. We kissed and chatted and I devoured some grapes in his room. Being close to him made me feel reassured that life would go on with some normality. Soon exhausted, I was wheeled back to my room where I immediately fell asleep.

On Saturday 1 September I was handed a note from my father: 'GOOD MORNING? SEE YOU SOON?' On the back was a list of things to be remembered, headed page '2'. The list had been crossed out, presumably accomplished. Even now he was 'humming like a top'[39] making plans, holding meetings and writing notes. He persuaded the hospital management to wheel a telephone in his room and this he used as much as the nurses would allow.

The stitches in my face, elbow and hip were taken out. When alone, I often wondered how my mother was getting on and desperately wanted to be with her. That day I wrote:

Dearest Mum

I hope you are really feeling better now. Everyone tells me you are making really marvellous progress. I am feeling fine and aren't in any pain. I've got Phi's radio, now, which is lovely, and I have books and cassettes galore.

I'm very near Dad, and pop along for meals, drinks and chats every so often. All the nurses, Doctors, Sisters etc. are <u>so</u> kind and nice to me. I am very spoilt by them, and am getting so lazy! Its lovely seeing everyone. I can't tell you how much I am looking forward to seeing you.

Masses + masses of love, Timmy.

A reply came back in the handwriting of my aunt Pamela:

1/9/79

My Darling Tim,

A special little line to thank you for your darling little letter. I know how good and brave you are being and an inspiration to us all. I am longing to see you and Daddy.

Very much love,

Mum

9

FRIENDS FROM ENGLAND

My aunt and siblings would soon have to travel to England for the funerals they were helping to plan. They were desperate at the idea of leaving us behind but there was no medically safe alternative. Their prayers were answered two days after the attack when Jamie Crathorne and David Dugdale called to offer their help. The two brothers thought and acted as we did and we trusted them utterly. Our family asked if they and their wives would come and look after us in hospital while the rest of the family went to England. There was nothing in it for them except danger, expense and trauma. Without hesitation they agreed to come. In his final years my father described it as the 'most shining example of friendship in my life'.[1]

Jamie and Sylvia lived in Yorkshire, close to David and Susie. Leaving their young children behind, they set off together the next afternoon, Saturday 1 September. Landing in Dublin, they were met by a warrant officer from the Irish Army and hired a car. For the best part of the next five hours they drove with a Garda escort through incessant rain until, nearing Sligo, they emerged into 'brilliant streaks of light and bright yellow sunshine'[2] shining straight into their eyes, the sun now lowering over the Atlantic. Classiebawn's steps were wet when at nine o'clock they were met there by my brothers and sisters whom Susie Dugdale later remembered as 'desperate for a cuddle'. The one thing Sylvia found herself 'totally unprepared for' was their state of shock.

'They were marvellous too, but we were the first of their friends from home & when we arrived they fell upon us.'[3]

They went straight into dinner where they discovered that life in the castle was going to be 'funny & sad, giggly & tearful'.[4] As they ate, the family told them stories, some of which made them 'roar with laughter' while the next would reduce them to tears. As usual, the family were very open with them and Susie quickly found herself 'drawn in'. Norton said, 'How will Tim ever live? How will he cope?' A discussion followed in which Tony Heenan's opinion was quoted: it was not me he was concerned about but my parents 'because young minds get over things; older ones find it more difficult'.[5]

Arriving at the hospital next morning, Sunday 2 September, Joanna went with Jamie to see my mother. Knowing what a gentle and sensitive man he was, she locked her arm in his, and as they approached Intensive Care she could feel him trembling. When they arrived at my mother's bedside, he found her barely recognisable.

Later that day my mother composed a letter to my father. She signed it in large childlike capitals, guided by my aunt to whom she had dictated it.

My darling Johnnie,

In all the 33 years we've spent together this is the first letter that I've wanted to write and haven't been able to do so.

I am sure it was your dear voice calling for me when I hit that piece of wood that made me realise you were all right and kept me going.

If ever any of us wanted proof of what an absolutely splendid family we all have, it was to find them all around us immediately giving comfort and support. My heart bleeds especially for little Timmy and he will need all the comfort every one of us can give him but I hear he is being quite marvellous in keeping his pecker up.

I long to see you soon and think of you both so much and look forward to our reunion soon although you must realise I look horrid but that is of no importance. Luckily I think being a sailor's daughter helped me escape with his Kelly technique I remembered, and it's

really nice to realise Dodo was in the boat with us. What a remarkable old lady she was and don't really feel she would have wanted
a different end. I'm very pleased Twiga was looked after properly
and I hope we can get a nice new one for Timmy which I might
be able to have in the term time.

Masses of kisses for you two from me until we can meet very
soon.

PATRICIA

The Crathornes and Dugdales had holidayed in Ireland with our
family for decades and never felt in danger but now the atmosphere
was different. They were told that the telephone was being tapped and
were given 'dire warnings about security (. . . what an uncomfortable &
uneasy feeling)'.[6] At dinner they found the dining-room curtains were
closed despite the beautiful Atlantic sunsets. They badly needed somewhere to escape and Roskeeragh Point seemed ideal, stretching from
Classiebawn to the Atlantic half a mile away. Even here the Gardai
and Army told them to be watchful as there could be a bomb hidden
anywhere. The four of them took a long Sunday-afternoon walk on the
Point while my father called my five brothers and sisters to his bedside
for a heartfelt farewell. He had by now accepted that he was too badly
wounded to travel to the funerals that were set for the coming days.
All week he had been insistent that nothing, no person, no reason was
going to stop him being there. This was wildly unrealistic but neither
the family nor Tony Heenan had been able to make him see sense.
Years later he told me that there had been an element of 'fuck you'[7] in
this as if in defiance of the attack.

Many of the most difficult decisions and tasks the family had to face
were now being passed through Norton who, as the eldest, had stepped
into a leading role. The extra strain seemed to be taking a toll on him.
One evening at dinner the family were so concerned that one of them
slipped away to ring Tony Heenan, who immediately set off from Sligo.
At the castle he asked for a bottle of whisky and to be left alone with
Norton. Behind the closed door of the Morning Room he got Norton
to pour out his feelings. When the two men left the room a long time
later, the bottle was much reduced, Norton much restored, and the
family much relieved. Tony packed my brother off to bed, reminding

the family, 'I don't want to see any stiff upper lips around here.' The resilience shown by Norton and the rest of the family was perhaps augmented by such brief episodes of release, without which they may have cracked. Years later I wondered whether I would have benefited from having a similar episode myself, a complete letting-go of my pent-up emotions as a way of venting what was building up inside me and which was later to surface chronically.

On Monday 3 September, one of my father's nurses noted: 'Sleeping for shorter periods. Perspiring at 4am. Restless this a.m. and complaining of deafness in left ear and soreness all over.' Another reported him 'depressed and agitated'. That day he entered two weeks without proper sleep. After breakfast I wrote: 'Morning Dad, Feeling fine, and liking having Phi's Radio. No visitors yet, but perhaps we'll be seeing the Dugdales before too long. See you soon, possibly for lunch? Love Tim.' As always, the morning was consumed with various treatments and tests. The nurses removed stitches from my elbow and thigh, but when they tried to take them out of my stomach I writhed in pain and they left them in place till the next day.

At Classiebawn, Jamie said goodbye to the family as they clambered into a British Army helicopter for the funerals. Norton had taken Jamie to one side and said that if my mother died before they returned, none of Jamie's family should feel in any way responsible. Meanwhile David, Susie and Sylvia were at the hospital where one of them handed my father an envelope from Joanna.

Darling Daddy

I'm sure you know all the things we wanted to say to you this afternoon when we all came to see you but didn't, for the two reasons of not wanting to tire you and the fact that you'd already said so much of what we would have anyway. As you can imagine we've done nothing but stick together and talk to each other through all this, but we know our individual and collective ways of thinking and approaches to life stem so totally from you and Mamma that we've never felt apart from you for one second. If there's one thing this horrible business has done, it's cemented our family together with a bond that was even stronger than before, if that was possible. I know that's one of the things you said to us, but I wanted you to know how strongly we all feel it too. How lucky we've all been these past years, lucky to have known and loved grandpapa and granny and Nicky, and lucky to have been so very, very happy with them and you and Mamma.

I can't say anymore now. It's midnight, and I'm not feeling very coherent, but we'll have time to say more later. We'll all be thinking of you and Mamma and Tim every minute we're away from you. We all love you so, so much, more than we can <u>ever</u> say, I'm sure you know.[8]

Believing the family had gone, I was slumped in bed, feeling low and talking quietly with David. Suddenly I heard an approaching helicopter. The family had persuaded the pilot to make a detour past the hospital. I struggled out of bed and stood at the window waving like mad. I wished I could hug them all goodbye but this was almost as good and my anguish evaporated. I stayed at the window and watched as they became a dot in the clouds. I was aware of David behind me but, feeling uplifted, I did not take my eye off the helicopter until it was gone. They had flown away to say goodbye to Nick; and in saying goodbye to them I had come as close as I could to saying goodbye to him. When I climbed back into bed, David seemed immensely relieved. If Sister Darcy had found me out of bed she would have given him a piece of her mind.

My father's mind was already on the future. 'John was absolutely determined not to let [the attack] disrupt the annual trips to Ireland,' Jamie later told me.[9] That afternoon his employees at Aasleagh joined him, the Crathornes and the Dugdales for a bedside tea party. 'I want to talk about next year's stocking programme,' he told them. He felt especially close to Mickey and Bridget Keane who personified the small community at Aasleagh which had always felt like a second family to him.

When Tony Heenan told me that afternoon that I would soon be reunited with my parents, I was over the moon with excitement. My father was as happy as I was when later we kissed hello and I climbed into a nearby bed. We talked incessantly. I described seeing the family fly by and how I had waved to them. He showed me a letter he had just received from my mother. It was an almost exact repeat of what she had written the day before but it warmed our hearts to get anything from her. Her closing words made us look at the empty bed beside us and long for it to be filled:

> I cannot wait until I am allowed to see you both and hope it won't be too long before we are all reunited.
>
> Meanwhile how proud and happy we are to have such a marvellous family and friends to rally round and look after us.
>
> This is not the end of a letter but the continuation of our loving relationship throughout the years in which Timmy will now have an even more special part.
> P/ MUM
> XOXO

Warmed and comforted, we wondered when she would arrive. The wait seemed interminable. At last two porters and some nurses wheeled my mother in on a bed. Despite all the warnings, nothing had prepared my father for what she looked like. Dozens of prickly black stitches protruded from her face. She turned her head but could not see us through her barely open eyes. Instinctively they wanted to kiss each other but my mother croaked, 'You can't kiss a hedgehog,' and broke into a laugh that suddenly switched into a coughing fit. As she fought for air, she moved one of her hands from beneath the sheets. 'I remember this hand coming out with this bandage all round it,' my father told me years later. 'I wanted to put out my hand to hold it and I got such a shock. All the bandages made it a very upsetting moment.'[10] I quickly got out of bed and went to my mother's side. I managed to find a spot to plant a kiss and she immediately wanted to touch me and try to get a glimpse of my face. It was difficult to know if her lacerated and stitched eyes saw anything, but they must have for she later wrote in her diary: 'What a joy to be taken up and reunited with my darling darling J & Timmy both of whose faces bruised and battered.' The nurses wrote in my father's file: 'More relaxed and happy [to see] wife.'

I sat on my father's bed talking quietly to both my parents. Soon it was time for me to sleep and the nurses pulled a curtain around my bed. My parents waited until I was asleep before they allowed themselves to share their grief. My mother's diary continues: 'at night our beds are pushed together and I can hold his hand when he wakes in terror. He is also suffering a lot of pain. But his memories so searing and we both cry a lot at night – & other times.' By day it was more difficult for them to hide their tears. I could remember seeing my mother cry only once before, when our young dog had yelped in pain and died in her arms of a sudden heart attack. I had never seen my father in tears. I wanted to ease their pain but had no way of doing so apart from being happy around them, and in this I busied myself. I avoided crying in front of my parents because I did not want them to worry about me.

Within hours my mother's recovery accelerated and her bodily functions started performing again. She later wrote in her diary: 'I had "severe diarrhoea" climbing on and off bedpan with leg in long plaster with no strength to do so, behind my curtains while life continues around me – poor things! We have an armed guard outside who must be learning a lot about nursing.' While thunderous noises emanated from behind her curtain, my father and I smiled at each other and cheerfully read our books and chatted with the steady flow of nurses and doctors and occasional visitors. We were just happy to have my mother back. The week before, we might have been appalled at the indignities foisted on her but now we were measuring everything on a different scale. Next day the nurses told us we would have a visit from 'His Lordship Dr Conway', who was the Bishop in Sligo. As he and an assistant entered, my mother was struck by another attack of diarrhoea. With lightning speed the nurses drew the curtain around her bed. The Bishop's conversation with my father was punctuated by explosive noises. My father found listening to someone talk about religion an uphill task in any circumstances; now it was all he could do to keep straight-faced. Watching from the other side of the room, I too fought giggles. My mother told me years later, 'It was the nearest I came to not caring.'

When my mother was allowed to start taking food by mouth, she was asked what she would like. She enquired what was on offer and a nurse said she could have absolutely anything. She insisted there must be a set menu but the nurse again told her to order whatever she wished. Determined to win, my mother asked jokingly if caviar was on the menu. 'That'll be fine,' said the nurse and started to walk away before my mother could stop her. From then on I invented a menu which I wrote out daily.

For several days my mother had believed the explosion on *Shadow V* had been caused by the engine overheating. When my aunt eventually told her that it had been a bomb she was 'interested' to find she still 'loved the lovely Irish voices all around us and the whole place'.[11]

Getting back from the hospital, the Crathornes and Dugdales walked together on Roskeeragh Point. They gathered beautifully rounded ancient stones. Carrying them back to the castle, they spent a long time sorting them and then building a little cairn over Twiga's grave. That afternoon Susie and Sylvia walked on the Point again, now in warm sunshine, and picked honeysuckle. They arranged this in vases which they placed in my grandfather's and Nick's bedrooms. They did not have enough for my grandmother's but later found some wild freesias and put them in her quiet, windblown room. Sylvia then started writing a letter to her sister.

> Oh Rachel, darling Rachel – if only I could talk to you – I can't tell you how devastating, how moving, how heartrending this nightmare is. It's impossible really to describe what a bomb victim looks like – not so as to let the other person feel the full sickening horror, & for us seeing Patricia a full 6 days after the event was apparently so different from the first few days. Norton had to have his own mother pointed out to him when he arrived at the intensive care unit late on Monday night – an unrecognisable object that did not even have a human shape. But so marvellous, so courageous and strong in spirit. Her first action when she could barely move her arms was to reach for Norton's chin to see if <u>he</u> was alright, after a recent operation on his jaw – & the first scrawl she managed to draw, was 'whe . . . sle . . .' & the family said 'when . . . , where . . .' & she nodded – & they made out she wanted to know where they were all sleeping to be sure they were all sleeping with someone else – no one on their own. And her first husky broken & somewhat drugged question to me was – 'What's happening with <u>your</u> family the children' &

'How nice it is that people should come all the way from England just to see us'. Always thinking of others first – after her own intense pain & anguish.

We heard that my grandfather's obituary was to be shown on Irish television. As we had missed it on the day of the attack, we wanted to see it, or in my mother's case, hear it. Two porters carried in a television which we watched after supper. For an hour I sat, sad but dry-eyed. The programme ended with a final question put to my grandfather by the interviewer: 'Do you think Prince Charles will be a good king?' My grandfather replied, 'Well if he doesn't, I'll eat my hat.' There was a long pause. After six seconds a small smile spread on his face. 'I'll eat my halo,' he said and the screen faded to black. Destroyed by the ending, I broke down. I could not remember the last thing he had said to me. Now I had something.

10

FUNERALS

At the beginning of August, Grace Ryan had never heard of Paul Maxwell. By the end of the month she found herself among the leading mourners at his funeral. She wrote in her diary:

August 29th 1979
Today was the day of Paul's funeral. It was very sad. Everything went as normal in the morning. At two pm we had to leave to go to Enniskillen. Libby, Siobhán, Sheela and I went with the Knatchbulls. Michael-John drove, Penny was in the front, behind them were Norton, Amanda and I and behind us were Libby, Siobhán and Sheela. We drove at about 80mph and had a Garda escort all the way which changed at the Border. When we arrived at the church everyone was waiting for us. There were crowds around the car when we got out and loads of reporters and cameramen. The Police took the car.

The church service was beautiful but so sad and upsetting. When we came out afterwards there were cameras everywhere, how could they at a funeral? . . . While we were driving away in the car reporters kept coming up to the windows but we just shut them.

The day was beautiful, Mrs Maxwell was very nice. She walked to the graveyard with her mother. She looked very Indian – she is dark skinned and long dark hair and wore a long mauve dress.

I felt most sorry for poor Mr Maxwell, he was really broken hearted, Paul was his only son. Everyone cried when they put a wreath in the shape of a boat from 'Big John and Little Mama' on his grave. Amanda and Penny were trying to comfort us but they were just as bad as us.

We left immediately after. Norton drove home. It was all very sad.

My mother spent her first morning out of Intensive Care being seen by doctors and nurses, after which she had her bed pushed against my father's. In my dressing gown I hopped in between them. We were talking quietly and she brought the subject around to Nick's funeral. She had first learned of the arrangements being made while in Intensive Care and had asked for the hymn 'To be A Pilgrim' to be added to the service. She had chosen it for our christening. The plans were now almost final but she wanted to know if I wanted anything included in the service. I said I did not think so. She asked me very softly if there was a hymn I would like. I thought for a few seconds and said 'Jerusalem'. 'OK,' said my mother, sounding slightly surprised that I had chosen so quickly. I explained it was a hymn we liked. In fact I had chosen it because it featured in a *Monty Python* sketch we loved. I knew in an instant that it was the way I would be able to blow him a kiss at his funeral without even being there. I did not want to talk about it but I was quietly pleased because now I had a part in his farewell.

My father opened a letter from his solicitor Robert Moorhead. The two men saw eye to eye on everything. Each respected the judgement of the other; they laughed a lot together and were unfailingly courteous to each other in an old-fashioned way which might easily be mistaken for a lack of affection. In fact they were the best of friends. Bobby Moorhead had learned of the attack from his wife not long after it was first reported. That night he got a phone call from Ireland and every evening after that my brother Joe called to update him and relay messages and requests from my father. 'That way I came to arrange the funeral in Mersham,'[1] Bobby Moorhead later explained. A joint funeral for Nick and my grandmother was to be held on Thursday, the day after my grandfather's funeral. Bobby Moorhead wrote to my father:

Dear John,

   . . . All four children have nattered to me on the phone except Philip – but it has mainly been Norton and Michael-John. As one would expect they have been wonderful – absolutely cool and calm and utterly in control of events. You really have no idea, and if you had been a fly on the wall you would have been terribly proud. Each time there is a conversation there are generally ten or twelve <u>decisions</u> to take and they are taken without fuss or pause. And I know very well that the discussions I have with them are only a drop in the ocean compared with all the other 101 matters which are going on for them all day – not least giving Jack Lynch tea! They have been truly magnificent – and you need have no fears about them not being able to cope . . .[2]

On holiday in the Bahamas once, my cousin Ashley had walked into our grandfather's room to find him leaning over the bed which was covered in papers. He explained proudly they were a new draft of his funeral arrangements. The fun he had in planning his last hurrah was evident to all the family, and he updated them a number of times in the last few years of his life. The main venue would be Westminster Abbey but he wanted to be buried at Romsey, near Broadlands, so he planned that his last journey should be on a train from Waterloo Station accompanied by family and a few close friends. For the trip he requested a snack lunch, specifying one menu for winter and another for summer.*

After the assassination, Bobby Moorhead spent two days at St James's Palace going through the plans 'which was an absolute eye-opener; I had never seen anything like it in my life,' he told me many years later. There were thirty or forty people at a horseshoe table headed by the Lord Chamberlain, Lord Maclean. 'They were all very well informed, the people around that table; very, very impressive.' Every part of the day was planned in detail:

---

* 'Lord Mountbatten's family paid for the drinks and sandwiches served on his funeral train because the government . . . would not meet the £1.50 a head cost.' *Daily Telegraph*, London, 2 January 2006.

When we got to Waterloo Station, Lord Maclean looked up and said 'Is anyone from British Rail here?' A little man held up his hand and said yes he was a Mr Simpson. So, Lord Maclean said he was so glad. 'Now, you are in charge of this special train we are having, aren't you?' The man said he was just a station master and Lord Maclean said, 'I don't mind. As far as I'm concerned you are looking after the train. I don't want to hear the thing has been held up between here and Romsey, you've got to see it has a clear run. I don't want it to go like the clappers; it's got to go at a stately speed.'[3]

When my brother Norton got home from Sligo on Monday 3 September, he pressed the 'play' button on his answerphone and suddenly heard our grandmother speaking. It was a message she had left a week or two earlier. He was finding it hard to get through those days and this 'did not help'.[4] In London he and the rest of the family were relieved to find they were swept along by the vast state machinery deployed for the upcoming ceremonial funeral.

By contrast, the funeral for Nick and our grandmother was to be a small private one in our village church in Mersham. Donald Coggan, the Archbishop of Canterbury, had christened Nick and me, and my mother wished him to lead the service. When Bobby Moorhead called Lambeth Palace, he immediately agreed and then my father wrote to him:

Dear Archbishop,

I am sure you will understand how sad my wife Patricia and I are that we cannot be at the funeral on Thursday of my mother and our little boy, Nicky . . . who is, as I am sure you know, one of our marvellous identical twin sons. We had 3 sons and 2 daughters between 17 and 3 when we started our last child, which turned out to be darling Nicholas and Timothy . . . Timothy of course adored his brother (who was 20 minutes older) and it nearly breaks our hearts to see only Timothy left. However he is recovering very fast and I know will make a marvellous life of his own . . .[5]

On Wednesday 5 September in Dublin's High Court, Francis McGirl applied for bail. Superintendent Patrick O'Connell told the court the murder was 'the most serious crime committed since the foundation of the Republic' and bail was refused.

In London my family was assembling at St James's Palace. Norton, Joe, Philip, my uncle David Hicks, and Ashley lined up behind my grandfather's coffin with Princes Philip and Charles and the Dukes of Kent and Gloucester. The coffin had arrived the previous day from Romsey Abbey where my grandfather's staff had mounted a day-and-night vigil. They had stood at each corner of the coffin while people passed in silence for two days. The coffin then went to the Queen's Chapel in St James's, where 25,000 people queued to file past. That evening the family visited in private. My cousin India wrote in her diary: 'We . . . say goodbye to Grandpapa. We all cry even the men.'[6]

Next morning, as dictated by tradition, the female members of the family waited at the Abbey while the men followed the coffin on foot as it was pulled mile after mile on a gun carriage by a hundred and twenty-two naval ratings. Alongside the coffin walked admirals from India, the United States and Burma, and a general from France. Ahead, riderless, was Dolly, my grandfather's black charger, with my grandfather's boots reversed in the stirrups. As they walked, she deposited a large pile of droppings. Seeing it ahead, Joe concentrated hard on how to avoid the mess without breaking step. A friend later wrote to my parents: 'The warmth & size of the crowds in London . . . was something never to be forgotten.'[7] The ceremony was televised in twenty-one countries.

The Queen led crowned heads and royalty from Norway, Sweden, Denmark, Holland, Greece, Italy, Luxembourg, Monaco, Liechtenstein, Bulgaria, Romania and Jordan. The Prime Minister, Margaret Thatcher, was followed by her predecessors James Callaghan, Harold Wilson, Edward Heath and Harold Macmillan, as well as the Irish Prime Minister Jack Lynch. Among the congregation of two thousand was John Maxwell. Simultaneously in Enniskillen Paul was being remembered that morning by a minute's silence at his school, the Portora Royal. In London, the Commissioner of the Metropolitan Police, Sir David McNee, posted four thousand officers to guard the funeral.

At Classiebawn, Peter Nicholson raised my grandfather's standard for the last time. While some chose to congregate at the television sets of Mullaghmore's two hotels, others said prayers at the convent chapel overlooking the harbour. At eleven o'clock, a two-minute silence began in Ireland, widely observed in workplaces north and south of the border.* One report estimated more than a million workers downed tools.[8] In south-west Belfast, a nationalist area, seven hundred workers at the De Lorean car factory stopped work. In Dublin, buses and cars pulled over to the side of the road and the Tricolor flew at half mast over the General Post Office in O'Connell Street, symbol of armed republicanism since the Easter Rising of 1916.

In Sligo Hospital that morning, my father was recovering from an operation. At ten o'clock the night before, the bones in his right leg had been re-set and a new plaster-of-Paris cast applied. Mindful of his cardiac history, Tony Heenan had put him to sleep not with the normal intravenous drugs but with gas. My father told me years later that it felt like asphyxiation. Like the doctors, however, he was pleased that it had reduced the stress on his heart. This morning he was complaining of 'flashing lights' before his eyes, a symptom I had for some time as well. We were reassured this was a sign of damaged nerve endings coming back to life.

The nurses wheeled my father's bed into the middle of the ward and put a vase of flowers on top of the television. When they told us a patient in a nearby ward could not get his radio to work, Jamie and I nipped down the corridor and managed to fix it so he could listen to the service. Back in the ward I took up position on my father's right side and Jamie went on his left. I felt as though I was in the front row of a rugby scrum expecting a tough match ahead. As my mother still had no useful sight, she stayed in her bed in the corner of the room with David and Susie on either side. Listening to the broadcast and knowing my grandfather's detailed plans, she said occasionally, 'Oh, that's not quite the way Daddy wanted it to be.' Mostly she was silent and tears rolled down her face from time to time.

I felt like a detached spectator watching a distant ceremony that

---

* The call for silence was made by the Irish Congress of Trade Unions in remembrance of the 1,958 people who had died in the Troubles that had then been ongoing for ten years. It was endorsed by major employers, the four main churches and many chambers of trade.

just happened to include my loved ones. It was as if something inside me had snapped and disconnected from reality. I was dry-eyed, not out of an effort to be strong for my parents, but because I was emotionally numb. It felt unnatural, and deep down I knew it was wrong. But it was also convenient as it allowed me to sail through the day and comfort my parents, as the Crathornes and Dugdales were doing. Susie looked at me from time to time, amazed at how unaffected I seemed.

The commentator said, 'How sad it must be for Lord and Lady Brabourne that they cannot attend this occasion. We send them our love in hospital in Sligo; and our particular sympathy for the fact they can't attend the funeral of their own son which will be held tomorrow.' I felt a crack open up inside me and I knew some latent emotion was beginning to stir.

My mother managed only one glimpse of the procession when she saw Dolly the horse and my grandfather's empty boots. My father was often overcome by what we were seeing. 'Darling, the procession is simply beautiful. The boys look marvellous,' he said as the camera panned along Norton, Joe, Philip and Ashley walking behind the coffin, and the vast silent crowds. Suddenly I felt a hot stab of emotion and wished I was there with them. When the Archbishop of Canterbury asked everyone to pray for us in Sligo Hospital, a horrible feeling of separation came over me and at last tears came to my eyes.

After the service the Crathornes and Dugdales suggested we have some time to ourselves and we checked on each other; my parents kissed me and I kissed them. After we moved the beds back into position, I sat between them again. Sylvia was touched by the 'brilliant, loving, strong & endlessly kind' staff as they set up 'a positive banquet', including two bottles of wine. My mother had not yet eaten any solid food but she now managed a little, later noting in her diary that it had been difficult 'to do justice' to it. She seemed very pleased and referred to the lunch as 'a proper wake'.[9] I was hungry and tucked in heartily.

Meanwhile my family joined the royal family and guests in order to travel with my grandfather's coffin to Romsey.* My aunt recalled, 'On the train the Queen asked me to sit in her carriage and tell her

---

* Acting as the on-board British Rail guard, William 'Sailor' Simpson knew the secret of the train's steady speed, as mandated by the Lord Chamberlain: other trains on the track had been ordered into sidings.

everything that had happened. She hardly commented but listened intently to everything I could tell her.'[10] Along the eighty-seven miles of track people could be seen in their back gardens, standing stiffly to attention. Union flags were commonplace, all at half mast. My grandfather's coffin was lowered into the ground in a private twelve-minute service which for some of the family was the most harrowing part of the day. When a bugler failed to hit quite the right notes during the last post, the family knew they were not the only ones affected. Later at the door of Broadlands, Joanna met the Queen who had managed as ever to maintain perfect composure in public. Now she was red-eyed. When Joanna asked her if she would like to go upstairs, she nodded and said, 'Yes, I think I will.'

For those who witnessed it, the day had been dominated by the simple enduring smile of a twelve-year-old girl. India had been standing in Westminster Abbey waiting for the funeral to begin. Princess Grace of Monaco walked over and bending down examined the little gold cross India was wearing around her neck, saying how beautiful it was. 'Thank you,' replied India with a toothy smile. 'It's new today, from my godmother Katharine over there. It's my birthday, you see.' Princess Grace smiled, straightened herself up, walked away and burst into tears.

My parents' solicitor and close friend Bobby Moorhead wrote to them:

After that service we brought Nicky and his grandmother down to their home. It was the brightest of summer afternoons and although it was not a time for talking one really felt they were there the whole time chatting away. We pulled into Newhouse to pick up two bunches of roses from the garden. We'd had an escort of a police car and three motorcyclists and I took the opportunity of thanking them on your behalf there. Each in turn said it had been the greatest privilege of their lives. We then went on to the church . . . Many of the men in the village quite properly stood to attention as the cars went by . . . At dusk the Vigil commenced and they spent the night in the Knatchbull Chapel.[11]

Lord Louis Mountbatten, known to us as Grandpapa and to his friends as Dickie, told a biographer, 'I am very, very lucky with my grandchildren … The happiest times of my life have been spent with the family together, and the thought about death that saddens me is that I shall miss them all very much.'

Stealing the limelight on the beach at Classiebawn. The film crew was meant to be following our grandfather for the 1966 television series *The Life and Times of Lord Mountbatten.* Nick is on the left.

Nick and me with our paternal grandmother, Doreen Brabourne, at Broadlands, December 1964.

My aunt, Pamela, and grandmother, Edwina, leaving Viceroy's House, New Delhi for the last time, June 1948. After she died in 1960 my grandfather described her as 'that beautiful, unique wonderful girl Edwina Ashley who was more than a wife to me, she was a partner in every sense of the word.'

With our Mountbatten grandfather at his Hampshire house, Broadlands. Nick and I were four weeks old when we decamped there with the rest of the family for Christmas 1964. It soon felt like a second home.

Our grandfather adored family picnics on Classiebawn beach. I remember the sandwiches as being crunchy from grains of sand. He has Nick in his arms.

My own snap of my grandmother, Doreen Brabourne, sitting in her customary position in the stern of *Shadow* V as we left Mullaghmore harbour, August 1976.

My grandfather's relationship with Classiebawn was one of love at first sight. In 1941 he wrote to his wife Edwina: 'You never told me how stupendously magnificent the surrounding scenery was. No place has ever thrilled me more and I can't wait to move in.'

With our mother on *Shadow V.*
Nick is on the left.

At Newhouse, Mersham, 1967. Nick is on the right. Twinhood was fun,
constant companionship and total empathy. It was central to our lives
and we were each other's closest friend, protector and partner.

On Classiebawn beach, 1973. Nick is on the left. We never doubted that our relationship was for life.

Shadow V, built from Classiebawn timber, owed her features to a combination of traditional Irish designs and my grandfather's inventiveness. From left: my grandfather, Norton, Joanna, my uncle David Hicks, my mother, Tom Duffy, Michael-John, Amanda and my father, August 1966.

With our grandfather and his Labrador, Juno, at Classiebawn, 1971. I remember being very pleased to have found a stick like his. He was happier there 'than anywhere else on earth' and we felt the same.

Classiebawn, 1966: Edwina, Ashley, my aunt Pamela, Michael-John, Norton, my mother, Nick and me, my father and Amanda, with our grandfather holding sway. After my grandmother's death, he made a point of filling his homes with his children and grandchildren as often and as much as he could.

I wrote in 1973: 'Dear Grandpapa, I hope you are very well.
Thank you for having me at Clasibawn. The thing I most liked
was the boat, but it was sad we didn't catch a shark. With lots
of love from Timmy.' The picture shows my older brother
Philip with our grandfather, fishing that year from *Shadow V*.

Classiebawn, 26 August 1979. The negative was damaged when my
father's camera sank with *Shadow V* the following day. Left to right:
Ashley, Edwina, Philip, my parents, grandparents and aunt, Freda Rooney,
Michael Connolly, Peter Nicholson, John O'Grady, Paul Maxwell. Front:
Siobhán Burgess, Sheela Rooney, Grace Ryan, Elizabeth O'Connor,
Amanda, India, me and Nick. Twiga is on my lap.

Hugh Tunney, my mother and grandfather photographed
by my father. On the back he wrote: 'Taken at about
11am, 45 minutes before the bomb exploded.'

From my father's photograph album: 'This was the last photograph of
Dickie, about 25 minutes before the bomb exploded. I stayed on the
quayside and took the photograph before getting on board.
The photograph went to the bottom of the sea and was brought
up the next day by police divers.'

Men who lived in the surrounding villages and worked on the estate had asked to be included in the all-night vigil. One of them was gamekeeper Ken Stokes with whom Nick and I had been rabbit-shooting just before we went to Ireland. Now Ken was among those volunteering to carry his coffin. The funeral director Richard Kenyon quickly explained he had arrived with eight pallbearers for this difficult job. When the local men insisted they would like to do it, Bobby Moorhead backed them up and Richard Kenyon brought out two dummy coffins filled with bricks for practice.

Next morning, when Prince Philip arrived at our home in Mersham, the first thing he saw was a pair of empty hearses, thoughtlessly parked the day before. Not wanting the family's homecoming to be any more painful than necessary, he quickly ensured the hearses were moved away.

Bobby Moorhead's account for my parents continues:

> . . . This morning [Nicky and his grandmother] were moved over to the chancel (still chatting I can promise it was such a strong feeling) and the flowers began to arrive when we did around 9.30. And they were so beautiful, I have never seen any so lovely.

As the funeral would take place without us being able to see or hear any of it, we decided to have a small service of our own. At 11:30 the Crathornes and Dugdales arrived at the hospital and met Canon Wood with a sheet outlining the service which he would lead. Written in Sylvia's neat handwriting, it had been created by her and Susie and had on the front page 'NICKY AND DOREEN'. Knowing we were not 'church-going people' Sylvia was struck by 'how important and incredibly supportive the discipline of a religion is to people at such cataclysmic times'. Nonetheless Jamie thought it prudent to ask the Canon to avoid being 'parsonical' during the service. His reply, that the only person in any danger of being 'parsonical' was Jamie, made them all laugh.*

---

* Canon Wood was a dependable source of mirth. A journalist at the hospital entrance saw his dog collar and asked if he was a cardinal. 'No, my dear, but I've many cardinal sins,' he replied.

Arriving in Mersham, Sir Charles Troughton went to the church. We knew him as Dick and his wife Gillean as Gosh, and, like the Crathornes and Dugdales, they and their children felt more like family than friends. He arrived early because he wanted to practise his role in the short service. 'I regard the fact that Joe asked me to read the lesson as one of the great privileges of my life – so that in some small way I could show my true love and friendship to you both', he wrote to my parents. In the church he saw one of the men who regularly helped Ken Stokes. He did not know his name but 'I shook hands with him and said I was just going to read one verse to see how it went and asked him to forgive me for interrupting his prayers. He said "You will do it very well, sir" – such words of comfort as I badly needed.'

By noon the congregation had overflowed into the churchyard. Seats had been set up in rows but soon there were nearly three hundred people standing outside, squinting in the warm sunshine. The light inside was soft, provided mainly by reflected sunbeams from the open door and from the stained-glass windows, their colours faded by the passage of six hundred years. Bobby Moorhead noted: 'The police presence was massive but discreet and not entirely without some after effects since alas it only came to my notice a few seconds before noon the pew in which the Hicks family sat had been used as a bed by the police Alsatian dog the night before and was covered in hairs.'

As the family wound their way through the village, 'there were knots of people at every corner and in every garden'. As they arrived, the organist started playing 'The Lord's My Shepherd', 'hitting a series of wrong notes after much practice which instantly brought a feeling of natural love & simplicity to the proceedings', wrote Dick Troughton. Soon he was at the lectern and delivered his reading: 'Who shall separate us from the love of Christ? Shall tribulation, or distress, or persecution, or famine, or nakedness, or peril, or sword?'

In our hospital room the fluorescent lights hummed and the yellow bed linen gave the room a jaundiced hue as Canon Wood quietly read the same passage that Dick was reading in Mersham. The Canon continued:

Lord, make me an instrument of thy peace;
Where there is hatred let me sow love;
Where there is injury, pardon;
Where there is discord, union;
Where there is doubt, faith;
Where there is despair, hope;
Where there is darkness, light;
Where there is sadness, joy.[12]

In seven minutes it was over and the Canon, the Crathornes and the Dugdales left me with my parents. As with my grandfather's funeral, I felt strange and horribly absent from my home, my siblings, and most of all from Nick. I was aware of the gulf that existed between what I was feeling and what I viscerally knew I needed to feel. My emotions were flat and muted. But I did not worry; I had my parents and that mattered to me more than anything.

In Mersham the Archbishop addressed the congregation:

Let us not, today, hark back to the tragedy which led to their deaths, except to register our determination not to let hate reign but rather to give ourselves, so far as we can, to the extermination of the conditions which led to these dreadful acts perpetrated by wicked men. Let us, rather, look up and look forward, for we are all of us in need of wisdom and strength.[13]

When the organist struck up with the music for 'And did those feet in ancient time . . .?' few people had much air in their lungs. This was the hymn I had chosen, privately inspired by Monty Python. The coffins passed by. On one was written 'Dodo' and the other 'Nicky' but Ashley could not see which was which and wailed, 'Which is Nicky? Which is Nicky?' My aunt hugged and held him.

Bring me my bow of burning gold!
Bring me my arrows of desire!
Bring me my spear! O clouds unfold!
Bring me my chariot of fire![14]

149

'Christ!' thought Joanna. '*Who* chose this hymn?' She and my siblings followed the coffins to the graves, supporting our Nanny, Helen Bowden, every step of the way. 'I am broken-hearted about darling Nicky,' Nanny had written to our parents a week earlier.[15] Now Ken Stokes and his fellow pallbearers did not falter and her flowers stayed on Nick's coffin. As the coffins were lowered into the ground, lambs played in the neighbouring field.

The throng of journalists and camera crews worried Bobby Moorhead. He had been told by the Queen's Press Secretary, Michael O'Shea, that the only way to control them was to bargain. 'So I did a deal . . . We said, "You can photograph the coffins coming out of the church as much as you like; once they go round the tower, you must stop."' He need not have worried because 'the press really did behave well'.

To my parents Dick Troughton wrote:

> The funeral itself was a terrible trial for the children but they held themselves together and so made it possible for everyone else . . . But you cannot steel yourself against the totally unexpected emotional sledge hammer. As I walked out I saw on an outside pew [retired gamekeeper] Mr Crouch. The white collar he always wore out shooting different only that this time the collar stud was covered by his tie. His eyes were full of tears and as I drew near him he gave me an enormous wink and put out his left hand secretly and touched mine as I passed. Gosh felt, when she saw this, that he might have given her a sweet, which he sometimes does out shooting, and if he had, all control would have left her.

It was a private funeral so Nick's school friends did not come, with one exception. Piers McGillycuddy had arrived at Gordonstoun with us the year before. He had a big frame, red hair and an outrageous sense of humour, and we quickly became close. At his home in Ireland the day before, he had packed his bag and sat in the car until his parents drove him, uninvited, to the church in Mersham, an overnight journey. They sat in the crowd outside listening to the service relayed over speakers. When, much later, I discovered this, I was immensely pleased that one of Nick's friends had penetrated the brouhaha surrounding his death and made it almost to his side. I felt desperately sad that he did not have a seat at the front of the church because I knew that is what Nick would have wanted.

My siblings and Penny, now a mainstay of the family, went back to Newhouse and gave lunch to everyone who had come. Gradually the mourners left and when Joanna went out to see the Troughtons off, Dick removed his jacket which revealed his hallmark red braces, the sight of which raised Joanna's spirits no end. In her childhood one of her favourite *Winnie the Pooh* passages had been when Piglet saw Christopher Robin's colourful braces and 'being a little over-excited by them, had had to go to bed half an hour earlier than usual'.[16]

By dinner time the house was quiet, and for the first time my siblings could sit down and relax together. They could have cried their eyes out; instead Amanda told them how she had delivered a deep curtsy to a very smartly dressed man whom she thought was probably a king. He turned out to be the head caterer.

Getting home, Dick Troughton wrote to my parents about their children. 'There was something so moving about them all – so long as they could stay together, one felt, nothing could break them.'

11

LEAVING IRELAND

Waking in Kent the morning after the funeral, Joanna's thoughts turned to Sligo Hospital and she immediately felt 'a dread, a real sickening dread . . . Much as I loved those doctors and nurses for what they had done, I never wanted to see the inside of that or any hospital again. For a long, long time afterwards I couldn't walk into a hospital and smell that smell without feeling physically sick.'[1]

Bobby Moorhead took my siblings and Penny to a plane waiting nearby to bring them back to Ireland. In his pocket he had a letter he had written to my parents:

> . . . Needless to say it was a terrible day for them but they really were in complete control. And it was good of them to let the local people come to the service rather than have a private service which would have been less taxing for them – but as ever with the Knatchbulls they put themselves last and I know the local people were grateful to be able to come and express their feelings.[2]

When my siblings landed at Classiebawn, they joined the Dugdales and the Crathornes for a 'lunch debriefing session'[3] in which the families swapped stories. My brothers described the 'awe-inspiring sensation of that procession through London – total silence from the crowds except clicking of cameras, tears all about them'.[4] Joanna noticed a proud and relieved glow on Jamie's face when he told them they were going to be agreeably surprised by the improvement in my mother. He was right. When they had said goodbye to her on Sunday afternoon she had seemed at death's door. Now they found she was 'a sort-of functioning human being again. That was a big difference. It was like she had woken up from something.'[5] My parents were noticing great change in their children as well. That summer my parents had often found themselves at loggerheads with Philip which they put down to his 'troublesome schoolboy period'. Now they found he had 'become a most gentle man overnight'.[6]

In Sligo we were following our normal hospital routine. My mother was frequently asked to 'expectorate'. This involved the nurses helping her to sit up, lean forward and force herself to cough, a process she later described as a 'horror' and one of the most difficult things about her time in hospital. Once she said to Tony Heenan, 'Do I have to?' He pondered for a while without saying anything and then said, 'Yes, I think you really should.'[7] Her efforts sometimes produced small quantities of phlegm from her lungs which the nurses found very pleasing.

As we had waited excitedly for the family to return that afternoon, my mother had tried standing up for the first time. My father and I cheered as she got to her feet, but soon the crutches made the wound on her right hand bleed and she had to give up and have her hand redressed. She was very disappointed.

The last of my stitches were removed and later the nurses noted that I was 'up and about' for the first time. In my father's file they wrote: 'Fairly good day.' The deep wound in his left leg had become infected and at one point gangrene had been suspected. By night he was 'frightened and anxious'.

When the Irish Prime Minister, President and Cabinet led the congregation at a Dublin memorial service for my grandfather that afternoon, it did not register with me at all. On the other hand, when a nurse told me that a school friend called Rory was on the phone that evening, I was immensely pleased. We spoke for five minutes and he told me he was buying a pet pig. I walked back from the nursing station feeling that life really was going to be OK. The hospital was now quiet and these last few minutes of the day were my favourite because I could move over to my parents' beds, which were now drawn together, and lie down with them. As normal, I asked if they would prefer Horlicks, Ovaltine or cocoa and then, having passed on the request, we stayed huddled together and chatted about the day, waiting happily for the hot drinks to arrive. After a goodnight kiss I crossed back to my bed and turned my light out.

The Dugdales' and Crathornes' presence at the hospital had prevented our spirits from sinking while the family were away. In this respect they might have contributed decisively to my mother's survival and therefore to the recovery of us all. On Saturday morning, 8 September, they left to be reunited with their children at home, where Sylvia finished the letter to her sister:

> I don't suppose the 4 of us will ever spend a more worthwhile 7 days in our lives – when every second of our time counted for so much for that family . . .
>
> People marvelled at their courage – Timmy's too, he's only ever spent 5 consecutive days apart from Nicky up until that Monday. Poor darling is now beginning to feel <u>that</u> so badly. His eye fortunately was already a very lazy one – he took the blast on the right side of his face & body – for a full week his eye was so swollen you could only see a slit . . . Well, why go on? It's just that all day & night, if I wake up, I find myself thinking about them.
>
> The other tragedy is the profound shame & sorrow of the kind & loving Irish, their unanimous phrase – 'it makes me so ashamed to be Irish'. And no matter how much one feels – well hell go & do something about it then – there's little one can do with Lynch in power & world opinion still demanding kid-glove leniency when dealing with international terrorists.[8]

While the Crathornes and Dugdales were driving home, Tony Heenan at last told me that I could return to Classiebawn. Being separated from my parents again was a wrench for us all but we told each other it would not be for long. They too were improving. That day my mother's left eye had healed enough for the doctors to probe it with forceps and remove a splinter three-quarters of an inch long. The surgeon did not rule out the possibility that there were more splinters.

My mother was very pleased with the trophy and kept it in a perspex container by her bedside, hoping she would one day be able to see it for herself. I examined it with fascination whereas Norton, very reasonably, found it upsetting and did not like even to look in the direction of her bedside.

For the trip back to Classiebawn, twelve days after the attack, I sat in the back of a car between my two sisters. They had warned me not to be frightened by the fact that the Garda driver, Maurice Hension, drove with his foot flat on the accelerator. They were now quite used to it and referred to him affectionately as 'Morris Engine'. I sat in the heavily armoured car cosseted between my sisters and feeling very cared for as we thundered and flew the fifteen miles down the bumpy road to Classiebawn. They both seemed very content and this heightened the warm, secure glow I was feeling. When I walked into the castle I felt elated just to be back.

A short while later the family suggested we go for a walk and I quickly agreed, but after a couple of minutes I began to feel very tired. I wondered how much further I could go but I said nothing. After another hundred yards I stopped and said I would go back. They asked if I wanted one of them to come with me but, not wanting to seem weak, I quickly said no, and turned back for the castle. Alone for the first time since the bomb, I soon found it difficult to keep walking and started to think I might collapse. I redoubled my efforts and concentrated very hard. Now really frightened, I reached the castle and aimed for the drawing-room door. Having managed to open it, I hauled myself the final few paces to the sofa and collapsed into a deep sleep. When I woke long after the family returned, I realised how weak and depleted my body had become in the past twelve days.

One day, some time after the bomb, Amanda had walked into the bedroom which Nick and I had shared, the Lower Tower Room. As she had packed away some of his possessions she had strongly sensed his presence, and the experience had made a deep impact on her. Now, as I walked into the same room for the first time since Nick's death, she watched but I gave no hint of what I was feeling inside. I walked around his bed and sat on mine. From his side of the bedside table I picked up a small plastic box on which was etched N.T.C. Knatchbull. When I shook the box it rattled. Opening it I saw Nick's mouth splint, a delicate wire and plastic assembly designed to give him a future with straightened teeth. I steadied myself. Outside on the walk with my family I had tried to hide my frailty. Now I was subconsciously doing the same with my emotions.

I had asked Joanna for my mouth splint in hospital. Next morning she handed me a box and I tried putting its contents in my mouth. When it did not fit I knew she had picked up Nick's box. It gave me a moment of stabbing emotional pain. I removed it from my mouth and put it back in the box, gently explaining to Joanna. 'Are you sure?' she said, aghast. I smiled to reassure her, knowing she was perfectly placed to share the black humour as well as the poignancy, and I did not want her to worry over the mistake. I accepted I was going to have many such moments, that there was nothing I could do to avoid them, and that if everyone else could put up with them so could I.

In the Lower Tower Room I felt I had to let something out. From first learning of the deaths I had been encouraged by the family to talk and cry as much as possible. On the rare occasions when I did cry they cuddled and soothed me. I liked that but it had the unfortunate consequence of quickly drying up my tears which were the best tonic of all. In this respect their support was having the opposite effect of what I needed, which was to cry and vent my emotions. For that I had to be under the sheets at night or in a deserted place. In the Lower Tower Room I shut the door and had the solitude I was looking for. I picked up some white string. Glimpsing it earlier, when Amanda was in the room, I had felt a contraction inside me because I knew what it was. Arriving at the castle, Nick had carefully removed the string from the box containing our favourite toy, Computer Battleships. I would have thrown away the string but Nick had carefully wound it up into a neat coil and stored it on the mantelpiece for the end of the holiday. He had been passionate about Computer Battleships. Now it sat in the corner and I was thinking that I would never play with him again. Heaving sobs and bucketing tears, I missed him then more than I had ever believed possible. Now I was feeling his death in a new way, as a pain, the pain which Nick and I had been unable to guess at, sitting in this room and looking into each other's eyes not long before.

I had not had a bath or shower since the bomb and my flat greasy hair stank of diesel oil. Before supper Amanda took me into our grandfather's bathroom and helped me undress. As I lay helplessly in the bath, looking out of the window towards Benbulben, she washed me as she had done when Nick and I had been tiny tots. I stuck my right leg on the edge of the tub and rested both arms clear of the water to keep the wounds dry in their dressings. Amanda was a natural nurse; she juggled my limbs and jostled my body; she wrapped me in towels; she ran here and fetched there. A seven-inch scar ran vertically up my stomach ending short and slightly to the right of my navel. It was red and hyper-sensitive and she dressed it with enormous care. For weeks I depended on my sisters in this way. Amanda helped me carry my clothes up to the Middle Tower Room. It was a nicer room and it felt like an upgrade, especially because I would share it with Philip who had always been my closest friend and ally in the family after Nick.

Philip and I were woken late the next morning, a Sunday, by Joanna. She opened the curtains and sat on my bed. As she talked about the plans for the day I sat up and pulled back the bed-sheets causing her to let out a cry of mock horror. Like a tree losing leaves in autumn, my trunk had shed a carpet of scabs which now littered the sheets. They had come away from the dozens of small tears in my skin, revealing a shiny new layer underneath. Joanna made me laugh aloud as I brushed my teeth and dressed while she examined my remaining scabs for signs of lift-off and marvelled at their quality and quantity.

As well as my scabs, I felt I was shedding a good part of my previous existence. My parents' absence was sad and strange but the lack of super-vision was exhilarating. My sisters had stepped into my mother's role but not in a domineering way. I felt grown-up and free. The world had been turned upside-down; now we were looking after our parents. The sudden obliteration of our grandparents heightened the feeling that we had moved up a generation. My siblings seemed to take everything in their stride and gave an appearance of confidence which is just what I needed. I felt secure and content, reassured by my family that I would be staying with them for a long time while my recovery continued. In the meantime Classiebawn was a familiar and cosy place to be. I cried very little and stayed optimistic. I did not ask questions about the long-term future and never contemplated that our visits to Classiebawn were at an end. The one great goal we all concentrated on was getting my parents back to England.

* * *

From Sligo Hospital my father wrote:

Dear Mr & Mrs Maxwell

My wife and I will be returning to London tomorrow morning and I felt I must write you a note before we left. We both wanted you to know how heart-broken we were for you when we heard about Paul. He had done an excellent job and my father-in-law and we had all grown very fond of him. Indeed, at a meeting held at the Castle on the Sunday evening to discuss our plans for the boat for 1980, my father-in-law said he would definitely like Paul to have the job again, if he wished to do so . . . My father-in-law and my mother had both had very full and wonderful lives, but poor Paul and Nicholas had only just begun theirs. We are naturally very sad about the older members of the family who died, but our hearts are broken for the two young boys . . .[9]

At a regular morning visit from Tony Heenan, my father asked whom he should talk to about settling our hospital bill. Tony replied very slowly and clearly, 'If anyone asks you to pay a penny they might very soon find themselves in need of treatment of their own.' My father smiled and shook his head slightly and I could tell he was deeply moved. The two men were from very different backgrounds yet they were well in tune with each other and had become good friends in less than two weeks. Tony Heenan walked away thinking, 'There is this common humanity that threads through us all. It doesn't matter where you've come from, from whatever background.'[10]

I spent two nights at Classiebawn, and then after breakfast on Monday morning it was time to go. Suddenly I felt as if I were leaving something vital behind but I did not know what. As my siblings started getting into the car, I ran back up the steps. The castle was deathly silent as I crossed the hall. In the bathroom I stared at a picture I had seen a thousand times before. It showed the profiles of Nelson and my grandfather; underneath were the words 'British Worthies'. I heard the car horn. As I walked out, I glimpsed pencil marks made on the wall each year by my grandfather, recording the height of each grandchild. I ran out of the castle and down the steps. Peter was holding open the door of our

Peugeot and said, 'Goodbye, Timmy' as I squeezed in and sat in the third row of seats. It was a seven-seat car with six of the seven children in it and an empty seat beside me. As we drove down the hill and along the drive, I looked back at Classiebawn and waved at Peter. When I said, 'We'll be back', there was a chorus from my five siblings saying we would not. Shocked, I countered, 'Yes we will.' They told me that we would never be allowed back and even if we were it would never be the same happy place. Upset, I stared stubbornly at Classiebawn and repeated myself. I was not sure how to explain it but I knew one day I would return.

In the village there was a clear expectation that we would do so. One letter my mother received told her: 'The natives of Mullaghmore will never forget the kindness of your family to them down the years . . . We look forward to you and your family coming again among us to Mullaghmore.'[11]

Our departure that day was sudden and final. I had the impression of being sucked down a whirlpool, wrenched from the places and people we loved. There was no ceremony and time for only a few snatched goodbyes. A Cliffoney shopkeeper wrote to my mother:

> With typical kindness and consideration your two sons, Norton and Michael-John with Miss [Penny] Eastwood, called to say goodbye and I had their permission to write to you . . . Those of us, who for over twenty five years enjoyed closer contact with your family will never look on Mullaghmore again, without sadly reliving, those dreadful days.[12]

Rodney Lomax was struck by our sudden 'disappearance'.[13] A boy my own age in the village who had occasionally come to play with us at the castle felt we had 'vanished' and found it 'hard to deal with . . . My family all cried many times afterwards'.[14] In Sligo Town Hall lay a book of condolences opened by the mayor. Three thousand people signed it.*

The Garda and Army had set up road blocks around Sligo Hospital and it felt like a war zone. We set down our bags, kicked our heels and waited. When two large Royal Air Force helicopters arrived, they

---

* Another 2,700 people signed a similar book in the British Embassy in Dublin, and 6,600 signed a declaration of sympathy in Waterford.

were surrounded by Irish troops and watched by crowds of onlookers. Upstairs an RAF doctor walked into my parents' room and explained he had come to supervise their removal. With the air of a parade ground instruction he announced, 'And now – empty – your – bladders.' As they were carried from the hospital on stretchers, my mother was 'almost sorry to leave this place which has been a haven to us, to face the world again' and was moved to find 'the whole hospital'[15] had turned out to see us off.

As the helicopters rose above the neighbouring grammar school, Tony Heenan reflected on the job the hospital had done and felt a deep satisfaction. Mary Lowry was watching with her Intensive Care colleagues, and as the two aircraft turned north towards Belfast she thought, 'Oh my God, they are gone. This is the end of an era.'[16]

12

LONDON

At Belfast's Aldergrove Airport we transferred to a Queen's Flight aircraft and were met by John Barratt, my grandfather's private secretary. We had not been expecting him, and when my mother saw him she wept. When we landed at Northolt in London, my parents did not have much time together before they were lifted into ambulances bound for different hospitals. It was horrible to see them parted again. Soon we were in a fast-moving convoy of ambulances, cars and motorcycles. At every traffic light, police were waiting to wave us through. The journey seemed to be reaching a dizzying crescendo when my mother's ambulance made an unexpected right turn onto a back road in Knightsbridge and we followed. The police convoy continued with my father's ambulance and suddenly we were stationary in a workaday London traffic jam. As the sirens receded and the engine hummed and the indicator ticked, I felt very cut off from the convoy, from my father, from Nick, from our past and from normality. I was physically weak, with one leg bandaged from the knee down, one eye out of action and a pair of punctured eardrums. My parents were headed for a long stay in hospital and my school friends were beyond my reach. I sat slumped in the back of my grandfather's Austin Princess and wondered what lay ahead.

I had been told the doctors would almost certainly want me to stay in hospital for tests, but not long after accompanying my mother into a room festooned with flowers in Moorfields Eye Hospital I was told I was free to go home with my sisters. As we walked to the car, a photographer snapped and flashed with a motor-driven camera from close range. Sitting in the car I stared ahead and clung to my Air India overnight case, one of a pair which Nick and I had been given by our parents, as the paparazzo continued shooting through the windows making it difficult for us to drive away.

Next morning the doorbell rang at our London home, and I opened the door to find a large box with my name on it. On the accompanying card headed 'Chocolates by Charbonnel Et Walker, Old Bond St' was a note in the curly handwriting of one of my godmothers: 'I am in America until next week but I hope to see you when I get back. All love, Amanda.' Tearing open the box I found the biggest array of chocolates I had ever seen.

That morning Joanna walked me to the nearby Brompton Road and into the nearest hair salon. Within minutes a highly sophisticated-looking stylist in designer clothes was expertly shaping, trimming and blow-drying my hair. Joanna sat nearby with a newspaper and occasionally glanced in my direction, outwardly enjoying the visit almost as much as I was. Inside she was 'really worried'.[1] I needed a great deal of mothering, our mother was clearly unable to do that and Joanna, aged twenty-four, doubted her own ability to do it in the meantime. My mother would have had kittens if she could have seen us. For a haircut she had always taken Nick and me to her our local hairdresser in Kent where a quick trim was swiftly accomplished for next to no cost. The bill for this cut required a hefty note from Joanna's wallet which made my eyes pop. The experience seemed like a rite of passage, symbolic of my move from the old, rural world of my childhood to the new urban one of my siblings.

My mother thought her eye surgeon at Moorfields was a 'charming and gentle man' even as he pulled two 'enormous pieces of wood' out of her left eye. She said it was 'not really painful' but nontheless it made her 'knees weak in bed'.[2] Soon Norton arrived and read out for her a letter which my grandfather had prepared for his death. She braced herself for tears and they duly came.

While at my parents' home in Kent, Penny had gone to my mother's room and collected *Other Men's Flowers*, a small book of poetry which my mother earlier that year had told her she kept by her bed and liked to dip into from time to time, when particularly happy or sad. Now her thoughtfulness meant my mother could again hear some of her favourite verse:

> . . . In the fell clutch of circumstance
> I have not winced nor cried aloud.
> Under the bludgeonings of chance
> My head is bloody, but unbow'd . . .
>
> It matters not how strait the gate,
> How charged with punishments the scroll,
> I am the master of my fate:
> I am the captain of my soul.[3]

My parents were 'pining for each other'.[4] They spoke by phone that day and were 'greatly cheered' when they heard that my mother would be moved in with my father at King Edward VII Hospital the next afternoon.

Thousands of letters had been arriving since the attack. They were drawn from people from all walks of life. The ones from Ireland mostly shared a common theme. They came from men, women and children, and the children mainly wrote to me. A card from Dundrum, Dublin, carried the words: 'Dear Timothy, I love you. I am sorry. I am shamed. I am Irish. I love you. I pray for you. From Sarah (8 years).' On the facing page was: 'Timothy – our little sister said it all. We love you. I am your age. We pray for a special light for you. Forgive us all. We love you. Fiona and Mary.' An employee of the Allied Irish Bank in Bundoran wrote to my aunt: 'My anger and disgust is such that I feel I must write . . . I am absolutely ashamed to be a member of a race which can commit such an outrage. I can assure you that this feeling is shared by everyone I have met in the past few days . . . Please try to forgive us.' My father opened a card which simply said: 'Saddened by your great tragedies. God bless you all. An Eire family living in Birmingham.' The number of letters arriving from well-wishers in Ireland was so great that my parents placed a message in the 'Social and Personal' section of the *Irish Times*:

Lord and Lady Brabourne and their family deeply appreciate the
thousands of comforting messages which they have received from
friends and strangers. They regret the delay in answering but hope
to do so in due course, after they are able to leave hospital in
London.[5]

Most of the letters came from closer to home. David Niven, who
had recently acted in my father's film *Death on the Nile*, wrote to him:

. . . Every millimetre you can drag yourself ahead <u>now</u> will mean
a mile later on.
   You are a very brave man with a lot of guts and NOW is the
time to dig deep – and your load is terrifying indeed – but keep
going, 'use' your friends (they all long to help) keep busy, don't
look at the empty chairs and above all talk about 'them'. Get
pissed, cry, shout, laugh, let it all out and much sooner than you
can ever believe now, <u>IT WILL GET BETTER</u>.[6]

My mailbag was a drop in the ocean compared to my parents' but it
made me realise how many people wanted to help. Piers McGillycuddy
wrote from his home in Kilchrohane, County Cork: 'I just pray to God
that you can be brave about it. Please come back to school next term
because I think I'll be rather lost without you . . . Don't give up, try to
get better, think happy things . . .' An unknown mother in Dorset and
her two young children sent me a record token and wrote: 'Maybe you
will be able to see when this letter reaches you. If not "keep going
youngster!!"' Visiting my parents in hospital and reading their letters
provided a seemingly endless supply of new variants on the messages of
support. From my father's bedside I picked up a card with dozens of
signatures, assuming it must be from one of the schools of which he
was a governor or perhaps a film studio. It was from an entirely anony-
mous group of Americans in Lincoln, Nebraska. I did not have any
schoolwork at the time so I worked instead at trying to reply to every
letter I received. It felt good to be busy.

On Wednesday morning, 12 September, my mother had a visit from
Solly Zuckerman who had helped assemble many of the doctors looking

after my parents. When he saw her, he wept. My mother knew that in the Second World War he had led a scientific inquiry into the effects of explosives on humans. She asked if he could explain why any of us had survived. He said that the energy released by a bomb radiates in spikes like fingers from a hand. A finger pointed at anyone nearby would devastate him or her; anyone else could survive.

Later that day my mother was taken to my father's hospital and put in the next-door room with a promise of a twin-bedded room the following Monday. She was 'thrilled' but still felt 'very comatose'.[7] Finding her small room 'overflowing with delicious flowers,' she asked the nurses to share them with their other patients. Soon more than a hundred arrangements of flowers had been delivered.

On the first day of term, Gordonstoun's headmaster Michael Mavor addressed the school in the chapel:

> Today I want you to remember not only Nicholas but the task that we who are living must pursue. I ask you, in the name of all the Knatchbulls, and the many others who suffered loss that day, whatever you do in the years to come, whatever your political beliefs, whatever searing thrusts Fate makes at you, never to say or to do anything that needlessly threatens human life. Instead strive to save life. And when there isn't the drama of a life to be saved there is still the task of preserving those qualities which go to make for a good life – faith, hope and love and – what Nicholas possessed so abundantly – a sense of fun.
>
> Yet on Saturday I received this letter: 'Dear Sir, It would appear from *The Press and Journal* that you have been heard to express some remarks about the loss of one of your pupils in an I.R.A. bomb explosion. In that case I look forward to what you have to say over the fact that I too lost a pupil in the Ireland troubles – ten-year-old John Clarke, who was summarily decapitated on 16th October, 1972. There are, however, two rather interesting differences between my case and yours: 1. John was a victim of your Westminster pals in the Army; 2. I got my information in a cat-out-of-the-bag admission by the Army supporters; whereas, I suspect, you got yours from a worthless propagandist effort by the

I.R.A.'s opponents. The hypocrisy of some of you people sickens me. Yours faithfully.' Then after the signature there is a postscript: 'the English Tommies are good men, they go to Church on Sunday, and pray to God to give them strength to axe a child on Monday.'

I wrote back to this man and the essence of my reply was: 1. I did not see how one was being hypocritical if one expressed exactly what one felt. 2. The death of his pupil in 1972 was also a tragedy. 3. The angry bitterness of his letter was precisely the furl that kept Ireland's problems simmering. I referred this man to the words of Lord Brabourne . . . There was a man who had lost his son, his mother and his father-in-law saying that the people of Ireland were his friends and that he was grateful to the staff of Sligo Hospital for their kindness. What a fine and right thing to say. It was an example of the faith, hope and love . . . so urgently needed in many current political situations.[8]

Next day, Thursday 13 September, Amanda drove me the sixty miles to our home in Kent. Our main purpose was to see our Nanny, Helen Bowden. At her bungalow in Mersham, I carried out small chores as usual, including watering a small grapefruit plant. Nick and I had collected grapefruit pips from the breakfast table at Easter that year in the Bahamas and planted three in a pot as a present for her.* Now each had sprouted into a strong green shoot. As I watered them I felt tears coming and went next door to wind the clock in her front room. From the window I looked past a magnolia tree where Nick and I had played as toddlers and towards a path that led to the church. I knew what was to come: Nick's grave.

The last time I had been to the cemetery was on a beautiful summer's evening when I was twelve years old. Nick and I had been fishing with our father, and after supper we bicycled through the village to the church, taking a short cut while our parents went ahead by car. At the church-yard they showed us a wooden bench they had had made. Nick and I did our best to sound excited but our imaginations were caught when we all walked over to a corner of the graveyard filled by generations of

---

* One seedling thrived and grew into a tree. I wrote much of this book close to its fruit-laden branches.

Knatchbulls. There were only two empty plots remaining and my father explained that he and our mother would be buried there. 'Then what will happen?' I asked, referring to the lack of space for the rest of the family. 'That's for you to worry about,' my father said, chuckling. That had been two years before and now the place looked very different. Gone was the neat area of undisturbed grass and in its place were two monstrous piles of raw brown earth, topped by grassed squares and the remains of flowers which had faded since the funeral seven days earlier. I sat and asked to be alone. I felt as though I had arrived at a station but the train had left. I wanted to feel pain but I was hit by numbness. I had been told Nick was killed instantly and that his body had not been badly damaged. I found myself trying to imagine what he looked like, inside the coffin. I sat in tears asking-myself had he really died? Had his funeral truly taken place? Was his coffin genuinely in that grave? It all seemed so unlikely. I was hopelessly out of my depth. I knew that the death of my twin meant something different to me than to anyone else. Years later, reading the words of another twin, I would understand my numbness was not from shock, grief or a psychopathic failure to emote, it was something much more complicated.

> For nontwins, the death of even the most beloved person is the death of another. For [my twin] and me there is no entirely discrete other. There is still a part of each of us that has not completely differentiated from the other. A part we share . . . And that part will die in the surviving twin, not as a cheap poetic, not as a simile but an actual deadening of some fraction of the living organism, some part of the will or the spirit or the mind or the body. That partial death of the surviving twin will leave him with the worst of all worlds: the fearful experience of death and the grief of the mourner for both his brother and for himself.[9]

That weekend our parents insisted that we should leave them behind and go to Broadlands to recharge. It felt very odd to be there without them and our grandfather but wonderful to be back in a place we loved so much. It now belonged to Norton. He and Penny had decided to go ahead with their wedding which was only five weeks away. On top of everything else, they were having to manage the arrangements for nine hundred guests. It also gave us all something to look forward to and, in particular, it presented a goal for my parents. The pressure on Norton and Penny was enormous but they seemed to rise to it as naturally as they had done in Ireland. Around them we thrived on the high-adrenalin atmosphere and the prospect of a major ceremony focused not on death but on a joyous new beginning.

On the Saturday evening, 15 September, we settled down at Broadlands and watched *Last Night of the Proms* on television. In hospital my mother was doing the same, noting in her diary that she:

> could just manage it as sight is much better – despite dilating drops every four hours (five varieties) which don't help focusing. Plastic surgeon Mr Broomhead only comes and picks large and small bits of poor *Shadow V* wood splinters and green paint out of my face and hands. Hopes I may need anaesthetic for some reason so he can really get at face!

She continued, 'Phi returned to Gordonstoun on Sunday but finds concentration difficult, and distressed – as we were – to find (rightly no doubt) all traces of Nicky's name, bicycle etc gone, except for initials on a desk. J and I cried of course – as we do daily.'

My parents were reunited on Monday 17 September and again the effect was enormous. They appeared to do more for each other than any doctor. My mother wrote:

> We were able to move down to just redecorated first floor (Sister Ford) into same rooms, 7 and 8 (9 left empty) and be reunited. I started feeling better that day (3 weeks after the bomb) and J slept from 11pm Monday to noon Wednesday and awoke from his thirty-six hours sleep – despite being fed, washed, sat out etc – including three or four crying fits, refreshed and with fear of sleep gone. I obviously had soporific effect on him.

For most of the past fourteen days my father had been unable to sleep. Each time he slumbered, he woke within minutes, often with a start or a scream from his memories of being in the water after the explosion. Seeing him now catch up on his sleep was impressive. He would open his eyes, talk and smile for a minute or two, and fall asleep again. It was soothing and reassuring and gave us the impression that he was now starting to heal in a way he had not before. Later the powerful restorative effect of this process became clear when his general health made a marked improvement. The episode became known as his 'dormouse period'. Visitors would come and go and he would miss them altogether. When Prince Charles flew down from Balmoral, my father snored through the entire visit.

13

FRIENDS IN SCOTLAND

In the second half of September my parents were making slow but steady progress in hospital where they had a regular flow of visitors, who tired them but lifted their spirits enormously. Among the visitors were Charlie and Kathy Pierce who had pulled them from the sea. My daily visits to them were punctuated with my own medical checks, mainly to eye and ear specialists. Of the many calls my parents received, one in particular was to prove a turning point for me. It was from Dick and Gosh Troughton, who lived in Ullapool on the west coast of Scotland. Aware that my parents were very worried about me, they suggested that my sisters and I should come and stay. At the time, I was listless, under-weight, hollow-eyed, physically debilitated and too weak for school. When my parents told me of the invitation, I jumped at it, particularly because I had heard my father talk about the wonderful salmon fishing there. The trip turned out to be the single greatest leap forward of my recovery.

Joanna, Amanda and I flew to Inverness in the north of Scotland, and then took to roads which became progressively smaller, evolving into single tracks. The skies grew leaden and it started to rain. I had been along part of this road once before, with Nick at the beginning of the summer when we had travelled in a Gordonstoun minibus for a camping expedition. As I went down the road again, I recognised the bends and passing places, the lochs and gorges, the hills and mountains, and I thought of my journey with Nick three months before; of the tent we had shared with Simon Jones; and the rain that had nearly washed us away. As we turned off the road and stopped in the gravelled driveway of the Troughtons' home, it was raining cats and dogs. Running into the house, I felt immediately sheltered from the rainstorm outside and warmed by the fire. The same feeling descended from Dick and Gosh; they were totally focused on my sisters and me, and I felt supremely safe and secure. I also adored being once again in a rugged west-coast hinterland.

Having said hello to Dick and Gosh's daughter Tina, who was about the same age as my sisters, we went straight to the dining room. Food was to be a major ingredient of the days ahead: delicious local produce served in copious quantities. Sleep was the second ingredient. After dinner I went straight to bed and was asleep instantly until a late breakfast the next morning. My sisters would then take it in turns to bath me, allowing me to keep my dressings above the waterline. Always thinking about my feelings, Tina quietly asked Joanna whether this embarrassed me, on which score Joanna was able to reassure her. The third ingredient was humour, with Dick playing the part of jester. Nonsensically he adopted the persona of Smith, my faithful fishing ghillie, while he called me Sir Leslie, frequently doffing his cap.

The first morning, Wednesday 19 September, the rain had stopped and Dick drove me a mile or two to the Broom, a beautiful river that was now in flood, perfect conditions for salmon fishing. He and Tina got the car as close to the river as they could, and carried the rods straight to the best spot on that beat of the river. Dick studied his fly box, took out a size six Hairy Mary and attached it to my line. Although I had tried for years, I had only ever caught two salmon, so Dick knew he would have to instruct me carefully. He did not say so but when I started to fish he immediately saw that there was little hope I would catch one. I did not have the strength. When I tried to cast I could not throw the line far enough, or control the fly when it landed. Dick was downcast, he later told me, but said nothing and encouraged and coached me all the while. A short time passed and my casting was not improving. My line, which had fallen clumsily and seemed certain to have scared any nearby fish, was uncoiling in the current. As it floated downstream it suddenly went ballistic. My heart missed a beat. 'Strike!' said Dick, reminding me to raise the rod tip sharply to set the hook into the fish's mouth. The rod bent, the reel sang and I let out a whoop of joy and surprise. I held the rod as I was meant to, keeping the tip well up. I knew that if I played the fish poorly, allowing the line to slacken or putting too much strain on it, the fish would escape in a flash.

I was weak. Try as I might, after the first few minutes I was struggling to keep the rod tip high enough. Dick steadied me on one side and Tina on the other, and I leant back allowing my trembling arm to keep the rod angle up against the pull of the salmon in the fast, dark current. The fish was strong enough to keep its head down and stay deep and we still had not seen it. Suddenly it made a violent dash, stripping line from the reel as it snaked downstream and then jumped well clear of the water and splashed back again. It was the largest salmon I had ever seen, and a brilliant silver colour indicating it had only recently arrived into the river from the sea and was in perfect condition. We all now lost our cool in a rush of excitement mixed with fear of losing the fish. At the back of my mind I felt I simply had to land this fish, for myself, for Dick and Gosh, for Tina, for my sisters, for my parents, for Nick.

As it jumped I had momentarily dipped the rod to even the strain on the line. Now I was reeling in like fury, half walking, half running back up stream as the fish started back. Up and down the bank I went, electrified with excitement and adrenalin. Midges from the nearby bracken had descended on my face while my hands were busy working the reel. Soon their bites were bringing my skin up in red spots and Tina started mopping them away from my brow as Dick carefully guided me along the edge of the river, as if the future of all humanity depended on landing this fish. After what seemed an eternity but was in fact twenty-five minutes, the gleaming salmon, all fifteen pounds of it, was in Dick's net and then on the bank beside me. Physically spent, unable even to sit up, I fell into a deep sleep by the fish. In the following years I never again fished so poorly nor caught a salmon so big. It was one of the best experiences of my life.

Dick had hated being unable to reach us in Ireland by telephone in the weeks following the attack. Now he could phone my parents easily in their London hospital, and on getting home he immediately called my father with the news. If Gosh had given birth he could not have sounded more proud. He knew he had done something remarkable and it would do my parents at least as much good as it was doing me. When I took the phone and gave my parents a blow-by-blow account, they already knew I was in the best possible place in the best possible hands, but my voice must have told them that my recovery was at last beginning to pick up. I was so proud of landing the mighty salmon that I did not mind admitting that my fishing had been atrociously awful. When my mother told me, and later wrote in her diary, that 'Nick must have arranged it' I did not disagree.

Soon Dick wrote to my mother:

Darling Patricia

Timmy's fish really was the answer to our prayers. I have never seen anyone so pleased in their lives unless it was Tina or his sisters! It has done him more good than several tons of Virol.* We did not let him fish today: too high a wind & he gets easily tired. My view is that mentally & spiritually he is absolutely all right; & emotionally very stable. I think he will need a long convalescence & absolutely nothing physically tiring at all. He is amazing about it & says hc feels tired going upstairs like me! We have a series of absolutely idiotic jokes which he loves & plays up to – & he and Tina became firm allies.[1]

The trip gave Joanna and Amanda their first break from the relentless pressures caused by the bomb and put us all in a holiday mood. Joanna sent a postcard which started 'Dearest Mum and Dad, Here's a picture of Gosh's shop, where we're about to go and spend far too much money. Tim is eating like a heavyweight wrestler in training. Unfortunately so are Amanda and I.'[2]

A couple of days later Dick updated my father about me:

I let him talk about anything that comes into his head. I never ask him questions as, in my old fashioned book, questions raise questions & he has enough to be going on with. My private guess

* A children's food supplement.

remains the same – substantially – mentally – spiritually – very stable & I would think not damaged. But certainly physically, on which the others so much depend, he has a good way to go & I personally would not let him go back to the 'world' until his resistance to cold & germs has been built up . . .

No more now. Very best love to darling Patricia. Insofar as this wing of the Army is doing: 'steady progress on a wide front'. And that is all we can ask.[3]

When the time came to leave for home, I found I had gained seven pounds in seven days. The visit had given me a physical and emotional boost and showed me that while my parents were still incapacitated, their friends were ready to step in, in loco parentis.

Tuesday 2 October was a watershed in my parents' recovery. My mother's diary reads:

Today, after 5 weeks in hospital, we went home, me with some misgivings of heartache. Family came in morning (and doctors of course) to get us packed up. At 2pm a Red Cross Ambulance with car and 4 men and Nursing Superintendent . . . came to drive us home on stretchers . . . [Joe, Amanda] and Timmy got there 30 seconds earlier. It is so nice to be home ([John] thrilled) but I dread later going to twins' room – Tim seems to want to go on sleeping there alone. Poor lamb, coping in his own way so well, but looks frail and not fit for school. After tea in our wheelchairs we went up to bed. Lovely to be back in one, even with 3 broken legs.[4]

On their first full day at home, while I spent the afternoon with my Nanny at her bungalow, they got themselves and their plastered legs into the back of a car and went to the church with Joe and Amanda, where the vicar read the prayers and lessons from the funeral. They then went to have their first look at the two graves. My mother wrote in her diary: 'Still do not believe our beloved Nicky & Dodo are there – but glad he is not alone. Their and Daddy's spirits so alive. Why, oh why did it happen? At least really are mourned on world-wide scale . . .'

Having had my own time alone at Nicky's grave, I felt that perhaps my parents would like to be there by themselves. Now I wish I had gone. It was why I was at home, to grow strong so I could restart my life. Becoming strong again did not mean physical strength alone, it also meant emotional strength. Had I spent more time actively mourning, then I would have healed more quickly and suffered less. Instead, I just let grief float over me on an occasional and passive basis.*

I admitted that I was having difficulty in accepting Nick was really dead. Subconsciously I felt he could walk into the room at any moment. In this I was not alone. My mother wrote in her diary: 'I heard the doorbell tonight and thought it might be Nick.' Without any first-hand proof, his death seemed little more than hearsay. An idea which I knew was absurd entered my mind: perhaps for some unfathomable reason everyone had conspired to make me think he was dead. I told my family this, adding that I knew it was rubbish. It was a useful metaphor to show how unreal his death seemed. In the course of being rescued I had been spared the trauma of seeing his body. Had I seen him, I might, however, have accepted his death more quickly. If I had been well enough to see his coffin, I would perhaps have said my goodbye then. His funeral would have given me a ceremony to mark the end of his life, a full stop. Instead I felt he was merely absent and I was still somehow sharing my life with him while he remained out of sight. Emotionally I had a deep pain that rarely rose to the surface. I was encouraged by some of my family, particularly my mother and Amanda, to talk about it whenever I felt like it. To some extent I did, but I was unsure to what extent I should let it out, or how. For this I would have needed more than permission and encouragement, I would have needed example and practice. The balance I struck was not a bad one; it got me through the toughest months and let me enjoy life.

Soon after we returned to London, the Queen invited Amanda and me for the weekend to Balmoral, her home in Scotland. I leapt at the

* 'Until now I had only been able to grieve, not mourn. Grief was passive. Grief happened. Mourning, the act of dealing with grief, required attention.' Joan Didion, *The Year of Magical Thinking*, (New York: Alfred A. Knopf), 2006, p. 143.

idea. I was especially keen as I remembered the times Nick and I had shared on the grouse moors there. Having seen the good done by our stay with the Troughtons, my parents quickly agreed to the proposal. Two days after their return home, I set off with Amanda. One of the things I most liked about my siblings was that they treated me as an adult. Amanda, at twenty-two, was particularly adept at this. She obviously had not forgotten what being fourteen was like. Our flight was scheduled to land at Aberdeen but the airport was closed and we were diverted to Glasgow. From there we made our way by coach through the thick fog to Aberdeen Airport, where a chauffeur was waiting for us. It was now late at night, and as he drove the fifty miles to Balmoral, the driver explained that everyone at the castle would be asleep but that if we wanted something to eat there were soup and sandwiches waiting.

I had stayed at Balmoral twice before and Amanda had been more often. We both knew the family did not stay up late. We were planning to shuffle like mice to our rooms, when suddenly we caught sight of the Queen striding down the corridor. She had the air of a mother duck gathering in lost young. Beside her was Prince Charles, Nick's and my godfather. He looked every bit as agitated, yet tender and concerned. As they kissed us hello, it felt wonderful to be back. The telegram Charles had sent me in Sligo came to mind and I concentrated on not becoming tearful. They led us into the drawing room and plied us with the soup and sandwiches. Amanda took the lead in thanking them and suggesting they go to bed but there was no persuading them, as they continued to bring food and drink and ask for news from home.

After a while we ambled down the corridor. We knew the form; at some point the Queen would break off and head in the direction of her bedroom. None of it. She shepherded us into our rooms and started to unpack. Here Amanda drew a line, removing a sweater from the Queen's hands, and convincing her that we really would be happier if she took herself to bed. She was in almost unstoppable mothering mode and I loved it. We kissed her goodnight and then unpacked as we chatted to Charles.

Next day there was heavy mist, drizzle and a northerly wind but in my eyes the day was nevertheless heavenly. The Queen and Prince

Philip took me and their other guests shooting. Prince Philip organised the day while the Queen worked her Labradors in the long heather. At lunch she kept an eye on me and afterwards sent me back to the castle. I slept all afternoon.

At dinner the Queen sat me beside her. After the meal was over, she let a short while pass in the drawing room before turning to me and saying, 'Timmy, don't you think it's about time for bed?' It was caring yet firm. Thinking about it years later, I recognised it was the instruction of a stand-in mother, made over and above the head of my sister. I said my goodnights and left for bed with a warm feeling towards the Queen that has stayed with me ever since.

Next day the Queen and Prince Philip suggested I stay in during the morning and come out onto the grouse moor at lunchtime. During the morning the Queen's doctor arrived to dress the wound on my right leg. I remember he looked rather concerned and treated me with kid gloves. 'May I take your boot off?' he asked in a strong Scottish accent. This set me thinking. The word 'boot' implied that they were for outdoor use only. To me they seemed very smart suede shoes but now I wondered whether my mother would disapprove of my wearing them at Balmoral. Suddenly I longed for her.

At midday Amanda and I went out with the Queen to a shooting lodge. I was particularly excited as my brother Philip was coming out from Gordonstoun to join us for the weekend. At lunch, the Queen put Philip and me on either side of her. It felt very cosy and we had a noisy lunch together. It was wonderful to see Philip after some weeks apart. 'Do you want more?' I asked after he had finished his pudding. 'Well, I wouldn't say no,' he replied, camping it up. The Queen giggled. 'But would you say yes?' I insisted, and the Queen giggled some more. Over lunch I talked to her about something that was on my mind: a vague memory of the sound of the bomb. I described it not so much as a noise but a feeling, 'percussive' and 'tangible'. I realised that I was not quite getting my meaning across but found she was a very good listener and drew things out of me that others had not. In the afternoon we went out onto the grouse moor, and that night I wrote in my diary proudly that I got two grouse, as I had the previous morning, and was exhausted.

The weekend went far too quickly. After tea on Sunday the family went out to say goodbye to Philip and Prince Edward, the Queen's youngest son, who were both going back to Gordonstoun. As they drove away, we waved. Just as my mother would, the Queen kept waving until the last moment. My thoughts drifted. I was very pleased not to be going back with them. Without Nick it was going to be a very different experience and I did not feel up to it. The Queen noticed I was looking a little lost and snapped me out of it. With mock force she knocked me with her arm. 'Go on,' she said, 'wave!' I burst into laughter.

Next day the Queen's mothering antennae were out again. I was a bit quiet and she zeroed in on me. 'Timmy, if you had *Britannia* and could choose anywhere in the world to go, where would you choose?' I gulped. It sounded like a good invitation. My grandfather and parents had sailed in the royal yacht *Britannia* for six weeks through the Pacific; was this my chance? Calculating this as unlikely, I decided I would tackle the question as purely academic. 'China,' I declared. 'Why China?' she asked, and soon she had me explaining my reasons and being at the centre of the conversation again.

Prince Philip's brand of support was quite different. He quietly included me at the heart of the weekend without ever making a fuss. His interest in me was unflashy. By now I was getting used to being spoiled and it was refreshing that he spoke and treated me in exactly the same way as when Nick had been alive. When everything in my life was out of balance, it was good to be about people who were rock steady.

At lunch one day, years later, I was sitting next to one of the family whom I had first got to know when Nick and I stayed at Balmoral as boys. This led me to talking about how the Queen had looked after me so lovingly in 1979. Suddenly my eyes filled with tears and I could not say any more. This was a very rare occurrence for me and later I wondered what it was locked up inside of me that had precipitated such a powerful reaction. It was an early pointer to a journey I did not yet know I would have to make, back to 1979.

14

HOME AND AWAY

England enjoyed an Indian summer that October, and each day one of my sisters and I pushed our parents around the garden in their wheelchairs, and sat with them for periods in the warm sunshine. My aunt Pamela came to stay for three days and continued what my mother referred to in her diary as their 'mutual therapy' as they told each other of their various experiences, especially those in Sligo Hospital. She added: 'Poor Timmy still very tired and looks a bit dazed and lost – not surprising.'[1] Plans had been made for me to return to school at the end of September, but when the time came I was far too weak.

At home I needed to fill my time and I threw myself at piles of books which my Gordonstoun housemaster had sent me. Completing the assignments made me feel satisfied and added to my daily routine at a time when I had little. I missed my school friends and was pleased when they wrote to me. Piers McGillycuddy wrote in late September: 'I am disappointed at you not coming back tomorrow but I understand how it must be . . . Hurry up and get better for we all miss you greatly. I can't wait to take you out in *Hunny Bunny* my Mirror dinghy.'[2] Simon Jones wrote several times with details of who was doing what at school and enclosing magazines and photographs. I replied with letters and phone calls. One evening during their study time, Nick's and my friends passed around a card on which they wrote messages. Mahin and Shirin were identical twins in our class, and Nick and I had grown very fond of them. Their letters that evening were signed 'all my love and kisses'.[3] I cried. I realised that they more than any of our friends understood what I was feeling.

As a result of being absent at boarding schools for six years, I did not have many friends in Kent. Philip and my cousins were at school; Norton was at Broadlands preparing for his wedding. Into this sudden void of companionship, previously unthinkable as a twin, stepped my brother Joe and my sisters. Joanna and Amanda split their time between their homes in London and our parents' home, Newhouse, in Kent. For my parents and me, they were our closest companions and carers.

Joe followed a similar routine, returning to Newhouse often from his London home. He had always been a childhood hero to Philip, Nick and me, playing with us and taking us in his Lotus sports car. Now I needed a playmate and Joe often took that role. He spent hours keeping me happily amused. During the afternoon he would play television games with me for long stretches; our favourite was Space Invaders. At dusk he sometimes took me out with a rifle to patrol the farm for vermin. Sometimes he let me drive the car while he took the rifle. Joe was twenty-nine years old but he could bring out in me a schoolboy sense of fun better than anyone. I was loath ever to see him leave. When his Australian girlfriend went home for a prolonged stay, she left me with her Yorkshire Terrier. He was named Basil after John Cleese's television character in *Fawlty Towers*. Basil and I became very attached to each other. He slept on Nick's bed beside mine and from morning to night followed me everywhere. I cared for and treasured him until his owner returned some months later.

One Friday afternoon my mother and I chatted about Nick as I pushed her wheelchair around the garden. She wrote in her diary: 'He dreams about him, and sometimes expects to find him upstairs when going to bed. Feels he must put his things tidy – as he did. I admire the way he is coping, but so heartbreaking.'[4] The next afternoon, while my father slept, she got out of her wheelchair and ventured around on crutches. When she came across Nick's Air India case, with his name in Dymo tape, she was 'in tears'. It was still packed with his possessions from Classiebawn and beside it lay his fishing bag, embossed *NTK*. She gave it to my father, who started to use it as his own. When she found the cartridge bag Nick used when shooting, also with his initials, she adopted it as her handbag and travelled the world with it for years to come.

My parents worked as a team on the mountain of letters that had built up. My father helped my mother with the ones that needed his knowledge of Ireland, business and politics while she helped him with the most emotional ones. She drafted his letter of thanks to the ushers, pall bearers, vigil keepers and flower arrangers at the Mersham funeral:

> Since we were still in hospital ourselves, it was a real comfort to us to know that they were being looked after to the very end not only by our immediate family, but also our larger 'family' of people who live and work on Mersham Hatch Estate.
>
> Our beloved Nicky has spent his short and happy life amongst you all. My mother had spent the first half of her married life here and still regarded her visits as 'coming home'.
>
> It is difficult to try and tell you what we feel, but I am sure you will understand how pleased and grateful we were that you could be with them to the end.[5]

It was now nearly two months since the bomb, and for weeks we had been focusing on the upcoming wedding of Norton and Penny, set for the third Saturday in October. On the Wednesday my parents were taken to Broadlands by ambulance. My mother had known the house all her life and seen it lived in by her grandparents and parents. Now, as she recorded in her diary, she was seeing it for the first time as 'Norton's home'. The homecoming was a mixture of happiness and pain for my mother. In a quiet moment she sat with our grandfather's butler George Daborn and his wife Mafalda and told them what she described as 'our end of the bomb story'.[6] Next morning, in wheelchairs, my parents sat in sunshine on the house steps and had a 'friendly chat' with the team who had managed the estate, all of whom were 'full of praise for Norton'. In the afternoon we visited my grandfather's grave in Romsey Abbey. 'Nice', my mother wrote in her diary,

'– but John and I felt "Bloody IRA".' What should have been an important moment for me made no impression. I have no recollection of the visit. It seems I was physically present but emotionally absent. In contrast, I remember being particularly happy that evening when Philip joined us from Gordonstoun. The excitement was mounting as family and friends streamed in from all directions and Broadlands began to take on the Clan Headquarters role which it had often filled in my grandfather's days. Cousins arrived, among them India, who was a bridesmaid, and Prince Charles, the best man. The house became a hive of activity.

The wedding day was warm and sunny. We forced my parents to stay in bed until noon as family and friends 'dashed in and out'[7] to see them while we helped them get ready. Oscar-winning designer Anthony Powell, who had worked for my father on *Death on the Nile*, arrived to sew my mother into the clothes he had created for her. A long, green tweed suit was set off with a cream blouse and a hat with an ostrich feather and a veil. 'Great success', she noted in her diary, 'and veil covers a multitude of other people's sins!' The sad air that had descended on the house since the bomb was replaced by excitement and energy. The press had noted this in the coverage they gave to the upcoming celebration, as if in search of an uplifting sequel to the bomb, a home-grown *Empire Strikes Back*. Norton and Penny were the stars of the day and were cheered by the crowds. When my parents arrived at the church in wheelchairs pushed by Joe and Philip, with my sisters and me walking behind, a huge cheer greeted us too. A national newspaper pictured my parents on its front page the next day with the headline 'Wedding joy of Lord and Lady Courage'.[8] My mother described Norton and Penny in her diary as 'marvellous & breathtaking – but how we missed darling Nick and our parents'. Of the nine hundred guests, the only ones she singled out for a mention in her diary were 'Drs Heenan and O'Connell from Sligo and 5 of our 6 rescuers from sea'.

Driving back through the town's cheering crowds made me feel like I was in a sports team being welcomed home after a famous victory. I felt energised, but the wedding photographs show me as small, thin and pale. I knew many people there and many others recognised me and introduced themselves. A man put out his hand

and said in the soft accent I was familiar with from the west of Ireland, 'Hello, Timothy, I don't think you know who I am.' His face meant nothing, but the moment I heard his voice I was transfixed and felt the hair on the back of my neck sticking up. For a moment the whole world seemed to stand still as a powerful, distant memory came back. I knew exactly where I had heard that voice before: in the boat, after I was pulled from the water following the explosion. His voice then had been strained and anxious. Now he was holding a champagne glass and smiling. 'My name is Dick Wood-Martin,' he continued. 'Yes, of course I know who you are,' I said. He, his wife Elizabeth and I chatted for a short while and I took the chance to quietly thank them for what they had done. When we parted I thought I had not betrayed the extraordinary sensation I had had when first hearing his voice. But unbeknownst to me Dick had then gone to my father and said, 'I'm sorry, I think I've given Timothy a terrible shock.'

When Penny and Norton left the reception for their honeymoon that evening, they slipped back into the Abbey where Penny placed her bouquet on my grandfather's grave.

After two more days together at Broadlands, the family dispersed and my father was re-admitted to hospital in London for more work on his right leg. This proved to be the most damaged part of his body and gave him pain for the rest of his life. My mother was by now strong enough to do some work, and that afternoon she chaired a meeting for an educational charity. The next day a letter arrived from one of those at the meeting:

> I wonder if you have any idea what an impression you made on us yesterday afternoon! The calmness with which you told us the story; the total absence of drama, or of self-concern; the total dedication to truth and decency – not the faintest suggestion of rancour or bitterness – only the sorrow that your dear son had been cut off at the very time when life was unfolding for him; the naturalness which pervaded everything you said – it was beyond everything![9]

When years later I read this letter, I realised the powerful impact my parents had on those around them and that I was perhaps the principal beneficiary of this. I learned my lack of bitterness from them.

Philip was on half term and due to go back to Gordonstoun soon. My parents decided and I agreed that the time had come when I should join him there. Joanna and Amanda helped me get my trunk ready on the top floor of Newhouse. My mother normally did this and it made her feel 'so helpless and frustrated' that she was only able to 'hobble about' on the ground floor, her only consolation being that my sisters were doing 'a grand job'[10] in her place.

In the days leading up to my return to school I opened a letter from Toni, a girl my own age from New Zealand who wrote: 'I don't know you but then you don't know me either so that makes us even. I am writing to you because I am an identical twin and I understand how you must feel.' I was touched and started to read the letter aloud to Philip. She explained she lived in a fruit-growing region in a small city which had the biggest cannery in the southern hemisphere. However, I mispronounced 'cannery' as 'canary'. After a moment of confusion we realised my mistake, and as our solemn mood was shattered we descended into uncontrollable laughter. Such gut-wrenchingly deep bouts of laughter seemed to be the flip side of the tears which continued to hit us unexpectedly. The imminent return to school was making me feel tense and worried, which made such laughter all the more therapeutic.

The Crathornes and Dugdales visited us for the weekend during half term and heard me talking about *The Life of Brian*, a *Monty Python* film which was soon due for release. Jamie Crathorne had been to university with John Cleese, and a few days after their stay a large package arrived. Inside was the *Life of Brian* book in which was written: 'Timmy, Jamie asked me if I had a pre-publication copy for you. Here it is (five weeks before it "hits the stands") with all our very best wishes and congratulations on your rapid recovery, John Cleese'. The thoughtfulness of this struck me deeply and reinforced the sense that everyone with whom we had contact, directly or indirectly, wanted to help. This transformed the months following the bomb.

When the day came for me to leave my parents and return to school

I was deeply sad. Our local doctor came to give me a check-up, re-dress my leg wound and write notes for the doctor at Gordonstoun. Philip and I had a final lunch with my mother and sisters in the nursery, while downstairs my father and Joe had a working lunch with their farming colleagues. When I walked in to say goodbye, I wanted to show I was strong and ready for the big step ahead, and to hide my doubt, fear and loneliness. Feeling weak and wretched, I kissed my father goodbye. Suddenly I lost control and burst into tears in front of his mortified employees. Later that afternoon my parents had a rest but found they were 'miserable'. My mother wrote in her diary: 'Wrings one's heart'.[11]

At Gordonstoun it was good to be among my friends again and I had no trouble in throwing myself at my work. I attended classes and some activities and then rested after lunch. A friend passed me a message from a new member of staff who was teaching our class that term. His name was McMahon and he wanted me to know that he was not in any way connected to Thomas McMahon. He proved to be a gifted teacher of whom I quickly grew fond. When I rang home at the end of the first day I 'sounded cheerful'[12] but underneath I was homesick with an extra twist: at the end of each class I had gathered my books and instinctively looked to the desk beside me for Nick. At night I went to the sanatorium and shared a room there with Philip. We talked in a way that would not have been possible in the large and rowdy dormitories of our boarding house.

Letters welcoming me back to school arrived regularly, some from people I barely knew. David Niven, whom Nick and I had met briefly the year before, wrote:

> Don't answer this! I'm just climbing aboard the 'Concord' for NY and heard such good news of your recovery and of your parents' too.
>
> You are all so full of guts over the whole terrible experience that I just had to drop you a note wishing you all good luck now you are back at school.
>
> I won't make any more boring noises but millions of people all over the world would like to have written a word to your whole family.[13]

I was a little unsure about the letter because it seemed very emotional for someone who hardly knew us. The envelope had a watery smudge on it and with the cynicism of a fourteen-year-old I suspected he might have been drinking. Years later I was writing a letter which unlocked powerful emotions in me and a tear nearly smudged my writing. Looking down, I remembered David Niven's letter and felt ashamed.

At lunch time one day, I was called to my housemaster's study and passed a bulky envelope which he explained had been intercepted by the police and tested for explosives. It turned out to be a letter from Susie Dugdale who had enclosed a Mars Bar. That security was still a concern had been brought home to me one afternoon the month before. Norton had taken me alone into our father's study to explain that the police were considering whether to send a detective with me when I returned to school, an offer I quickly declined.

After a few days at school I realised I was missing some of the clothes I needed and asked my mother to post them. It happened to be the first day that my siblings had felt it safe to leave my parents alone for a few hours. My mother wrote in her diary: 'Quite nice to have house to ourselves. I went up to Joe's room to try and find some clothes Tim wanted in Nick's school trunk – but found it impossible physically – and emotionally. Had a good, lone, loud, long cry.'[14]

That morning the trial of Thomas McMahon and Francis McGirl opened in Dublin and the media started to cover it. My mother noted: 'John finds it more upsetting than I do – I still feel rather stunned by it all. John O'Grady (17) in thank you letter for our late tip for helping Peter in Castle put it so tellingly. "It was the most disgusting and cruelsome act any human being could ever do."'[15]

I read the newspaper reports each day but happily my classes and activities gave me little time to dwell on them. In the evening Philip and I had a hot drink together while we watched the television news in the sanatorium. The proceedings in Dublin seemed remote and unreal.

One of the many strangers thanked by my father for a letter of condolence wrote to him a second time:

Please do not get the idea you are going to be plagued by my illeg-
ible scrawl but I do want to ask you if you can help by word of
encouragement a young boy who was seriously injured at
Warrenpoint on the same day of your tragedy.

Paul is 18 & was one of the four injured when the 17 were
killed – his mother is a widow.

Paul is now in the burns intensive care unit of the Queen Elizabeth
Hospital at Woolwich. He has extensive burns. One leg has been
amputated below the knee – the other foot might have to come off –
now they have decided the remainder of the amputated leg must also
come off. His ear drum has been perforated – all his front teeth gone
– a broken elbow was discovered last week. Up till now he has had
operations every Monday & Thursday – now & for weeks to come he
will be having skins grafts every Monday, the skin having to come
from his back as his hips are so burnt.

You & your wife will know what this boy must be suffering –
I can only guess, but I do know his morale is now <u>very</u>, <u>very</u> low.

. . . I appreciate you cannot go but could you find the time to
write a few lines to him – I think the fact that you can identify
yourself with his suffering would help enormously – he is <u>Pte Paul
Burns</u> & at the same time his great friend – aged 18 – is also with
him – badly burnt but no limbs lost – his parents live in Ireland
& so he has no one over here now. They have been living in the
hospital but had to return to Ireland because there are their other
children – he is called <u>Thomas Caughey (Pte)</u> & his father an ex
paratrooper himself.

The parents of both boys are going through hell watching the
suffering their sons are having to endure. People so easily forget
the injured when their dead have been buried – <u>please</u> write to
them both – they are so young.[16]

Joe and Amanda immediately went to see the two soldiers in hospital
and my mother then wrote to one of her own Red Cross colleagues
who agreed to 'keep a special eye on the two boys'.[17] On the same
day my father sent a letter to each soldier. A reply from Paul Burns
stated:

. . . I'm glad to hear that you are all recovering well and are back at home. It was great that your children came to visit me.

I had a terrible time at first but now that I'm out of the intensive care unit things have improved a lot. It's great to be able to get around the hospital and I go to the gym for physiotherapy. They've started me walking on crutches but I'm finding it very hard at the moment, but it makes a difference to know that people are thinking about me.[18]

Joe, Joanna and Amanda visited the men a number of times in hospital over the coming months, and Amanda corresponded with them.

When eventually this petered out, we followed their progress in occasional news reports. Although I never met them, I felt bonded, and realised how lucky I was to have been so comparatively free of injury. The strength they showed during their recovery lifted our spirits and earned our respect.*

My birthday that year fell on a Sunday and as the day approached I was feeling low. Amanda flew up to Gordonstoun the day before. She collected me, Philip, Prince Edward and our cousin Ivar Mountbatten and we all went for a meal at a favourite local restaurant. Later she took Philip and me to spend the night with family friends nearby. I felt very far from my parents who were at Broadlands with Norton, Penny and a large gathering of the family. My mother went to sleep

---

* Attached to the correspondence in my parents' files are two press cuttings from 14 March 1986. *The Times* carried a photograph of a parachutist touching down and reported 'Lance Corporal Paul Burns, aged 24, who lost his leg in an IRA bombing at Warrenpoint in 1979, making a perfect landing at Aldershot yesterday after qualifying as a parachutist and becoming a member of the Red Devils (Display Team). He had made 240 jumps to get his free fall licence.' He became a jump instructor and left the army in 1991. His later career included being a Ski Bob instructor, a qualified Yachtmaster and a Hollywood body double. In 2006 the *Daily Telegraph* reported that Paul, a father of three, had 'used his disability to land roles in blockbusters such as *Gladiators* and *Band of Brothers*' and had helped to set up the agency Amputees in Action. Amanda noted his list of qualifications and added 'and a cool dude'.

that night 'thoroughly miserable', asking herself, 'Why, oh why isn't Nick here?'[19] I dreaded the next day and that night had a nightmare in which I heard the explosion and then the sound of water and pieces of boat raining into the sea. I woke 'very frightened'.[20] Next day I could not lift my spirits for long. Each time I opened a card it seemed there was an error as the cards were addressed 'Darling Timmy' instead of 'Darling Nicky and Timmy'.

It was horrible to open presents of my own rather than ones to share with Nick as normal. I started to find each hour increasingly hard to get through. The day wore on and as the shadows lengthened I knew the time was coming when Amanda would leave. I cut a cake all my own and rang our parents at Broadlands before returning to school. It was the only day I felt nothing but sadness from start to end. My mother's account of the day states: 'rang Nan [Helen Bowden, our nanny] this evening as she will be as sad & to give her news after speaking to Tim and Phi & she finished me by asking if I had arranged for flowers for Nick's grave. Derek [gardener] goes before weekends with flowers but hadn't thought of this as to me he isn't there but all around us.'[21] My mother would have been able to reassure our nanny that I was doing well at school because my parents had received what my mother called 'such a wonderful letter from Phi, with most thoughtful and touching "report on Tim" at school – sad moments he of course finds at Nick's absence'.

When Philip and I moved back into our boarding house I quickly found dormitory life too boisterous. I was unable to get enough sleep and soon my housemaster switched me back to the sanatorium. It was here at bedtime on 23 November that I watched the Dublin trial come to an end and learned the verdicts. As I sipped my bedtime Ovaltine with the nurse and watched a small black and white television, I had the sensation of a storm raging above my head while I sheltered in the safety, peace and privacy of the sanatorium. Thomas McMahon was found guilty and Francis McGirl not guilty. In a detached, clinical way I felt satisfied. McMahon was clearly the senior of the pair and the Garda had done a good job in catching him. I was philosophical about Francis McGirl's acquittal; I quietly accepted that the evidence had not convinced the court.

It seemed there was a widespread feeling that he had escaped justice so I was not altogether surprised when two men tried to kill him within a week of his acquittal. On Thursday 29 November, Gardai arrested two members of the Ulster Defence Association, a Protestant paramilitary group who had decided to take justice into their own hands. One was a 32-year-old fork lift operator from Rathcoole and the other a 25-year-old bus conductor from Newtown-abbey, both in County Antrim. They checked into the Bush Hotel in Carrick-on-Shannon, County Leitrim, at 3pm on Wednesday 28 November, posing as fishermen visiting the area. Next, two men arrived with weapons and further instructions. They were to wait at Francis McGirl's regular pub in Ballinamore, owned by his uncle, John Joe McGirl. When Francis McGirl arrived they were to leave, put on balaclavas and go back in to shoot him. What saved Francis McGirl was an unconnected explosion on the border, which poured Gardai into the area. The murder was called off but the would-be assassins drove into a checkpoint south of Swanlinbar, County Cavan. When Gardai searched the elder man they found a newspaper picture of his intended target. It was not long before he directed them to a ditch were they had left their weapons and provided the names of other UDA men in the area. They were taken to Dublin and on 1 December charged in the same court that had acquitted Francis McGirl eight days earlier. On 15 February 1980 they were both convicted and sentenced to prison, the elder man for seven years, his accomplice for five.

A few days after the trial, my parents received a reassuring letter from a recent guest speaker at Gordonstoun, Norris McWhirter. He and his identical twin Ross had created the *Guinness Book of Records** and were celebrated lawyers, broadcasters and campaigners for the liberty of the individual against oppression whatever the source – corporate, state or terrorist. In 1975 Ross McWhirter offered £50,000 for the capture of terrorist bombers, and the IRA responded by sending two men to his home in Enfield, near London. When he opened the door he was shot dead. Norris McWhirter described it as 'not a bereavement, an ampu-

---

* The bestselling work of non-fiction after the Bible. Source: Norris McWhirter's *Daily Telegraph* obituary, 21 April 2004.

tation' and stepped into his twin's shoes as founding deputy chairman of the National Association for Freedom. He said, 'I am resigned to be a target. I take the view that I have had a good life and that I owe something to Ross's memory.'[22] When in November 1979 the head-master Michael Mavor told me Norris McWhirter was visiting the school to give a lecture, I quickly accepted the chance to meet him in private. Over tea after the lecture, we talked at some length with Philip beside me for support. I found his optimism and energy inspiring. It was re-assuring simply to be in his presence. He did not use the term 'lone twin' but he was the first such person I had met and he was evidently enjoying a great life. That his brother had been killed by the IRA made Norris's survival all the more valid as an illustration for me. He wrote to my parents:

> I was able to say two things which I hope might have been helpful – first that recuperation is a very up and down process and secondly it is no good just living in hope that time will cure the hurt. This being so the only plan is to double rather than to half one's aspiration for the future. It was heart-warming to witness the way Philip is trying to shoulder the role of being a 'deputy twin'.[23]

The bomb may have put my father's film production work on hold but it did not stop him adding to his long line of awards. When London cinema-goers voted *Death on the Nile* the best film of the year, Norton collected the award on his behalf.* His voice was charged with emotion as he stood at the podium holding the award and told the audience that the reason our father could not come in person was that he was still recovering 'from the IRA's murderous attack on my family'.

In Ireland my parents had carefully collated a list of fifty doctors and nurses at Sligo General Hospital whom they wanted to thank. On 6 December they wrote to them individually and enclosed a recently published book, *Mountbatten: Eighty Years in Pictures*, or a small commem-

---

* London Evening Standard Awards, 27 November 1979. Norton was associate producer of the film.

orative Wedgwood dish containing my grandfather's likeness. That weekend my parents were hosting a large family party at Newhouse. In her diary my mother wrote: 'stumped about in the nursery floor trying to tidy Twins' room for Norton and Penny! Seeing Nicky's clothes totally devastates me. How does poor Timmy surmount it without wanting to move out?'[24]

On Friday 30 November the last of my wounds surrendered its scab and at long last I could get rid of the bandage on my lower right leg and lie full-length in a bath tub, which felt wonderful. I rang home and shared the news with my parents, my mother duly noting it in her diary. My body was beginning to undergo the effects of puberty. My voice was breaking and for some time had the annoying habit of suddenly switching from a man's voice to a boy's and back again. On the last day of term I got up early in the sanatorium to go and stand nervously in front of the mirror and shave for the first time. I used a disposable Bic razor which Philip had provided. I removed the few unsightly hairs from my upper lip without cutting myself. It felt good to be moving into a new stage of life. When I felt a pang of grief that Nick was not taking the same step, I thought about it for a moment then turned my mind to the day ahead and the flight home with Philip for the holidays. The relief at having got through my first term without Nick was enormous and I was longing for the fun and excitement of Christmas.

At home my parents sat with me to go over my school report. Michael Mavor wrote: 'it is a great pleasure to see that Timothy's enquiring mind and zest for learning have in no way been blunted. He has shown great courage and good sense and deserves a happy and restful holiday. If he is not delighted with his exam results, I am!'[25] My housemaster Peter Larkman wrote:

When Timothy came to me towards the end of term and said that he did not wish his exam results to be made public I felt that he was being a little over sensitive and told him so. I know that he is a perfectionist but I believe that even he will be pleased by the enclosed set of exam results . . . All the staff who teach him are delighted with them.

No praise is too high for him for the way he has coped this term.[26]

My father gave his boyish grin as my mother read this out. I knew we were all relieved that I could do well without Nick at my side; and how desperately sad we all were that Nick was not at my side doing well.

15

STEPS OF ST PAUL'S

On the first day of the school holidays Philip and I were full of high jinks as we flew south from Gordonstoun. Noticing that someone in the row behind was eavesdropping, I put on a show. For our chemistry classes Nick and I had memorised the Periodic Table of Elements in which each element was abbreviated to a letter or two. The first, Hydrogen, was abbreviated to H; next was Helium, He. Reading across the chart provided a nonsensical flow of letters. I now intonated these as if speaking a foreign language: 'H He, Li BeBCNOFNe? NaMgAL SiPSCLAr! KCaScTiV, CrMn FeCoNiCuZn GaGe AsSeBrKr SnSb TeXi CsBaLaHfTa? WReOsIrPtAu!! HgTiPbBiPoAtRn . . .' Soon Philip was in stitches. A stewardess came by and spoke to us. As she did so, Philip's annoyingly-difficult-to-open plastic container of airline coffee cream spurted onto my jacket. I dabbed the milk without drawing breath and then Philip, oblivious to the mess, made a fresh assault on the pot, sending another spurt onto the same spot. I rolled my eyes at the stewardess and kept on wiping. Philip may not have been a twin but I had just as many laughs with him and adored the heightened bond we now shared. From London we sped home to Mersham. My mother wrote in her diary: 'Our two darling boys arrived (Oh! for the third).'[1]

As always, our traditional family Christmas was due at Broadlands. I was longing to be there again, but first there was a major event on our horizon in the form of a memorial service. Originally it had been proposed for my grandfather alone, but when Prince Philip suggested that it should be made for my grandmother and Nick as well, everyone agreed.[2] On Thursday morning, 20 December, we joined a congregation of two thousand in St Paul's Cathedral for the service. 'Norton read the Lesson,' my mother noted in her diary, 'and Charles gave outstanding 25 minute address . . .'

I arrived at the service steeled for what I knew would be a very large event; I was sure I was going to keep my composure under the public gaze, and when Joanna asked if I had remembered to bring a handkerchief I told her I did not need one. When Prince Charles spoke about my grandparents I was moved but kept my feelings under control. He started to talk about Nick. The music, the architecture, the stillness all came together. A few seats away my mother found the 'singing of anthem by young choirboys – like Nick – so moving'. I broke down suddenly. It was all too much and I had nowhere to turn and no hanky to cry into. My aunt Pamela quietly reached out from the row behind and gave me hers. From that day I carried a handkerchief in my pocket wherever I went.

My mother wrote to Prince Charles to tell him how deeply he had touched and soothed us. His reply to his 'Dearest Godmama' said how much her words meant to him and he enclosed the address. Its closing words spoke about Nick:

Here was a young boy of such enormous promise and potential – one minute an innocent, laughing, affectionate personality, the next a lifeless reminder of that dark, inexplicable side of man's nature, which brings death and misery to countless people all over the world. Nicky was the absolute antithesis to all that is dark and miserable. He had great sensitivity. He had an infectious sense of humour. He showed infinite concern and understanding for others and he was extremely bright and intelligent. Last year he and his identical brother Timothy (I could never tell them apart) came to stay at Balmoral. At one meal I had them both sitting beside me and rarely have I enjoyed anything more. At the age of thirteen their conversation was extraordinarily interesting and highly intelligent. Not only were they incredibly funny, but both of them were well-read and interested in so many subjects. Nicky was becoming

a very promising photographer and at school he displayed perse-
verance in all he undertook making, as one of the masters said, a
good, neat job of whatever he applied himself to. Both twins ran
their school ciné club and did so with such efficiency and enthu-
siasm that they could be left in charge of the film shows with
complete confidence on the part of the staff. At my old school,
Gordonstoun, Nicky was earning glowing reports each term and
there is little doubt that he would have excelled in whatever field
he had chosen to operate.

We have been deprived of the kind of stalwart character the
world needs. Nicky has departed with both his grandparents,
leaving us to face that awful, gaping emptiness which remains
behind – a memorial to all those truly innocent young people
who have died as a result of man's unholy extremism. A part of
his spirit, I am sure, lives on in his brother Timothy. We have
lost part of ourselves with all of them, but one day we shall find
it again.[3]

Simon Jones struggled through the crowds and found me outside the
church doors with my parents and Warrenpoint survivor Paul Burns in
their wheelchairs. Simon called me to go with him and his father. They
were carrying, broken down into parts, a large model aeroplane which
Nick and I had spent hours helping Simon to build at the Dragon
School. I was not entirely comfortable in accepting such a valuable gift,
with its expensive radio-control circuitry and two-stroke engine, but
when I looked at Simon I immediately knew he really wanted me to
have it. Overjoyed, I helped carry it to our parked car. On its side were
the registration markings, derived from our initials, which Simon, Nick
and I had steamed on the year before, SJ1-TN, longing for the day
when we would fly it. I was determined that day would now soon come.
I returned to my parents outside the cathedral door and joined them
in speaking to crowds of friends and well-wishers. Among them was
Paul Maxwell's mother, Mary, who was struck by my mother's 'courage
and generosity of spirit'.[4]

I felt uplifted by the service and powerfully energised. Somehow it
seemed we had reached a symbolic turning point. For me the day was
particularly important because I felt I had shared some form of farewell

with my family and friends. I felt relieved. When my parents decided they wanted to leave, Norton and Philip were ready to wheel them via a circuitous route to their car, but they had other ideas. The most direct way was down the magnificent flight of steps leading from the front of the cathedral. This was hazardous terrain for a couple with three broken legs and bodies still riddled with bomb injuries, but my parents were having one of their 'in for a penny, in for a pound' days. The route was sheer madness but their minds were made up. They seemed as energised as I was. A large number of photographers had been hovering in the vicinity and, sensing a photo opportunity, they now formed up like a flock of starlings.

'We got out of those wheelchairs and we walked,' my mother reminisced over breakfast with me and my father nearly a quarter of a century later. Gazing at her, my father continued, 'It was an incredible moment, going down the steps of St Paul's. You were wonderful. How you made it I really don't know.' She replied, 'There were only two moments in my life that I had been rather frightened – *very* frightened: at Gandhi's funeral, being pushed [towards the pyre].* And standing at the top of those steps with a battery of reporters and going down and feeling, "I don't think I'm going to make it but I've got to."'[5] As we walked down, the photographers went in reverse, snapping and calling out and jostling like fury. Those few seconds captured my parents' utter determination. It was a happy, simple, end-of-saga message. Next day, the pictures were plastered across newspapers.

After the service we went home for a family lunch. In the previous months the family had attended a stream of funerals, memorial services and other religious ceremonies. Amanda told us that her godfather, who shared our sense of humour but not our lax attitude to churchgoing, had murmured to her, 'Nice to see you in church so much these days.' By 6:30pm we were at Broadlands for the Christmas holidays with the Hickses. The Queen and Prince Philip had invited us all to stay at Windsor for Christmas, perhaps imagining what it would be like to be

---

* Mahatma Gandhi was cremated the day after his Delhi assassination in 1948. As the pyre was lit, the crowd, estimated at a million, surged forward and the dignitaries at the front were pushed towards the flames. My grandfather called for everyone to sit down, which helped restore order.

at Broadlands without my grandparents and Nick. My parents grate-fully turned them down; it would not be the happiest of Christmases but we were all keen to get back to some form of normality as quickly as possible.

At Broadlands we settled into a routine similar to that of previous years, although my mother noted in her diary: 'Daddy very missed.' On the third day we were shocked by something that happened at our Irish fishing lodge. The entry in my mother's diary reads: 'Heard on the news that Aasleagh had been "vandalised" and thousands of pounds of damage done. Terribly upsetting especially to poor John who in our low state was reduced to tears.' When we learned that the vandalism had taken place on the final day of the trial in Dublin, it seemed likely that the two were connected. My parents reached the local Gardai by phone and were 'astounded' to learn that the culprit was a young man whom we knew from the local area. Apparently he had walked around the house smashing ground-floor windows 'in a drunken stupor'. We all felt sad for his parents, to whom we were close, but as my mother wrote in her diary: 'Relieved it was not IRA.'[6] The Gardai explained that the youngster had no connection to the organisation but liked to give that impression in the pub where he spent a great deal of his time. In truth he was little more than a wild young man seeking attention and rebelling against his parents. The Gardai 'made him sweat for a few weeks'[7] before telling him that my father was taking no further action. The episode made me think back to a day when a farmer had shouted at us as we walked over his land to reach the river bank. His shouts left us in no doubt that we were not welcome. In the past we had shrugged off such incidents, but if we were to return in the future our presence would perhaps seem like a challenge to such animosity. When my father learned of the damage to Aasleagh, it might have been the moment that he accepted it was no longer safe to return to Ireland. Since childhood he had spent some of his happiest days there and the idea that he would have to give the place up must have seemed like a further bereavement. It did to me.

We did not doubt that the overwhelming majority of people around us in Ireland were friendly. One of the Irishmen who regularly fished at Aasleagh wrote: 'old Martin Nee of Bundorragha Bridge put it further when he spoke to me and said "when I heard it I had to go out and get sick". This would convey what regret and horror was in the hearts and minds of the people in the area from [shopkeeper] Eddie Hamilton to even the poacher and I can assure you that it was sincere.'[8] Another fisherman wrote to my father: 'I may say that nearly all to whom I spoke . . . were visibly affected and were just unable to speak of Lady Brabourne and yourself without a wee tear gathering to the eyes.'[9]

Despite assurances of the warmth of feelings towards us, the unavoidable truth was that while Ireland harboured killing and violence, we would not be safe, let alone able to relax. If we had any doubt about the division and resentment in Ireland we only had to consider the stories we heard in England. My mother was told that, following the Mullaghmore bomb, Irishmen working on the construction of the M20 motorway close to our home in Kent were told by fellow workers to leave for their own safety. Apparently they did. A friend in London wrote to my father that 'even in the supermarkets the sales assistants say that not one ounce of Irish butter and cheese has been sold'.[10] Firms in Ireland were feeling the effect of a grass-roots boycott of Irish exports. A man who had been employed in Limerick wrote to a national newspaper many years later: 'I worked for a firm that exported nearly all its products to the UK; the firm lost most of this market and closed down. I lost my job, as did many others.'[11] A man I knew in later life was so ashamed of his Irish name that he seriously considered dropping the 'O' from his surname, O'Brien.

Over the months, the volume of post had reduced but still each day brought new letters and Christmas cards. I opened one from the Protocol and Conference Department at the Foreign Office. Inside was a compliments slip from 'Her Majesty's ambassador, Rangoon' saying 'for forwarding to the Hon Timothy Knatchbull if you think fit'. The Christmas card included such comments as: 'although you have no great noblest grand Pa, you have very merciful Uncle Philip . . . and very merciful aunty who is my favourite queen of the world.'

My parents and aunt had been dealing with my grandfather's will for some weeks. In November my mother and aunt had spent a morning clearing his bedside table of his belongings. I was sitting on my parents' bed at Broadlands when they explained our grandfather had written a letter to each of his grandchildren and his great-nephews George Milford Haven and Ivar Mountbatten. My mother handed me a large brown envelope with *Timothy* typed on the front. Inside was an undated letter in my grandfather's handwriting.

> My Dear Timmy
> You will receive this letter after my death.
> I want you to know of the great affection which I felt towards you.
> All my possessions will pass eventually to Norton and his heirs, but I was keen for you to have some personal souvenirs of me and the Mountbatten Family, and I enclose a list of what I have set aside for you.
> Not all the grandchildren have exactly the same list because I was not always able to get hold of sufficient copies of some of the items for you all.
> It will be nice to think that you may want to pass on some of these things to your own children in due course.
> They come with my deepest affection and love
> Your devoted old
> Grandpapa

The letter was a complete surprise and I treasured it. It was so very *Grandpapa*. Attached was a list of things he had left me. The contents of this were not a surprise because over the years he had shown us the boxes he was filling for each of us. Each box had a sheet sellotaped to it, identifying the intended recipient. The boxes were the size of large briefcases, and as each was filled another was started. He added to them steadily over the years and the piles grew. By 1979 there were approaching ninety boxes, stacked against a wall in a laundry room at the top of Broadlands. Eight were for me and were augmented by a number of bequests too large to fit inside, such as a bust of him. My boxes remained untouched at Broadlands for another decade until I moved them to my first permanent home. They contained one hundred and forty-nine items which were listed:

Set of three volumes on Naval Medals by the 1st Marquess of Milford Haven.
The Mountbattens by Alden Hatch

L'Amiral Mountbatten by John Terraine (French Edition)

Transcript of T.V. Interview with Duke of Edinburgh and Lord Mountbatten, 23rd/24th November 1967.

'Sunday Times' magazine, three copies, 10th, 17th and 24th November 1968. (Summary of 'Life and Times of Lord Mountbatten') . . .

Viceregal Dessert Plate

The Encyclopaedia of Naval Warfare

An Introduction to polo by 'Marco'. (Nom de plume of Lord Mountbatten).

Cypher of the Last Viceroy of India, worn by servants on liveries.

Royal Sailors by Cecil Hampshire

Mission with Mountbatten by Alan Campbell-Johnson

Gold Sovereign

Silver Ash Tray, with Coat of Arms

Signed photograph of Lord Mountbatten in leather frame.

The Murder of Roger Ackroyd by Agatha Christie (paperback edition)*

Earl Mountbatten. One of many notebooks compiled by school-children about Lord Mountbatten.

The list went on to include cufflinks, gramophone records, magazines, lecture transcripts, postcards, a menu card, embroidery, a local newspaper, medallions, and finally a pair of shotguns. If he had wanted to reach out from beyond the grave, he seemed to have achieved this, for the two final entries on the list were dated September and October 1979, probably inserted by his private secretary John Barratt.

Separately my grandfather left me a note with some gold and amethyst cufflinks explaining they had belonged to his father. Every time I wore them I thought of him and his father, who had died in my grandfather's youth. I knew how he loved, admired and later missed his father, and nothing he left me gave me more pleasure.

Christmas was much as we expected. My mother wrote on Christmas Day: 'Woke at 7am & a few tears, but we are trying not to be too sad for Penny's sake whose first Christmas it is away from home.' Physically

---

* My grandfather wrote to Agatha Christie in 1969 and secured her confirmation that he had contributed to the plot of this novel in 1924.

exhausted and emotionally drained, my father succumbed to a bad cold and spent the holidays in bed. For the New Year we returned to Newhouse, as usual accompanied by my aunt and Hicks cousins. My mother wrote in her diary for New Year's Day 1980:

> Despite the horror of this past year I somehow dread it ending because Darling Nick was with us for 2/3 of it. What pleasure is there in welcoming a New Year of which he is not a part? But of course the miracle is that John and I – as well as Timmy – did survive together and so well really but for which life would be intolerable. Perhaps I should make more effort to be jolly (I am at times but tears at others) as well as cheerful. How wonderful all our family (and Penny) have been.

16

NEW DECADE

'Thank goodness it's 1980 shortly – I have an odd feeling that a new decade will help,' wrote Bobby Moorhead to my father.[1] He was right. The 1980s brought to fruition much of the healing my parents sought for themselves and the family. They gained a further two daughters-in-law, two sons-in-law and the first five of eighteen grandchildren. My father carried on producing feature films. My mother was given a pair of miniature Dachshunds, hoping to fill the hole left by Twiga. She continued to expand her charitable work until she held the position of president, chairman or patron of over fifty organisations. The corresponding figure for my father was only slightly less. They bought New Kelso, a rambling fishing lodge on the west coast of Scotland, large enough to accommodate their steadily increasing family.

In the early weeks of 1980, the results of the bomb were still being reported in the press. On Wednesday 9 January the Sligo coroner, Desmond Moran, completed the formality of the inquest. Among those willing to comment afterwards was the family's Sligo solicitor, Charlie Browne, who said it was ironic that people looking for freedom for Ireland should assassinate a man who gave India her freedom, and was 'a great friend to Ireland'. The coroner issued a statement:

> . . . I believe it is important to stress again the great responsibility
> that parents and teachers of any nation have in the way they

interpret history and pass it on to the youth of the country. I believe that if history could be taught in such a fashion that it would help to create harmony among people rather than division and hatred it would serve this and all other nations better. It must also be stated that churchmen and politicians have indeed a great responsibility to renew and add to their efforts for peace and harmony in this country. I know these are very general recommendations but I feel they must be made . . .'[2]

A short while later he wrote letters of sympathy to the families involved. To my aunt, he wrote: 'When people suffer together it creates a very special type of bond, and while the personal intensity of your suffering was in the extreme, the people of Sligo were in communion with you through the terrible nightmare . . .'[3]

More press interest was generated on 21 January when Thomas McMahon and Francis McGirl appeared again in a Dublin court to be tried for membership of the Provisional IRA, an illegal organisation. The only evidence offered was the 'belief' of a chief superintendent. Often this had been sufficient for a conviction but this time, without any cross-examination of the men, the judge acquitted them both.

During the Christmas holidays I had worked on a project close to my heart: the radio-controlled plane which Nick and I had helped Simon Jones to complete at the Dragon School. Sometimes when I looked at the plane I felt sad and unsure whether I wanted to finish the model and make it fly. But when I reminded myself that Nick would undoubtedly have completed the job, I realised just how much it meant to me. In the new year of 1980, I therefore made contact with Mike Duell, a model enthusiast, who agreed to help. Having made some last-minute amendments to the model, he managed to coax the engine to life and soon my heart was leaping as I found myself at the controls. It was a dream which Nick and I had shared, and I was now elated as the aircraft spiralled and looped through the sky, while Mike watched over my shoulder and coached me. On the second flight the radio-control circuitry failed and we watched helplessly as the model flew at top speed into the branches of an enormous tree. As the sound of splintering balsa wood filled the air, the engine tore itself free from its mounting and continued forward for several seconds like a whining banshee. Then there was a silence. Everyone looked at me and when I burst into laughter, Mike, my parents and my brother Joe followed suit. On the spot Joe offered to buy a replacement, and with his and Mike's help over the coming months I learned to fly model aircraft. It proved to be a nexus in my life as I started on a life-long love affair with aviation. The next year I took my lessons as a glider pilot at Gordonstoun. At university I qualified as a private pilot and in later life as a professional. Without the model I might never have found the path to the exhilaration, freedom and fulfilment of flying.

Back at school I continued to receive letters from well-wishers but found, as Norris McWhirter had predicted, recuperation was 'a very up and down process'.[4] One morning in the spring of 1980, I awoke early at Gordonstoun from a dream in which *Shadow V* was blown up and Nick was dead. I was shaken to the core by what I thought was just a nightmare. As I calmed down, a nagging doubt entered my mind: Was it just a nightmare? I came close to panic as I tried and failed to sort out nightmare from reality. Slowly the truth spread over me like a cold dawn. In a dormitory of sixteen sleeping boys, I lay there struggling to control my tears. Those were some of the hardest minutes of all.

As the months passed, my damaged right eye was going downhill. A vital process of fluid circulation within the eye had been interrupted by the bomb injuries and over the following months the lens became opaque. My iris became eerily white. The sight in that eye, bad since birth, became worse as a cataract formed and blocked out the light. The only solution was an operation. Fed up with hospitals and wanting to get on with life, I told the family one day that I was not going to have the surgery. Luckily Philip was on hand to change my mind. Late in the summer term, I travelled home from Gordonstoun and had the cataract removed. When I came around from the anaesthetic and opened my right eye, I could see astonishingly bright and colourful light whereas before I had been able to see only a dim and cloudy grey. However, I now had to wear a thick contact lens which irritated my eye. I also found the eye very sensitive to light, and direct sunlight made me squint. Worse, the poor image from my right eye clashed with the good image from my left eye, giving me double vision. I struggled with exercises designed to improve the sight but they came to nothing, and eventually I resigned myself to abandoning the contact lens. I found the remaining sight was enough for almost everything I wanted.

One lasting bonus of the operation was that the eye no longer had a ghostly white look to it, which others had found unsettling. After the operation I was left with a stitch in my eyeball which I longed to have removed, a task that was left to the last moment before we left London for our August holidays. I sat in the specialist's chair with sweaty palms as he approached my eye with a razor blade and told me not to move. I was very pleased not to have to repeat the experience.

The family had by now accepted it was not safe to return to Ireland for our summer holiday, and went instead to Glen Affric, a beautiful valley in the Scottish Highlands. We travelled in our usual large family group and invited friends including the Crathornes, Dugdales and Troughtons. It turned out to be a happy few weeks. The scenery was sometimes 'heart-achingly like Ireland' and elicited what my mother referred to as 'shades – or rather shadows'[5] of the previous summer. After four days she recorded that my father was 'now really enjoying himself having worried (quite unnecessarily) that the boys and everyone else would be happy – and of course mourning Aasleagh most of all of us. So cruel to be kept away from the place he has always most loved after [Mersham] Hatch.'[6] On 27 August my mother woke early 'so conscious of this awful anniversary' and 'tried to write a little piece about Nicky. Tim talked a lot about it all to John.'[7] I found this very therapeutic and my parents were uniquely good listeners. In turn, I listened to their memories, questions and reflections, which sometimes proved too much for others in the family.

In the run-up to my O-Level exams, I had my one and only episode of fury at the IRA. During a mid-morning break between lessons, I walked into my study and as usual turned on my radio to catch the eleven o'clock news. It was Friday 24 April 1981 and the bulletin told of protestors having taken over Classiebawn in support of the IRA. I swore and kicked, venting my anger in private. It seemed the IRA wanted to add insult to injury. I calmed myself down and resolved to get back to classes, but midway down a flight of stairs I was hit by another blinding rage and found myself talking aloud and swearing. I sat in classes seething and only relaxed later when I heard, again on the radio, that the siege had ended quickly and peacefully.

The occupation had been staged by three men calling themselves the 'Bundoran H Block Committee' led by a militant from Bundoran.

Their protest was in support of Bobby Sands, the IRA hunger striker in prison in Northern Ireland.* They went onto the roof and unfurled a banner saying 'Bundoran Sinn Féin supports the Hunger Strike'. They settled in the Upper Tower Room and when they demanded food, Hugh Tunney's partner Caroline Devine took them hard boiled eggs and orange juice. They also asked for a phone and with this their leader told reporters that they had selected Classiebawn as a 'symbol of British Imperialism in Ireland'. He went on:

> We entered the building through the front door at 7 o'clock this morning and locked ourselves into the tower room. There has been no damage done to any of the property in the castle and we have taken no hostages. We have no quarrel with the owner of the castle, Mr Tunney, and we explained the purpose of the protest to him. Neither have we a quarrel with the forces of the Free State [the Irish Government].'8

They assured reporters that Hugh Tunney, Caroline Devine, and employees Peter Nicholson and Michael Connolly had free movement within the castle. They ended the sit-in at 1pm and were taken to Cliffoney Garda Station where they were released without charge. A group calling themselves 'The Sligo H-Block/Armagh Committee' said similar action would be carried out against British landlords and firms in Sligo.†

---

* Bobby Sands died eleven days later on 5 May 1981 after sixty-six days without food. By October when the hunger strike was called off, ten IRA men were dead. The British Government of Margaret Thatcher refused throughout to reinstate political status and privileges to IRA prisoners.
† On Sunday 3 May at 10am, five members of the group entered Tanrago House, Beltra, near Sligo, the home of Lieutenant Commander John Farr, Conservative MP for Harborough. The group, which included a County Councillor, unfurled a banner and displayed protest posters from an upstairs window. Twenty others picketed the entrance. By 11am Gardai including a Chief Superintendent, a Superintendent and five Special Branch men armed with Uzi machine guns demanded that the protestors leave. Proclaiming that John Farr should be refused entry to Ireland and his 400 acres be nationalised, the protestors left by 2pm. They were not charged. Source: *Sligo Journal*, 8 May 1981.

My father took the sad decision to sell Aasleagh and look instead for a replacement in Scotland. Not wanting to put it on the open market, he let the Irish government buy it quietly in June 1982. He entrusted it to the state because he wanted it to be protected from commercial exploitation and the relentless nets of poachers. During the Troubles it seemed only the government had the economic weight and political clout to ensure this.* He did not, however, trust the politicians to look after Mickey and Bridget Keane and as a parting gift he gave them the cottage they lived in.

Had it not been for the bombing, I believe my father would have spent more and more of his time at Aasleagh as he approached retirement. When he and I read in the newspaper of an elderly fisherman who had hooked a salmon so mighty that he had been swept away and never heard of again, we agreed it was a good end to his life. I think he would have been happy to grow old and die at Aasleagh. I suspected how keenly he felt its loss because, as with the deaths of his brother, mother and son, he rarely spoke about it and when he did his whole body took on a heaviness. My mother was much better at articulating the loss. Decades later, researching this book, I found some notes she had prepared for an interview in September 1983. One section dealt with her psychological injuries and included: 'no Ireland and [Irish] friends'. I too felt the loss of contact with Ireland and our Irish friends keenly, and both of us wanted to return, but in this we were alone in the family. Perhaps we had been anaesthetised against the trauma by our prolonged lack of consciousness in the water and in hospital, a mercy not extended to my father and wider family. Ireland was a bereavement I felt I would somehow undo one day, by returning and learning how to enjoy the place again.

My mother's interview notes also contained the words 'expect bombs'. My parents and I feared that one of the many attacks then being launched by the IRA would be directed at our family. After each attack my father urged my mother and me to check under our cars before driving away,

---

* By the time my father returned in 1995, a ceasefire was in effect and Ireland was a much-changed place, as was the Erriff Fishery. The stocking programme he had restarted in the 1970s had thrived and the annual catch had risen from under a hundred salmon to over eight hundred, making it one of Ireland's most notable fisheries.

and reminded us of the warning from the security services that we remained potential targets. I used to look under my car by leaning out while holding onto the steering wheel. Not wanting to draw the attention of colleagues or friends, I did this nonchalantly as if I was looking for my keys or a coin. I also disciplined myself to be on the look-out each time I walked towards my car. I had read of an attack in which a traffic cone had been attached by transparent fishing nylon to a car. When it was driven away it detonated explosives inside the cone.

In 1980 my parents asked me if I had considered attending Atlantic College in Wales, the first in the chain of United World Colleges which my grandfather had made the focus of his retirement. Joanna had studied there and had adored the experience. It was a progressive sixth form college which seemed more like a university than a school. It promoted the idea that a 'united world' was possible, in which peace was given an extra chance through the helping hand of an international approach to education. The lofty aim was that if promising young students from around the world could be brought together, they would return to their homelands with a mutual understanding which might over time help to reduce tensions and conflict. To my grandfather the Colleges seemed to offer an educational experiment that was well worth pursuing and he lobbied governments, philanthropists, institutions, charities and educationalists around the world to support it. Critics lampooned it as at best impractical, at worst a dangerous piece of elitism. They said it would soon fade into obscurity; instead it spread to a dozen campuses on all continents and attracted students on scholarships from over a hundred and eighty countries.

I had never expected to leave Gordonstoun, but after I first visited Atlantic College my mind was immediately made up. I did not think about it at the time but everywhere I went I was faced with reminders of Nick. The peg in the locker room where he had hung his clothes caught my eye each time I walked past. I was good at ignoring such reminders but inevitably they coloured my perceptions of the school and dampened my spirits. At Gordonstoun I would always be thought of as One of the Twins; at Atlantic College I would have a fresh start, untainted by sad reminders or sympathy. The College seemed like an open door through which I would find the rest of my life.

Every place at the college was funded by a scholarship and the competition was fierce. I was shortlisted for an interview and when, a few weeks later, I was offered a place I was more excited than ever. Arriving at the College in September 1981, I immediately fell in love with the place. The students arrived from around the world and were accommodated in dormitories of four. Usually all four were from different continents, religions, languages and races. The college placed Arabs and Israelis together, Americans and Russians, Catholics and Protestants, British and Irish, black and white, rich and poor, communist and capitalist, tall and short. It was a place of dazzling diversity and giddy idealism, and I was hooked from my first hours. The campus was centred on a twelfth-century moated castle perched on treacherous cliffs overlooking the Bristol Channel.

Although both schools were started by the same man, Kurt Hahn, Atlantic College felt very different from Gordonstoun. The rules were written by the students, and boarding houses were mixed with boys on the ground floor and girls upstairs. I was in a dormitory with Frits from Holland, Andy from Australia, and Phinjo from Nepal, and I soon had a lovely South African girlfriend. I was being pushed to my academic limit, studying six subjects for the International Baccalaureate. When not in the classroom I underwent intensive training on an RNLI lifeboat. With students from a Beach Rescue Unit, and a Cliff Rescue Team, we guarded the dangerous coastline which claimed a number of lives each year. The experience bound us together in a powerful esprit de corps. With so many new friends and activities, I had little time to think about my former life.

As part of the college's programme for stimulating debate on international affairs, I soon attended a lecture by the head of the BBC in Northern Ireland, James Hawthorne. Among the things he said was that peace in Ireland would ultimately come from a marriage of the Catholic and Protestant communities. There could be no marriage until there was an engagement; before that a courtship was needed; and prior to that a friendship. First, he said, they had to get to know each other. I left the lecture hall deep in thought and wondering if I would ever see peace in Ireland.

Atlantic College gave me a great sense of freedom, not least because most of the students had no idea of my past. Sometimes publicity was inevitable. During the final school holidays I went with the rest of my family to a public unveiling of a statue of my grandfather. The ceremony was performed by the Queen in Whitehall, London, in front of a large gathering of international politicians, royalty and civic leaders. Because it was so public and so orchestrated, the day was largely ceremonial and the emotions were restrained. Inevitably logistics dominated, and as usual the security services were planning for every eventuality. They rang my father's office to ask for the blood type of each member of the family. His devoted secretary Hilary Etchells, always with a caring touch, went around the family noting our requirements. It felt as though I had placed an order for coffee rather than blood.* We all returned with stories, some sad and some funny and some surreal. Philip described how Mrs Thatcher had told him with great conviction, 'But Philip, you know it is so very *difficult* to sculpt.' As usual under the glare of publicity and the might of the state, the day left me with a customary sense of disconnect between the show we made for the public and the emotional turmoil beneath.

One day at Newhouse, I opened a book I had not touched since my Dragon School days and a note dropped out. I opened it and saw half a dozen sentences which Nick had penned to me. Seeing his perfectly formed handwriting was enough to make my heart miss a beat. The note said nothing of any great significance but nonetheless it made me cry at length. My eyes grew red and my face became blotchy, and when my mother walked into the room she immediately knew I had been crying. I handed my mother the note and it had the same effect on her. Like me, she found talking about Nick comforting. But what we found comforting, others found upsetting. For Norton, reminders of absent family served not to soothe him but to stir up his grief. Without being unsympathetic he candidly explained this to his siblings. My father always tenderly permitted my mother to speak and share her thoughts as she needed. To me it did not matter how many times she spoke about Nick, I was happy to hear her thoughts each time and share her memories.

* Such precautions did not seem misplaced after the IRA blew up Margaret Thatcher and many of her government the following year. She survived but the bomb killed five and injured thirty-four.

I also felt comfortable to correct her gently if she remembered something inaccurately. She was inclined to recall an achievement by one of her children and automatically attribute it to Nick. She was invariably gracious when I pointed out an error.

A number of memorials sprang up after Nick's death. Instead of flowers for his funeral my mother asked that money should be sent to the National Society for the Prevention of Cruelty to Children. As a Vice President of the charity she later helped to raise funds for Protestant and Catholic children in Northern Ireland whose families had been affected by the Troubles, directly or indirectly. At the Dragon School she helped endow and supervise a fund to provide grants to young people for travel or humanitarian work. The school created an annual prize in Nick's name for the best academic scholar, and Gordonstoun also created a prize, awarded periodically for outstanding service to the community.

When the Dean of Westminster Abbey suggested a plaque in memory of my Mountbatten grandparents, my mother asked if Nick's name could be added. She was told this would not be possible because it was to be a public memorial rather than a private one. The magnificent brass plaque was unveiled by Prince Philip in February 1985. All the family attended but what none of us realised was that the plaque's designer had taken a dim view of the Dean's stance and had quietly amended the design to incorporate the letter N. When I discovered this years later, the memorial meant all the more to me.*

One day in the dining hall at Gordonstoun, Nick and I were asked by one of our teachers which university we would like to attend. 'Come on!' he said. 'You two could get in anywhere. Where would you really like to go?' I had never expressed it before but secretly I wanted to go to Cambridge and I now told him so, and Nick agreed. Suddenly we had an academic goal and from that moment on we were set on it. The teacher seemed pleased with my answer. I did not tell him that an additional reason for my choice was that Cambridge University was where

---

* In 2004, after the designer Christopher Ironside had died, his daughter told us about this. My brother Joe and I went to have another look and found the N hidden in the top-left and top-right quadrants, a message lost to anyone not admitted to the conspiracy.

John Cleese and others of the *Monty Python* team had met. After Nick's death I became very focused on reaching the university; it was the last milestone on which we had jointly planned and I very much wanted to accomplish our goal.

Halfway through my time at Atlantic College, Amanda accompanied me to Cambridge for an interview at Christ's College. A few weeks later I was offered a place to study Economics, but there was a catch: the offer was conditional on getting very high marks in my International Baccalaureate exams. Privately I was terrified of failing and I realised that I needed a Plan B in case I did not get the required grades. I went to the Student Counselling Office at Atlantic College and started to look at the mass of prospectuses housed there. The office was in the bowels of the ancient castle, and as I plodded through the paperwork it got later and later until it was the dead of night. In all my time at Atlantic College those were the hours when I most wished Nick was with me. The loneliness was almost overpowering. I came away realising that there was no other university that I wanted to go to and from that day I worked harder than ever. After my examinations were over, I waited in suspense for weeks for the results to arrive. When an official envelope arrived one day at Newhouse, I retreated with it alone into the spinney at the end of the garden where Nick and I used to play. After contemplating the envelope for a long while, I opened it with dread, only to discover the contents had nothing to do with my exams. When soon afterwords another envelope arrived, I tore it open without thinking and to my absolute delight discovered that I had achieved the required grades – with one mark to spare.

When in October 1983 I drove into Cambridge to take up my place, I felt as if I had arrived at the last crossroads which Nick and I had been able to see in the road then ahead of us. From here on I would be making my own way. Instead of going straight to the college and unpacking my bags, I meandered through the narrow streets and down the beautiful lane that looked onto the River Cam and the backs of the colleges. I was reluctant to plunge in without a friend by my side, and then suddenly a familiar face caught my attention. Ian, a good friend from Atlantic College, had also been accepted by Christ's College and by chance was now walking into the town for the first time. I hollered at him from across the street and ran over to greet him, happy and relieved not to be walking into the college alone.

Cambridge helped shape my future. After a year of Economics I studied Social and Political Science for two years while in my spare time learning about film-making and television production. Slowly I came to realise that I wanted a career in documentaries and journalism rather than in feature films, which until then had been the career path I had expected, following in the footsteps of my father and brothers.

I loved the academic atmosphere in Cambridge, but even more exciting was the emotional development into which I suddenly plunged. During the first few weeks of term, I found myself drawn more and more towards another of the students. She was a deep-thinking woman with an exceptionally warm and caring character and infectious sense of humour. Very soon I started to fall in love. It was my first long-term relationship and the constant companionship, trust and intimacy we shared made me feel happier than at any time since Nick's death.

Cambridge was where I developed my passion for flying. In my first week I applied to the University Air Squadron, a part of the Royal Air Force. I was very disappointed when they rejected me on the grounds of my damaged right eye. I crossed the airfield and enlisted instead at a civilian flying school where the eyesight test was less stringent. After my first lesson in a tiny two-seat Cessna, I was hooked.

I graduated from university with a degree in Social and Political Science, a grounding in film-making, and a pilot's licence. I decided to make 1987 a gap year in which I would travel and work. I also wanted to return to Ireland for the first time since the bomb; I did not know what I would do there but I felt drawn to half-developed thoughts lingering at the back of my mind. I had an uneasy feeling about the hole in my life left by Nick's death. I was aware that I needed to sort out my incomplete and confused emotions but I did not know how to proceed or how to explain those feelings to others. I decided the only thing to do was to take a first step by going back to Classiebawn and starting where I had left off in 1979.

While at university I had met an American friend of Amanda's. Jeff Bennett had been flying as a hobby for several years and was then training for a professional licence. He became one of my closest friends and inspired me to take my own flying much more seriously. When he was asked to pilot a light aircraft in a four-week race from Paris to Peking, he suggested I should come too. A television documentary was being made and I was invited to join as a cameraman and stand-by pilot. As I had no experience in the aircraft being used, a single-engine Piper Malibu, I underwent a week's intensive training at the Piper Aircraft Company in Vero Beach, Florida, after which I was told to report to Paris for the start of the race.

Suddenly I saw an opportunity to return to Ireland. Finishing my training in Florida, I boarded an Aer Lingus flight from New York, and at dawn the next morning landed at Shannon on Ireland's west coast. I had the impression I was landing behind some form of invisible barrier, a sort of emotional Iron Curtain. I planned to spend a few hours at Aasleagh then drive on to Sligo and spend a night near Classiebawn. I did not know what I would do other than spend some time alone with my thoughts and feelings. Not knowing how to articulate this, or what reaction I would get from my family, I decided not to tell them of my plans.

As I drove towards Aasleagh I felt the emotional tension mounting, and I stopped in a Galway hotel to wash, shave and change from my crumpled clothes. I had an enormous breakfast before driving on. The scenery started to become familiar, and I was struck by how completely unchanged it was, which made me reflect on how much I had changed. In 1979 I had been one of a pair of twin boys; now I was a man on my own. I felt strong and bold. However, when I drove up and stopped the car in front of the house at Aasleagh, I suddenly knew I did not want to meet or talk to anyone, I just wanted to be alone with my memories. I reversed out of the driveway and drove instead to the nearby village, Leenane. It was a freezing-cold day with a blue sky and blinding sun. There were very few people to be seen and the place seemed so unlike the bustling summer idyll of my memories. Wanting to talk to someone about what I was seeing and feeling, I decided to call Jeff in America. I stepped into a telephone box expecting to speak to the village operator and book a line to America. Instead I found a gleaming new payphone. I dialled Jeff's number and within seconds was speaking to him on a crystal-clear line. Ireland, like me, had undergone enormous change.

Driving towards Sligo, I passed the neighbouring fishery, Delphi, which had also belonged to my Anglo-Irish forebears and in which I had stayed as a small boy. I pulled over and spoke to a man working on the renovation of an outbuilding. He told me the lodge had been bought by an Englishman who would soon be restoring it and re-launching its fishery. I felt as if I was floating on a magic carpet above an emotional landscape that would turn to dust if I set foot on it. I wound the window up and drove on. On an impulse I turned up a single-track road that led to another valley, its sides covered in a thick pine plantation. Suddenly I felt oppressed, remembering the IRA camp which had been discovered during my childhood further up this valley at a spot called Glenummera. Most days we had driven close by with our Garda escort, on our way to fish on Tawnyard Lough. Only much later was I to learn that at least some of the locals knew what was going on because each day IRA men would walk down to nearby houses for milk. In 1976 a helicopter had flown over the camp, after which it was abandoned.

Emerging out of the pine trees, I was treated to the sight of Tawnyard nestling in the valley ahead. I crawled up the lane and, seeing a man walking through the fields, stopped and watched. It was the old farmer and ghillie Martin Joyce, who had first taken my father fishing more than fifty years before. I was staggered at how he had changed. In 1979 he had been unable to hobble more than a few yards, crippled by pain from his hips. Ireland's new prosperity had filtered down to these valleys and he had received two new hips and been restored to an active life. Part of me wanted to run over and shake him by the hand and tell him all our family news and find out his. But I knew I would break down and come away having failed even to scratch the surface of what I wanted to say. I did not know where to begin or how to tune myself once more to the very different frequency on which the west of Ireland operates. Martin turned and looked in my direction. Slowly I reversed and turned around, driving away with a lump in my throat, and my eyes on my mirror, as he returned to his work in the field.

I drove on to Mullaghmore passing the harbour and stood at the cliff tops overlooking where the bomb had exploded. For minute after minute I swayed in the wind, appalled at the numbness I was feeling. I had heard of a man whose arm was severed by machinery and who looked down and picked it up, registering what was happening but without feeling any pain. I knew inside me there was a pain that had not yet hit me, and I knew when it did it would be overpowering. For now, all I could detect was a cold, raw numbness. I dreaded the pain but I was mystified that even here it would not come. I had planned to go next to Classiebawn but, acting on instinct, I returned instead to Sligo and checked in to a small hotel from where I phoned our old friend Aideen Gore-Booth at Lissadell.

Aideen answered the phone and we spoke for several minutes. When I told her that I was in Sligo, her voice faltered and she asked me to repeat myself. A short while later I was at her home, a once proud and stately house from which her family had for generations held sway over this part of the county. We sat in her tiny kitchen, the one room in the ghostly mansion she kept heated. She told me stories about the house in its heyday, of her parents and grandparents, her four brothers and three sisters. Her eyes lit up with details of scandals and intrigues. I loved listening to her talk but I was in no position to retain or record the stories, and when I left I urged her to make a written account of her memories.

Next morning I awoke thinking about Classiebawn and I had an idea. I had discovered from Aideen that Sligo now had a small airfield. I drove to the strip and found I was able to hire a Cessna. Soon I was flying along the coast spotting the beaches and islands, bays and by-ways of my childhood. I flew low and then out to the island of Inishmurray and back to the castle. When it came time to land, I knew that I wanted to go up close to the castle. I drove to Cliffoney and parked at the cottage that had been home to Mrs Kennedy, the cook. It was now boarded up. I walked down to the rolling Atlantic beach and gathered my thoughts looking at the castle. I was feeling the same unnatural numbness that I had felt the day before. I was longing to take some small keepsake away with me, and when I came across a flat sheet of hardened sand, I carried it back to the car. Later I framed it and hung it on my wall, its beauty heightened by its provenance.

I was still cautious about approaching the castle directly so I parked a quarter of a mile away and walked across the fields and up the long driveway. With little more than a hundred yards to go, I had a fleeting glimpse from the corner of my eye of a figure standing on the hill behind me above some rocks. As children we had believed fairies lived there.

Classiebawn had been sold to Hugh Tunney in February 1991, and I was aware I was now trespassing on his property but I decided to walk on. A minute later, on reaching a bend in the driveway, I turned to face whoever was behind me and was surprised to find the skyline bare. Whoever had been standing there seemed to have disappeared into thin air. I walked on. The castle was apparently unoccupied, which suited me. In the cold wind I strolled past the stables and into the fields stretching towards the sea. I was pleased to see the place again but I had no desire to prolong my stay or the strange numbness I was feeling. As I left, I kept wondering: Whose presence had I detected from the corner of my eye? It troubled me.

When I left Ireland the next day, I felt as if I had started something difficult but necessary. I also had a sense that one day I would return, and that there was something there which I needed to go back for, though I had no idea what it was.

17

LONE TWIN

Five years after the attack a retrospective newspaper article had concluded with a summary of what had become of the survivors. About me it said: 'Last heard of studying Economics at Cambridge University.' I was pleased to have disappeared off the media radar and to be getting on with my life. After my gap year I found work in a succession of jobs in television production, working in agreeable anonymity on the other side of the camera.

In 1989 I heard from Susie Dugdale about an extraordinary meeting that had recently occurred. Thirty bereaved people had met; each was a twin whose twin had died. They had been brought together by Joan Woodward, a psychotherapist in Birmingham who was herself a 'lone twin'. I learned she had 'recently made a study of 219 such twins and discovered that for some the emotional impact of bereavement was savage and almost impossible for others to understand. For some it led to chronic grief, a sense of never quite feeling whole again. "I am nothing as one," was how one woman expressed this.'[1] The thirty twins who had met had found the experience very helpful and a support group called The Lone Twin Network was now being proposed. When I was asked if I would help launch the initiative through an interview in *The Times* I decided to do so. It was the first time I had spoken about Nick's death to anyone other than family or friends. As the journalist noted, I did not find it easy:

As far as one can see, Knatchbull after 10 years is fully recovered. When he discusses his physical injuries – his blindness in one eye, loss of hearing in one ear, occasional pains – it is with a dryness, a lightness of tone that Lord Louis would applaud.

But losing Nicky has been another matter altogether. When he talks of him it hurts to observe how carefully he controls his voice. He has a look of concentrated passion, and his hand presses his chest as though his heart is in imminent danger of leaping out.[2]

I thought I was doing the organisation a favour by talking to the newspaper but as things turned out it was the other way around. A short while after the interview was published, I was contacted by a doctor at Queen Charlotte's and Chelsea Hospital in London. Elizabeth Bryan was director of the Multiple Births Foundation under whose auspices The Lone Twin Network was being established, and was calling on behalf of a colleague who was the mother of identical twins. John and David Loftus were a year older than me. The year before, while John was undergoing treatment for a brain tumour, the twins had celebrated their twenty-fifth birthday in John's hospital room. After they opened their presents a doctor arrived and administered an injection for John. Tragically he gave the wrong dose by a factor of eighty. When David came into the room minutes later, John was already starting to deteriorate. Shouting for help, David held his brother as he vomited and then sank into a coma. He was rushed to Intensive Care but died ten days later. In the months since then David had been inconsolable, and was now struggling to resume his own life. Elizabeth Bryan asked if I would meet him. I took his number and she gave him mine. For months I meant to telephone him but failed to do so. I had met other lone twins and, although it had been interesting, I did not think that I had been able to do or say much to help them. David stalled as well. 'I did not want to revive your feelings,' he later told me.

Eventually in September 1989 we agreed to meet in a London pub. I was doubtful that our meeting would last long or that we would see each other again but I was mistaken. I had almost never until then spoken at length to someone who totally understood what it felt like to have one's twin killed. The exception had been Norris McWhirter, but at the time I had been too young and too traumatised to benefit fully. With David it was different. As we described our feelings and experiences, I found I was able to fast-forward through the conversation in a way I had with Nick. It felt like rediscovering a long-lost faculty. It was liberating, invigorating, intoxicating. David later said of that evening:

> We talked for hours like long lost friends, reunited after forever apart. Twin-ship: youth, muddles, mix-ups, shared loves, life, childhood experiences. The fear it would be a meeting of tears and pain was completely unfounded. And instead I found myself laughing like I hadn't laughed for ages. We became very close, very quickly. Tim helped fill the large chasm that had opened in my life.[3]

David's experience of twinhood was different from mine in one fundamental aspect: his twin, John, had lived long enough for them to want to go their own ways. I had always wondered how Nick and I would have dealt with that seemingly inevitable stage of twin development. In talking with David, I was able to bridge an important missing link in my conception of how Nick's and my lives might have progressed. I learned from David about a side of twinship which I had never known and it sounded painful. He spoke about how they had started to go in separate directions. When John gained a girlfriend, it caused difficulties because she did not like David; and when David found a girlfriend, she disliked John. The tensions did not stop there. The happy and healthy competition that had existed between David and his twin, as it had between Nick and me, evolved into something which became a source of sadness. By the time they were in their mid-teens they no longer wanted to be identical. John let his hair grow and had surgery to stop his ears sticking out. When John became engaged, David became jealous. 'I would have married anyone to get there first,'[4] he said. In their childhood David had seen himself as the dominant twin, but John gained confidence as they matured. Professionally as well as socially David felt under pressure. Both were graphic designers and David suspected that his work was not as good as his brother's. When I later heard this, I was sceptical because I already knew David was highly successful. Nonetheless I was fascinated by the description he gave of him and John maturing into adults. Until then I had assumed that

Nick's and my experience of twinhood would have been an extension of our childhood. David made me realise that in adolescence and adulthood our lives might have been very different. I was able to ask questions of David I had never been able to ask anyone else, and the way he was able to intuit what lay at the core of my questions made me realise how deeply he understood me.

At our first meeting we talked uninterrupted for several hours, and when we left we knew without doubt that we had started a unique and lifelong friendship. The Lone Twin Network had brought us together but we soon found there was only so much talking about twinhood which we wanted to do. Although our shared experiences remained at the core of our friendship, we also found we shared a love of the absurd. One day we were at an airport together and while paying for our tickets were mistakenly handed each other's credit card slips. Without hesitating I forged David's signature and he forged mine. The sales clerk looked at the two slips. She smiled and said, 'Blimey, you two must be twins!'

Although our personalities were in some respects polar opposites, we complemented each other very well and this echoed something of the relationship we had shared with our twins. We soon got to know each other's families. When I heard my mother one day refer to David and me as 'her youngest', I realised just how much a part of the family he had become. Within six months of meeting him, I was best man at his wedding to Debbie.

Anniversaries mattered, especially to my mother and me. The tenth anniversary of the attack fell on 27 August 1989 and resulted in a number of newspaper articles which I skimmed while on holiday with my family in Scotland. As I did so, a headline caught my eye: 'Was Mountbatten betrayed?' The leading paragraph proclaimed: 'Ten years on, a member of the security service voices his suspicion that Lord Mountbatten was betrayed by a man known to be a Provisional IRA sympathiser by intelligence chiefs – who have since kept silent to cover their error.'[5] We had heard of such stories before, and as a family we had learned to accept that they sold newspapers and fuelled gossip but were ill-informed and hopelessly unreliable. In this case my father had received word from a number of people that the person in question should be checked out and he had passed this on at the highest levels. My father was reassured that the man had been cleared using every means possible, and there was nothing to suggest he was anything other than innocent of the whispers against him. Notwithstanding that, the effect of reading the article was a realisation of just how little I knew about what had happened to us in Ireland. I did not like the veil of ignorance that we had allowed to descend on us, even though it was comfortable.

In August 1991 I joined my parents for a summer holiday at New Kelso, where my family now came each August. Jeff Bennett was visiting from America and one night he and I sat up late talking about Classiebawn. I reminded him of the one visit I had made since the bomb and how it had left me with a strong feeling that I wanted to go back. During that visit I had been unable to do more than scratch the surface of the place, and in the four years since then an uneasy sensation had built up in my mind that I should go back again. When Jeff said that he would like to see the place, we agreed to make a brief visit the next day.

Landing in Sligo Airport, I felt jubilant to be back. I took Jeff and two other friends from New Kelso and showed them around. In the few hours we spent in the area, I again felt as if there was something important and fundamental that I needed to be doing there, but I did not know what. I did not dwell on it. I took my friends up to the castle. Hugh Tunney and Caroline Devine were very welcoming and we spent half an hour in the castle before heading back to the airport. I enjoyed the day but found the trip ultimately unsatisfying; emotionally I was not ready to do more than dip my toe in the water.

Aasleagh seemed a very different proposition, not having been directly linked to the 1979 attack, and the following year I decided to return for a fishing trip with Simon Jones. We booked our accommodation, and when we arrived we were shown to our room by Mary, wife of the fishery manager, Jim. She asked if this was our first time in Ireland, and when we said we had known the lodge well in the 1970s, she fetched the housekeeper, our old friend Bridget Keane. When Bridget walked into the room, she looked at me and wept.

Simon and I fished for two days but the water was low and we went home without a salmon. However, in our bags we carried loaves of soda bread baked by Bridget. The visit had been fun but it had also allowed me to take my first tentative step towards reconnecting with the unresolved emotions with which I had left Ireland as a boy. The time I had spent talking to Bridget had given both her and me the chance to say some of the things we had never been able to say in 1979. I realised that if I wanted to get back to Classiebawn in any meaningful way, I would first have to gradually acclimatise myself to being in Ireland again by spending time at Aasleagh and Delphi. Whereas at Classiebawn I had found it impossible to connect with the feelings which I viscerally knew were seized up inside me, at Aasleagh I found emotions were gently beginning to unlock. I felt as if I were climbing a gentle hill on which I could keep my foothold and make some progress. In contrast, Classiebawn appeared to be a sheer-sided cliff which left me at its base, unable to take even the first step.

After Simon and I drove away from Aasleagh, we passed along the valley to Delphi where we stopped and talked at length with the new owner, Peter Mantle. He had renovated the lodge and its cottages, recommissioned the salmon hatchery and breathed new life into the almost defunct fishery. My great-grandmother had lived there during the Second World War after the death of her husband, but when she had moved out the place had slowly become run-down. To see it blossoming again made me happy and optimistic for the future. Simon and I decided we would stay here on our next trip, and in 1993 we returned. The Delphi Fishery manager David McEvoy was a man my own age. Soon after we started talking I realised this was the same David whom I remembered fishing at Aasleagh in my childhood. The realisation had a profound effect on me, and long-lost childhood memories came rushing back, all very welcome and happy, like unexpected gifts. It was good to rekindle the friendship with David and others in the area: the Heneghans who were the ghillies at nearby Doolough, the Joyces who farmed and fished at Tawnyard, and the Hamiltons who ran the shop in Leenane. Most of them showed me to a drawer or a cupboard where they kept Christmas cards from my parents which still arrived annually; and without exception they sent me away with warm messages for the family.

Back in England, reporters rang me several times about rumours that Thomas McMahon was being reviewed for parole from prison. As normal

I chose not to say anything, but soon I read a letter in *The Times* from my cousin George Milford Haven who wrote that he was 'shocked and horrified' that the idea was being considered. He pointed out that Thomas McMahon had twice tried to escape, using a gun the first time and explosives the next.

> This is utterly contemptible . . . That a cold-blooded murderer who has wreaked untold damage on to my relatives and those of Paul Maxwell can be considered a changed man and let loose into the outside world makes a total mockery of the judicial system.
>
> It is only by a quirk of fate that I was not in that same boat with my cousins and great-uncle. Only days earlier, Paul Maxwell and I were out on the bay laying the lobster pots for their collection on that fateful sunny Monday. No doubt our every move was watched and monitored by the evil eye of McMahon or his partners in crime. He too should be watched and monitored for the rest of his life; he should never be allowed out of the prison gates until he is driven out in a hearse.[6]

By the time the letter was published, the Irish prison service had already ruled out an early release. Despite that, I agreed to write an article for *The Times* because I wanted to offer a different view. In the article I stated that while it was important that the public should be protected from Thomas McMahon and that he deserved 'the stiffest sentence possible', he should nonetheless 'at some point, some years in the future . . . be released to live out the autumn years of his life with his family, his children and grandchildren'.[7]

On 31 August 1994 the IRA announced a ceasefire, and the following year Prince Charles' office contacted my father to say that he was due to make a visit to the Irish Republic and asked if we could help arrange a few days for him to enjoy the parts of Ireland we loved so much. It was felt unwise for him to visit Classiebawn, so instead I called Peter Mantle, who immediately arranged for him and my parents to spend two nights at Delphi. He and my father fished, they all relaxed and Prince Charles painted. Meanwhile hundreds of Irish troops hid in the mountains above the fishery and its two loughs, Finlough and Doolough. They had reason to be cautious. The day before Charles arrived in Ireland, the caretaker at Classiebawn had discovered the lock and chain on the front gates had been broken and found two barrels at the front door of the castle. In one was a leaking gas cylinder with materials heavily soaked in petrol attached to a power unit and a running timer. The second barrel contained forty-five gallons of fuel. A bomb disposal team from Finner Camp dealt with the device. No one claimed responsibility.

Public opinion was sharply divided. An article in Ireland's *Sunday Independent* concluded:

Whether by design or, more probably, by accident, Prince Charles could have chosen few more appropriate places in Ireland to relive the pain and suffering he felt at the death of Lord Mountbatten who, by all accounts, was more like a second father than his uncle. For Doolough was the scene of one of the most harrowing episodes in the famine, when people died like flies when they tried to walk through this desolate valley in their search for food.

The reunion of Prince Charles and the Brabournes at Delphi Lodge should prompt us to think henceforth of Doolough not just as a monument to Irish pain, but as a monument to English forgiveness.

Perhaps Sinn Féin might contemplate not only that parity of esteem which is so high on their agenda, but also parity of forgiveness. Or is it too much to hope that if Prince Charles can forgive what happened at Mullaghmore, that Sinn Féin may some day forgive what happened on Bloody Sunday?

If so, there can be no real reconciliation or lasting peace on this island.[8]

A few days later a letter was published in *The Irish Times*:

I was disgusted at the news that Charles Windsor spent the 'private' days of his visit at Delphi Lodge . . . Having not once given even token acknowledgement of the wrongs done by his crown and his class against our country, Charles Windsor had the effrontery to trample on the graves of the 'Famine' dead in Mayo. No doubt not even this insult will give pause for thought to the pathetic crew who fell over themselves to welcome him.[9]

My parents stayed on after Prince Charles left, and asked Philip and me to join them for a weekend. It was a happy time; my father guided me down the salmon pools he had fished since the 1930s, and I hooked a salmon only to lose it a short while later. My father's disappointment was as great as mine. We called in at nearby Aasleagh and saw Bridget Keane in her cottage. Later we drove up to Tawnyard and had tea with Martin Joyce and his wife while they showed us their photograph albums. My father adored the afternoon but from the way he spoke it was clear this was his farewell to the area and his life-long friends.

At the end of the weekend we were about to leave for the airport when I unexpectedly broke down and wept. It was perhaps the first time my father had seen me cry since 1979. Later I asked myself time and again why I had found leaving so difficult. I could not yet answer the question.

18

THE SOUND OF THE BOMB

'Goodbye,' I said to Berenice, standing on the doorstep of her house in Swiss Cottage, London, in June 1997. I had been seeing her for weekly sessions of psychotherapy for the past eighteen months. Normally she would not have come out to say goodbye, but this was my final appointment. The sun was setting slowly over West London. 'Thank you for everything you've done,' I said. 'Yes,' she replied, 'but there's still something holding you back, isn't there?' I knew she understood. I had come as far as I could for now. At some point I would be ready to tackle her question. I did not know when.

Some years previously I had told Martin, my doctor, that I was suffering from occasional mood swings, some days being on top of the world, others miserable. Sometimes so miserable that even speaking on the phone or going to the shops was difficult. When I described this to a friend, his shock and pity and loud 'How awful' had helped me decide that it was a subject I would not raise too often or too publicly.

Martin, a gifted communicator as well as General Practitioner, described how he had gone through a period of psychotherapy some years previously, and how he had found it useful and interesting. He had known when it was time to finish. It sounded so easy, so uncomplicated. I was struck by the fact that someone so sane could benefit from seeing a shrink and began to feel more comfortable with the concept. From time to time over the following months I thought about his words. One day I phoned and asked him to refer me to someone. He recommended a counselling therapist and before long I was at the first appointment.

It started with questions. 'Do you have nightmares? Do you feel sad when you think about your twin? Do you feel anxious when you say goodbye to loved ones?' 'No' was my reply each time. 'So you really don't suffer any symptoms you can describe?' I thought very hard. 'Just the normal things that everyone has,' I said. 'Such as?' he replied; another pause. 'Well, I hear the sound of the bomb from time to time.'

It happened the first time just before Christmas in 1979, when I was staying at Broadlands. As a fifteen-year-old boy I was always hankering to be behind the wheel of a car. Appealingly, there was an old Land-Rover there in which I was allowed to practise my driving. As ever, my parents were firm but fair: If I were to drive the car, it must be under the supervision of my brother Philip who had got his licence the year before.

At twilight one afternoon, I twisted Philip's arm and he agreed to come out with me so I could drive the Land-Rover. I mistimed the use of the clutch when changing up a gear, and as I did so I suddenly had an extraordinary sensation. It was as if a very loud bang had occurred. I thought maybe I had damaged the engine or the gearbox, but when I looked at Philip I saw no reaction. I said nothing. That night in bed I thought about driving the Land-Rover again. Suddenly a bang filled my head. I was surprised, slightly scared at first, and completely perplexed. Again and again in the coming months the sound returned to me. I had no idea why.

In July 1980 my parents took us on a family holiday to the South of France. I was playing golf with my brother Joe at the Mandelieu Golf Club near Cannes. We had to cross a small river in a boat and walk to the next hole, passing under a railway bridge. As I did so a fast-moving train passed overhead. The suddenness of it took me completely by surprise, terrifying me. As suddenly as the noise arrived, it disappeared and I realised I was screaming in fear. I walked on shaking like a leaf, and as soon as I could I made a big joke out of it with Joe and left it at that.

I started to think more and more about what was going on in my head. Why had the sound of this train unnerved me so much? The episode persuaded me that the sound of the bomb was somehow travelling around with me every day, suppressed in my mind but waiting to pop up when a stimulus came along. It was almost impossible for me to predict when I would hear it but I began to notice patterns, and the more I noticed the patterns, the more familiar I felt with my own psyche. I had many almost invisible scars from the bomb, and this mental scar seemed of little more significance than the scar on my left thumb. Just as I might roll a pebble around in my pocket, I sometimes found myself in moments of solitude, reflection or just boredom, looking down and touching the familiar old scar. It is like the wrapper off a childhood toy found in the back of a cupboard; the toy and childhood have long since gone but the memories are summoned.

I began to settle in with this mental scar. I knew that I could not predict or control it. I knew that no one else could tell when I was experiencing it. Strangely, as well as being eerie, I found it almost reassuring. I was so lacking in symptoms, and so often complimented for being so 'strong' that I sometimes wondered if I had a screw loose and had turned into a psychopath. Nicky was dead and I had not had any sort of breakdown. The sound in my head proved I was feeling something. It was intriguing, perhaps satisfying; in a macabre way, sometimes it almost entertained me. When would it go off next?

In about 1990 I bought a mobile phone and a car kit. I knew when it was about to ring because the box of electrics in the back of the car made a *click* a couple of seconds before the phone rang. I learned to listen for this click. If I had a passenger I would say, 'The phone is about to ring,' and he or she would be amazed when it did. What they did not know was that very often the click would also trigger the sound of the bomb. Subconsciously I must have been connecting the click with a radio signal, and hence with the bomb, which was almost certainly detonated by radio control. If I received half a dozen phone calls during a car journey, more often than not I would hear the bomb each time. Opening a fridge door and knowing a light was coming on inside would occasionally trigger the sound in my head. Turning a light switch on or off would sometimes do it. Subconsciously I was connecting electrical circuitry with detonation.

By the time I started going to therapy, the sound of the bomb had come back to me so often and for so long that I had stopped thinking of it as anything other than normal. It was like the mole under my chin, hidden from view.

Sitting in the therapist's consulting room, for the first time I was starting to admit that having flashbacks to the sound of a bomb was not normal. And maybe it was connected to my mood swings. The revelation helped me to become proactive about looking after my mental and emotional health rather than taking them for granted. Beyond that I made little progress and after some months I stopped the sessions.

Later that year, I found I still wanted to understand more about what was going on in my head. When I was alone and peaceful, I felt terribly sad and lonely. I knew this was unhealthy and abnormal. I wanted to find a way out of this mindset and I knew it was down to me to make the first move. I rang Martin again and this time he suggested I try seeing Berenice. The difference was marked. She practised in a style which suited me better. At her suggestion, I would start preparing myself for her weekly appointments by having some quiet time in the car on my way to her. This was after I finished work in the early evening. I turned off the car radio and my telephone and started to focus on the events of the previous week. I felt tense before the appointments because I did not find them easy; they required a lot of concentration and were hardly a barrelful of laughs.

I found the mechanics fascinating. I did not come away with the answers to deep questions, but I slowly learned to see connections and recognise processes, conscious and subconscious, that I had overlooked before. After my appointments I would normally feel relieved they were over and sometimes pleased, even elated, that I had completed a difficult and unpleasant task. I knew it was doing me good. I would often stop at a petrol station on my way home and have a snack or drink while turning on my mobile phone and reconnecting myself to my routine and plans for the evening ahead. To my surprise I noticed that I was hearing the bomb less and less. Eighteen months rolled by and I recognised I was looking for less therapy and more new departures in my life.

In the summer of 1996, aged thirty-one, I had been visiting my new therapist weekly for about six months. I was in no doubt that Berenice was doing a good job, and I was feeling good about life. I was single with a number of broken relationships behind me, some of them long-lasting. I was longing to find a soul mate, settle down and have children. But over the years, one after another I had brought my relationships to an end. Now I started to feel optimistic that my next relationship would be different.

I had not been able to go to the funerals of 1979 and did not experience a full process of bereavement and mourning. Post Traumatic Stress counselling was virtually unheard of in the England of 1979. Possibly, so the thinking goes, I had been left subconsciously anxious about committing to other close relationships and my therapy was dispelling that anxiety. I am sceptical of any such neat explanation but I did start to feel differently, more confident, more optimistic, more energetic. In spring the days lengthen, nature blooms and the human body and mind respond. I felt as if springtime had arrived in my life, late but welcome.

I had been a BBC journalist for six years, first as a researcher and latterly as a film director. I had been assigned for the last two years to *Crimewatch UK*. During the programme's summer break I booked a week's holiday in California. At the end of the week I had no reason to hurry back to England. I called Jeff Bennett in New York and asked him if he could take any time off. The answer was no. 'But,' he told me, 'if I were you, I would get yourself down to India's house in the Bahamas. She has two beautiful women staying with her.'

The trip started unpromisingly. I changed planes in Miami and arrived too late to catch the last flight to the Bahamas. That night was spent in a mildly rancid hotel room at the airport, made even worse by three hours of jet-lag and some mind-numbingly awful programmes on television while I lay wondering if this trip had been such a good idea. By lunch the following day, I was on Harbour Island off Eleuthera, one of the lesser developed of the Bahama Islands. I walked into Pink Sands, a small hotel where India had told me to come, and saw a large table of young people having a merry time. Lunch had already started. Some of the faces were new to me. I was jet-lagged, pale, and travel-weary. I stood in the sun, blinking. India had always been loud; our grandfather had nicknamed her Decibel. 'Hello, Mr Blobby!' she called out in a voice that made half the restaurant look around.

I saw one empty chair and quickly sat down in it. I turned to my left and someone stuck a very large strawberry daiquiri in my hand with the words 'Hello, I'm Isabella'. She was a primary school teacher in

London and had arrived with her sister Anna Norman to spend a month with India. Anna and India had been friends since their schooldays and India was now modelling and had just started living in the Bahamas. Both sisters were strikingly beautiful and tremendous fun but at that stage I had no inkling that Isabella was going to change my life. Next day India, her two friends and I crossed by water taxi to Eleuthera. We drove south to Windermere Island, reaching it across a small bridge just wide enough for the car. It was five miles long with a deserted beach of white and pink sand and surrounded by seemingly endless coral reefs which stretched out into the Atlantic.

I had been going there since I was seven years old, when my parents had built a beach house on the island and India's parents had built another nearby. It was to the Hickses' house that we now came. By the time dinner was over, we were tired. When I asked if anyone wanted a walk along the beach, only Isabella accepted. She had come to recover from the break-up of a relationship, and India warned me it was the one subject to avoid. I started our walk by asking her how she was getting over it. The previous thirty-six hours had served as just enough of an introduction for her to speak openly. The dark beach gave a sense of privacy and she talked in an uninterrupted flow and with a frankness that might have been much less easy elsewhere. I listened as she talked about her emotions, her childhood, her parents and family, her work as a teacher, the children she taught, love and life. We walked down the beach and sat together at its far end. By the time we started walking home I was clear that I had reached a turning point in my life. Never before had I been so profoundly drawn to another person. I remember feeling stunned by two things. First, that I had found someone who could have such an overwhelming effect on me. Over the years I had occasionally wondered if my childhood experiences had left me unable to feel the depths of love that I viscerally knew were possible. Second, I could not believe my luck that she was single and unattached. Even a few years before, my mind had often been confused about my priorities and feelings. Had I met Isabella then I might well have made the fatal mistake of hesitation. The past few years had helped me gain a great deal of self-knowledge. I was much clearer about my values, inner strength and emotional health. I firmly decided that from that moment Isabella was my absolute, overriding and all-consuming priority.

That night I lay staring at the ceiling and listening to cicadas. I quickly decided what to do. Next morning at breakfast I told India, Isabella and Anna that unfortunately I had to return to England immediately. I did not give the real reason, which was my conviction that if I stayed for even a day longer I might get drawn into a holiday romance. Much better that Isabella complete her holiday, recover from the knock she had taken and we would soon meet again in London.

I waited day by day until the summer was over. I was planning to make contact with Isabella again when she rang me and said I had left some clothes behind the previous month and India had asked her to bring them back to London. We lived less than five minutes' walk apart and I insisted on coming over to collect them. I also offered to bring over some photographs from our few days together. From that one meeting I was able to stay in contact. She was evidently not interested in me romantically. I asked her to join me and friends for dinner, for lunch and for a weekend in France but she declined them all. I could only interest her by inviting her sister Anna as well. My parents were very confused when I appeared at Newhouse one weekend with two sisters. Happily they liked both of them very much. Over the course of the weekend they could tell that I was in love but they could not tell with which. Other than David Loftus, I had not told anyone that I was passionately in love with Isabella, and I decided to keep the secret even from my parents. I was determined that nothing would derail my plans.

I discovered that Isabella had no end of admirers but very few listeners, so I made listening my top priority, even when she wanted to talk at length about a lovely American man whom she had recently met. I was not unduly worried because I knew from experience how difficult it was to maintain a transatlantic relationship. When she asked for my advice about whether to accept an invitation to see the man in New York, I urged her to accept. The weekend was a disaster and when she returned she was very downcast. I was not.

Sometimes she did not return my calls. I forced myself to wait for a few days and then found another excuse to call her. One night I went to the cinema with a friend but all through the film I could only think about Isabella. For the first time she had returned my calls two nights running. After the film I parted from my friend and went straight to check my answerphone. I found a long and warm message from her.

No voice had ever made me so happy. Although she did not say so, at last she was clearly taking some interest in me and it was from then that our relationship bloomed. Soon we were both head over heels in love.

Professionally I was looking for a change. Wanting to prepare for a future step in my career, I started planning for a master's degree. I looked at all the possibilities and found a perfect one-year course at Harvard. Stuck in a Sunday-night traffic jam on the way into London that winter, I asked Isabella quite suddenly if she would like to spend a year in America. I passed some exams, resigned from my job and in August 1997 we climbed onto a plane for Boston, utterly happy.

Before leaving England I had rung India and asked her to send a shell from her Bahamian beach. When it arrived I banged it onto some paper and out rolled a small pile of pink sand. I contacted a jeweller and created a diamond and sapphire ring packed with messages. Examined closely, the design revealed '10', '8' and '96', together making the date we met. The shank of the ring was hollow and filled with the sand. On a Sunday-afternoon walk I gave her the ring and asked her to marry me. Her hugs and kisses were all the answers I needed.

At Harvard I split my time between the Kennedy School of Government and the Business School. Isabella picked undergraduate courses and we lived in a small clapboard house in Cambridge. That year forged our relationship as well as our love of America and its people. Isabella had an American grandmother and we travelled extensively to meet a host of American cousins. By the time I graduated we had decided to return to America for the first part of our married life and for me to pursue the next stage of my career there.

In the meantime we returned to England and were married. Isabella's family was as large as mine and together we would never fit in her Hampshire village church so we chose instead the nearby cathedral in Winchester. Before the wedding service I met my parents, siblings and David Loftus whom I had asked to be best man alongside my brother Philip. We all went quietly to the cathedral's Lady Chapel and held a brief service of prayers and readings of remembrance. The service was not just for Nick but also Leonora, the five-year-old daughter of Norton and Penny who had died in 1991 of cancer; and David's brother, John Loftus.

An hour later the church filled with family and friends for an intensely uplifting service. As favourite hymns echoed in the nearly thousand-year-old architecture the effect was almost overpowering. Towards the end of the service I felt a transition occurring. As Isabella and I knelt alone at the front of the church, the choir sang an ancient Gaelic blessing:

> Deep peace of the running wave to you
> Deep peace of the flowing air to you
> Deep peace of the quiet earth to you
> Deep peace of the shining stars to you
> Deep peace of the gentle night to you

Until then my deepest bond had been with Nick; now it was with Isabella.

At the reception I said:

I have thought of Anna much this year as I have contemplated what she must feel as she sees Isabella marry today. For those of you who don't know their relationship, it's more like twinhood than sisterhood, and that's a relationship I understand more than most.

It is nearly nineteen years since Nicky was killed, and I have spent those years feeling strangely alone. I never really dared to allow myself to believe the day would come when I would find someone with whom I could truly share all the highs and lows life offers. But that day has come and I was supremely moved earlier today when the choir sang from the Song of Solomon:

Rise up, my love, my fair one, and come away.

For, lo, the winter is past, the rain is over and gone.

I feel my winter *is* past and as I go forward in life with Isabella, I want you, Anna, and indeed all of you, Isabella's family and friends, to know that I will take every step of the path ahead aware of my debt to you in helping to make Isabella the person she is; and aware that if she is to burn as bright in the future as she does now, she will need your continued presence, love and support.

From earlier hilarity, the room had fallen very silent. Isabella's hand trembled in mine. Many of those listening had helped me recover from the lowest days of my life and had never heard me speak like this. I caught a glimpse of the Dugdales; Susie was holding David tightly. A mutual friend standing next to the Queen told us years later that it was the only time he saw her with tears in her eyes.

After an evening of partying, we left at midnight and next day flew to Delphi in Ireland. I could not have imagined a happier start to married life. We continued our honeymoon in Kenya. I had a sudden jolt into the past when we were handed a newspaper which announced the release from prison of Thomas McMahon. I was partly prepared for this. Eighteen months earlier I had unfolded my Sunday newspaper over breakfast to be greeted by the headline 'Mountbatten's killer to be freed':

> Thomas McMahon, 48 . . . is already allowed out of Dublin's Mountjoy prison to work as a carpenter on local building sites and spends one weekend a month at home in County Monaghan with his wife Rose and two sons. Rose said this weekend that her husband had turned against terrorism and severed his links with the IRA six years ago . . . Speaking for the first time since her husband's arrest, Mrs McMahon said last week 'Tommy never talks about Mountbatten, only the boys who died. He does have genuine remorse. Oh God, yes.' She and her two grown-up sons still live in the family home at Lisanisk, a hamlet outside Carrickmacross. 'He has no connections with anybody now' she said . . .[1]

I did not know if the words attributed to Rose McMahon were either accurate or sincere, but it made little difference because by then I had no wish to impede Thomas McMahon's path to freedom. The situation in Ireland had shown clear signs of progress. In July 1997 the IRA had announced a new ceasefire, and in October they had entered peace negotiations. As Easter 1998 approached there was a nail-biting finish. Behind the scenes President Clinton phoned the parties from the White House to urge them not to let this chance of peace slip away like so many others in the previous three decades. Ominously a final deadline came and went without agreement. Then, seventeen hours beyond the deadline, at 5:36pm on 10 April 1998 the long-awaited agreement was signed by the British and Irish governments and endorsed by most of the parties in Northern Ireland. It was Good Friday and the document became known as the Good Friday Agreement. It called for a wide range of measures including a locally elected Northern Ireland Assembly; prisoner release; British troop reductions; decommissioning of paramilitary weapons; polls on Irish reunification; and the introduction of new civil rights. A referendum to ratify its measures was successfully held in May 1998. Against this background the release of Thomas McMahon, by then the longest-serving republican prisoner in Ireland, seemed sensibly timed. Nevertheless it left me with a strange feeling that I might one day run into him in the street, and I realised I was not yet prepared for that.

As we continued our honeymoon, I felt buoyed up with optimism for peace in Ireland. Then came a sickening blow. On Saturday 15 August 1998 we were enjoying an idyllic stay in Rajasthan when we saw television reports from Omagh in Northern Ireland of a bomb which had killed twenty-nine people and injured two hundred and twenty. It was the bloodiest attack of the entire Troubles and was claimed as the work of a splinter group, the Real IRA who along with Continuity IRA were opposed to the peace agreement. Thankfully, as the months and years were to show, their attempts failed to knock the peace process off course.

Returning to America, I joined the *Discovery Channel* based outside Washington, DC. We lived in Georgetown with Grove, our Labrador. Here, away from the ties of home and family, we again had the freedom and time to travel and make new friends.

Isabella and I longed for children and we did not have to wait long. Our parents came to visit us in Georgetown for the Millennium celebrations of 2000 and while they were with us Isabella gave birth to a girl, Amber.

After a short night of sleep at the foot of Isabella's hospital bed, with Amber swaddled in a bassinette beside us, I walked to the adjoining bathroom. Isabella was asleep. As I came out I glimpsed a nurse walking away with our baby. Some impulse made me rush after her and I had to restrain myself from grabbing Amber back. It was my first experience of the deep parental instinct to protect.

Happily at home, I often found myself sitting alone with Amber. Like Isabella, I was in love. I wondered what would happen to our child. Would she have a long life? How high would the crests of her waves reach and how low the troughs? Above all, I wanted to protect her. I knew it was a futile desire. She would have to lead her life without my minute-by-minute protection.

Being a parent myself, in moments of quietness I found myself thinking again of what it must have been like for my parents when Nick had been killed. I realised that many questions about Nick's death still hung unanswered at the back of my mind, and that as I went forward in life as a father, I needed to answer them. I wanted to be emotionally strong for the family I was starting and for that I needed to exorcise the remaining unresolved grief that lingered from Nick. In previous years I had occasionally considered a church service in his memory but it had not felt right and I had not found any other solution.

As the weeks following Amber's birth went by, I realised that above all I was thankful for the gift of her life. That made me all the more aware that my own life was a gift. I had once come within a hair's breadth of losing it. I owed my life to the couple who had pulled me from the water. Sitting by Amber's cot, I decided to write them a letter. I walked to my study desk and took out a sheet of paper.

Dear Mr and Mrs Wood-Martin,

How easy it is in the hurly burly of life to hurry past the important things and leave them undone. In the more than 20 years of life I have had since you saved me from drowning after the bomb, it amazes me that I have failed to reach out and singularly thank you for doing for me the greatest service it is possible for one person to render another: to save his life.

Of course I remember talking to you at the wedding of Norton and Penny, and signing my parents' Christmas cards many times since, but these are incidental. Only in recent years have I reached that point in my underlying emotional recovery to be able to understand enough about life, and surviving the bomb, to know that small steps like this one are vital in the ongoing process of integrating the past into a fulfilled and happy present.

Many a time in the several years of therapy I did in the mid nineties did I find myself talking about you, and resolving to write this letter. But I never did.

I remember reading an interview with you, and being fascinated to learn things about the bomb only you could have known. It was helpful, as indeed is writing this letter. I think others in my family have different ways of coping with the grief. Of all of us, I think my mother and I share most closely the need to discover small and important truths, and to communicate with others about them. Occasionally, even publicly, because I've learnt how often it helps others.

One of my greatest frustrations is how rarely I am able to cry the deep cry I need to. Perhaps only a couple of times a year. And some people mistake the tears for pain, when of course they're not, they're the pain coming out. Writing this letter has been like pulling a big splinter of grief and emotion out of me, and the tears and relief have been enormous in so doing.

I recognise that no demonstration of gratitude could adequately repay the gift of continued life you gave me in 1979, nor express sufficiently what I feel. So all I will say is thank you. And ask you to bear in mind every day that somewhere else in the world is someone loving the miracle of life thanks to you.

And what a miracle it is; my wife Isabella gave birth to our first child, Amber, on January 3rd, and never have I known a baby smile so much, reflecting back perhaps our own happiness.

When and if our paths will cross I do not know; either by design, or chance as they did once before. But somehow I feel they will. Until then my love and every good wish,

Timothy[2]

Two things surprised me. First, it was a very quick letter to write; it flowed almost as if by reflex. Second, writing it made me cry. I had difficulty in keeping the writing paper dry, just managing to keep it away from my waterfall. I was determined not to make the letter look ridiculous by smudging it with tears. I stifled the noise of my crying because I did not want to upset Isabella, or interrupt either the letter or my tears, both of which were very therapeutic. I sat back thinking that if this letter to people I hardly knew had produced such a powerful reaction, then I must go back to Ireland and explore everything that had lain dormant in my psyche for so long. I was beginning to answer the question posed by Berenice after my last session of therapy: 'There's something holding you back, isn't there?' I knew I needed to return to Ireland. Slowly I started to think through the best way to do this, made cautious by my previous lightweight visits which had been largely unsatisfying.

To our complete joy, in February 2001 Isabella gave birth to a son, Milo. Soon we decided that we should move back to Europe to be close to our extended families. Settling back in London, I realised that if ever the time was right to go back to Sligo it was now, with Ireland in peace and my life transformed by the deeply fulfilling and inspiring love which Isabella had brought into my life. In marriage and fatherhood I had found a new level of emotional security. This was crucial as I contemplated what I knew was going to be an almost impossibly difficult but necessary step ahead: to return to Ireland and finally address what had been holding me back for so long.

PART THREE

RETURN TO SLIGO

2003–2004

19

CASTLE REVISITED

The small commuter aircraft touched down and braked sharply. As the propellers whined in reverse thrust, I peered out and saw sand dunes rushing past the window. I felt very close to Classiebawn. It was August 2003 and this was the first time I had returned to Sligo in many years. My mind raced as I contemplated what it would feel like to wander the labyrinthine lanes of my childhood again and search for the inner peace I had lost there. As I walked from the plane and smelled the sea, I felt the surge of excitement that I had often experienced as a boy. Throughout my childhood I had absorbed my holidays at Classiebawn unquestioningly. After the bomb the feel of the place had remained in my mind but the details had become blurred. Now I wanted to piece together a clear picture of the place and events that had shaped so much of my childhood. For that I planned to visit Sligo regularly over the coming year and to immerse myself in the process.

I hired a car and spent my first night at a holiday-let cottage not far from the airport. I awoke in the middle of the night with an uneasy feeling. I lay in bed, unable to fathom my whereabouts. When I remembered where I was, and that the door of the cottage had no lock, I felt something I had never before felt in Sligo: fear, as if someone might be coming to get me. I turned over and drifted uneasily to sleep. In the morning I set off by car for Classiebawn. I gazed at views which

quickly came back to mind like long-forgotten tunes. In my journal
I wrote:

I became aware that the castle would come into view at any
moment. I started to feel quiet and knotted up as if shrinking
inwards somehow. Then I said 'There it is' and suddenly I was not
sitting in the car in 2003, I was looking at it as I had as a child.
It was utterly unique, distinctive and unchanged.[1]

I drove on through open countryside then pulled in at the side of
the road with the castle still a mile or two away. I did not yet want to
go any further. Slouched on a stone pillar beside a gate, I suddenly
dissolved into tears. As traffic rushed past I thought of my brother Joe.
When he had returned here years after the bomb and first glimpsed the
castle, he had stood by his car and felt physically sick.

I got back in the car and continued. The tumbledown stone wall
that had run for a mile or more around the estate had been beautifully repaired. Beyond it the woods I remembered had vanished and
now beef cattle were grazing on neat paddocks. Much of the tall, wild
Marram grass which had spread over the land from the sand dunes
had been removed, and in its place was lush new pasture. The face
of the landscape had changed but I was pleased it was being cared
for by its new owner, Hugh Tunney. I was aware that many people
in the area disapproved of him and the changes he had brought.
Within months of his first leasing the castle, Molly Kennedy, the
cook of more than twenty years, had walked out of her job after a
fierce row. A long dispute had ensued, resulting in legal action, after
which she left her cottage on the estate and moved away. Hugh's
uncompromising stance as a landlord made him unpopular; when the
IRA bombed us, his enemies made wild claims that he had had some
foreknowledge of the attack, although investigations on both sides
of the Irish border reassured us that these rumours were baseless and
untrue. Nearly three years later, my family's Sligo lawyer, Charlie
Browne, wrote that he himself was amongst those who suffered 'a
prejudice'[2] against Hugh.

After my grandfather's death, the castle had passed to my aunt,
who confirmed with Hugh Tunney that she wished to retain the right

246

to use it each August. Some people were surprised by this. One friend had suggested that she might like to give it to the United World Colleges of which my grandfather had been President. She had been 'horrified' by the idea and had thought, 'But I love Classiebawn. I don't want them to have it, it's ours.' She explained, 'It is all happy memories. When they went fishing that day it was a lovely sunny day and I remember them all on the porch of the house and going off down the drive in a very happy group. The ghastliness happened right out at sea. It's a family house with years of happy memories.'[3] In the years that followed, the security situation showed little improvement, and despite her hopes she was never able to use the castle again. However, she and my uncle stayed in contact with Hugh and when their son Ashley was married, Hugh and Caroline came to the wedding.

When I contacted Hugh in August 2003 and told him I wished to come to Classiebawn, I was astonished when he immediately offered to leave the castle so I could move in. I quickly reassured him that I had no such intention but I accepted his invitation to come and see him as often as I liked. Within weeks I was driving through the castle gates, and the first thing I noticed was that my grandparents' initials and crests were still on the gate pillars. When I reached the brow of the hill, I found Hugh waiting on the castle steps. He greeted me emphatically with a warm 'Well-come'. As I walked into the castle, I saw near the front door the wooden-handled nets in which we used to catch prawns. A rush of memories and emotions swept over me. I felt that I had dived in at the deep end and that I needed to go back outside to acclimatise. Having briefly met Caroline Devine, I walked out again into the sunshine.

Hugh followed me outside and we walked together around the castle. I made tracks towards the spot where Twiga had been buried and soon found her small grave and headstone hidden in long grass. In the stables I saw our old saddles. When I passed my grandfather's, hanging in its normal spot, I felt my insides flare up, as they did when I touched the harness which had been worn by my favourite pony, Timmy, born during the Second World War. In his old age he had pulled us grandchildren around the lanes in our great-grandmother's pony trap, which still lay in a nearby shed.

When I walked into the castle I had steeled myself for more of the same. It was not long before Caroline pointed to a collection of bottles and explained these had been on the drinks trolley when we walked out of the castle twenty-four years before. She said, 'Every year we were waiting. We were so scared to touch anything and this is exactly what was left. We never touched it.'[4] I held the bottles in my hand and felt as if I was aboard the *Mary Celeste*. The gins and whiskies were crystal clear; the lemon cordial had clouded.

When we walked into the dining room for lunch, Hugh pulled open a sideboard drawer which contained four small brown envelopes. I recognised them instantly. Each morning my grandfather had removed one such envelope which contained his daily intake of vitamin and mineral supplements. The surviving envelopes were evidently for the four days of the holiday still remaining when he was killed. As Hugh sat down at the head of the table, I had the momentary sensation that he was in the wrong seat and my grandfather would walk in at any moment, collecting an envelope of pills as he passed, and sit down in his rightful seat at the head of the table.

That afternoon I wandered the castle for three hours and later wrote:

Had I been alone I would have allowed the breath to leave my lungs as it wanted to, and the tears to flow . . . Each of these places – a room or a spot offering a familiar view – has something locked up in it, like a sweet fragrance. On opening it up for the first time, there is an evanescent and fragile sensation, soon scattered to the wind. From every corner the rooms whisper memories of sensations, noises and smells.[5]

I returned to the castle the next day, happy at last to be taking the first steps that I hoped would lead me to understand the process that so changed my life and ended Nick's. I wrote in my journal:

After leaving the castle I felt a surge of emotion like a great weight in the lower part of my ribcage. Bizarrely the scar on my stomach (left by the operation on the day of the bomb) started to hurt which it has not done for a year or more.[6]

From Classiebawn I drove into the edge of Mullaghmore. The approach road had not changed much in twenty-four years. The warm sunny weather was exactly as it had been on the day of the bomb and the atmosphere was strikingly similar. There was a throng of holidaymakers in shirtsleeves and T-shirts. The salty, fishy smell of the harbour wafted over the village. The sea shimmered beside the sand dunes and in the background lay the mountains of Benwiskin and Benbulben.

I had made an appointment to see Dick and Elizabeth Wood-Martin, but when I parked outside their home I found myself unable to get out of the car. Later I wrote in my journal:

> Suddenly I was crying. The sight of the village in the beautiful August sunshine was too much; to meet Mr and Mrs Wood-Martin in its midst was an impossibly tall mountain to climb on the energy left to me. I needed to be alone.

Driving back towards Sligo, I got out at the now vacant house in which Mrs Kennedy had lived. I walked down the track towards the Atlantic. As I passed over a small dune, and the enormous beach beyond came into view, I suddenly had a powerful feeling I was going to stumble upon one of my childhood family picnics, the sandwiches crunchy from grains of child-scattered, wind-borne sand. Behind my sunglasses my tears came in a silent, constant stream. I passed three children playing in the sand; their lives seemingly innocent, untouched, uncomplicated. My own small children, far away in England, filled my mind; I longed to hug them and Isabella. I walked to the top of the highest dune and for half an hour sat alone, the beach a channel for my tears.

Soon I was on a plane from Sligo Airport, then an airliner from Dublin to London. I felt each stage of the journey was like an airlocked decompression chamber, as if I was a diver coming up from a great depth. Getting home before midnight, I silently kissed my children and tucked myself up in bed, an arm around Isabella as she slept. My trip had been painful at times but I had come away feeling uplifted. I felt I had worked loose some splinters which had lain deeply embedded in my psyche for years and I found myself eagerly looking forward to the next trip which I had scheduled for later that month.

I returned to Sligo in time for the twenty-fourth anniversary of the attack and, as before, I started at Classiebawn. As soon as I got out of my car, Hugh Tunney walked me over to Twiga's grave. It was now neat and tidy with a small fence to keep away the cattle. I was touched and pleased. This was the thoughtful and charming side of Hugh which I had seen in my childhood and which I heard about from a small number of his friends. However, as time passed I came to understand what a complex man he was.

When Hugh had retired, sold his home in Clones and moved to the castle full-time in 1991, he had directed his energy, time and money at making improvements on the estate. This produced tensions with the local community which resulted in court action and press reports. Hugh felt many of the local people were untrustworthy. He told me that my grandfather had been a victim of pilfering and unauthorised grazing, and that when it had come to light my grandfather had been unduly lenient. Hugh wanted it to be known that he would not tolerate any such behaviour. A number of local residents pointed out the irony that my grandfather, a British landlord, had treated employees, tenants and neighbours generously, but when he had been succeeded by Hugh, an Irish nationalist, the same people felt poorly treated.

Over the years Hugh had become increasingly isolated from village life. Although he went to church daily, he told me that in the previous twenty years he had only been to a local pub twice. One by one the staff left or were dismissed. Aideen Gore-Booth was a placid and congenial person but one day she told him, 'Mr Tunney, I'll never stand in this castle again' and she was as good as her word. When I asked Hugh what had prompted this, he replied sadly, 'I don't know. I don't know. I just don't know.'[7]

He chose to minimise the number of people who were allowed up to the castle. Caroline seemed to do most, if not all, of the housework, cooking and cleaning. Most of the castle was shuttered, dusty, damp and cold. Many rooms were crammed with objects bought by Hugh and slotted in and around the furniture, pictures and possessions we had left behind. The effect was ghostly and gave me the impression of visiting a monument, even a mausoleum. Hugh was now seventy-five. His memory was poor and he was in a weak state of health. I wrote in my journal: 'Mostly I am sorry for him. Occasionally I can't help but be touched by his desperate attempts to please and be kind, all wrapped in the charm of the Irish to which I am susceptible.'[8]

When I asked Hugh how he had felt after we were attacked, he said that he had 'nearly lost two stone' in weight in the following two weeks:

That's how much it affected me . . . It was a mixture of shock, horror and possibly guilt. You might well ask 'Where did the guilt come from?' The guilt was that in my ignorant mind I wondered all day long, and agonised all day long, as to whether this horrible thing that had happened was because the engine for which I was responsible had blown up . . .

He told me that by 1979 he had been worrying for some time about the way my grandfather put to sea in such an old boat and with such a young skipper. As a Roman Catholic from Northern Ireland, and a nationalist, he pointed out to my grandfather how bad it would look if there was an accident at sea while he was responsible for the boat:

I told him exactly what I thought and said, 'Well now, my Lord, I have to tell you that I want to be excused from the caveat in the lease which makes me responsible in law to have *Shadow* V seaworthy. Only on one condition will I be prepared to continue that and that is if you bring an experienced seaman from England with you which, given your status, should not be extraordinarily difficult.' And I went on say I didn't understand anything about boats, or engines of any kind, I still don't except that I know a decent engine could not explode.

At Hugh's invitation, I spent hours during my second visit wandering around the castle. In the larder opposite the kitchen was a high shelf where I found an ancient Imperial typewriter. As a youngster I had often sat beside Gabrielle Gore-Booth in the library and watched mesmerised by the rush of her fingers and the clickety-clack of the keys as she typed menu cards for Peter to place in the dining room. In a corridor not far away I found a page of her typing which listed our collection of gramophone records. Her energetic voice sprang into my mind and then her softly rolling laugh. Beside the list lay a large stack of vinyl discs in their colourful sleeves. I leafed through dozens of them looking for my childhood favourite. As I went through the pile I feared it had not survived. Instead I came across *The King and I; Annie Get Your Gun; West Side Story; Oklahoma; Camelot; The Grand Prix of Gibraltar* by Peter Ustinov; and *Let's Sing with the Irish*. I found a note in my grandfather's handwriting on one of them: 'The outer inch of this record has become warped but if the needle is started one inch from the edge, the rest of the record plays very well.' It was so *him*. I laughed aloud and then as I felt close to him a lump grew in my throat. I continued flicking through the records until a burst of pleasure came over me as I found what I had been looking for. The cover, a classic piece of 1970s kitsch, was a photograph of a shapely young woman clad only in a bikini and cricket pads and gripping a bat. At the top in garish red letters was the title *Hot Hits*. I had played the record, released when I was eight years old, ad infinitum, through successive Augusts at Classiebawn. I let out a whoop of joy to have found it. I felt sure that its music, unheard since my childhood, would unlock a whole range of feelings that were dormant within me and which I was desperate to dig out and expel. I flipped over the record cover and when I saw the names of the songs, some of them started to play in my mind: 'Pied Piper'; 'Banner Man'; 'When You Are a King'; 'Me and You and a Dog named Boo'; and 'River Deep, Mountain High'.

Walking into the library, my attention was immediately drawn to the door in the corner into whose keyhole we had stuffed cornflakes, confident that leprechauns and other fairies would enjoy them. The door which had beckoned so tantalisingly then still held me in awe. As I looked at it, a spine-tingling sensation overcame me as I remembered what it had felt like to sit in front of it as a boy: the thrill of endless possibilities.

I walked out of the library and stood at a window facing Inishmurray. I closed my eyes and found an ancient muscle-memory guided my hand to a spot on the wall. Opening my eyes, I made out two tiny holes in the sun-faded woodwork. Now I remembered: it was here that had been suspended a cradle for the microphone of the Pye wireless set which connected the castle to *Shadow V*. There was no sign of the radio but close by hung instructions from my grandfather:

SHADOW V EMERGENCY

In event of breakdown or trouble send someone to Mullaghmore Harbour to see if any motorboat is available to go out to her assistance.

If none is available quickly or SHADOW V is far out ring up Donegal Co-operative Fisheries at:-
KILLYBEGS 94
and ask if any trawlers are in the neighbourhood who could go to her assistance quickly.

If no trawler is available ring up the Duty Officer at HMS SEA EAGLE at:-
LONDONDERRY 3211
and ask if air sea rescue helicopter could be sent.

Final alternative ring up lifeboat which is 45 miles away:-
ARRANMORE 3
Note: If touch is lost by direct radio-telephone ring Malin Head Radio Station to call SHADOW V:-
BALLYGORMAN 2

I asked Hugh if any of *Shadow V*'s wreckage had survived.* He gave me a key and directions to a small room in the basement. As I unlocked the door and turned on a dim bulb, I felt a strange stirring as my eyes slowly adjusted and picked out faint shapes in the dusty recesses of the room. Sticking up proudly was the swivel fishing seat on which my grandfather sat when not at *Shadow V*'s wheel. Its green cushion smelled of the diesel oil which had covered the sea after the explosion. I quietly handled the few parts of *Shadow V* that had survived and let my

---

* In 1987 the remains of the boat had been burned by Gardai in Dublin.

feelings rise and fall with the memories that flooded back. I felt I was closing in on the purpose of my visits but that I still had a long way to go. I decided that next day I would go into Mullaghmore and out to sea.

20

VILLAGE REVISITED

I ambled through a sun-drenched Mullaghmore in my shirtsleeves. The village was filled with holidaymakers, many of them day-trippers from the North making the most of their August bank holiday. The scene was eerily similar to the bank holiday Monday of 1979. I was wandering on automatic pilot and now found that I was on the small beach beneath the Pier Head Hotel in the heart of the harbour. Under my dark glasses and cap I was on a sea of emotion. I screened out the noise and activity around me and tuned myself to an inner frequency. In my journal I wrote later:

> Strangely I remember feeling as if the many holidaymakers and locals around me didn't exist. They were in one dimension and I was in another and they never troubled me . . . I just wanted to float on the winds blowing from 1979, from childhood, from innocence, from Nicky . . .
>
> This was the spot on which the boats had landed us ashore minutes after the bomb. Standing there this August Monday, 24 years to the day, my face wet with tears, I sensed life and death: my life being saved; Nick's death in the water a few hundred yards away. His coin had come down 'death up, life down' and with it all possibilities had been denied him. When told, 3 days after the bomb, of his death, I had some dim inner suspicion that

wrapped up in the unintelligible sick-making horror of the destruction, was a piece of joyous get-up-and-sing good news: that I had survived to receive the greatest lottery win ever accorded to any human, the chance to live again. That had been on the second floor of Sligo General Hospital in August 1979. Now, August 2004, here I was standing on the beach and quite unexpectedly finding the spot gave me at one and the same time violently opposing emotions. On the one hand I had extreme grief and a mental picture of Nicky's body just off Mullaghmore Head, lifeless beneath the flat calm surface. On the other hand I felt this spot was the place of my lottery win. I felt a pulse-quickening sensation of being rocket propelled, which made me look up, and feel in awe.[1]

I studied the white of the clouds and the blue of the sky and enjoyed the 'incredible lightness of being' I was feeling. I had only felt this way a few times before, once as a small boy feeling excited about something that was due to happen, my birthday perhaps, or Christmas. I climbed onto my bed so I could see myself in the mirror. It was like having butterflies in my tummy and I wanted to know if the glow I was feeling was visible on the outside. Now I was having the same sensation. A memory suddenly came to me from a hot summer's day in the garden at home when I had been a toddler. I had watched Norton get into his car, drive to the gates at the entrance to our home and disappear from sight. In the silence that followed I thought about following him. I did not do so but I wondered what lay beyond. Standing now in Mullaghmore, I felt a similar tingling sense of being at the edge of something. I had a rush of excitement and hope. I felt inspired by simply being alive. It was the feeling I had felt looking into Amber's newborn eyes which had then prompted me to write to the Wood-Martins and tell them how I felt about the gift of life they had handed back to me. I felt a total excitement about the limitless possibilities of the day, the year, the life ahead of me. I had a sense that something special was going to happen but I had no idea what or when.

A few minutes later I walked up the hill to a bungalow overlooking the harbour. Now I had the strength to knock on its door and meet the people to whom I owed my life: Dick and Elizabeth Wood-Martin. They were expecting me and immediately welcomed me into their home. When I brought the conversation around to the subject of the bomb, I made the mistake of trying to run before I could walk. I choked on emotion and sat for a few moments in silence feeling foolish.

We spoke instead about a lifetime of memories from Dick and Elizabeth. We had been talking for more than two hours when Dick said he was going out that afternoon in his boat and asked if I would like to go with him. He went ahead by car to prepare and I followed a short while later, entering the harbour on foot.

I walked very slowly and felt the sensation of 1979 rise slowly in my chest. I stopped and heaved. I felt like I was wearing lead-lined boots about to jump off the Atlantic Shelf. I had to stop again when I looked down and saw the seaweed, the stones of the harbour wall, the colour of the water, translucent green, and smelt the salty, boaty smells. Nothing had changed. I felt like I would see *Shadow V* in a few seconds and be with Grandpapa, Granny, Paul, Nick, Mum and Dad again. I crumpled as quietly as I could. We put out to sea and I sat on the roof and wept.[2]

Getting close to the spot where *Shadow V* had exploded, I came down from the roof and started talking to Dick in earnest about my memories of the day and asked him for his. He told me exactly what he had seen and done.

Next day I travelled by car, plane and train to my parents' holiday home in Scotland. Early the following morning I gathered with several siblings around my parents' bed with mugs of tea and told them stories from Classiebawn. I knew they would enjoy Dick and Elizabeth's dry sense of humour and gave them a verbatim account of their last sight of me in 1979 being carried away towards the Pier Head Hotel on the bottom-board of their little boat, wrapped in a multicoloured towel. She had finished her account with 'and I never saw that towel again'.[3]

I wrote to the Wood-Martins: 'After a long time not asking questions, my mind is now making up for lost time and is asking questions all the time. I hope you don't mind too much.'⁴ I returned to Mullaghmore as soon as I could. I wrote in my journal:

> I shook Dick's hand long and hard and kissed Elizabeth on both cheeks, big smackers of kisses, and she and he reciprocated equally warmly. What hit me immediately was the delicious smell of the peat, 'turf' as it is known here, on the fire. I can't remember the last time I saw it, and it transported me magically back to boyhood, Classiebawn's drawing room and the 1960s and 70s. I picked up a piece and turned it over and over before dropping it into the embers, mesmerised by the effect.⁵

I had brought Elizabeth a present and she laughed aloud when she unwrapped it to reveal several multicoloured beach towels.

Building my relationship with the Wood-Martins through 2003 and 2004 removed a fear I had carried with me since the day of the bomb. In the months following the attack, memories had returned without warning but none had been visual. I had flashbacks of talking with the Wood-Martins: the vibration of their outboard engine; the cold; the stinging taste of the saltwater mixed with diesel and blood; the pungent smell of the oil on my skin; but never did I remember the sights that accompanied these memories. In hospital the doctors explained that the human mind seemed to have a facility to suppress memories which are too traumatic and release them only in small doses. I dreaded what sights might come back. The Wood-Martins dispelled this dread at a stroke when they told me that at first I had not been able to see at all. It seems my sight did not come back until well after I had been returned ashore. The first sight I remember is that of my father as he was lifted into the ambulance forty-five minutes after the explosion. Another piece of the jigsaw fell into place as I realised for the first time why the next day's newspapers had reported that I had been blinded.

Each time I visited Mullaghmore harbour that summer I was struck by how it continued to be a magnet for activity as it had been in the days of my four-greats-grandfather Harry Palmerston who had built it. Fishing boats were now far outnumbered by pleasure craft and sailing

Debris from *Shadow V* minutes after the explosion, seen from
Gus Mulligan's boat.

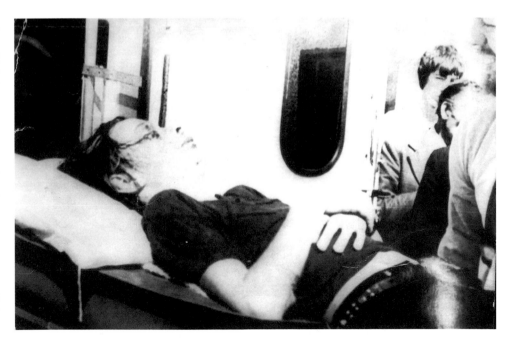

Terry Baker (right) carries me into his ambulance in Mullaghmore.
Seeing my father being carried towards me on a stretcher, I propped
myself up using my arms but fainted instantly.

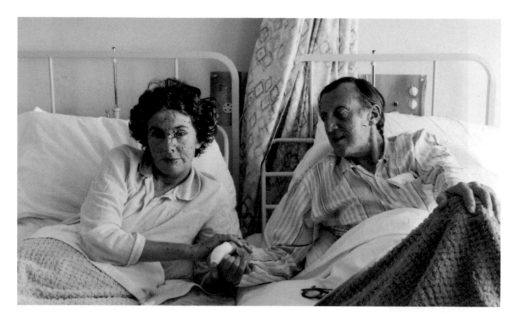

My parents, Patricia and John Brabourne, shortly before leaving Sligo Hospital, September 1979. A week earlier the nurses had put their beds together and wheeled mine opposite. At night they held hands. It was the first time I saw my father cry.

Sligo Hospital felt like a war zone. When it was time to leave, Philip and I set down our bags and waited. Two large Royal Air Force helicopters landed and were immediately surrounded by Irish troops and watched by a crowd.

Francis McGirl walks free from the
1979 trial which had convicted
Thomas McMahon. 'I'm delighted,'
he told reporters, '... but I'm unhappy
that he did not get off too.'

Thomas McMahon leaves Dublin's
High Court in 1988 after claiming
compensation for a broken arm
received in prison. He produced and
fired a handgun in the courthouse in
what was his second escape attempt.

Inspector Patrick Jordan (centre) with the remains of *Shadow V*. The
investigation concluded that four to five pounds of gelignite had been
placed between the engine and the cabin. With him are Sergeants
Gerard Carroll (left) and Michael Niland.

'Sad Tim Is Home Again' is how the *Daily Mirror* headlined the story which accompanied this photo, taken as I left Moorfields Eye Hospital in London with my sisters Amanda (left) and Joanna.

With Dick Troughton by the River Broom, Ross-shire, 19 September 1979. I was so proud of landing the salmon and smiled happily when my mother told me that 'Nick must have arranged it'.

Philip, my mother, Norton, my father and me, St Paul's Cathedral, 20 December 1979. My mother told me years later, 'Standing at the top of those steps with a battery of reporters, and going down feeling "I don't think I'm going to make it but I've got to", I was rather frightened – very frightened.'

Returning to Sligo in August 2003 and seeing Classiebawn for the first time, unchanged by the passing decades, I slouched on a stone pillar and suddenly dissolved into tears.

Nick's body arrives in Mullaghmore, held by 'Whitie' Gilbride and Sean Brennan (behind). Talking to Sean in 2003 I was handed this photograph. I stared and stared. It was as terrible a photograph as I had ever seen but also gave me what I wanted: a sense of being there.

On the beach at Classiebawn in August 2004, I put Ludo on my shoulders and joined Amber and Milo in their running and splashing, laughter and screams. My wife, Isabella, videoed us. Like me, she sensed that the shadows of my past were lifting.

dinghies. Children splashed. In early childhood Paul Maxwell and his elder sister Donna had started their holidays with a ceremony they shared with their friends Rachel and Matthew Johnson, jumping off the stone steps that led down from the harbour wall and splashing into the water below. Each year they would jump from one step higher. In 1979 Rachel had been 'incredibly jealous' when Paul got a job at the castle. One morning she went to the castle kitchens with him knowing he had no right to take her there, but she had got so used to my grandfather's presence in the village that he seemed 'a distant grandfather figure' and she did not worry. She knew from experience that when he paddled around the harbour at low tide, fishing for prawns, he let the children join in and 'always had a few spare nets if necessary'.[6] Rachel was pleased that Paul had *Shadow V* to look after because he loved boats.

Paul Maxwell's parents had also been very pleased he had landed the job. I visited his mother Mary, now divorced, remarried and living in County Down, Northern Ireland. She told me that initially Paul had got off to a bad start with my grandfather. She had kept a diary of the things he told her that summer. At the beginning of August Paul said, 'I just can't bear him', but he decided to stick at the job and quickly changed his opinion. 'He really grew to like him very, very much,' his mother told me. It was little things that brought about the change. Paul invented a gadget to help my grandfather catch shrimps and for this he praised Paul. 'Paul liked praise. I suppose all of us respond to a bit of praise,' his mother said. One day Paul came home from a trip in *Shadow V* and told her that my grandfather had been 'just staring out to sea' and that he had looked sad. Talking about my grandfather's time in the Navy, he had asked if he had ever been frightened, to which my grandfather had replied: 'Yes but you bloody well don't show it.' One night Paul came home 'so pleased' because my grandfather had sent him home with some salmon for his mother. She told me, 'Paul had just wonderful little ways. In his latter years as he was getting big, if I would be annoyed with him about something he would just lift me up off my feet and say, "Now little mother, calm yourself down." He always called me "Little Mother" and of course that made me even crosser in a way. And I miss that.'[7]

In November 2003 I arranged to meet Paul's father for the first time.

In 1979 he had been a lecturer in Enniskillen. He was now retired. My journal entry records:

This morning at 9.30 I met Paul's father, John Maxwell. I leapt out of the car in bright sunshine in Mullaghmore and said 'Hello Paul'. How many times have I been introduced as Nick? Countless, and never once has it upset me; so I didn't feel bad when I recovered myself and put my arm around him and he put his arm around me and said not to worry at all and we laughed, firm friends after 10 seconds. Having spent 4½ hours in his company I felt completely bonded . . . He told me of two men in the area about whom he had always had his doubts, indeed men whom he has reason to believe were connected to the bomb. He points out that it doesn't make any practical difference today what might have happened or might have been prevented and I share his attitude. At one point, standing together in spitting rain at the end of the harbour pier, I told him that I had heard from Dad that the security services believed a number of men and a woman were involved. He had not heard from anyone about the possibility of a woman apart from what his present wife, Marion, had told him after the bomb. She had seen a woman moving around Mullaghmore very nervously and obviously alone, at around 10am that morning. Marion had given a statement to the Garda but nothing had ever come of it. It was a thunderbolt to hear this from John, not because it proves or changes anything but because sightings by people as close make the facts real and personal and the feelings are revived again, now even more vividly.

I was fascinated that John had tried to contact Thomas McMahon . . . to see if there was any 'common humanity'. I so admire John's openness to the possibility of good from such a meeting. Twice McMahon had replied that he wasn't interested in meeting. Once had been prior to 1998 via a priest who saw him in jail, and the later time through someone else with the same effect.[8]

When I asked John what he might gain from meeting Thomas McMahon, he said:

You can't quantify it. You're not going to kiss the guys that did it; but I would try and get him to put himself in my shoes or your parents' shoes. One of the things I would say is, 'You've got boys, Thomas, how would you feel if I had done it to your boys?' I wonder what he would say to that? Be interesting to see. My theory is, and I don't know if it is right or not, if you feel guilty about things, at some point it comes out again and you worry about it. That was a terrible thing for him to have done and somewhere the full realisation has been damped down otherwise he couldn't live with himself. I have a theory it will come out at some point in his life. I think that's the way the human mind works.[9]

John described how after the explosion:

suddenly I got in a tremendous rage and if Thomas McMahon had been on the harbour wall at that time I am sure I would have killed him. I've never felt it since. It just left me and I was left with a complete feeling of desolation and a kind of ache in my stomach. The rational mind came kicking in at that point. And the realisation that I had just talked to Paul, waved at him and he was never coming back. I thought, 'For the rest of my life I am not going to do anything that would exacerbate the situation.' I was determined not to look for retribution because no matter how bad somebody is they don't deserve to feel like that; and that has been my philosophy ever since.

As Paul's body was being carried to an ambulance John reasoned that he could not do anything more for him and decided not to accompany his body to hospital. He regretted the decision. 'To this day I feel I should have gone with him to the morgue,' he told me. Instead he wandered about aimlessly until he was reunited with his family at the cottage. Later a friend came and told him he was needed to identify Paul's body and drove him to the mortuary at Sligo Hospital. John told me:

They just pulled the sheet back from Paul's face and he was covered in pock marks from the explosion. I didn't look at the rest of his body as the sheet was over it but his hair was all sticky and salty and I rubbed his head. There was a guy there who said, 'Would you like a lock of his hair?' And I said yes so he gave it to me. Up to that point I was really in shock and when I came out my friend said to me 'OK, we'll go back now' and I sat down and I started to cry and I cried and cried for a very long time. And it was many years after that – eighteen years in fact – before I cried again. The reason for that I think, Timothy, is that the male feels he has to look after the females. Crazy, isn't it? But I figured I would have to be strong particularly for my two daughters and I tried to do that. It wasn't a good thing for me but it might have been a good thing for them.

Later I learned that among his symptoms after the attack had been migraines, several times or more per week, and nightmares. Years later, with two children from his second marriage, he started to feel a great guilt about the attention he was giving to his son Robbie, born in 1985. Robbie would walk into a room and look just like Paul and have the same way of sitting and turning. John felt bad that he seemed to be supplanting Paul in his mind. He solved the problem by getting out old home movies showing Paul as a young boy. It reconnected him to the sort of boy Paul had been and allowed him to accept that he had been completely different. His difficulties went away and he was left wishing he had looked at the home movies years earlier. His feelings of grief finally started to flow again eighteen years after Paul's death. He saw a psychotherapist who persuaded him to set down his memories of the day.*

John Maxwell told me about an incident which nearly destroyed *Shadow V* before the attack. During a spell of stormy weather in the fourth week of August, Paul had asked John to come out on the boat to help him. Also on board were three of my cousins: Edwina and Ashley Hicks and George Milford Haven. John knew Ashley and Edwina and they introduced him to George before they all set off. 'George wanted to take the helm and opened her up. We were going fast and there were

---

* He did this in the form of an essay and a poem. See pages 132 and 133 of *Bear in Mind*, published in 2000 in Belfast by a group known as An Cran (The Tree).

a lot of pots about,' John told me. He warned him that the buoys marking the pots had ropes attached to them that could foul the propeller. 'I said to George to go a wee bit wider but he said no.' John did not feel comfortable telling the eighteen-year-old how to handle the boat and let him continue. After a short while they hit a rope and the engine cut out. 'It was quite a big wave that day and we were drifting onto the reef and rocks. It was potentially dangerous. So there was a bit of panic on board. Paul produced a knife and I dived overboard.' At this point John got up, rummaged in the kitchen drawer beside me and held up a knife saying, 'That's the actual knife.' He continued, 'The boat landed on my head a couple of times, I thought I was going to get knocked out. I managed to cut the rope from around the propeller and clear it. I got on board again and George got the boat started just in time. If I had been a few minutes later the boat would have been on the rocks and Nicholas and Paul might be alive today.'

As he returned the knife to the drawer, it struck me that while his world and mine had been re-ordered in the twenty-four years since the explosion, his kitchen drawer had not. He opened another little wormhole through time when he took from his wallet a photograph of Paul. I studied it, unmoved. I turned it over and was devastated. In a child's handwriting was: 'A not very good photo of me. Oxxoo Paul. To Eileen oxxoo'. 'I've no idea who Eileen is,' said John as he put it away. 'She's out there somewhere,' I replied, and in the moment that followed I felt we were both torn between laughter and tears.

John mentioned that when he held Paul's body there was no watch on his wrist because, as usual, he had taken it off before going out on the boat to keep it safe. When John got home it was in its normal place. I described to John my last conversation with Paul. Paul had been very focused on the time because the engine needed water every fifteen minutes. Paul had laughed when I told him it was eleven thirty-nine and forty seconds. In my journal that evening I wrote: 'John laughed and smiled and his eyes were eager as I spoke.' The previous evening I had met someone who had been able to tell me what had happened to Nick after I last saw him alive. 'Any little detail helps,' I wrote in my journal.[10] I guessed that John was probably as keen to learn about Paul as I had been to learn about Nick.

*   *   *

Among those I made a point of seeking out was Peter Nicholson. To refer to him as the butler misses the point. As a teenager, he had inherited his work on the estate from his retiring uncle and his life became inextricably caught up with the place. He evolved into a mainstay of Classiebawn, a trusted friend to both staff and family. His had been the last face I had seen when I had finally walked out of the castle as a boy. He had stood alone on the steps as we drove away. He was in his thirties then and had black hair. Now as he opened the door of his cottage, his hair was grey. 'I was shocked at how lined and pained he looked. He was the personification of the Classiebawn of my childhood,' I wrote in my journal. 'He knows about leprechauns and fairies and keyholes of cornflakes, he calls me Timmy and is as much a part of Classiebawn as the sand is of the dunes. Part of me just wanted to give him a hug and cry.'[11]

In the years following the bomb, we were dismayed at the way Hugh Tunney had fallen out with many of our former employees, including Peter. After an acrimonious dispute, Peter's employment came to an end and Hugh then pursued him through the courts for more than twenty years until Peter was forced to relinquish his claim to the cottage he and his wife had long believed was theirs. Some years later, Hugh had a dispute with our long-time employee Michael Connolly who lived in the gatehouse. Relations between the men deteriorated badly and in 1998 they had a violent argument at the castle gates.

When I met Peter in 2003, he was working at Lissadell. Aideen Gore-Booth had died nine years earlier and her nephew Sir Josslyn Gore-Booth had inherited the house. I went to meet him and his wife Jane there and had lunch in their comfortable flat. Afterwards I found Peter and walked the house with him. He seemed very pleased that I had come back and said, 'Miss Aideen would be pleased, wouldn't she? She would, she would.' The only time I had seen her at Lissadell since the attack had been when I was a young man. I had urged her then to write her memoirs but I had not believed she would do it. I was therefore all the more surprised during this trip when a friend put into my hand a document which Aideen had written shortly before her death in 1994. Of the attack she wrote:

I was so dreadfully depressed before it happened as I had dinner at Classiebawn on Sunday night and I suppose the evil of what was happening overshadowed it. The next day I felt worse and said I would go for a swim, and I cried twice on the shore. Then when I returned to the house Peter Nicholson phoned me to say Shadow V was bombed and Paul Maxwell dead. I went to Mullaghmore and met two ambulances and then I saw John Maxwell and he told me all. I went to Classiebawn. When I returned to Lissadell as it got dark there were shots all round the house.[12]

It seemed the gunshots were part celebration, part warning to Aideen from IRA sympathisers in her area, and when I read her description I imagined how vulnerable she must have felt. If she felt that way, she never told us, nor did she say so in her memoirs. She closed her recollections by dedicating them to me, among others. Suddenly the unbound manuscript seemed like a postcard from her. That night in 1987 she had told me a great many things which she had not repeated in her memoirs. I took this to mean either that what she had told me had been unsubstantiated or that she felt it was best to let some things be forgotten. Either way I missed her greatly.

During my visits of 2003 and 2004 I made time to read the local newspapers, and by chance one day an article caught my eye: 'As a regular customer in my father's fishing tackle shop in Castle Street ...' wrote one journalist, 'Lord Louis never put on airs and graces and was courteous and charming at all times.'[13] I came across evidence of goodwill towards my grandfather from many who had come into contact with him. Mary Lowry, who had nursed us at Sligo Hospital, told me of the day when my grandfather had arrived at the hospital in a borrowed Mini. He explained he wanted to be as low-key as possible as he was just popping in to see one of his household staff who had been admitted.[14] It seemed that those who had indirect links to him also felt an attachment. An artist friend* of my grandfather with a house on Tory Island off the Donegal coast wrote after

---

* Derek Hill had lunch at Classiebawn two days before the attack and took away a portrait of my grandfather he had painted years before for varnishing. He was looking at it when news of the bomb arrived.

the attack: 'When my housekeeper heard, at her family home, she said the whole family burst into tears, outraged that such a thing could happen in Donegal where the family were so esteemed and loved.'[15]

When Cliffoney shopkeeper Teresa Daly had written to my mother after the bomb, she stated she was doing so with the 'permission' of Norton, Penny and Joe. I wondered if she had thought we wanted to cut off our Irish friends. In 2003 one of my earliest local journeys had been to look for her shop, The Chalet Marietta. The sign which had hung above the door had gone, the spinning wheel had been removed from the window and the shop reconverted once more into a home. The whitewashed walls were now a peachy orange. A Mullaghmore homeowner had written to my father in 1979: 'To us and others like us who are regular visitors to Mullaghmore, the absence of Lord Louis and his family will remain as an unhappy memory for life.'[16] This seemed to be the case, at least for some. When I wandered into the front yard of boat-builder Rodney Lomax and his wife Trudy, they seemed pleased to see me and we sat talking at length. He told me he had two portholes in his store that he had removed from *Shadow V* when he had rebuilt her cabin in the winter of 1966. Together we dug them out from his yard and I carried one home. I called on them several times after that and came away with a sense they were relieved by my visits, as if an old sorrow, briefly reminded, had been put away, and a wound healed.

In 1988 an English colleague asked me how much was known ahead of the attack in the local area. He told me about a friend who had holidayed elsewhere in Ireland and one day had been approached in the pub and told very quietly and firmly that he and his family should leave the area for their own safety, immediately and without any questions. They took the advice and left. The story caused me to recognise that while we brushed shoulders with villagers, we did not drink in the pubs. We may not have lived in an ivory tower, but in our granite castle behind an estate wall and crested gates we were divided physically and socially from the community, and this reduced the opportunity for any such warning.

I had seriously doubted the likelihood of anyone in the village having known about the attack beforehand. However, considering what the place had been like in 1979, it was a distinct possibility. Life in the west of Ireland moved slowly. There were very few cars, telephones, televisions or credit cards, and there were a large number of subsistence farmers, donkeys and carts, nuns in habits and turf-burning fires. Above all else, there seemed more time: time to walk rather than drive; time to talk rather than pass someone in the street; time to sit and look about; time to notice. The economy was smaller, incomes lower, the airport had not been built, and roads were narrower and quieter. While visitors to the area gave a decent local trade in the summer months, there was nothing like the volume or diversity of people on holiday or on business. In this environment outsiders were conspicuous from the way they spoke, behaved and spent their money. And in this slow-paced, observant, communicative fishing village, where the bush telegraph hummed with all the energy of today's cyberspace, repeated visits by IRA volunteers would have been noticed by some and shared with others.

I discussed this with a Sligo resident who accepted this but pointed out that even if some locals knew an IRA unit was active in the area, they would have guessed the target was a member of the military or security forces visiting from the North. Although such attacks had not taken place in this part of Ireland, it was well known that security personnel holidaying south of the border were seen as legitimate targets by the IRA.

In Northern Ireland, I gained the perspective of a man who had come into contact directly and indirectly with the men doing the killing on both sides, British and Irish, Catholic and Protestant. In my journal I wrote:

He had dealt with SAS* and IRA men . . . and said they were the hardest of men and the most ruthless of killers, and there was no difference between them in this respect. He recounted some of the techniques used by the IRA intelligence gathering teams, for example sending a bogus dustcart down a target's street, to act as eyes and ears and literally gather up useful information

* Special Air Service, variously seen in Ireland as the most famous or infamous unit of the British Army.

put out in the rubbish. He said that British military intelligence officers had told him how they wished some of the IRA operatives would work for them, so high was their regard for the IRA's techniques. On that basis he did not think the IRA's information gathering machine would have alerted anyone in Mullaghmore to the fact that we were under surveillance.

Being back in Mullaghmore gave me the chance to reassess a memory which had come back to me either while still in hospital or shortly afterwards. The afternoon before the attack, Ashley, Nick and I had wandered into Mullaghmore in glorious sunshine, tailed by a guard, to mull around and perhaps buy an ice cream. In the village I walked into a small shop. A man and woman, apparently customers, were inside and as I entered they visibly tensed up, as if shocked. The man stared at me and after a few moments mumbled something nervously at me. I had never known anything like this before and was very disconcerted. Shyly I said, 'Hello.' I wanted to get out but I was determined not to look frightened. In the awkward silence I kept calm and peered with an air of nonchalance at the shelves before walking out, relieved to be heading back to Nick and Ashley. Not knowing how to account for it, I said nothing. Staring and uneasy silences were completely at odds with normality in Mullaghmore. Over the years I thought of that moment many times. When I returned in 2003, the shop looked just as I remembered it. From its doorway I turned and looked towards the harbour. When I realised that from here you had a clear view of *Shadow V*'s mooring, the hair rose on the back of my neck and I walked on in something of a daze. In my journal I wrote:

> I will never forget the 2 people freezing on seeing me. They recognised me instantly. They must have thought I was a dead child walking. Their terror was, in hindsight, pathetic. From their reaction you would have thought I was six-foot-six combat-dressed SAS commando. I was a scrawny, doe-eyed fourteen-year-old boy whose voice hadn't broken. They could not possibly have known which twin I was. Next day they would have known that one of us was killed but they would not have known if it was the polite, timid little boy who had spent a minute or so in their presence,

before looking them each in the eye and saying 'goodbye' with a smile before walking out into the sunshine.[17]

After the attack, local people were understandably cautious about talking to the Gardai. A local man, interviewed for this book in January 2004 and requesting anonymity, admitted that he had decided not to tell the Garda what he had seen and heard on the day of the attack. A small white boat had been anchored the whole day about half a mile out. When the village emptied, a man walked along to the end of the pier. The boat came over to him and there was a conversation between him and a man on the boat. 'That went very well, didn't it?' 'Yes it did, it went very well.' Some days later the same man received a letter from someone unknown to him, naming a man as responsible for the bomb. Again he decided not to pass the information on. When I learned stories such as this I was initially tempted to research them further. I chose not to because I recognised they were red herrings. The purpose of my return to Sligo was to heal old wounds, not open them.

As my research revealed more and more about the activities and attitudes of the local population, I became clearer about the complex pattern of conflicting loyalties which they had accommodated for generations. On the one hand, they valued the friendship and support of my family; on the other, they remained constant to the overarching goals of republicanism. In leading their daily lives, they picked a delicate path, guided ultimately by a discretion that was the underpinning of their own physical safety. They knew how the IRA dealt with anyone suspected of informing and this further guaranteed the silence which enabled the IRA to mount the attack.

It seems the cultural touchstone that enabled so many Irish to balance their conflicting loyalties was their knack of accepting ambiguity. Foreigners, perhaps used to an exactness in their own culture, are sometimes confused or frustrated in Ireland when they come across loosely defined answers, such as 'a few' or 'a couple', to questions they would like answered precisely. Equally, during the Troubles, the unpredictable response of some Irish to illegal activity aroused deep discomfort among outsiders. It upset the Swiss tourism facilitators in Bundoran, Robert and Christiane Graf. Their antiseptic approach to law and order was in stark contrast to the prevailing culture in which they were visitors. Robert felt that if he saw a crime, he might be expected to 'shut up'.[18] This went against their own moral code and left them feeling isolated.

Learning this made me reflect on the well-established fact that any home-grown insurgency depends on the support, albeit tacit, of the population. By failing to report illegal or suspicious activities a citizenry can sustain a violent struggle carried on by a minority in their midst.

That there were proud nationalists in the area was never doubted by my grandfather, but they seemed to tolerate him. 'For the most part they minded their business and we minded ours,' was the 2004 recollection of Joe McGowan, a Mullaghmore resident, local historian and republican activist:

> We had nothing in common with them nor they with us. Most had no idea of his close relationship to the royal family, nor cared. Little snippets of casual gossip circulated. The Boy Scouts who often camped in the woods on castle grounds flew the tricolour over their camp.
>
> 'Did ye hear Mountbatten and the wife were driving out the road in their car. Lady Mountbatten saw the tricolour and was complaining it shouldn't be flown on their property?'
>
> 'Go on!'
>
> 'Aye, the chauffeur heard her, but Mountbatten said to her: Why shouldn't they fly it? It might be our property, but it's their country.' That went down well.
>
> 'Oh, I wouldn't be surprised. I heard he wore an Easter lily the last time he was here?'
>
> 'Well ye know there's no badness in him.'[19]

Undoubtedly those who knew the back-ways and by-ways of the local area would have seen and heard things we did not, but rarely was open hostility visible to us. After the attack, Aideen Gore-Booth told the Garda about a day she had been showing a group of tourists around Lissadell. 'There was a book of Lord Mountbatten's *Life and Times* in the house and one visitor, a man of the visiting party, referred to him as "an old bastard" or the likes and was told to shut up.

Otherwise I have not heard any other derogatory remarks about the family and I have known and been associated with them for at least twenty years.'[20]

One of the old friends with whom we had lost contact was Liam Carey, who had lived in the gatehouse. In May 2004 my brother Philip phoned me to say that he had visited Mullaghmore and while in the harbour had seen a man working on a boat. It had turned out to be Liam, and they had had a long conversation which Philip had much enjoyed. He was calling me to pass on Liam's best wishes and encourage me to look him up. Then Philip said something that intrigued me: Liam's only son had *Louis* as his middle name.

During a subsequent visit to Mullaghmore I went to see Liam and his wife Yvonne. He told me how much it had meant to see Philip. Then he started to talk about his life. He was born in 1951 and that year his parents had moved into the lodge at Classiebawn's gates. Liam showed me a framed photograph of himself aged about six in a small boat with my grandfather. His job had been to hold a bucket while my grandfather caught prawns. Next he showed me another photo of him aged about ten standing in a newly built *Shadow V*. One day he had been peeling potatoes in the kitchen at Classiebawn when my grandfather had walked in and said, 'That's no place for a young man. You! Come with me. You're on *Shadow V* this year.' He had done some of the boat-handling from his early teens and was given the summer job of boatman when he was sixteen. He wanted to leave school that year but my grandfather tried to persuade him to stay on and then go to university. He offered to pay for his tuition and asked in return that he work on *Shadow V* in the summer. Liam refused. By that time they had been talking for an hour and in the end my grandfather accepted defeat gracefully, telling Liam he was 'very stubborn' in a tone of voice which Liam liked.

Liam worked on *Shadow V* for three summers. When in 1969 the Irish Navy placed newspaper adverts, Liam went for an interview and with an old school friend from Mullaghmore was accepted as a cadet that September. Training was initially at the Irish Defence Forces College in Dublin. To their surprise the pair were then sent to England for training at the Royal Naval College in Dartmouth. I do not know if my grandfather pulled any strings but they were the only two Irishmen to enter the college that year. My grandfather invited them to Broadlands during their first mid-term break and walked down the staircase with them to greet the family who had gathered below. After two years as a cadet, Liam entered the Irish Navy for a year. My grandfather prevailed on him to stay on, but in 1972 he quietly resigned. He was in the gatehouse at Classiebawn when my grandfather arrived in August that year. All he said was, 'You could have made Admiral, you know', before driving on.

Liam lived in the gatehouse with his mother for another two years but left in 1975. In July 1979 he married Yvonne, a trainee nurse from New Zealand working in Dublin. When the IRA attacked in Mullaghmore the next month, Liam learned of it from a television newsflash. Later that day, a friend who had been best man at his wedding said something about my grandfather. According to Liam it was 'the wrong thing at the wrong time' and Liam punched him. After a series of varied jobs in different cities, Liam returned to Mullaghmore in 1998 and started once more to make his living as a seaman. Now he owned -and captained a charter boat in Mullaghmore.

In my conversation with Liam I felt there was a bear in the room which we were all pretending was not there: the IRA. I gently raised the subject of the girlfriend with IRA connections many years before. When Liam hesitated, Yvonne intervened to confirm that the girl-friend in question had been closely related to a local IRA boss. Liam seemed to relax as we talked on. His life appeared to have had its fair share of paradoxes, complexities and regrets. He painted a picture of difficulties, many of them overcome, and opportunities, some of them missed. There were parts I understood he simply had to keep private. I was in Ireland to heal and be healed. My desire was for that to be underpinned by a process of truth and reconciliation, but I accepted that it had to be allowed to take its time and I should not press him further. The next month I wrote to him and his wife: 'It meant a great deal to me to be able to sit, talk and learn so much from you both . . . The highpoint for me was hearing about [your son], and seeing the pride you both rightly take in him.' He replied:

This past year has been very good for me, with the new boat been launched and the season been very successful. But the two high points of the year was meeting both you and Philip, seeing you both again was truly marvellous. I really felt so much sorrow and sympathy for all members of your family for every minute of the past 25 years, and I never had the chance to express my feelings to you all. Your visits laid all that to rest. I suppose I, like you, was waiting for a form of closure also . . .

I reflected a lot after your visit on my own past. Looking back I now realise that the happiest moments in my life were as a child living in the Gate House, as a young man on Shadow V . . .[21]

Liam was one of the many men and women I met in Ireland that year who demonstrated a skill necessary for the success of their community. When he spoke, he did so with a sensitivity, mindful of the many claims on his loyalty and the views of the person with whom he was speaking. When I watched a television interview he gave in 1998 for a German documentary about the day of the bomb, he had described my grandfather in a clinical, detached way.[22]

The same documentary interviewed a Bundoran man. I had seen the interview years before, but after my Irish trips I watched it with new eyes. He spoke from behind the bar of a Bundoran pub which I had often driven past. His voice and face were animated with passion and anger as he spoke:

There has never been any English blood innocently spilt in this country. The only innocent blood that was ever spilt in this country was the Irish innocent blood. The people that caused it have been the English. They have been in our country for the last 829 years. And while they are here you will always have a war situation in this country. It was the same in 1979, it was a war situation. And while you have an occupation force in a country you will always have a war situation. And we want peace. Everybody wants peace but they want it with justice, and they want to decide their own destiny without any interference from the English. We in Ireland want to see our country free. When all over Irish people can decide their own destiny without any interference from England. So it's about time to decide the declaration to get out of our country, be it one year or however long it be, they get out of our country.

The film-maker later spoke to my father and told him that he had come away from the area shocked by the private views of many of the people he had interviewed. People had started by saying what a dreadful tragedy the bomb had been. However, after an hour or so, a change came over a good number of them and they explained that in the privacy of homes and pubs in the area there had been great celebration after the bomb. A number of interviewees asked him about the Second World War, and when they discovered that his father had been a soldier in the German Army, they asked if he did not gladly support the fact that his father had taken part in the war against the British. He told my father, 'At one pub a number of people . . . at the end of their talk, stood up and gave the Heil Hitler sign!'[23]

As a German journalist, the documentary-maker had glimpses of local undercurrents which I did not. However, the idea of overwhelming local support for the IRA is difficult to sustain. Despite the type of IRA statements which had long made clear that people should 'weigh up the political company' they kept, Florence Rowlette, for five years until 1973 assistant to the cook Molly Kennedy, arrived at the castle almost immediately after the bomb.[24] She had come, un-invited, from her home in Sligo to help with the cooking. That she had been retired for six years, had a heart condition and had not got her doctor's approval for her return to work, did not deter her. Others rallied too, including Catherine Doherty, who had managed the castle in August 1977 and arrived to help to clear bills, refusing payment for her work.

Further, in what might be seen as defiance of the IRA, both Protestant and Catholic members of the local community assembled on the grass by the harbour in Mullaghmore at six o'clock on the Sunday evening following the attack.* Here they held what they called a 'Service For Peace'. Years later my aunt told me, 'It was particularly brave as being held out in the open, the IRA could easily identify everyone taking part.'[25] Evidently uncowed, over three thousand people attended from a parish of about one thousand. Afterwards they filed into the adjacent convent to sign a

---

* The day before, London's *Evening News* had reported that the British-born organiser of a memorial service in Los Angeles, planned for that Sunday, had been threatened by IRA sympathisers.

book of condolences. Father Sean Kelly of Cliffoney, speaking from a platform hastily built by the villagers, told them, 'The family regret they cannot be here today but they send their thanks and love to you all for coming here and for your great kindness over the past week.'[26]

Undoubtedly the IRA commanded support in the area and some of those who chose not to join in the support were coerced or forced to move away. Restaurant owner Elizabeth Duffy, who had accompanied my father and me to Sligo Hospital in the ambulance, told me that she and her husband William had 'plenty of worries and plenty of threats'.[27] Each time an IRA hunger-striker in Northern Ireland was buried, Mullaghmore shopkeepers were told by the local IRA to close for half a day. Elizabeth told me, 'They came around and I just said, "No, absolutely not, I am not closing." I was the only one who said no. That didn't go down too well.' Later one of her neighbours rushed up and spluttered something about her house and 'they've painted it'. When she went to look she saw 'Scottish pigs go home' daubed over the walls. She stayed in Ireland for more than another ten years before eventually moving to Scotland.

After 1979 the IRA saw Mullaghmore as a rallying point for their supporters. Nearly four years after the attack, they held a march there to commemorate the 1981 deaths of Bobby Sands and his fellow hunger-strikers. A thousand people, mostly from Northern Ireland, attended and were accompanied by sixty Gardai. As they marched passed the castle they 'raised their fists and shouted "IRA, IRA, IRA" . . . Speakers included Joe McGowan, a former member of H-Blocks Committee in Mullaghmore, and Leitrim republican John Joe McGirl.'[28] He was the uncle of Francis McGirl who was acquitted of the bombing. If the visitors thought they were going to be welcomed, they were in for a surprise. Local hotels, shops and restaurants stayed closed and then suddenly the local doctor, Evelyn Flannagan, drove her car at the marchers, honking her horn. The march was not repeated.

January 2004 brought storms. In the depths of these Amanda agreed to accompany me on one of my trips to Classiebawn. I wanted to see it through her eyes and get her views and memories. After work one evening, we met at Heathrow and flew to Dublin in a blizzard, renting a four-wheel-drive car for the drive across Ireland in the dark. We stopped at Longford for soup and sandwiches in the hotel where we had habitually broken the journey in previous decades. We spent the night at a Sligo hotel, and next day at Classiebawn Amanda started to share her innermost memories and thoughts.

Leaving the castle behind us, we walked for two and a half hours on Roskeeragh Point, sitting and sheltering for a while against an ancient tumbledown wall and eating a snack. She told me that in the late 1970s when she had been in her early twenties, she had been aware of the catalogue of injustices committed in Ireland by generations of English. This had often made her feel uncomfortable, as if there had been an unseen barrier to us truly integrating into village life. I had been untouched by any such knowledge and therefore had had neither her grasp of the situation nor the feelings of unease which had accompanied it. Listening to her memories helped me see our former visits with new eyes and understand a little more the very different experience of Ireland which she had taken away. We circled back through the dunes and then through the weather-beaten little strip of trees that lay beneath the castle beside the drive. As I recorded in my journal:

> I had not set foot in here since the bomb, and suddenly the sights and sounds and smells from this spot of my childhood summers rushed up on me. I could almost hear the buzzing of flies and smell the soft cow pats that attracted them. In my mind's eye I could see the dew in the cobwebs that clung to the silvery, moss-speckled branches. I remembered the early morning mushrooms that we collected for Mrs Kennedy's frying pan. We passed a spot where Philip, Nick and I and our cousins had made a camp as children. I could not resist reminding Amanda to keep her eye out for the golf ball Nick had lost here before leaving for the harbour on the morning of the bomb.

> We emerged from the wood and stopped, leaning on the beautiful old stone wall that ran along its edge and up to the cattle grid, fifty yards from the front door. Looking at the castle Amanda said, 'It's so beautiful. I've looked at it so often but not as we are now', and we just stared and admired its features. I was happy and tired and mildly amused when Hugh Tunney appeared out of the front door, and failed to see us while obviously scanning the horizon,

mystified at how we could have disappeared for so long on such a bitterly cold January day. We waved at him and he climbed into his Mercedes and drove down assuming we didn't know where to find the hidden steps that were constructed into the stone wall. We could have found them with our eyes closed. Each day we had spent here as children we had invested with madcap energy and laser-beam intensity, and the sights, sounds, smells, feels and tastes of the place were hardwired into our heads. Classiebawn was in our DNA.

Amanda and I had precious few minutes of daylight left. We drove down to the headland where *Shadow V* had exploded. We walked up to the cliff edge and Amanda produced two pieces of stone she had brought from her home in England, a place Nicky, Grandpapa and Granny never knew. She had shown them to me earlier and I now took one, happy to have a role to play in the ritual we would now perform. Amanda couldn't bring her special ones home, but she could bring bits from her home to this special place. I took the stone and shivering in the cold wind I said, 'When Nick and I used to go to sleep, I said to him, "Goodnight Nick." "Night Tim; sleep well." "Sleep well; God bless." "God bless."' I threw the stone high into the air and lost sight of it. A couple of seconds passed, and a good way out it splashed into the sea. Amanda said, 'I'm not sure I'm going to be able to throw mine that far', and she threw hers, and it splashed down far beneath us. The wind was blowing hard, and the splashes made no noise, and the ripples were quickly lost in the fading light and gently moving sea.[29]

At the end of this trip I wrote:

I looked around the little commuter turbo prop sitting in Sligo's airport (1 ¼ hours late this morning) and smelt through its open door the salt air coming off the rocks and sea a hundred yards off the end of the runway. The sand dunes a few hundred yards away would, just a few months ago, have made me feel I might turn around and see my brothers and sisters as children at any moment . . . But that thought never entered my head. I simply thought, 'What a beautiful spot.'[30]

21

RESCUE REVISITED

Brian Best was one of the two doctors who helped save my parents. As I rang his doorbell near Belfast at the end of 2003, I wondered if he would be the heroic figure I had attached to his name over the decades. He lived up to the stature with a relaxed and informal confidence. I spent that December evening with him and his wife Heather in an unhurried flow of memories and reflections. We pored over photograph albums and cine films, now transferred to videotape, taken in a late-1950s Mullaghmore that looked as if it came from another era, the silent, jerky footage showing cars, clothes, haircuts and boats that were enjoyably dated.

Brian had first come to Mullaghmore in the late 1970s, introduced by Heather who continued to be known there as Miss Craig for some time after their marriage on 7 September 1979. Brian had arrived in the village that year after a draining summer. He had just finished a series of exams; his father had died three months earlier; and the visit offered him the chance to unwind and recharge prior to the wedding.

Brian was an identical twin, his brother Derek being vice-principal of a college in England. One day, Brian told me, he had been staying with Derek when Derek's young daughter had come into breakfast and climbed onto Brian's lap; delighted, he had put his arms around her. After a few minutes, when Brian spoke to someone, the little girl looked at him, realised he was not her father, shrieked and fled. Hearing Brian describe this made me think of the fun I would have had with Nick's children.

My journal:

Brian's account led me to believe that on the day of the bomb he had been very assertive and had 'led' those around him, but he certainly didn't claim that, he gently steered me away from that idea. But the facts he gave me had a highly credible ring to them, and when put together, painted a picture of him having been a leader in the minutes following the explosion.[1]

Brian's detailed account of the day culminated with him watching a small child playing in a pool of my grandfather's blood that had collected in the sand. I wrote:

I had got what I needed: a shocking and disgusting image from the scene of the butchery. The fog that had hung for years around my conception of Grandpapa's death was suddenly and brutally penetrated by this spike of information. It helped in the same way that, on discovering you have done yourself a physical injury, you are relieved to find the object that caused the injury. You are better equipped to understand the situation. Horrified but spellbound, I was also pleased. Brian had proved himself a generous man, because it would have been easier for him to stick to vague generalisations, despite my request for the truth, even the upsetting bits.

In describing the survivors Brian drew my attention to the way my father had moved himself from one boat to another without complaint. It was only later that Brian discovered that both my father's legs were broken. Brian was astounded he had been able to move, and said that when later he read my father had had combat experience in the Second World War, he had wondered if this explained his calm endurance and physical courage. My father had briefly spoken a handful of times about the day when he had been injured fighting one Saturday morning in September 1944, three months after the D-Day landings in northern France. He was then an infantry lieutenant. His regiment, the Coldstream Guards, had been severely depleted and he was the only platoon commander left in his squadron, the others having been killed or injured. He was talking to his sergeant on the edge of the village of Heppen when a flash from a wood drew his attention and he saw a Panzer tank which had just fired at them. He shouted but the shell blew the sergeant to pieces and left a gash in my father's left arm. Taking the morphine from his officer's medical kit, he numbed the pain of his wounded men, leaving none for himself. Later, his own pain became almost unbearable. His sergeant major rallied the company and they successfully fought their way into the village ahead, leaving my father to be evacuated to a hospital in England. He later rejoined his regiment on the Rhine and started the fight across Germany.

Brian had received Christmas cards each year from my parents; but true to form he had not kept them. He was not a 'hoarder'. His approach to the cards was the same as to his memories of the bomb: the essence he stripped out and carried in his head; the rest he simply let go. His gift to me is that essence, that I too might let go of what is the accompanying chaff.

Brian told me that while he was busy with the wounded, he was 'very much working in the mode that I'd done over so many years of bombs'. After the activity died down, he went up from the harbour to Heather and found she was with Mary Maxwell. 'I was seeing the raw emotion of Mary having lost her son, that brought in the raw emotion of me having lost my father three months earlier and my father's memory crowded in on me then. After that it was anger, frustration, despair and almost embarrassment at being classed alongside these killers, being Irish, and whether you call it Northern Irish or Southern Irish, it doesn't matter. Almost a feeling of shame that you are in the same country.'[2]

On the same trip to Northern Ireland, I called on Brian Best's colleague Richard Wallace, who also lived near Belfast. We started talking over tea at 4:30 and did not finish until after midnight.

In describing the medical triage that he and Brian had hastily improvised in the harbour, Richard said, 'It wasn't a big deal from our point of view. It was something that we'd experienced before, but it was a heck of a difference doing it in your swimming trunks on a lovely sunny day in the sea, to having your white coat on in a Casualty department with nurses who will run and get you whatever bit of equipment you instantly asked for.'[3]

Apart from his account, I learned that at Norton and Penny's wedding he had found my parents waiting for him at the reception in their wheelchairs with a copy of the recently published book *Eighty Years in Pictures* about my grandfather. They also handed him a copy for Brian, who was unable to get to the wedding. When Richard came out of the reception he found Prince Charles at his elbow. He did not speak to him because he did not want to upset him by talking about what had happened in Mullaghmore.

Richard showed me some old Christmas cards from my parents. The 1979 card had a note from my father providing his phone number and urging him to call next time he was in London. My father was a shy man and it was unlike him to have added such an emphatic note. When Richard did call him, they had a pleasant conversation but it did not seem to lead in any particular direction. What, I wondered, had my father been looking for? He did not choose to talk about the bomb often, yet he wanted something from Richard, more so than from the other rescuers. In my father's archives lay the answer. He wanted to know more about what his mother had said after she had been left with Richard in the Pierces' boat. Evidently in need of information, my father asked Richard to set down what he could remember. Richard replied:

Following the transfer of yourself and Lady Brabourne to Brian Best's boat, I stayed with your mother. She was quite conscious as we made for the harbour and in answer to my questions she told me that her forearm and hip were painful. Once she had been made as comfortable as was possible considering the circumstances, she asked about Lord Mountbatten, yourself and Lady Brabourne. She was, however, most concerned about your sons and repeatedly asked about 'the twins'.

On the journey ashore she was very weak and I had to support her head in my arms. While our journey was slow, the motion of the boat undoubtedly caused some considerable discomfort to your mother, yet her thoughts were always for others and not for herself. She never complained about her own injuries and perhaps it was this which impressed me the most, making a young man feel very humble in the presence of such a dignified lady.

I am unable to recall any further details of the conversation, however the Dowager Lady Brabourne made an impression on me which defies my ability to commit to paper. I shall never forget her.[4]

The first people on the scene of the attack in 1979 were Charles Pierce and his wife of two months, Kathryn. When I wrote to them in October 2003, Kathy replied that my letter had evoked very sad memories but that they would be willing to meet if that helped my process of healing. Charlie wrote: 'I have always seen our role in its most simple terms as that of "helpful bystander".'[5] When we met for dinner at their home, I found I was able to understand more of what had gone on that day, and weave what they had seen and heard into the chronology that was emerging. The grey areas were progressively being slimmed and restricted by the cross-section of accounts. As the first on the scene they and their brother-in-law William Wilkinson had seen things no one else had. It was from them I discovered that my parents had been face-down in the water when they were pulled out.

Ever since the bomb, the slightest whiff of diesel oil had made my mind spin back to the minutes following the explosion. In meeting Kathy, I discovered that I was not alone in this.* She told me, 'It's not significant any more to me but for years afterwards the smell would just bring the whole memory back.'[6] After her account, Kathy looked desolate. 'There's something that still hasn't quite healed over for me, probably will never quite heal over. Talking definitely helps though, doesn't it?'

The accounts of Charlie and Kathy were vivid up to the arrival of the doctors, Brian Best and Richard Wallace. At that point, it seemed, a fog descended on their memories. Perhaps with the arrival of the doctors they succumbed to delayed shock. They had difficulty recalling almost anything of the subsequent journey to the harbour. Only one moment stood out. As they entered the harbour they saw Paul Maxwell's

---

* I later discovered that my sister Joanna experienced a similar feeling whenever smelling diesel oil, a result of the smell that clung to the hair and bodies of my parents and me in hospital.

friend Rachel Johnson standing on the pier. She looked 'wild' and was calling out to boats, 'Have you seen Paul?'

Towards the end of our conversation Kathy said, 'I've actually found it very difficult to talk about the whole thing. When we talk about it with people it's normally Charlie who does the talking', and she left it to him to close. 'In it all,' he said, 'I think we both have a Christian faith. You believe there is a greater power at work and you're just a part of it rather than having to bear the responsibility yourself.' He sounded regretful. 'It's hard to grasp the horror of the situation, sitting in an armchair: the sense of shock; and compromise; and also the futility of being there with such an inadequate boat. We were very badly equipped and you look back and feel that you stumbled.'[7] I had assembled enough information from others to know that, far from stumbling, he had reacted instantaneously and with his wife and their brother-in-law had saved my parents. Afterwards I wrote to them: 'Your tasks were carried out effectively, quickly and quietly and for twenty-four years I have been reaping an hourly dividend.'[8]

I had met the Pierces's brother-in-law William Wilkinson the month before. Strangely his name had not been familiar, whereas the names Wood-Martin, Pierce, Best and Wallace were etched into my mind. Despite this, our meeting at his home in Northern Ireland felt strangely like a reunion. His wife Ruth, the sister of Kathryn, made coffee while Billy spread out letters, photographs and cuttings about the bomb and our family, collected as the years went by. I wrote in my journal that it seemed:

that our lives tangled on the day of the bomb in such a way that, long after one might have expected, our brief coming-together to have faded from memory we still felt connected. To meet Billy, whose name I hadn't known a few weeks earlier, made me feel like meeting a long-lost relative. He was also entertaining with the ability to tell a story with a direct intensity that was gripping. I turned on my recorder and, unlike any other person I interviewed, he responded as if I had thrown a switch inside him. He suddenly became intense and focused, and he delivered a straightforward account of everything he could remember. It was as if an electric charge passed into him as he described the moment of the explosion. At this point he looked shocked, horrified, lost almost, as if he was seeing it again. He stopped briefly once or twice, for his emotions. He acted out the movements he made on the day with his arms and I could almost see him pulling Mummy, Granny and Daddy into the boat, and holding Grandpapa's body . . . His account suddenly dropped off at that point. Until then he had been a man possessed by the scene inside his head. When he finished it was as if the electricity went out of him and he was exhausted. His body sagged, his voice dropped in pitch and volume and he could recall only patchy and generalised scenes.[9]

Billy said, 'It was an experience that nobody would want to pass again, to witness it. It will be in our minds for the rest of our days.'[10]

Billy Wilkinson had passed my grandfather into the arms of Edward Dawson, another name which meant nothing to me. I arranged to meet him at his office in Northern Ireland and followed him to his home where we talked at length. After the attack he never returned to Mullaghmore with his caravan, nor did he proceed with a plan to build a bungalow there, feeling that the peace and beauty of the place had been spoiled for him and his family. He told me that he had found a life jacket floating on the sea after the attack and that it was now in his garage; would I like it back? When he handed it to me, ponging of diesel oil, I recognised it instantly and thought of Arran jumpers and cream crackers and Bovril and the cabin of *Shadow V*. I quietly put it on the passenger seat of my small hire car and drove away thinking about what I had learned. My thoughts were interrupted by a loud buzzing noise. I thought it might be coming from the radio when suddenly a large bumble bee crawled sleepily from the life jacket beside me. I was driving at speed with traffic all around. With one hand on the wheel I reached across the passenger seat and managed to wind down the window. After a while the bee staggered into the air and was carried away in the breeze. Its disappearance brought a smile to my face, its liberation echoing the feeling I got each time I met one of the people who had been involved in our rescue.

I returned home to London and spent a happy weekend with Isabella and our children. As usual, on the Sunday evening I was the last to go to bed. Before doing so, I remembered the life jacket and stood by the dustbin contemplating throwing it away. Instead an impulse led me downstairs to the basement of our home and here I washed it down in a big sink at the back of our kitchen. As I removed the oil and gunge, salt and stains from the life jacket, its surface pockmarked, peppered and punctured by the shrapnel and splinters from the explosion, just as our bodies had been, I had a strange but therapeutic feeling that I was washing down human skin. The life jacket came up a satisfying yellow and I tucked it away quietly into a cupboard along with bric-a-brac where nobody would notice it. When we moved house the following year, it made it into the pantechnicon with us and ended up in the cellar of our new home, fodder for a spring clean one day, no doubt.

For three months after the attack, my father pieced together an outline of the events and on 9 December 1979 at his home in Kent he set these down in an eight-page account accompanied by a sketch which he drew showing our positions in the boat at the moment of the explosion. To help my research, he handed this to me in November 2003. When his account reached the part where he was carried to a waiting ambulance, he wrote:

> I was astonished and delighted to see Timmy lying in the ambulance and I was laid on the second bunk. I asked him if he had seen Nicky, but he did not reply. He was in a terrible condition but seemed very pleased and relieved to hear me talking. He was lying on his front, with both eyes swollen very badly, and I am told kept calling out 'Daddy, speak to me, speak to me', so I must have been unconscious part of the time in the ambulance on the way to Sligo, which took about twenty minutes. A nurse . . . called Elizabeth Duffy travelled with us and the ambulance attendant, and I asked her what had happened to Dickie and she told me that he was dead. I had really known this already so it only confirmed my worst fears. No one was able to give me any news of Nicky. I asked after Paul and was told that he was dead.

At that point I did not know anything about Elizabeth Duffy, and it was then that I sought her out. She was born in Dublin and lived in

County Kerry and Scotland. She gave up being a nurse after the birth of her third child in 1975, and the following year she and her second husband William bought a property in Mullaghmore and opened the Ceol-Na-Mara restaurant. Most of their business came from the German tourists who visited in the summer, and they soon found they loved the new start in life they made there, with their daughter and the two sons from Elizabeth's first marriage. Two more daughters followed. 'It was just a great place until the tragedy happened. The best way to describe it is: if you have a brand-new car and you really love it and somebody bangs into it, it is never the same. For an awful lot of people even now it's not the same.'[11]

Elizabeth Duffy told me the atmosphere in their restaurant on the day of the attack was 'unbelievable, terrible, dreadful'. As usual they had many German customers.

> They were devastated; they couldn't wait to get away. There was absolutely no way I could think of cooking or doing anything. Then the police from Sligo asked if they could use our house as their headquarters for the investigations and they persuaded me to continue with the function that night because it wasn't just Makem and Clancy to cancel, there were other bookings.

Elizabeth asked her bed-and-breakfast clients to move to other lodgings and she let the Garda use the bedrooms to change. 'Some of them went out as walkers to mingle in the Pier Head Hotel. The entertainment went on that night but there was Special Branch on different tables. I think they stayed at our place for a couple of weeks.' The attack was 'the end of our business', according to Elizabeth. 'We relied on the Germans and they stopped coming after 1979.'

The Swiss couple Robert and Christiane Graf had settled in Bundoran the same year as Elizabeth and William Duffy. I tracked them down, and Christiane told me that on the day of the attack, coming back into harbour, she 'came to' and became 'very, very angry. What was very much in my mind was that those people which do such things should see for themselves what they have done. What does it solve? I was incredibly sour.'[12] Her husband was visibly upset by the memories he described of using a large pair of gloves to help haul Paul's body into the boat, much of his clothing blown off by the blast. He had felt the same anger as his wife, and on getting home they had not felt like doing anything other than sitting 'numb' in the back garden of their large Georgian house. 'The Irish we had contact with were all disgusted,' said Christiane. 'When you live amongst them you know the undertones and the way they put things, you can read what they are saying. They were really upset and angry at this horrible, senseless act.'

The week before Christmas 2003, I sat by the fire with David and Susie Dugdale at their home in Yorkshire. We spoke about the attack and later I wrote in my journal that he said:

> It was a life-changing experience because it changed your prior-
> ities.' He paused. 'Of course, in my case, it didn't actually change
> much;' another pause. 'But that's because I'm not nearly well
> enough organised.' There's something about this man you just want
> to hug. He's the sort of man you'd want to come and be with you
> if someone had just detonated a bomb under you and half your
> family.[13]

When Susie spoke about their arrival at the castle five days after the bomb, and the state of shock in which they found the family, her words set me thinking. Later I wrote: 'The family were taking heavy blows on a minute-by-minute basis with no sedation, and no sense of having taken any of the physical injuries themselves. That comfort was available only to Mum, Dad and me.'

I spent the night at David and Susie's house, and next morning, having watched the sun rise, I crossed the valley and called on Jamie and Sylvia Crathorne. After a morning spent raiding their memories and files, I caught an almost empty train to London. As the English countryside rumbled past, my thoughts lengthened and finally settled on one story. After their first two children were born, Jamie and Sylvia had tried unsuccessfully for a third. Eventually Sylvia's gynaecologist recommended medication but they decided against this and another five years passed without a pregnancy. Arriving at Classiebawn after the bomb and seeing the way my brothers and sisters were supporting each other proved decisive. Sylvia told me, 'After that first evening I felt very strongly that I'd love to have another child.' Jamie continued, 'We talked about it at Classiebawn and we said, "We are going back to the doctor."' Before they could do so there occurred what Jamie called 'something of a miracle'. Sylvia was taken ill in London and was rushed off to hospital. 'They kept me in overnight and wouldn't allow me home till they had the results of tests. When they said "pregnant" I said, "Don't be silly!."'[14] When their second daughter Katharine was born the next year, for a middle name they chose Nicola in memory of Nicholas.

22

HOSPITAL REVISITED

'We will call them Micky and Pat. They are people just like anyone else: they are born, they die, they suffer,' Tony Heenan told staff following our admission into hospital. It was a highly unusual situation and he was a highly unusual doctor. In effect, the whole family came under his care, both in hospital and at Classiebawn, over the next fifteen days and nights. By the time we left, he had become a friend in whose advice and judgement we had complete trust.

On my return to Sligo in 2003 he was one of the first people I sought, only to find he was working in England. I arranged to see him when he next returned home, and in the meantime I met one of the nurses who had looked after us in Intensive Care. Mary Lowry told me:

> He opened the unit, he was in charge and he ran a tight ship. He has a great brain, tremendous for making diagnoses very, very quickly, no messing, excellent. And he worked hard; he wanted everything perfect. He could be very cross sometimes but I was never afraid of him because he was too fatherly for that; we were his babies really. We used to call him 'Daddy Bear'.[1]

Tony Heenan was thirty-two in 1969, when he arrived in Sligo with his wife Mary and their children, having trained in Ireland, England,

Northern Ireland and the United States. The west of Ireland was relatively undeveloped at the time, and he was dismayed at the lack of facilities and staff at the then two-storey 1940s building to which he was posted. In 1970 their son Patrick was born with severe disabilities. Tony might have soon left Sligo had it not been for Patrick's condition and his need for continuous care. As a result of the ten years he and his colleagues spent building up the hospital, in 1979 we received a standard of care and expertise that was in every way world-class and without doubt saved my mother's life, and probably mine and my father's. Patrick died in 1985 never having learned to recognise anyone. Tony was then working in a hospital in Riyadh, Saudi Arabia, and immediately returned home, devastated.

One Sunday evening in November 2003, I arrived at Tony and Mary's house. I had seen Tony briefly in London ten years before, and the moment I was with him again I felt the deep bond of affection and respect that he always inspired in me. We sat talking until past midnight. He was soon explaining that on the day of the bomb he had wanted the hospital staff to keep their feet on the ground and not be affected by the drama that was unfolding around them. He admitted, however, that there were times when even he felt the pressure. 'It was the arrival of the Queen's representative at me bloody door that fazed me,' he explained. 'I was going on gently up till then and it was at that time I realised the kind of political significance of the whole thing.' His job was made easier by what he called 'a couple of good allies'. One was a Sister in the Intensive Care Unit, Maureen Gateley. 'She was a very level-headed solid citizen, a good professional and a great sounding board for me. Ask her something and she'd say in her sharp Donegal accent, "Of course, what else would you do?" No prevarication, no long-winded discussion; she was a great help.' Tony also paid tribute to his anaesthetics partner in 1979, Jim Nolan, whose role, Tony felt, was forgotten at the time. 'Jim would say everything I would say but he would say it with a smile. He was a very diplomatic kind of a guy and he was the best partner I ever had because he got on with the rest of the work in the hospital. He said, "You started it, you finish it", and that's how I came to manage the whole thing.'

It was not long before Tony and his colleagues ran into their first criticism. 'There were politically motivated people who were whinging, "There is far too much being done for these people." I took those guys on full-frontal by saying, "They haven't had any damn thing that any patient would not get from us in this hospital." That stopped them in their tracks because it was correct. I was so glad.' Some were angry that physicians from another hospital had been let into Sligo General. The opposition did not stop at the hospital door. Arriving at home late one night, he picked up the phone to hear a voice say, 'We're watching you, be careful.' He replied, 'Fuck off', and put the phone down.

The medical staff in Sligo were evidently as dedicated to saving us as the rescuers in Mullaghmore had been. Tony said, 'There was a feeling that "some of us have done these people badly and we must make some kind of restitution". Now, it wouldn't be expressed in those terms but that's exactly what it was.'[2]

Next day Tony and I walked into Sligo General Hospital. A vast new building had been constructed beside the old hospital, dwarfing it and covering the car park from which the helicopters had taken us away in 1979. As Tony led me in, he spotted a nurse he knew. Clearly happy to see him, she stopped to talk. He said to her, 'There's somebody I would like you to meet. This is a patient from 1979 you might remember: Nicholas Knatchbull.' I avoided bursting into laughter and shook her warmly by the hand. It seemed surprisingly natural, even after so long, for Nick's name and mine to be mixed up.

I noted in my journal:

Tony took me to the oldest part of the hospital on the first floor where a microbiology lab now exists. He showed me exactly where the Intensive Care Unit had been and I was able to map out the position of my bed. I was amazed to learn from Tony that it was in her bed beside mine that Granny had died. I have no recollection of her being in the ICU but found myself looking out of the window beside which she ended her life's journey, and thinking what a small and claustrophobic spot to end a life that had taken in such a panoramic sweep of the world and the twentieth century. I felt very close to her and very pleased that

Tony had not ventilated her and turned her into a pitiful creature whose machine Dad would have had to authorise the doctors to turn off days later.[3]

I had a sense of her life coming full circle; my grandmother had survived the Troubles following the First World War only to die in their return sixty years later. One of her friends later wrote: 'Fate decreed that the daughter of the Marquess of Sligo, after a life of public service and residence in other countries, should die at Sligo.'[4] I thought how fortunate my grandfather was to have gone out like a light, his last moments supremely happy. My grandmother suffered trauma and pain and succumbed slowly to death, aware of the butchery around her. Since I had started to piece together her final twenty-four hours, I had come to realise how desperately I had missed her and the opportunity to say goodbye. Writing in my journal, I had a sudden vision of her putting Nick and me as small boys on a train in London for our return to our Oxford boarding school.

> The idea of Granny dressing in fur to take us to the school train at Paddington has just made me shake and howl with laughter; at the end of which I broke into tears. I could turn around and fully expect to see Granny sitting in the chair beside mine.
>
> Tony showed me a window that looked over a grassy patch where he had spotted a journalist and a photographer. The Sister, Maureen Gateley, had snapped the venetian blinds down to frustrate them.[5]

I felt very lucky when I learned that our medical records were still in the hospital. From these I started putting together a detailed picture of our time there. I wrote:

> Sister Gateley writes at 1pm, 75 minutes after the bomb, that I was conscious on admission to ICU.
>
> This makes me think of Nicky and how, at about 1pm or 1.30pm, he was being found about 2 feet beneath the surface just to the north by a few yards, and just inshore of the floating wreckage of *Shadow V*. I was not capable of even missing him then I suppose,

being in and out of consciousness, but oh my God how it makes me cry today to think of his little body in the water, uncared for, while I was being looked after, 20 miles away, my life's path diverging from his irrevocably but without my knowledge. It is impossible, impossible, impossible.

Assembling the facts made me realise what a miraculous combination of factors allowed my mother to live. In just fifty minutes she was found, pulled from the water, stabilised by two doctors with experience of bomb injuries, taken ashore, tended to by nurses, and transported to a world-class Intensive Care Unit supervised by a doctor whose training in Northern Ireland had given him vital knowledge of her type of blast-lung injury. Remove any one of those factors and it is likely she would have died.

The records confirmed that I had been unaware of Nick's death on the day his body was sent to England. In my journal I wrote:

Nicky's body had breathed for 14 ¾ years mostly within a few yards of mine. Dead, he had been brought to the morgue in this hospital, a matter of yards from the ICU in which I was being treated. When he was taken away for burial, I now learn that everyone was able to see him depart on live TV and yet I didn't know he was going. I didn't even know he was dead. I remember the days and nights in that ward and I resent not having been compos mentis enough not to have seen my Nicky off. And that's what I'm doing now.

My hospital records show that I spent three nights in the Intensive Care Unit. An entry written in the Eye Unit on the night of Thursday 30 August states: 'Transferred from ICU at 6:30pm.' I asked Tony if I could go to the Eye Unit and we set off together, climbing stairs to the second floor which had housed the ophthalmic department in 1979. I recognised the corridor we were walking down and felt myself approaching the single room I had occupied. Suddenly the corridor came to a disappointing end. New walls had gone up and ahead of me was a door with a glazed panel. I peered inside to find a darkened store room, and as I did so memories came darting back. This was the place where Joanna had told me that Nick was dead. At my father's request she had done so with my aunt in the room. Years later she told me, 'It was typical Dad; he didn't want me to do it on my own. It was interesting that he said Aunt Pammy rather than Amanda. In a way, he was right because I would have worried more about Amanda – and worrying about you was quite enough.'[6]

My father trusted Joanna's judgement and his trust was well placed. She broke the news to me with a blend of directness and gentleness which was just right. She remembers looking into my face and seeing 'complete shock; complete desperation; just a flash as though it was the worst thing that could ever have happened to you, which of course it was . . .' Sitting next to me, holding my hand, she could tell that I had never considered the possibility.

It was in 2003 after one of my trips to Sligo that Joanna, now a trained psychotherapist, first talked to me about that evening. She said:

> I have always felt bad that I just left you after a very short time. 'Sorry Tim, Nicky's dead. There, there. Night, night.' Looking back now, that's what it felt like, which just goes to show I really wasn't functioning. I think it took so much of my resources to tell you, I had none left to think about what was going to happen to you after. I could only just think about what was going to happen to me. I knew I was going to have to go back to Classiebawn and lie awake thinking how I told you and how you looked. That's why I feel so awful.

I was astonished to hear her speak in these terms and immediately told her that I had never felt she had left me too early. I had wanted to curl up in my bed alone and cry until I fell asleep. When I told her to wipe the feelings of regret and guilt from her mind, she said it was a huge relief. I left her house feeling soothed but also amazed. I was discovering just how much healing had gone undone through the years.

The next time I returned to the hospital was in 2004. Amanda was with me and she told me that she had been waiting quietly in the corridor outside while Joanna had broken the news to me. As they had left me, she had felt they were making a mistake. In the same situation today, she told me, she would have stayed through the night. But that was the mature mother of three children speaking in 2004. In 1979 none of my siblings was married and none had children; none had been through an intense bereavement; none had been through a trauma of the sort we were now facing. They were under enormous strain and in considerable danger, dealing with a major crisis in a foreign country with poor communications while being shunted around in army helicopters and Garda cars. I wrote to Amanda that, far from doing poorly in 1979, her extraordinary gifts had served me well and she should never forget that because I never did.

Sitting with Tony at his home, I had talked about Nick and my need to revisit the circumstances of his death in order to find peace. A short while later he said:

> Anybody that has had serious loss is lucky if they have a spiritual dimension because there is nothing else. And if you don't believe me, you listen to the people today who want revenge, not justice. You hear it almost every day: that somebody 'doesn't get enough time in jail'. That's revenge, not justice.[7]

Everything his colleagues told me about Tony indicated a man who was kind at a personal level. What I had not understood was that he viewed kindness as an integral part of the practice of medicine. His decision not to prolong my grandmother's life by intubating her and placing her on a ventilator had been informed by a number of considerations, one of which was his conviction that to have stretched her misery out by a few more days would have amounted to little more than 'cruelty'. He told me that practising in this way today would be impossible. He evidently felt isolated in his ethos. 'I ruffled a few feathers recently at a faculty meeting in Dublin,' he went on. 'I said: One of the things I miss in hospital is *kindness*. Kindness comes from gentleness; gentleness comes from strength; and strength comes from discipline and work. That's about the size of it.'

From the first news of the attack, Tony knew family would start arriving from Classiebawn:

I was expecting the worst. I was expecting people who were spaced out and totally alien because, dealing with some of the famous and better-off people from around here, a lot of the time they project themselves like that, or *are* like that. I don't mind saying it now, twenty years later, when I first came across the girls Amanda and Joanna I said to myself, 'Christ! We've two right flighty socialites. Now Jesus, what'll we do with them?' Wrong! Wrong, wrong, wrong. And very glad to be wrong I was. In the whole thing Amanda and Joanna were stars; they were brilliant. They were *focused*, they were *persistent* and they were *reliable*. I was star-struck; I never met two people quite like them. [He paused.] I'd be happy enough with this description of our experience: we met these people that had dignity without arrogance and style without pomposity; real people with real feelings and real gratitude. That's it. That took us apart a bit.

At the end of many hours of talking, he finished pensively. 'It's a terrible way to put it but I would not have missed it for the world.'

Travelling home, I thought about his final comment and realised that although the attack had placed enormous strain on the hospital, it had also helped its development, and possibly even provided a tipping point. The Irish government was acutely aware that the attack had been a diplomatic disaster for the nation, made worse by the sluggish response of the state. Sligo General had been the notable exception. When the international press had arrived, Tony had invited them in and provided an office. They reported what they saw: a superb medical team saving lives. After the helicopters flew us out and the last of the press corps departed, the government's commitment to the hospital was vividly underscored by a visit from the future Prime Minister, Charles Haughey, who was then Minister for Health. Nearly twenty-five years later Tony Heenan told me, 'I haven't forgotten it. He came to thank the staff for dealing well with the crisis. He said, "We will give you a hospital worthy of your talents."' Over the next few years Sligo General Hospital received unprecedented investment. Plans were approved for a five-year building programme from which an eight-storey colossus emerged, housing a range of new departments and a greatly increased staff. Much of this had been approved years before but, as Tony Heenan told me, the 1979 crisis did no harm in helping the hospital's upward trajectory. Suddenly I grasped what had escaped me until then: that despite the horror of the bomb, a great deal of good had come to the people of Sligo, and this was the lasting legacy of Tony and his colleagues.

23

TRIAL: THE PEOPLE VERSUS THOMAS MCMAHON AND FRANCIS MCGIRL

A week after the attack a Garda superintendent described it as 'the most serious crime committed since the foundation of the republic'.[1] The Irish state needed a swift resolution of the domestic and international turmoil in which it found itself. Nine weeks after the superintendent spoke, a high-speed trial opened, lasting just fourteen days. As a boy I had read the newspaper reports of the trial but my grasp of it had been vague. In 2003 I read a transcript of the trial for the first time.

As Thomas McMahon and Francis McGirl sat in the dock in Dublin on Monday 5 November 1979, prosecution lawyers produced Admiralty Chart Number 2702 to show the spot where the bomb had exploded. My grandfather would have taken great pleasure that the chart had been produced by his beloved Royal Navy.

The Troubles of the 1970s had produced trial after trial at which juries had been intimidated by the paramilitary organisations. In 1972 the Irish government had responded by re-opening the Special Criminal Court in Dublin, in which the jury was replaced by a panel of three judges. Thomas McMahon and Francis McGirl were tried by Ireland's Chief Justice, Liam Hamilton, and two colleagues.

The trial got under way with Edward Comyn, Senior Counsel for the prosecution, outlining the case against the men and stating that the evidence he would rely on was largely circumstantial. He planned to show that *Shadow V* had been blown up by gelignite which had been hidden on board sometime after five in the afternoon of Sunday 26 August. He would show that a yellow Ford Cortina had been in the area and that the two defendants could be linked to this car. He would then show that they had driven it to a nearby town and exchanged it for a red Ford Escort in which they had been arrested by chance. On their clothes were traces of gelignite and, on one defendant, paint from *Shadow* V. In their shoes was sand of the same type found at the harbour slipway in Mullaghmore. Having outlined his case, Edward Comyn brought into the court a series of witnesses who described the Mullaghmore area, *Shadow* V and the scene that had unfolded on the morning of the attack.

Detective Garda Kevin Henry described the moment of the explosion as seen from his vantage point on the cliff tops close by. The doctors, Brian Best and Richard Wallace, described their role in bringing survivors ashore, as did Richard Wood-Martin. Retired Irish Army officer, Commandant William 'Gus' Mulligan, described bringing the body of Paul Maxwell ashore, and Sergeant Patrick Joseph Ward described identifying my grandfather in the harbour after he had been pronounced dead by Dr Wallace.

Reporting from the court was strictly controlled and, while journalists were allowed to report the proceedings, no pictures were allowed. A cartoonist was expelled and his drawings confiscated after he was noticed sketching key characters in the court for one of the American television networks.[2]

Garda James Lohan described stopping the men in a red Ford Escort, registered LZO 915, at a routine checkpoint in Granard. His suspicions were first aroused when Francis McGirl became extremely nervous. When they told him a story which did not make sense he became even more suspicious. At the local police station two hundred and fifty yards away, Gardai made enquiries for nearly two hours, keeping the men in the Garda station but not arresting them until 11:50am. They would later find out that *Shadow* V had exploded at about 11:45am. Garda Michael Hughes, from the Special Detective Unit in Dublin, testified that when he had arrived in Granard and saw Francis McGirl, he had immediately been able to bring to an end his pretence of being Patrick Rehill, a man whose appearance was known to him. Francis McGirl had then admitted his identity and provided his account for where he had spent the twenty-four hours prior to his arrest. It did not include any visit to the Mullaghmore area. He said the man in the car with him was a hitchhiker whom he had picked up shortly before he was arrested and that he did not know his name.

Sergeant Thomas Dunne, also from the Special Detective Unit, testified that he had been in the room while Francis McGirl was smoking and going through the account he had given of his movements that day. At 1:40 on the Tuesday morning, the day after the attack, he suddenly jumped up and shouted, 'I put no bomb on the boat.' The detective had cautioned him, at which he had clenched a fist and said, 'Fuck you.'³ When the detective wrote down what had been said, Francis McGirl refused to sign.

During his testimony, the detective said that the Gardai were aware that Thomas McMahon and Patrick Rehill, the pseudonym being used by Francis McGirl, were known bomb-makers. This brought about an interruption to the trial lasting three hours. The Chief Justice ruled that this statement was extremely prejudicial to both defendants and if it had been made in another court the jury would have been discharged. He banned the press from reporting on the statement and allowed the trial to continue on the basis that the judges had the necessary experience, knowledge and skill to put the comments out of their minds.

Detective Inspector Michael Canavan from the Garda Technical Bureau in Dublin described the alibi Francis McGirl gave and his account of his movements in the twenty-four hours preceding his arrest. He said that he had got up at 11am and made tea for himself and read the papers. He had dinner and at about 2pm went to a sports event in Mohill, a small town twelve miles from his home. After a tug-of-war competition, he visited some pubs in Mohill and then went to a pub in Ballinamore belonging to his uncle, John Joe McGirl. At 9:30pm he met the real Patrick Rehill and asked to borrow his car. Patrick Rehill gave him keys to his brother's car, a red Ford Escort. McGirl was only going to borrow it to go home to change but went back to the pubs in Mohill. Later he 'got sick' on a bottle of whisky and fell asleep. He woke at 7am on the Monday and drove to Longford to buy a car. When he got there the garages were closed. Driving on, he went through Edgeworthstown and then, as he drove towards Granard, he saw a hitchhiker. He picked him up and was stopped by a guard as he drove through Granard. He gave his name as Pat Rehill because he was borrowing the car.

Francis McGirl's solicitor from Mohill, Kevin P. Kilraine, took the stand and, amongst other things, said that two Gardai from County Leitrim had told his client that they were protecting him from being beaten by other officers.

Detective Garda John P. (Jack) Reynolds from Mullingar told the court that Thomas McMahon had provided him with his alibi. He had apparently hitchhiked in three different vehicles from his home in Carrickmacross, near Ireland's east coast, on the Sunday evening to Mullingar, where he had a date with a married woman. He refused to give any more details. When served with his evening meal he told the officer, 'The firm is strong that is supplying me.'[4]

At times the trial took unexpected and bizarre turns. Car salesman J. Dermot Mullooly was called as a witness on the third day. He had agreed to testify for the prosecution but changed his mind before the trial got under way. The prosecution therefore brought him into court as a hostile witness whose evidence would serve their case even though he was reluctant to cooperate. In court he tried to avoid going into the witness box on a last-minute technicality, but the prosecution overcame this, and the judge directed him to testify. He said he lived near Strokestown in County Roscommon, an hour and a half's drive from Mullaghmore. He had been trying to sell a second-hand yellow Ford Cortina, and one day he brought this home from the garage where he worked and parked it outside his house in Lisheen. This disappeared during the night of 26 August and in its place was left a red Ford Escort. Next morning he saw two men return the yellow Cortina and get into the red Escort. One of the men called out to him, 'It's OK, we are going down to the quarry.'[5] He put his shoes on and by the time he went outside the men and red Escort had gone.* He told Garda that he had recognised one of the men as Francis McGirl but later he withdrew this. This was despite a statement he gave which said he had known Francis

---

* When he did so he could not get the car to start. He said a mechanic later found a disconnected wire in the ignition column. Either it was unreliable, in which case Francis McGirl and Thomas McMahon were lucky to get to Mullaghmore, or maybe the wire was deliberately disconnected to put the car out of use.

McGirl and his brother for up to five years, the brother having bought his cars from him; and that he had seen Francis McGirl in the red Escort a month before in Ballinamore. He recalled the Gardai's allegation: that Francis McGirl had collected the Cortina from Mullooly's home and picked up Thomas McMahon there, while eating their evening meal and freshening up. All through his testimony he gave reluctant and wary answers. He suggested Gardai had put words in his mouth. He said his earlier statements to the Garda were obtained after they gave him 'a terrible interrogation, thumping the table' and calling him 'a thick-headed pig and all sorts of names'[6] and even threatening to arrest his elderly mother and sack his brother-in-law who worked in the Garda.* The prosecution combated these points and pointed to holes in his argument. He left the witness box sounding, at best, unreliable.

The prosecution called Inspector Patrick Jordan, the detective who had attempted to reconstruct the boat from the wreckage they had removed from the seabed. From this, he and his colleagues had concluded that the bomb had been placed in a central area between the engine and the cabin. They estimated the explosive would have weighed about four to five pounds and was gelignite. Although not certain, it was overwhelmingly likely that it had been detonated by radio control using a transmitter on the 27 megahertz waveband over a maximum range of about half a mile.

The main part of the trial involved forensic evidence, and for this the prosecution called Dr James Donovan, the director of the State Forensic Laboratory who had been called to Mullaghmore on the day of the attack. He gave extensive evidence at various stages of the trial showing the court the footwear and clothes of the accused men. In Thomas McMahon's case they revealed smears of paint from *Shadow V*, components of gelignite, and sand linking him to Mullaghmore. In Francis McGirl's case he found traces of explosives and sand he believed was from Mullaghmore, but no paint from *Shadow V*. Going into detail, he showed that on Thomas McMahon's right boot he had found a paint flake within the sand. On examination under a microscope, the paint consisted of two layers, dark green and lime green, the colours matching

---

* The judge asked if he had made a formal complaint and discovered he had not, nor did he do so after the trial.

the layers of paint on *Shadow V*. He found another flake of paint on the outside right upper part of the boot, and a thick smear of dark green paint about a fifth of an inch long, matching the layers of paint on the boat. The boot also had a smear of white paint on its toecap, a quarter of an inch long and matching in composition and shade white paint found on *Shadow V*. When he examined the yellow Cortina and the red Escort, he found dark green paint flakes in both cars. He testified that he had taken sand from the boots of Thomas McMahon and the shoes of Francis McGirl.

His colleague from the forensic science laboratory Dr Sheila Willis gave testimony about the paint she found on Thomas McMahon's jacket and trousers. She compared the paint flakes using a microscope and solvent tests, concluding that the paint came from *Shadow V* and estimating the probability of any other explanation at 1 in 250,000.

Another forensic scientist, Michael Norton, testified that he had found components of gelignite on Thomas McMahon's jacket and trousers and Francis McGirl's jacket. His colleague Liam Fleury, also a forensic scientist at the State Laboratory, testified at length about the tests he had carried out, principally on flakes of paint found on the suspects and in the cars they were alleged to have used.

On day twelve, the defence brought in their witnesses starting with Dr Dieter Gross, director of special organic tests at the Federal Institute for Testing Materials in Berlin, Germany. He expressed doubt about Dr Donovan's work, portraying him as having not gone far enough in his examinations and too far in his interpretations. His evidence did not, however, seem to deliver a knockout blow to Dr Donovan's testimony.

The defence called as a witness Thomas McMahon's brother-in-law, Felix McArdle, who testified that, as an upholsterer, he had employed his brother-in-law for about a year preceding the attack, making and painting furniture frames, and this brought him into contact with paints including green paint. This was backed up by Thomas McMahon's mother, Bernadette McMahon, who appeared as a witness.

The eighth and final witness called by the defence was Dr David John Cardin, a chemist at Trinity College, Dublin. He testified that when he looked at the sand on Thomas McMahon's boots and compared it to samples from Mullaghmore, he found significant differences. But when he compared it to samples taken from another beach in a different part of Ireland, he found no differences. By this he hoped to call into question the sand-based evidence against Thomas McMahon.

Closing the defence for Francis McGirl, Senior Counsel Seamus Egan said, among other things, that the traces of explosives found on his clothing were not recent, that no paint had been found on him and that the evidence relating to sand was tenuous. Thomas McMahon's Senior Counsel Patrick McEntee included in his closing submission that no safe conclusions could be drawn from the evidence relating to the sand or the paint, and there were plenty of other possible sources for the paint which had been found on his client's clothes. Similarly, he could have picked up traces of gelignite from other sources in the previous twelve months, including possibly from the quarrying or road cratering taking place in the area in which he lived. He concluded by saying the prosecution's case had been full of logical flaws and evidential short-comings and had done nothing more than cast suspicion.

On Friday 23 November, the court assembled to hear the verdicts. The judges found Thomas McMahon guilty of my grandfather's murder and sentenced him to penal servitude for life. They had not been satisfied that sand found on his boots and socks came from Mullaghmore. However, they had been satisfied that the paint on his clothes came from his presence on *Shadow V*, and his contact with explosives 'clearly establishes ... that he, either alone or in combination with other persons, intended to kill or cause serious bodily injury to any person on or in the vicinity of the boat'.[7] It later turned out that it was his third time in front of that court. In March 1972 he had been accused of IRA membership and being in possession of an incriminating document, but was found not guilty. When in February 1975 he was again accused with IRA membership, he swore this was not the case and the charges were dismissed.

The judges found Francis McGirl not guilty based on their having 'a doubt'. The law did not permit a conviction based on 'the very real suspicion surrounding this case' or on the basis of his association with Thomas McMahon.

Thomas McMahon was taken to prison and planned to appeal against his conviction. Life sentences in the Republic of Ireland were commonly accepted to be twenty years with a quarter deducted for good behaviour. Francis McGirl was released on bail with the condition that he would stay with his father and return to the court in the new year to face a charge of IRA membership, alongside Thomas McMahon. When the men did appear for that hearing, they were found not guilty.

On 24 November 1979, a newspaper reported that Gardai were still looking for at least three other men believed to have been involved in the operation. The trial was estimated to have cost £250,000.

Some aspects of the trial surprised me. The court spent days listening to evidence about sand, yet neither side produced an expert on sand. Much time was spent on evidence relating to paint from *Shadow V*, yet when the defence asked for a delay to the proceedings so their expert witness, Dr Dieter Gross from Germany, could examine samples highlighted by the prosecution, he was given only one day. He later said that he could have done with 'a month'.[8]

Reading the transcript more than twenty-five years after the trial, I was relieved my family had not been obliged to appear. Some of the evidence was gruesome. When the prosecution asked if there was any further debris of the boat which the Garda thought relevant, the detective who had been present for the post mortems said, 'Debris from the body of Nicholas Knatchbull. This is exhibit 2C(3) and it consists of three bags my Lord.'[9] Later a bag of Nick's clothes was held up in court as Exhibit 2(d). I felt sorry for Michael Connolly, the Classiebawn stockman, who had to appear as a witness. A gentle man already traumatised by the attack, he would rarely if ever have been to Dublin before. As the barristers cross-examined him about the paint he had applied to the boat that August, he soon became confused by their questions. The Chief Justice intervened, evidently keen to make the experience less harrowing. The buzz of the assembled international media, the intense security and the presence of Thomas McMahon and Francis McGirl a few feet away must have been a bewildering, upsetting and intimidating experience.

The trial offered a possible explanation of where Nick was at the moment he was killed. Kevin Murray, the technician who came out from Sligo to look at *Shadow V*'s ship-to-shore radio in the afternoon preceding the attack, testified that it was his third time on the boat and that on this occasion he had removed the radio for testing. The first time had been earlier in the month when he was summoned to

Classiebawn and then sent down to the boat with 'Paul and, I think it was, Timothy, one of the two brothers'.[10] In fact it was almost certainly Nick who went with them. I remember him taking an intense interest in the boat's radio that month and tinkering with it throughout the holiday, determined to master it. In the seconds preceding the explosion neither my parents nor I could later recall seeing him. It is likely he was in the cabin, most probably examining the wiring which the engineer had left behind. This would have put Nick just underneath me, his feet on the floorboards close to where the bomb was concealed.

The trial answered another of my questions: Where was the bomb hidden? Although this seemed inconsequential, it was one of the basic facts I wanted to know. The forensic evidence of Jim Donovan was that it must have been behind a white and green wooden structure, judging by the debris blown into the bodies of the dead. This strongly suggests that it was very close to, or possibly within, the cabin, the only large part of the boat painted white. Examination of the wreckage and bodies showed it was hidden low, almost certainly under the green-painted deck. When *Shadow V*'s remains were gathered, the hull between the cabin and the engine was largely missing. Taken together, the evidence points to the hiding place as being under the deck near the white cabin doors which were latched open.

When Thomas McMahon was arrested, he followed a standard IRA procedure and refused to answer any questions without his lawyer. At the trial he said his requests for his lawyer were ignored, an allegation denied by the Garda sergeant in concern who said he called his solicitor Martin Crilly shortly after he was asked to.[11] As was his right, Thomas McMahon chose not to speak at his trial. From the transcript I learned that when he had been questioned by Garda, he had said, 'I am a fitter.' Francis McGirl had said, 'I work at everything and anything.'[12] I thought how well these descriptions covered their activities the night before the bomb.

The trial yielded useful as well as evocative information. Rodney Lomax's meticulous description of the boat included the detail that 90 per cent of *Shadow V*'s floorboards were 'kept in place by gravity'[13] rather than nailed down, making them quick and easy to lift and providing access to an eighteen-inch void underneath, a perfect place to conceal a bomb. As a hiding place, the only disadvantage was how easy it would be for the Gardai to check but, as the IRA unit must have known from surveillance, this was academic because the Gardai never inspected the boat. Rodney's description of the cabin included a 'Tintawn carpet' and suddenly I could see and smell it, rough and fish-smelly, its loose construction trapping biscuit crumbs from my childhood snacks as I sheltered from the Atlantic spray and sipped from a thermos cup, rocking in the swell, my hands too chilled to fish.

Francis McGirl's lawyers painted a picture of the Garda having abused him and his legal rights. They pointed out that on the day of his arrest the Gardai had kept him up until 4:30am with two Gardai in the room at any time, rotating to keep themselves fresh while he grew sleep-deprived. Taking the stand himself, he admitted he had been allowed to lie down in a cell that afternoon but described the guards as 'coming in every 15 or 20 minutes and opening the door and banging and saying "Are you all right there?". . . and they'd flush the toilet.'[14] He claimed the Gardai repeatedly asked him the same questions, a practice prohibited under guidelines known as Judges' Rules. He said that the Gardai 'were banging the table with their fists, and shouting at me, roaring at me I was an IRA murderer and poking me with their fingers . . . I was told I would see no solicitor until I would make a statement admitting that I killed Lord Mountbatten and the rest of his family'.[15] Referring to his words 'I put no bomb on the boat', he explained he had only said this after he had been accused of it 'a rake of times'.[16] 'I remember them writing something down and they said, "Sign that you murdering bastard you" – something to that effect,' he claimed.[17] He said the Gardai had told him he was only 'good for blowing up children and old women'.[18]

Certainly it seems the senior Garda officer on the case, John Courtney, was a no-nonsense, go-getting investigator and the team he brought in from Dublin Castle and elsewhere were no softies. Francis McGirl's lawyer said that the Garda had brought in a detective who had immediately shouted at McGirl, 'You are not Patrick Rehill, you are an IRA murderer and you will never see the outside world again.'[19] The lawyer said that his client had been denied legal advice on the first day of his detention. His solicitor Kevin Kilraine had told Gardai that his client was 'afraid' of what they were going to do to him. The solicitor warned one Garda that when he next returned to see his client, he 'wanted to see him in the same condition',[20] implying that he suspected they were going to physically abuse him.

The Chief Justice stated that the Garda questioning appeared not to have followed Judges' Rules and insisted on an explanation.[21] One of the Garda team said the accounts Francis McGirl was giving 'weren't tying in' and 'we felt that if he could give a proper account of his movements he could eliminate himself from the investigation'.[22] The prosecution then began to discredit Francis McGirl's description of the Garda techniques, revealing cracks in the picture he and his lawyers had presented. His lawyers said that the Gardai removed their watches to prevent him from knowing the time but under cross-examination Francis McGirl contradicted this.

The prosecution painted a very different picture of their treatment of the prisoner. They specified when they served meals and said they allowed him to smoke, drink tea and rest. When he asked for an evening newspaper the day after the attack, a detective bought him an *Evening Herald*.[23] His allegation of being denied legal representation seemed weak. The fact he was still pretending to be Patrick Rehill made it unlikely he would summon a solicitor. He later admitted that he asked for a solicitor only when his true identity came to light.[24]

Reading the trial transcript helped me assemble more of the facts I was looking for, but it also made me aware how small a tip of the iceberg had broken the surface in 1979. As my trips to Ireland continued, I learned very much more.

24

GARDA REVISITED

The danger of a bomb in Mullaghmore was in the back of the minds of many of those who lived and holidayed there. When a 'tremendously loud bang' reverberated around the Bay of Donegal on 27 August 1979 a German tourist on Mullaghmore beach immediately joked to her six-year-old daughter, 'They've blown up Mounty.'[1]

Few people if any had taken the possibility of an attack very seriously and this seemed to include the Garda. They gave the impression of not understanding the significance of the man they were protecting. After the attack, senior Garda officers were perplexed at the world reaction and surprised that questions were being asked about his security. One superintendent told the press: 'This man was not used to security. He did not have it in Britain. After all, he was just a retired citizen.'[2] The possibility of an attack seems to have been pushed further and further back in everyone's minds.

Even when a strange package was accidentally discovered underneath *Shadow V*'s floorboards three days before the attack, it did not set alarm bells ringing. In the summer of 1979 Shane Rodgers from Bundoran was twenty years old and working for Rodney Lomax. At about 3:45pm on Saturday 25 August, he and another trainee, Trevor Henry, were working in the harbour with their boss when they noticed Paul pumping water out of *Shadow V*'s hull. Concerned she may have sprung a leak, Paul asked for help and Rodney directed Shane to lift the floorboards.

He looked under the cabin floor and found it dry, but when he looked between the cabin and the engine he found 'a good lot of water'. While making a thorough search for a possible leak he saw 'a see-through plastic bag tucked away to the left as you looked forward' between the cabin and the engine. It was 'the thickness of three pounds of sugar and it looked like putty, half dried'. The bag had no writing on it and when he said, 'What's this?', Rodney leaned over and had a look. Shane asked Paul what he thought it was and he replied, 'I think it's putty.'[3] They had a lot of other things to be getting on with so they decided to leave it alone and return to their work.

The Garda Technical Bureau later concluded that the bomb weighed four to five pounds and was placed under the floorboards between the engine and cabin. Learning of Shane Rodgers' discovery made my mind turn to the possibility that he had uncovered explosives which had failed to go off, perhaps due to the flooding in the hull. In any case, when Shane unblocked a drain and Paul operated the bilge pumps, the water started to flow away. Shane replaced the floorboards and fifteen minutes later my grandfather went out to sea.* What was the package? Had the IRA intended to attack us earlier in the month? Did they later send one of their foremost bomb-makers to fix a previous failure? The answers, even if they had been available, would not have helped me and I did not want to pursue them.

When I asked Rodney about it in 2004, he dismissed the package as nothing more than some rubbish floating around in the water, but he did say that it had played on his mind during a short break with his family after the attack. 'About four days after we came back from holiday I rang Norton at the castle and met him in the library.' He passed on his memory of what he had seen and Norton was interested but said he knew nothing about it. 'And that was the last we saw of the family,'[4] Rodney told me. The Garda felt the incident was not worth pursuing and when Rodney gave a statement to them on 11 September 1979 he did not refer to it.

It seems obvious that the boat should have been guarded around the clock and checked regularly for explosives; but to what degree was that obvious in 1979? Some say it was blindingly obvious even then. In the

* After Shadow V was blown up Shane Rodgers told the Garda what he had seen and they took a detailed statement on 30 August 1979.

late 1970s, Britain's military were assessing what they could expect from the IRA in future. Nine months before the attack a senior intelligence officer compiled a classified report which included references to the IRA's use of radio-controlled bombs.[5] By 1978 these were being used between fifteen and twenty-five times annually, and the report predicted their use would become more common.

The IRA had been experimenting with radio control for some time but had run into difficulties when the British Army devised counter-measures. Sometimes the military jammed the radio frequencies. Worse for the IRA, they started sending out rogue signals to prematurely detonate devices. This risked killing the IRA personnel handling them. The IRA had therefore learned to encode their radio signals so that only their own transmitters would cause detonation. By 1978 their preferred equipment was an inexpensive kit manufactured for model enthusiasts by a British company called McGregor. Simon Jones, Nick and I had installed similar equipment in Simon's model plane the year before. The transmitter was a small handheld box with a telescopic aerial. An IRA transmitter differed to ours only in that theirs had a matchbox-sized encoder added to it. Wired into the bomb's ignition circuit would be a small receiver with a decoder, again about the size of a matchbox.

By 1979 the British and Irish authorities had the technical knowledge and local intelligence to thwart an attack of the type planned for Mullaghmore. It is tempting to ask how much of this was passed to the team guarding my grandfather. But the real point is more fundamental. It would have been no more than common sense to put a round-the-clock guard on *Shadow V*.

From 1960 until 1987, the face of law and order in the area was the sergeant living in Cliffoney, John Hennessy. In 2004 I called on him at his Cliffoney home where he lived in retirement. He said that it was the Garda who decided what security was put in place and, contrary to what was sometimes reported in the press, not my grandfather. He confirmed that on 3 August 1975 a day-and-night guard was stationed on *Shadow V*, consisting of two men in a car. This lasted until 18 August when it was stopped. The instructions were issued by the superintendent in Sligo, and John Hennessy never knew the reason.

Standing at his large window, John Hennessy and I looked out to

Classiebawn on the hill beyond. He showed me letters he had kept from my grandfather, written at the end of each summer, thanking him for his help. He also had a copy of the book *Freedom at Midnight* signed by my grandfather, documenting the end of imperial rule in India. Before I left he said quietly, 'I apologise, as far as you can for something you didn't have control over.'[6]

Shadow V had attracted sabotage in previous years and on each occasion a Garda watch had been placed on the boat at night. But the Garda had been prepared to do this for limited periods only. In 1979 the boat was unguarded and this worried my grandfather, so much so that he mentioned it to my aunt.[7] It seems that had he been in control of his own security, he would have ordered it, but the decision was not his.

Just how much Garda security was on the boat in 1979 has never been fully explained. The issue arose briefly at the trial of the bombers. When the detective on duty at the time of the attack was asked what security arrangements had been in place at the boat, he did not know. The senior counsel then asked who could tell the court and when he said he did not know the answer to that either, the matter was quickly dropped.[8] It seems there was some provision for monitoring the boat at night but it was sporadic and no record has come to light of how it was managed.

About a week or ten days before the attack, an incident occurred that caused lasting questions to be raised. I learned this from Paul Maxwell's father when I met him for the first time in November 2003. He told me that something had 'niggled him' at the back of his mind ever since the attack. On the night in question he had been woken by Paul at about midnight. There was a terrible storm and Paul said, 'I think we should go down and look at the boat.' John got out of bed 'rather reluctantly' and got into his car. John went on:

It was a terrible night; the wind was howling, the rain was lashing and we went down to the harbour. There wasn't a soul about the place, a few cars parked here and there. We drove up onto the arm of the harbour and across the bridge to where the boat was. Headlights came on behind us and flashed a couple of times. We drove on about another twenty yards and then stopped. There was a Garda car with two guards in it and they asked us what we were doing out that time of night.[9]

When Paul explained the situation, the guards were satisfied. By the time John was back in his bed he was reassured for his son's safety by the 'very tight' security. 'They were so sharp on it,' he told me, 'and they must have been sitting there when we arrived.' Then he stopped and looked at me pointedly. 'This isn't going to make any difference to anything,' he said, 'but on the night the bomb was placed, the tide was out, it was a lovely night, there was a barbecue on the beach, my eldest daughter Donna was down and her friend Rachel. How did the guy get to place the bomb and not be noticed?' The answer is that the security was not continuous. When I met him in 2004, the superintendent who led the investigation told me, 'The boat was not under constant Garda protection, but was visited by Garda patrols from Kinlough, Cliffoney and Sligo Garda Stations, including [Special Branch].'[10]

Throughout my childhood the faces at Classiebawn changed little. As old retainers retired or died their jobs were often inherited by relatives or friends from the local community. When a new member of the team was recruited, such as Paul Maxwell, it was done through word of mouth. At Classiebawn everyone knew everyone, directly or indirectly: where they came from, where they drank, and what their politics were.

This norm was interrupted briefly for a few weeks in the summer of 1976 soon after the tempestuous cook, Molly Kennedy, had walked out. Hugh Tunney's lease of the castle stipulated that he must provide a cook so he quickly dispatched a chef from the Gresham Hotel in Dublin, which he conveniently owned. The arrangement worked well for the month but as Hugh was living in Dublin it made little sense for him to recruit a permanent cook at Classiebawn and it was therefore agreed that my grandfather would pay for a chef in future. In 1978 when 'Ted', an instructor at Dublin's College of Catering in Cathal Brugha Street, was found, he was duly signed up.

It seems 'Ted' distanced himself from the regulars at Classiebawn. He arrived unknown and when he left, little more was known about him, either by the family or by the staff. I do not remember him at all. Paul Maxwell's predecessor on *Shadow V*, Fionn McArthur, could only recall him as 'a fit, tough old bird, ex-Army' with 'some great stories'.[11] The Housekeeper Catherine Doherty could remember only occasional conversations with him, and only in connection with the requirements of the job. When my grandfather took his annual group photograph of the staff in 1978, 'Ted' is seen standing apart from his colleagues. His pay packet was much larger than anyone else's and this alone may have been enough to set him apart; or there may have been other reasons.

After the 1978 holiday, my grandfather wrote to 'Ted': 'Thank you so much for all you did during the month of August without ever taking a day off, indeed hardly an hour off, and with very little help. Those young men in your school in Dublin are lucky to have you as their teacher.'[12] He also wrote to thank Aideen Gore-Booth, adding:

> To try and reduce the immense cost of our month's stay in Ireland, we discussed, you may remember, various steps that could be taken. The first one is that the chef apparently undertook to try and find a really high class student from his Cookery School who could do the job, although perhaps rather less efficiently, for about £40 instead of £105 (per week) which really has broken the bank![13]

Over the coming months she complied with my grandfather's request to contact 'Ted'. Early in 1979 she reported that: 'I wrote and when I got no reply, I phoned . . . he said he would do his best to find one but had no one yet.'[14] This is the last entry for 'Ted' in my grandfather's archives, but as he disappeared from my grandfather's radar he appeared on that of the British and Irish authorities. Four months after he had worked at Classiebawn, staff at the British Embassy were alerted that something might not be quite right and they soon started investigations. By 18 April 1979 they were alarmed enough to send a confidential letter to the Foreign Office in London:

> 1. We do not yet know whether Lord Louis Mountbatten and his family plan to spend part of the summer at Classiebawn this year but if so they may need to take account of some potenti-

ally disturbing information which has come to our attention.

2. The ambassador was approached at the end of last year by [someone at] the Government Catering College who said that one of the students, a man called ['Ted'], who he understood was perfectly innocuous, had been employed as chef at Classiebawn. The problem was that ['Ted'] was friendly with another student . . . whom he thought was a Provo.

3. We duly asked the Garda to check this and they told us that their records show that [the student] had indeed been an active IRA supporter up to about four years ago when certain unspecified family troubles had caused him to cease his active involvement in politics. But more worrying was the fact that ['Ted'], far from being blameless is, according to the Garda, a listed member of the PIRA.

4. May I leave it to you to pass this information discreetly to the person responsible for hiring staff for the Mountbattens for the summer?[15]

If the Foreign Office did anything in response to this report, there is no evidence of it. Three months passed and when my grandfather wrote for security guidance to the Metropolitan Police, the Garda and the ambassador, there is no indication that a warning was passed to him. Ten days before the ambassador was due to receive the family at his Leopardstown residence for breakfast, he telegrammed London:

CONFIDENTIAL

1. BEFORE GOING BACK TO THE GARDA TO CONFIRM THE SECURITY ARRANGEMENTS FOR LORD MOUNT-BATTEN'S HOLIDAY, WE SHOULD BE GRATEFUL IF YOU WOULD FIND OUT WHETHER ['TED']. IS STILL EMPLOYED AT CLASSIEBAWN . . .

2. ['TED']'S CONTINUED PRESENCE AT CLASSIEBAWN WOULD IN OUR OPINION, GIVE GROUNDS FOR CONCERN ABOUT THE SAFETY OF LORD MOUNT-BATTEN AND HIS PARTY, ESPECIALLY IN VIEW OF THE FACT THAT THE PROVISIONALS ARE NOW STEPPING UP THEIR PROPAGANDA ACTIVITIES AS A PRELUDE

TO THE DEMONSTRATIONS MARKING THE TENTH
ANNIVERSARY OF BLOODY SUNDAY ON THE WEEKEND
ON 11/12 AUGUST WHEN LORD MOUNTBATTEN AND
HIS PARTY WILL BE IN THE MIDDLE OF THEIR STAY
IN IRELAND.
HAYDON.[16]

In a letter dated two days before we were due to arrive in Ireland,
the Foreign Office in London passed on some minor changes to our
itinerary which had been telephoned by John Barratt, my grandfather's
private secretary, the previous evening. The letter contained five short
paragraphs, including:

> 4. Mr Barrett was also able to confirm that ['Ted'] was no longer
> employed at Classiebawn.[17]

I first learned about the concerns over 'Ted' while sitting alone in
an archive vault during the research of this book. I was astonished.
When I discussed it with my parents and family, they too had never
heard about how close the IRA had come to us in 1978. As this was
precisely the type of information which my grandfather sought annually, it seemed a dreadful omission if he had not been made aware of
it; and it seemed unlikely he was told about it for he recorded and
archived even the smallest details of his visits, right down to the
clothes he required for his trip. The intelligence on 'Ted' was exactly
the sort of early warning signal that he looked for each year. For him
to have failed to discuss it, record it and act on it is difficult to
believe.

Recognising there was nothing proven against 'Ted', I asked myself
how likely it was that he had been there innocently. Given the efficiency of the IRA's intelligence-gathering system, it seemed highly
unlikely. For the information not to have been directly communicated
to my grandfather appeared to be a serious failure on the part of the
authorities, British and Irish, but I recognised that the picture I was
assembling was with the luxury of hindsight.

My mother's diary referred to him briefly. Reading this and the file
of correspondence made me wonder what had been going through 'Ted's'

head as he received requests to send a less expensive trainee. The answer will never be known; he died in November 2002 after a long illness.

Immediately after the attack, the Garda had called in Detective Superintendent John Courtney. Aged forty-nine, he had developed his own style as an investigator and had by then been leading the Garda's Murder Squad for two years.* When the call came, he was on holiday with his wife and children near his home village in County Kerry. He immediately started pulling together a team of about twenty investigators and a similar number of specialists from the Garda's Technical Bureau for fingerprinting, photography and ballistics. Having briefly returned to Dublin, he headed for Granard where Thomas McMahon and Francis McGirl were being held. Hoping their hands and clothes would yield vital evidence, he called in Dr James Donovan, Director of the State Forensic Laboratory. When the Scenes of Crime Officer pointed out that the men's boots were encrusted with sand, despite the fact they were in the middle of Ireland, John Courtney hoped the forensic laboratory would be able to identify where the sand had come from.

The press were already descending on Sligo. To avoid them, John Courtney booked into a small hotel just outside Sligo, and from there he later moved into a private house. He held team conferences in Sligo every morning and then, to give himself time to think, he walked for a couple of miles at a time before deciding on his next move. He found local people 'above average' in their willingness to help, and soon he had a picture of how the attack had been set up and carried out. But 'above average' helpfulness often did not extend to giving formal statements or providing hard evidence and, other than Thomas McMahon and Francis McGirl, John found himself unable to charge any of the people involved.

He told me that he had 'no doubt whatsoever' that one particular IRA leader in Bundoran was part of the team but he could not get the

---

* John Courtney headed the Murder Squad for another ten years until he was promoted to Chief Superintendent in charge of west Dublin. He retired in 1993. I met him in 2004. He was then aged seventy-four and running his own investigations business in Dublin.

evidence he needed. 'Well, you could say people wouldn't want to get involved,' he told me. One man, 'Conor', came up time and time again in John Courtney's investigations. Before long he learned that the IRA surveillance team had reported their findings to a man known to them only by a codename. From intelligence sources John was soon able to match the codename to 'Conor'. Despite questioning him for 'days and days', he failed to get anything he could use as evidence. When Gardai examined his car they found he had carried out the 'forensic cleaning'[18] which had by then become a standard practice of the IRA. This involved vacuuming the car before investigators arrived.

John Courtney desperately wanted to question 'Flynn' from County Tyrone who had been employed by 'Conor'. Gardai had called at his workplace soon after the attack only to be told that 'Flynn' was no longer working there. Investigations revealed he had gone to America, but three weeks later Gardai arrested him in Monaghan town. They confronted him with Garda Davey whose suspicions had been raised three days before the attack, when he had seen 'Flynn' driving the yellow Ford Cortina which was later used by the bombers. Forensic tests showed that Thomas McMahon and Francis McGirl had used that car and the Gardai must have hoped that 'Flynn' would incriminate himself during the course of questioning. Instead he refused to make any comment other than to deny it was him in the car and that he had any involvement in the murders. In the absence of more evidence, the Gardai were obliged to release him.

John Courtney's investigations into the IRA surveillance team led to 'Flynn's' girlfriend, who also came from County Tyrone. When she and another woman were brought in for questioning they 'never spoke a word. They simply stared at a spot on the wall and were eventually released.'[19] Gardai identified another team member from Lucan, County Dublin, but again failed to get the evidence they would need to secure a conviction.

As John Courtney dug deeper, he uncovered an IRA plan from an earlier year. 'Flynn' had been part of a three-man team dispatched to shoot my grandfather at Classiebawn under the cover of darkness. As was often the case in the Mullaghmore inquiry, the Garda investigations leaked into the press. A newspaper reported that the IRA had cancelled the operation because they felt the risk of arrest was too high.[20] In fact the Gardai believed the plan was thwarted by faulty intelligence. When the team assembled for the assassination, they found they had everyone they needed apart from my grandfather. He was apparently dining that night at Hugh Tunney's Dublin hotel, the Gresham.

Every Senior Investigating Officer hopes for a lucky break, and for John Courtney this was the arrest of Thomas McMahon and Francis McGirl before the bomb had even detonated. One week later his inquiry seemed to take another lucky leap forward. On the evening of 3 September 1979, a Garda patrol in the Smithfield area of central Dublin came across a car which seemed to have been abandoned. They ran some inquiries and soon found it had been reported stolen in County Donegal. They searched it and found a map which had been hidden in its boot and which clearly pinpointed the scene of the crime. The story leaked into the press and by the following afternoon it was reported that detectives were looking for a County Donegal man. In fact they were interested in a secretive IRA leader from Monaghan. Within forty-eight hours they were questioning him but once more they found the trail went cold and they were forced to release him despite being convinced he was the man who had orchestrated the attack.

When Dr James Donovan reached Sligo in the early evening following the attack, he expected to find it a hub of Garda activity. Instead the Garda presence was 'pretty minimal in view of the enormity of the crime'.[21] Those Garda he did meet gave the impression of not knowing what to do, which was hardly surprising given the almost unprecedented events that were unfolding. More unexpected was the impression they gave of not wanting to be too closely involved, as if their reputations might be tarnished. 'It was like a ghost town,' he told me. 'Everybody including the Gardai disappeared, they just cleared out. They didn't know where to go and one or two may have taken a drink to steady their nerves.' This included one of their most senior officers. When Jim met him at the Imperial Hotel, he left with the impression that the man might not remember their meeting the next day. Aghast, and knowing how much work lay ahead, Jim went on to Mullaghmore. Later he returned to Sligo and went to the hospital for the post-mortem examinations.

When John Courtney's investigation led to a caravan site on the other side of the bay from Mullaghmore harbour, Jim went along and started work. The trail led to the first or second caravan from the sea, facing the harbour. It seemed an IRA surveillance team comprising of three women had been based there but they had not left anything behind which could incriminate them.

Jim Donovan returned to his Dublin laboratory and started examining the clothes and boots of the suspects held in Granard. In September he was called back to Bundoran to examine a large house that the IRA used for personnel visiting from the North. Again he found nothing he could use but when the Garda showed him a yellow Cortina he was able to link that forensically with the red Escort that the suspects had been arrested in, proving they had used both cars. The investigation wore on and work piled up on Jim. The fast-approaching trial, set for November, added further to the tension. Stressed and overworked, he succumbed to a violent illness. 'I got more gloriously sick than I can ever remember. I brought the soles of my feet up,' he told me. But he quickly returned to work, where by now it was well recognised that the IRA might go to great lengths to bring his work to a halt. 'Tommy McMahon was by far and away the most adept bomber they had at that time,' Jim Donovan explained, 'and McGirl was very important insofar as all his people had major roles in the power structure of the IRA.' The role of analysing the evidence and presenting it in court was shared between him and three colleagues, in part to make it more difficult for the IRA to target them for assassination or intimidation. Two nights before going into the witness box, Jim Donovan left his laboratory to go home. He gave a lift to a detective who lived across the road. As they drove out of the gates, a car followed them. They drove round and round the city but could not shake it off. After a while Jim told the detective, Sergeant Michael Niland, that he had had enough:

> The guard took his revolver out and I decided to die at home. I thought my wife might as well know she was a widow as quickly as possible, so we drove into my driveway. I was sure I was going to die but they didn't do anything. The detective sergeant held

up his very large revolver so they could see there was a gun in the car. Then after about a quarter of an hour they reversed out.*

At various stages of my time in Ireland, I heard allegations not just of acquiescence to the IRA on the part of the Irish state but of active collusion. The Garda and Irish Defence Forces were long regarded by their British counterparts as infiltrated by the IRA. Such generalisations depend on simplifications; the reality is more complex and nuanced. One of the detectives, later a superintendent, who had been posted to the Mullaghmore investigation told me about the years he had spent in uniform in republican strongholds. When the father of one of his colleagues died, the superintendent in question went to the funeral. There he found that the undertaker was senior IRA man John Joe McGirl. When the superintendent asked his colleague about this, the man said, 'My father would not have it any other way.'[22] It was an example of the weave of allegiances that was then commonplace. To the superintendent and his peers, such stories were normal.

---

* Jim Donovan later survived two assassination attempts. In December 1981 his car was booby trapped but the petrol device failed to fully detonate; the following month he narrowly escaped death when his car was blown up, leaving him severely injured and in lifelong pain.

25

IRA

My grandfather did not involve himself in Irish politics. However, his general outlook betrayed a leaning towards the nationalism evident around us in Ireland in the 1970s. This should not be surprising given that his most radical ideas stemmed from nationalism; not English nationalism, but the nationalism he had encountered through much of his career. When he was Supreme Allied Commander in South East Asia from 1943 until 1946, he recognised that the future of the Empire lay not in the hands of the political masters in London but with local people, specifically the nationalists who wished to rid their country of the imperial power. This was seen by the status quo as at best the rantings of an ill-informed young hot-head (he was twenty years younger than most of the senior commanders he led), at worst the dangerous tendencies of an idealist whose actions could encourage revolution. When wanting to bring order to Burma after the defeat of the Japanese in 1945, he insisted that the Burmese nationalist leader Aung San, aged thirty, was to lead the government. The British civilian governor remonstrated and my grandfather fought him, even having him temporarily sent back to London. In India as Viceroy in 1947 he took a similar line, insisting that power be handed to the very nationalists who had previously been locked up by the British. He was being more than practical; he was following his own instincts and ethics.

One day in 1975 he went for a drive in the area around Benbulben, the mountain that dominates the Sligo skyline. He took pleasure in discovering for himself a piece of IRA history from earlier in the century. A monument nearby was inscribed: 'On this spot Captain Harry Benson and Volunteer Thomas Langan gave their lives for the republic, 20 September 1922.' He discovered that they had been killed during the Civil War by forces of the Free State and that a wooden cross had been erected on the mountain that year which had been replaced by a granite one in 1947. He photographed it and put the print in his photograph album with the caption: 'Grave of 2 IRA officers killed on the estate in 1922 on Ben Whiskin, opposite Ben Bulbin'.*

Finding this photograph in 2003, I was struck by three points. First, that he should take the trouble to find the spot on the top of a mountain, miles from the main road. Second, that he should want to put a photograph of it in his album. Third, that he should use the same term for these men as for those on earlier pages of his album who had died under his command in the Second World War: 'officers'.

He plainly loved and respected Ireland's political and cultural heritage and had not been put off returning to Classiebawn even when the Cabinet Office in London had pointed out: 'If you had no IRA man on your estate you would probably be the only landowner in the Republic of whom this could be said!'[1] When he invited local musicians to play after dinner at the castle, it was for pleasure, not public relations. Occasionally as a small boy I was allowed downstairs to watch the proceedings from the staircase. My grandfather and some of the family and guests danced to the Gaelic tunes and he seemed at his happiest. Many times I witnessed him listening to military bands with unalloyed pleasure but these pipes, fiddles and accordions produced just as much glee.

Late one night in the 1970s, my grandfather went into the Classiebawn kitchen and started talking to the Gardai he found there. One was Jim Kelly, the colourful detective whom we children had befriended. They had a long lighthearted conversation during which

* It was not in fact a grave. The men were buried in the republican plot in Sligo Cemetery.

the detective was full of his customary high jinks. When the subject came round to the Troubles, my grandfather asked him what he would do if he were in charge of security in the north. Jokingly the Garda motioned as if he were picking up one of the machine guns that were lying nearby and theatrically gestured as if he were mowing down imaginary militants lined up in front of him. My grandfather boomed, 'My God, Kelly, you'd not be in charge.'[2]

If he had been involved in Irish politics, it is likely that his opinions would have been radical and in favour of policies that incorporated the new generation of nationalists who had appeared in the form of the Provisional IRA. While men such as Gerry Adams and Martin McGuiness might have been bogeymen to the political establishment in London, it is likely my grandfather would have countered such mindsets by insisting that if a peaceful solution were to arise, the very men and women labelled as the revolutionaries and criminals would have to be seminal contributors to whatever solution lay ahead.

When he met the Irish ambassador Donal O'Sullivan at a banquet at Windsor Castle on 11 April 1972, he made comments about the political situation in Ireland which so pleased and surprised the ambassador that he made a report to Dublin.* My grandfather apparently indicated he hoped that an initiative of the then Conservative British government would lead to the reunification of Ireland. As this was the ultimate aim of republicanism, the comments would have caused a furore if they had become public and would no doubt have surprised and pleased the IRA as much as anyone. When the Irish government released the report three decades later it caused a minor sensation.[3]

Twenty-five years after the bomb, my ongoing visits to Sligo slowly yielded a picture of how the IRA targeted and attacked us. It was part of what I needed to know. I found it difficult to feel forgiveness when I did not know whom I was forgiving and what they had done.

---

* The ambassador wrote: 'Lord Mountbatten said he wished me to know that he and many of his friends have been deeply impressed by the positive Dublin reaction to the [British government] initiative . . . They hope that this can be developed into a "major advance towards the final solution". Reunification is the only eventual solution . . . If there is anything he can do to help he will be most happy to cooperate.'

The local hub for the IRA's attack in Mullaghmore had been Bundoran. The Garda were able to establish that Thomas McMahon and Francis McGirl had been in the town prior to the attack. For a considerable part of August they watched my grandfather's movements, driven around by 'Flynn', employed in Bundoran. This put them within easy range of the surveillance team in the caravan park nearby. According to a press report, the Garda believed the women there 'also provided a more basic service. According to intelligence obtained by the security forces, active service units now take one or two girls with them. These modern-day camp followers prevent unit members breaking out and meeting local girls with all the security dangers that entails.'[4]

Another centre of the conspiracy was the small town of Ballinamore in neighbouring County Leitrim. The focal point was an IRA watering hole, McGirl's pub. Its owner John Joe McGirl was a veteran republican and one-time member of the IRA army council. Gardai investigations showed that intelligence gathered at Mullaghmore was also delivered to his pub. His nephew Francis McGirl was well known for his IRA activities and had been involved in skirmishes with the Garda. One Friday night in January 1974, John Joe's son Liam McGirl was driving a car carrying his cousin, Francis, and two other men when they were stopped by Gardai at 1:20am. The Gardai asked for their identities and on getting unsatisfactory answers told the men they were arresting them. One of the passengers pulled out a revolver and ran off with a second man. The two McGirls were taken to the Garda station but soon afterwards the two fugitives arrived, now in the company of three further men, all armed with sticks, and seized them. The Gardai did not see Francis McGirl for quite a while and believed he had gone to ground in Dublin. When he reappeared he was not charged. In April 1978 he was arrested and questioned about a mail train robbery at Sligo and charged with IRA membership but avoided prosecution.

Ever mindful of leaks, moles and the possibility of arrest, the IRA carefully restricted knowledge of upcoming attacks even among the team involved. Francis McGirl was young, inexperienced, nervous, had difficulty controlling his drinking and was something of a hot-head, not traits that cut him out for paramilitary work. His IRA commanders may have been cautious about telling him too much too early. It is possible that when he was told to be in McGirl's pub on the evening of Sunday 26 August 1979, he did not know the exact details of what was coming next. All that is known from Francis McGirl's own testimony is that he met Patrick Rehill there that evening and was given the keys to Rehill's brother's car, the red Ford Escort.[5]

Thomas McMahon and Francis McGirl planted the bomb that night and then drove in the team's yellow Ford Cortina to Dermot Mullooly's smallholding in Lisheen, just outside Strokestown in County Roscommon. Here they switched into the red Ford Escort which they had left earlier. A short while later they had the bad luck to be waved down by Garda James Lohan in Granard. If Francis McGirl had kept his cool, the IRA would have kept one of their top bomb-makers.

Meanwhile the bomb they had left on Shadow V was ready to be detonated. Even after the arrests, the IRA left nothing to chance and maintained their surveillance right up to the end. The tension obviously got to one of the young women. She paced up and down the village and around the harbour so nervously that she drew the attention of one of the witnesses I spoke to. The Gardai investigations led them to believe that two of the IRA team, a man and a woman, both outsiders masquerading as holidaymakers, made their way to the top of the hill overlooking the bay. Together they watched our progress along the coast, two hundred yards offshore until at 11:46am we approached our first lobster pot. At that moment the man pressed the button, detonating the bomb.*

The IRA personnel on the ground were of course only a small part of the story. When John Courtney reported to his senior officers, he was emphatic that the attack was carried out with the total backing of what he called 'the Godfathers of the Provisional IRA'.[6] Although Sligo

---

* On 28 June 2004 a Sunday Life newspaper article in Belfast told readers to expect the identity of the man who detonated the bomb to be published by Scotland's Sunday Herald website on 27 August 2004, the twenty-fifth anniversary of the attack. The same site had exposed the IRA's Freddie 'Stakeknife' Scappaticci as a British informer. The Sunday Life article named a suspect but provided no evidence and never repeated the allegation. The anniversary came and went and no such unmasking took place.

fell just outside the IRA's Northern Command, most of the volunteers who carried out the Mullaghmore bombing came under its remit. The IRA's new system of internal discipline and cell structure enabled senior commanders to exercise far more control and coordination of their operations. That the devastating IRA attacks in Mullaghmore and Warrenpoint occurred on the same day demonstrated the IRA's new-found strategic skills. The bombs killed twenty-two people yet only one man was convicted, allowing the leadership to show how well the new set-up was working.

At Mullaghmore the IRA used their improved command structure to deploy personnel from many areas. The attack was to occur in County Sligo but much of the central planning was done by a County Tyrone commander. The bomb was built by Thomas McMahon, from County Monaghan but with strong links to the IRA's South Armagh Brigade.* He was driven to Mullaghmore by Francis McGirl, a native of County Leitrim, but under the control of Northern Command. A change of cars was provided in County Roscommon, under Southern Command. Meanwhile the operation depended on IRA men in Bundoran, County Donegal. Such elaborate coordination was made possible only through the central direction of the IRA's General Headquarters. GHQ staff organised the operation while drawing on volunteers from counties in both the Southern and Northern Commands. To facilitate this they called on the planning skills of one of their most successful commanders, 'Brendan'. According to a leading author on the IRA, 'It was very rare to involve different geographical areas in this way. An attack on a royal target was a major step and had to be sanctioned from the top. It had to be done right and this man had the authority to coordinate between the separate IRA elements.'[7] Another author on the IRA told me:

My understanding is that Belfast was the central fulcrum for the operation. The division of the organisation into formal sections (whether Northern versus Southern Command, or cells) was never entirely systematic. There was flexibility and this was often oper-

---

* By the end of the Troubles this Brigade had killed one hundred and fourteen British soldiers, more than any other unit of the IRA.

ation-driven. If an 'op' was to go ahead and needed some blurring of areas and roles, then so be it. An operation as high-level as this one would certainly have required the highest IRA sanction and involvement, and also would have been able to draw on central funds.[8]

It was 'Brendan' who brought in Thomas McMahon. One of seven children, Thomas McMahon appears to have been the only one drawn to the IRA, joining them soon after the Troubles restarted in 1969 when he was twenty-one. I have not been able to ascertain anything about his motivation at the time but my attention was caught by the words of another IRA man, Eamon Collins, who described his own mindset when joining the IRA as a young man in the 1970s.* Years later he wrote about his love of the Newry landscape in Northern Ireland:

> Whenever I came here I felt an emotional pull to the past. Tall pine trees stood guard beside abandoned stone houses where labourers and small farmers had reared large families for gener-ations until they had been driven out to fill the factories, armies and servants' quarters of the industrial nations. These abandoned ruins dotted a landscape that had once been densely populated. I felt that we in the IRA were the offspring of their humilia-tion: at that time I regarded myself and my comrades as history's vengeful children, come to exact the price for a society built on injustice. I believed that in our actions we gave form to the stifled rage of our ancestors . . . It certainly reflected my own rage and frustration.[9]

By the late 1970s Thomas McMahon was among the IRA's most capable bomb-makers. A carpenter by trade, he married Rose McArdle on 6 July 1975 in Carrickmacross, County Monaghan. The married couple moved into a bungalow he built in nearby Lisanisk in County Monaghan.

---

* Eamon Collins later broke from the IRA. He was beaten and stabbed to death in January 1999. Police stated their belief that the IRA was responsible. No one was charged.

Soon afterwards he underwent training in Libya at the arrangement of the country's dictator, Colonel Gaddafi. As his reputation as an IRA man grew, so would his stature within his community. One writer describes the process:

> Political activists, even those who may be secretive extremists, generally derive sustenance and gratification from their activities, which are, after all, voluntary, and which inevitably attract a certain kudos. To outsiders, IRA men personified menace; but to those inside the movement, they were good-hearted and lovable figures invested with a certain high minded nobility – cavaliers, even.[10]

When journalists investigated Thomas McMahon's past, they discovered that years earlier 'he became a hero when he saved a child who fell into a Dublin canal. He dived in fully clothed and swam with the child to safety'.[11]

Thomas McMahon had been making bombs even before his specialist training in Libya. He was 'behind a string of landmine attacks in South Armagh in the 1970s. Intelligence documents name him as the man who made the landmine that killed Corporal Harrison and Lance Corporal Brown near Newtownhamilton in March 1973; he was also suspected of being one of the gunmen who shot Sam Malcolmson in 1972'.[12] He was questioned numerous times but the Garda failed even to prove he was an IRA member let alone his role in the attacks. By 1979 he had two sons and apparently was working for his brother-in-law Felix McArdle as a carpenter taking home forty Irish Punts per week.* Meanwhile 'Brendan' had risen to become a senior member of their Northern Command.

After the Mullaghmore attack, as with any operation, the IRA took extreme care to ensure its personnel would not get caught. Francis McGirl gave his name as Patrick Rehill but by the time Gardai arrived at the home of the real Patrick Rehill he was gone. Later they heard

* Equivalent to about GB £160 in 2009. The average for a skilled Irish worker in 1979 was twenty-four Irish Punts.

he was on holiday in Australia and they did not see him again until the trial was in its closing stage and the investigation had been scaled back.

There were a number of factors against the Garda. First was a reluctance on the part of the general public to become officially involved in the investigation. Many were prepared to provide information but only on the basis that it would not be attributable to them. Such information allowed the Garda to piece together a picture of what had happened and who had been involved, but the Book of Evidence they compiled was far too thin for criminal proceedings. Second, the IRA were highly effective at enlisting the support of that part of the population who were prepared to turn a blind eye, and intimidating those who might be tempted otherwise. They could rely on safe houses and extensive networks of supporters to help IRA volunteers hide from the authorities until their trail went cold. Third, the IRA had the contacts and money to move their members around and even to send them overseas, as they did with 'Flynn'. Fourth, many of those who were arrested deployed anti-interrogation training to good effect, refusing to answer questions or even make eye contact with their questioners. Fifth, those accused of IRA membership employed excellent lawyers. This undoubtedly helped Francis McGirl escape conviction. It also nearly caused the collapse of the trial even before it had begun. On 29 August 1979 defence lawyers successfully asked the court to release the two men on a technicality. They had been arrested using anti-terror legislation which permitted them to be held for a maximum of forty-eight hours, after which they had to be charged or released. By some oversight the men had been re-arrested for the same offence one time more than the law permitted, and when the court realised this it ordered their immediate release. As the men left the courthouse and walked down the street they were suddenly re-arrested and charged with membership of the IRA. Gardai marched them back in front of the judge who remanded them in custody. The following day the two men reappeared in the court and were charged with murdering my grandfather.

For the IRA to have run two such lethal attacks in one day and then so thoroughly frustrated the work of the Garda and Royal Ulster Constabulary gives the impression they had massed ranks of men and women available for duty. In fact the number on whom they could call for operations was very limited. A claim that was deemed credible by a respected historian of the IRA put the number of experienced IRA gunmen and bombers in 1988 at 'no more than thirty . . . with perhaps twenty apprentices and up to five hundred volunteers who can be called upon to support their operations'.[13] Their ability to mount operations effectively and get away largely untouched was due to their ability to move personnel and arms around the country and across the border and, when needed, make them disappear. This gives the impression of active collusion by the general public. More accurately, what hampered the security forces most was the preparedness of the general public to turn a blind eye to the IRA operations in their midst.

This passive acceptance of the IRA was born out of a cultural phenomenon of incomparable power in the Ireland of the late twentieth century: republicanism. It is difficult to think of a tradition in Britain that was remotely similar and few countries had anything directly comparable. Republicanism was not simply a political movement; it was a cultural force which for generations had permeated into daily life in homes, shops, schools, offices, sports grounds, music halls and pubs. A polished and romanticised version of republicanism was celebrated in Irish literature, history, folklore and even religion. Easter was seen by some as a republican festival rather than a Christian one. 'I thought Easter was to celebrate the Rising. I knew nothing about the Resurrection',[14] was how one West Cork resident put it, as if the Easter Rising of 1916 against the British had eclipsed the Christian feast.

The vast majority of people in the Irish Republic, whatever their politics, at least tacitly supported the goal of one day seeing Ireland reunited and free from British rule. This was not just an article of faith, it was written into the Irish constitution. As unpalatable as IRA violence seemed to many, it was the only force which seemed remotely likely to achieve this goal. The IRA was seen by many as having the means and the ruthlessness necessary to deliver that goal, and in Mullaghmore there were enough people willing to turn a blind eye for them to mount their attack and escape virtually unpunished. Local reaction to the attack might have been summed up as it was in many other cases of shocking IRA violence:

'What has happened . . . is dreadful, they shouldn't have done it. But it's the IRA and you have to forgive them, for the community's sake.'[15]

Thomas McMahon and Francis McGirl were remanded in Portlaoise Prison. Its officers described it as the highest-security prison in Western Europe. The prisoners, almost all convicted of terror-related crimes, were housed on four landings known as 'E blocks'. Members of the Provisional IRA and Official IRA were on the top two floors; Irish National Liberation Army members were on the second floor; and beneath them on the first floor were those who had become disaffected with the paramilitary organisations. The only other inmates were petty criminals who worked hard for the IRA, cleaning their floors and toilets and delivering their food. They volunteered for this work and were rewarded with half remission of their sentence.

Thomas McMahon and Francis McGirl were interviewed at the prison reception by the IRA Officer Commanding, or 'OC', who verified their allegiance and accepted them onto the IRA floors. Francis McGirl did not have to stay long. After his acquittal on 23 November 1979 he shook hands with Thomas McMahon and walked out of the court with supporters towards a pub in Dublin's market area, telling reporters, 'I'm delighted . . . but I'm unhappy that he did not get off too.'[16] Prominent in those celebrating with him was his famous uncle John Joe McGirl.

Thomas McMahon had smiled as his own verdict and sentence were read out by the Chief Justice and then waved to his wife as he left to begin a life sentence in Portlaoise. Here he very soon seemed to assume an iconic stature within the Provisional IRA. His reputation fitted that of a 'proper' Provo: he did not womanise; he drank in moderation; he was even-tempered and he did not talk loosely. His wife, Rose, seemed to be a hundred per cent behind him. She visited regularly and they were obviously close. His carpentry skills were evident in the workshop, where he consistently produced the best work in the prison. Very soon he became an Officer Commanding. One prison officer described him as having 'small man syndrome', by which he meant he did not have a lot to say but from his demeanour he was the boss. He met the prison governor regularly and negotiated on behalf of the Provisional prisoners.

Thomas McMahon was intent on not staying inside longer than necessary and had immediately started the long process of appeal. When a prisoner's appeal was ready to be heard in court, he or she would, perhaps for the first time in years, leave the prison for the hearing. The prison service learned to its cost that such journeys provided the perfect opportunity for escape or the smuggling of arms. Portlaoise's chief prison officer Brian Stack was adamant that no one, not even a senior inmate such as Thomas McMahon, was exempt. He led by example, and when he encountered opposition from prisoners he did not hesitate to subdue inmates with whatever physical force was necessary. Some prisoners were offended by the process and, feeling their human rights were being abused, grew to hate him and the policy he implemented so effectively.

As Thomas McMahon left Portlaoise Prison for the Criminal Appeals Court on Monday 21 March 1983, he was subjected to a strip search. A violent struggle ensued. According to Thomas McMahon, the search was carried out by four men supervised by an officer called John. When McMahon was down to his underpants, he was turned upside down and his genitals were examined. When he was returned upright, he claimed John grabbed his arm until it cracked. The prison officers said that McMahon was kicking and pushing during the search, forcing John to hold him in an arm-lock while he fought back and shouted abuse. After the fracas he was driven to the courthouse, and when the hearing was over he was taken to hospital. Here it was discovered his arm had been broken; a surgeon later said the break was the result of a violent jerk. He was taken back to prison, and when he appeared in court again four days later, he learned his appeal had failed. There is no indication of a connection, but that evening prison officer Brian Stack was shot in the back of the neck. At the time he was walking away from Dublin's National Stadium, having just watched a boxing contest. The gunman ran off leaving him in a pool of blood. He survived for eighteen months, paralysed and severely brain damaged, until he died from complications in 1984. No one was charged with his murder.*

* A report published in 2007 stated: 'Now, almost a quarter of a century after his death his family are urging a fresh investigation under the Gardaí's recently established Cold Case Unit. And after talks with Garda Commissioner Noel Conroy, they are meeting with detectives about re-opening the unresolved inquiry.' Source: www.breakingnews.ie, 30 September 2007.

Thomas McMahon later lodged a complaint and started a claim for compensation for his broken arm. This took time to come to fruition and meanwhile, on 24 November 1985, the sixth anniversary of his conviction, he led an attempted mass break-out. He and ten of the IRA prisoners under him, including four who were serving life sentences, used an arsenal of smuggled arms to work their way towards the outer gate. Here they used PETN explosives to blow up the lock. It seems in their hurry they placed the explosive on the wrong side of the bolt, causing it to jam instead of fly off. As Portlaoise's unarmed officers ran out of the prison church, they were confronted by inmate Martin Ferris pointing a handgun at them.* Meanwhile another prisoner, Peter Rogers, used a pistol to take staff hostage on the IRA landing. Outside, his fellow conspirators were soon cornered and their self-confessed leader Thomas McMahon started to negotiate with prison governor William Reilly. McMahon agreed to return to the IRA block and remove the pistol from Peter Rogers, bringing the escape attempt to an ignominious end.

The attempted break-out, which had so nearly succeeded, hit the headlines and two inquiries were launched. A Garda investigation resulted in six of the men being convicted and having three years added to their sentences.† Of the five men not charged, Thomas McMahon was the most conspicuous. The Prison Service held an inquiry of their own, led by the prison governor. He examined how the inmates had managed to get hold of three pounds of explosives, electrical detonators, a .25 self-loading pistol, a .32 revolver, more than twenty rounds of ammunition, Mace gas canisters, imitation prison uniforms and copies of prison keys. The Prison Service report was never published. The Department of Justice, which had responsibility for prisons, refused to hold a public inquiry and suggested that prison officers had assisted the escape by smuggling in the materials. This compounded suspicions that there was an IRA volunteer working in the prison or the IRA had

---

* He had been convicted of smuggling guns and explosives from Libya onboard the Merchant Vessel *Marita Ann*, an operation he was in charge of. In 2002 he was elected to the Dáil.

† The six included Martin Ferris and John Patrick Crawley, each serving ten years for gun-running on the *Marita Ann*; and Peter Gerard Lynch, serving fourteen years for the attempted kidnap of Canadian businessman Galen Weston.

coerced staff. Some prison officers began to fear their service was seriously compromised; one interviewed for this book said there were rumours that senior officers were involved. His own experience shocked him. Shortly after the Garda inquiry he was stopped on the IRA landing by Thomas McMahon who asked after his wife, using her first name. 'What do you mean?' asked the officer nervously. McMahon took the officer to his cell where he showed him the officer's entire statement relating to the escape attempt, as given to Special Branch. 'It was very detailed and with sensitive information. He appeared to have the whole Garda file,' he told me.[17] It seemed that Thomas McMahon was hoping to recruit him.

Through the 1980s Thomas McMahon's family and supporters had been lobbying for his early release. The campaign was led from his family's hometown Carrickmacross and seemed to be gaining momentum. When his elderly mother Bernadette died in June 1988, he was paroled for three days of mourning after which he returned to Portlaoise. The next month he made a second escape attempt, this time while claiming compensation for the break to his arm. The proceedings began in Dublin's High Court on 19 July and he spent that night back in his cell at Portlaoise, leaving his clothes outside his cell as required for a detailed search. When he left his cell the next morning, he was escorted with another prisoner back to the courthouse in a prison van that had previously been searched, accompanied by three prison officers and two armed detectives. At the courthouse the same men escorted him to a lift to go to the second floor. The lift was small so only the prison officers went with him. On reaching the second floor he was led into a holding cell. Once inside he asked to be alone to use the toilet. One officer checked the toilet while the other unlocked McMahon's handcuffs. At this point he pulled out a handgun. The officers struggled with him and a shot was fired into the ceiling, after which McMahon was quickly overpowered. When calm had been restored, he was led into court and awarded £4,000 compensation for his broken arm.* With the prisoner safely back in Portlaoise, and the story appearing internationally, the Garda

* £4,000 was equivalent to almost two years' earnings at the rate of pay he declared at his 1979 trial.

appointed a superintendent that evening to investigate how he had managed to produce what turned out to be a Browning pistol. The Garda never published the report and Thomas McMahon was never charged.

Thomas McMahon's relationship with the IRA changed as the years progressed. He moved from Portlaoise's top landing to the bottom landing, reserved for what the prison officers called the 'Mavericks', the men who were disassociated from the illegal organisations housed above. He reportedly signed a declaration severing his links with the IRA in 1992[18] and in June that year was transferred to Arbour Hill Prison in Dublin. The following year he was moved to Mountjoy Prison Training Unit. In 1996 he started receiving daily parole from Mountjoy and undergoing further training as a carpenter. This was far from the normal progression of an IRA prisoner. In March 1997 he was photographed working on a building site near the jail, under a programme designed to prepare prisoners for release. His wife Rose had by then claimed that he had 'thought for a long time before giving up his IRA membership in prison and rejecting terrorism'.[19]

Four months later, on 20 July 1997, the IRA declared a ceasefire. When the peace agreement was signed in Belfast on Good Friday, 10 April 1998, one of the many issues it addressed was the accelerated release of paramilitary prisoners, and under its terms Thomas McMahon was set free on Thursday 6 August 1998. At 9:40 that evening he climbed into a Monaghan-registered car and was driven away by an unknown woman. He had served almost nineteen years, longer than any other republican prisoner in an Irish prison at that time.

It was a normal practice for returning republican prisoners to be honoured at a homecoming reception. McMahon's was held on 23 October that year in a Dundalk hotel. The IRA's political wing, Sinn Féin, sent a senior representative as guest speaker. The first IRA event he attended in public was the 1999 Easter Commemorations at Inniskeen in County Monaghan, when he laid a wreath on the graves of local IRA men 'on behalf of the republican movement'.[20] A hardline IRA strategist addressed the crowd of two hundred and called for the previous year's peace agreement to be rejected. Thomas McMahon, however, seemed to detach himself from the IRA and the dissident offshoots it sprouted, the Real IRA and Continuity IRA. One historian commented later: 'Quite a few ex-IRA people who carried out serious attacks decided to become semi-detached, not engaged politically, not joining rival groups, but living rather quiet and in some cases sullen lives. If that was Thomas McMahon's position it would have fitted a wider pattern.'[21]

After his release Thomas McMahon drew little publicity, with one notable exception. In September 2006 he pushed his way to the front of an angry demonstration about cuts proposed in his local hospital in Monaghan. As he had a finger-wagging confrontation with a government minister he was snapped by a photographer. His face was plastered in the national press under the headline: 'Hospital protester has dark terrorist past.'[22]

Francis McGirl was by nature very different from Thomas McMahon. When detectives from Dublin descended on Granard within hours of the attack, they soon realised that while Thomas McMahon was long in the tooth and well able to resist their questioning, his accomplice was the opposite. Superintendent John Courtney described him as 'very highly strung, aggressive, truculent if not slightly mental'. He was also aware that he was liable to 'drink to excess on occasions'.[23] It appears that in the early hours of the investigation the detectives patiently kept up the pressure, and before they retired for bed on the first day Francis McGirl had incriminated himself with the later famous slip of the tongue: 'I put no bomb on the boat' before anyone had mentioned either a bomb or a boat. He was unquestionably the weakest leak in the chain, and the IRA and Thomas McMahon paid a price for including him.

After his release he continued to work on his father's farm and kept up his IRA activities. Most notable of these was his involvement in what became one of Ireland's most notorious kidnappings. On Thursday 24 November 1983, Don Tidey, an American citizen working in Ireland as head of Associated British Foods, was kidnapped by the IRA when he stopped at what turned out to be a bogus Garda checkpoint near his home in the Dublin suburb of Rathfarnham. He was held for twenty-three days before information allegedly supplied by IRA informer Sean

O'Callaghan led the security forces to Derrada Woods at Ballinamore, Country Leitrim. When the Garda and Army approached the hideout, they were met by gunfire from four IRA men inside. In the ensuing shoot-out one Garda trainee and one army private were killed. After the kidnapping Francis McGirl went on the run. He narrowly escaped from soldiers and Gardai in the Ballinamore area and then fled across neighbouring counties. In County Mayo he was confronted by armed detectives but again managed to escape.[24]

In the early hours of Wednesday 15 March 1995, ten days before he was due to celebrate his fortieth birthday, Francis McGirl died in an unusual motor accident. The tractor he was driving crashed on a bend at Callow Hill near his home. It overturned, trapping him underneath in a ditch where he died. At his funeral two days later, St Patrick's Day, it was said he had been returning from the pub and was worse for wear.[25] A British newspaper reported:

> Fr Charles Heerey, the parish priest, called for divine forgiveness for sins committed by McGirl, a farmer, builder and former grave-digger, and reward for his neighbourliness, love of children and other qualities. Fr Heerey said: 'In his stumbling way, Francis tried to reflect God's goodness. He often failed.' . . . He was buried beside the graves of relatives, not in the cemetery's republican plot, no volley was fired and no paramilitary items were placed on the coffin . . . McGirl's cousin, Mr Liam McGirl, a Sinn Féin Leitrim county councillor, son of John Joe McGirl and Ballinamore's undertaker, said outside the church that the family maintained his relative played no part in Lord Mountbatten's murder.[26]

In reviewing the operations carried out in 1979, including Mullaghmore and Warrenpoint, An Phoblacht/Republican News wrote: 'last year was one of resounding republican success, when the IRA's cellular reorganisation was operationally vindicated, particularly through the devastating use of remote-control bombs'.[27]

In truth, as has been pointed out by historians of the period, An Phoblacht/Republican News had overlooked the fact that the cell system was mainly a Belfast phenomenon. The South Armagh Brigade, who carried out the Warrenpoint attack and were involved at Mullaghmore, were a good example of a rural unit who had successfully kept to their old structures and local control. This did not stop the leadership being perceived as behind a reorganisation that had saved the IRA from its disastrous performance of earlier years, most notably 1974 and 1975.

If 27 August 1979 helped to re-allocate power at the top of the IRA, the same could be said for its middle management. According to one historian, 'Brendan' had acted as 'intelligence officer' at Warrenpoint: 'Although the blowing up of Mountbatten had been an operation organised by GHQ staff, he had played a key role in the planning. That August day had made his reputation within the IRA.'[28] Both attacks that day were tremendously well received in republican circles. 'Mountbatten was a beautiful target', is how one supporter later described it.[29] Another said, 'I don't glorify death but I had personal pride in what happened because it was a military operation and they took him out.'[30]

The short-term international reaction might well have stung the IRA. The leaders of nation after nation rallied to Britain's side to express their dismay. They evidently remembered my grandfather as an outstanding wartime leader who became one of the prime architects of the ending of empire. The IRA was a pragmatic organisation. It is possible that some of their leadership foresaw the political costs and decided they were justified. Perhaps they took the view that has been ascribed to an earlier set of republicans who had assassinated a retired British Vice-Admiral in 1936, a killing which caused enormous shock and resentment at the time.*

A justification of this kind entailed rationalising the assassination as a form of *notice*. The purpose of such violence was not to bring about direct or immediate change or to make a measurable military gain but, rather, to alert the world to the existence of a wrongful political injury – in this case, the continuing trespass of the English in the north of Ireland.[31]

* Vice-Admiral Somerville was shot dead when he opened the door of his Skibbereen home to IRA gunmen.

If such a mindset existed in the republican leadership, it might explain an interview Gerry Adams gave to *Time* magazine in November 1979 when officially Vice President of Provisional Sinn Féin, the IRA's political arm:

> The IRA gave clear reasons for the execution. I think it is unfortunate that anyone has to be killed, but the furor created by Mountbatten's death showed up the hypocritical attitude of the media establishment. As a member of the House of Lords, Mountbatten was an emotional figure in both British and Irish politics. What the IRA did to him is what Mountbatten had been doing all his life to other people; and with his war record I don't think he could have objected to dying in what was clearly a war situation. He knew the danger involved in coming to this country. In my opinion, the IRA achieved its objective: people started paying attention to what was happening in Ireland.[32]

This was billed as the first interview he had given to any American publication. If so, it is possible he was reacting to reports that the IRA had suffered financially as a result of the Mullaghmore attack. These centred on claims that Irish-American donors had withdrawn support which had been channelled through Irish Northern Aid, better known as Noraid and later Friends of Sinn Féin. US government figures do not back this up. In 1979 Noraid declared income only slightly down from 1978 and 1977.* In any case, the flow of funds from Noraid, although welcome, was not vital to the IRA, amounting to $168,000 in 1978, less than 10 per cent of its annual income.†

---

* The total for 1979 was $140,000 but the data for the first six months is missing. If Noraid raised $140,000 in only six months it was their best performance since early 1973.

† In 1980 they raised $195,000; in the first half of 1981 $251,000. For a while fundraising in the USA did then seem to experience trouble after a judicial hearing in 1982 declared Noraid a foreign agent of the IRA. It is difficult, however, to attribute this to more than the close conservative ties that existed between President Ronald Reagan and the British Prime Minister, Margaret Thatcher. When Noraid started filing returns again in 1984, the figures showed an upward trend, rising from $226,000 in 1984 to $416,000 in, 1988.

In 1997 I saw the reception that republican leaders could expect in the United States. While at Harvard, I heard that Martin McGuinness would be a visiting speaker at the Kennedy School of Government, the very school in which I was enrolled. I walked through a blizzard to get there early, hoping he would describe the path which had led from killing and maiming to working for peace. At the time he was Sinn Féin's chief negotiator.

An academic moved to the podium and explained she was part of a programme at Harvard for the study of Northern Ireland. She then introduced Martin McGuinness: 'His reputation for integrity, for a personal incorruptibility . . . is unrivalled in Northern Ireland,' she said. Then she grinned and hinted that she could not speak freely. She continued:

> It is widely believed that Mr McGuinness was and became in 1976 the Director of Operations of the Northern Command of the IRA. He is widely credited with overhauling the organisation, getting rid of its formerly archaic structure . . . In the late 1970s and early 1980s, Mr McGuinness, it is widely believed (*laughter from the audience*) served as chief of staff of the IRA . . .[33]

I was now more optimistic than ever of learning from the mind of a man who was proving instrumental to the peace process but who apparently had been centrally involved in the violence that had brought so much suffering in Ireland in the late 1970s.

However, the evening turned out to be little more than an exercise to showcase Martin McGuinness. He received prolonged bursts of applause and cheering at various points, giving the appearance of one of the fundraising events at which he often appeared. I turned behind me and studied the audience which was unlike anything I experienced before or after at Harvard. It seemed to contain a large number of young men who had come from nearby Boston. They stamped their feet and wolf-whistled in a way that I had only seen before for film stars. A series of breathless fans rose to their feet and it was soon clear that none of them had any idea of the complexity of the man on the stage. Any attempt to raise the sort of difficult issues into which Martin McGuinness might have been able to offer insight would have been quickly drowned out by the mob. I left disgusted, not by Martin McGuinness but by the presiding academic.*

Critics of the IRA liked to sling mud at them for what they saw as behaviour akin to that of the fascists who had plagued Germany. John Hume, leader of Northern Ireland's Social Democratic Labour Party, said of the IRA in 1988:

> They are more Irish than the rest of us, they believe. They are the pure master race of Irish. They are the keepers of the Holy Grail of the nation. That deep-seated attitude, married to their method, has all the hallmarks of undiluted fascism. They have also the other hallmarks of the fascist – the scapegoat – the Brits are to blame for everything, even their own atrocities. They know better than the rest of us. They know so much better that they take onto themselves the right, without consultation with anyone, to dispense death and destruction.'[34]

Only time will reveal whether the men who were later to replace the IRA's Armalite rifles with Armani suits[†] realised in 1979 that what played well in west Belfast did not necessarily do so in Washington. What is clear is that the IRA leaders knew they could not afford to concentrate on explosions and forget about expressions; that gunning the presses was just as important as pressing the guns. By 1979 the IRA were using their marketing skills to full effect, already adept at leveraging their attacks through creative press relations. Pictures of the

---

* I later went to see the Dean of the school, formerly a member of the Clinton administration. I put a photograph of Nick on his desk and played a recording of the evening which I had bought from the school. He soon shared my opinion that it had been, at best, a cock-up, and although the Institute of Politics which had run the evening did not come under his remit, he promised action. Three years later I accepted his invitation to serve on the Dean's Council.

† In 2006 a doctor from Northern Ireland was treating my bomb-damaged eye. He asked me how it had been injured and soon we were talking about the peace process. He told me that the popular republican phrase *Tiocfaidh ár lá* (meaning 'our day will come') had been turned into *Tiocfaidh Armani*, a reference to the designer suits in which some liked to claim IRA leaders had been seen.

Mullaghmore and Warrenpoint murders were being published around the world within hours.

The IRA knew who to expect on the boat the day they blew it up, and by maintaining a minute-by-minute watch right up to the moment the man pressed the button with the woman at his side, they were able to confirm with absolute certainty who was on board. It was of course politically expedient to claim otherwise and within five days an IRA representative said in a newspaper interview:

> Young Maxwell shouldn't have been there. Latest intelligence before the attack said that there would be additional members of the Royal Family, not civilians, on the boat. Their presence would still not have inhibited the operation going ahead . . . But Paul Maxwell was not scheduled to be there. It should have been a more mature man, an older man who would have been able to weigh up the political company he was keeping and the repercussions of it . . . We're not out to kill civilians but take this as an example. Saracen [armoured] vehicles are known as targets: if the British Army carried a 13-year-old-boy and we hit it, who's responsible for his death?[35]

On the same day *An Phoblacht/Republican News* in Dublin published an article headed 'The Execution of Soldier Mountbatten' which included:

> Also killed as a result of the explosion were Mountbatten's fifteen-year-old grandson and the pilot, a teenager from Enniskillen, as well as the Dowager Baroness of Brabourne. Lady Brabourne, Lord Brabourne and another son were injured. The IRA has confirmed that they were not expected to board the boat at Mullaghmore, County Sligo. Paul Maxwell from Enniskillen was a late replacement pilot for an older man.[36]

By returning to Sligo I was able to find little pieces of the story behind the attack and piece them together for myself. In years to come perhaps more of the story will be revealed by those at the plot's centre or closely connected to them. As one author wrote of his

IRA uncle: 'He was the son my grandfather trusted, and to whom he vouchsafed knowledge of certain matters so that he might bear witness to them and, it could be inferred, keep them in memory until they might safely emerge at the lit surface of history. But when is this kind of disclosure timely?'[37]

26

FACE TO FACE

It was afternoon when I arrived at Finner Camp, on the other side of Donegal Bay from Classiebawn, but the clouds were so low and thick that it felt like night. It was Monday 11 November 2003. At the entrance barrier, soldiers took my name and directed me towards a modern building. In its doorway, sheltering from the rain and wind were two men: Sean Brennan and John O'Brien, both in uniform.

Sean, aged fifty-two, was a Quartermaster Sergeant. Born within a few miles of Classiebawn, in Cliffoney, he was one of sixteen children from his father's first marriage. When his mother died, his father remarried and produced a further seven offspring. Sean's grandfather had been a fisherman in Mullaghmore, and his mother worked in the castle for a season in the 1940s. In 1970 Sean left for England. Four years later he was back, married with two children and serving in the 28th Infantry at Finner Camp. Three years younger than Sean, John O'Brien was raised in County Mayo. Soon after leaving school he joined the Army during the large-scale recruitment that followed the return of the Troubles to Northern Ireland. In 1973, now a Company Sergeant, he joined the same battalion as Sean at Finner Camp. As we went upstairs to the non-commissioned officers' mess, Sean was looking shaken. In 1979 he had been one of the men who found Nick's body. Nick's lifeless face had stayed with him ever since, and nothing had prepared him for seeing my identical face this afternoon.

I had never discovered what had happened to Nick immediately after the bomb. I wanted to know, deeply and achingly. I wanted to hear it first-hand and in detail. Here at last was a man who could tell me. I told Sean and John how I felt. I had come too far, waited too long, to have this opportunity go off half-cock. They looked surprised and relieved.

John started by saying he had very vivid memories and wanted forgiveness for the words he was about to use. I was spellbound. In August 1979 John had been twenty-four. He worked in operations, the central hub of the camp. They had a special radio to listen to the Garda frequencies in case they were needed. As he spoke, it was clear John was visualising the scene down to the smallest detail. 'It was a blue radio – in the corner. I could clearly hear the guard in an awful panic: "Classiebawn Car calling Seven Five Two, come in, urgent, urgent",'[1] John explained. They were aware of Classiebawn and that my grandfather was always accompanied by a Garda vehicle with the call-sign 'Classiebawn Car'. The radio call was a guard in that car trying to reach the local Garda headquarters in Sligo, call-sign Seven-Five-Two.

A Garda station transmitted, 'Go ahead, over', and the response came, 'Mountbatten's boat has exploded in the water, send help.' The army base's Commanding Officer was sitting outside, taking in the sun. His response was, 'Now the shit's hit the fan.' He told John to get three Land-Rovers to the scene and call in a helicopter from Baldonnel, the government airfield near Dublin.

At 11:50 that morning, Sean was working in the ration store, issuing food, when a colleague put his head around the door. He knew that Sean had a role in Bundoran's lifeboat and he had come to tell him that he had heard something about a boat in trouble in Mullaghmore. Sean quickly got permission to leave the camp and drove down to the lifeboat two miles away.

The lifeboat was a relatively new addition to Bundoran and was crewed by a group of volunteers. During a call-out they would all get to the boat as quickly as possible. It carried a crew of three but at twenty-one feet long it was too heavy to get into the water without half a dozen men to guide it down the slipway. When Sean reached the quay he discovered that only one person had turned up. It was the coxswain, Denis O'Hara, a local teacher. Then another man arrived and said, 'Lord Mountbatten's boat has been blown up and there are casualties and people lost off Mullaghmore.' Sean told me, 'This news had an awful effect on me. My reaction was, "How can we get this boat out as quickly as possible?"'[2] But he was dismayed to realise that they might not be able to launch the boat with so few crew available to help.

Michael 'Whitie' Gilbride, a stonemason and farmer, was one of the lifeboat crew and he soon arrived. Sean described him as 'a good Irishman'. Listening to Sean speak about Whitie reminded me of the way my father had described his friend, Joe, the builder in County Galway. He had been a long-standing family friend as well as a proud supporter of the old IRA. My father had cautioned me not to mistake that for the Provisional IRA. Apparently when Whitie had arrived on the scene and discovered the nature of the call-out, he had expressed some doubt, saying, 'I wonder should I be here at all?' but he decided to join the crew in launching the boat. Sean told me, 'He done his damnedest that day' but they still needed more men. Whitie was accompanied by Martin Shelbourne, his seventeen-year-old nephew from England who had often helped launch the lifeboat. When Martin first arrived and offered his help, there was a silence. 'What's going on?' he asked. Then one of them said, 'The bastards have blown Mountbatten up.'

Sean Brennan, Denis O'Hara and Whitie Gilbride launched the boat themselves, with Martin's help. It took time. The boat was heavy, and with the tide low it was a long way to the shoreline. Whitie pulled from the front, Denis and Sean pushed at the back and Martin helped steer towards the water's edge. Their problems did not end there. The propeller became stuck in seaweed and Sean struggled to unravel it. The crew got on board and took Martin on as well. Whitie did not want his young nephew to be in any doubt as to the dangers involved: 'They booby trap things. There'll be a booby trap on the boat,' he warned. When I later met Martin, he told me he had thought, 'Bloody hell, I'm going to get blown up here. It is bank holiday Monday and I'm going to die.'[3]

Denis O'Hara was a skilful coxswain and eventually got the boat into deeper water. About twenty minutes later, at around one o'clock, they arrived on the other side of the bay near Mullaghmore, where they could see a number of boats gathered. There was no sign of *Shadow V*. There was scum on the water, bits of boat, matchwood and a bit of rope. When they approached some men in a fishing boat, they were told that there was still one person missing.

They had been searching for about ten minutes when they saw a helicopter flying towards them. This was an Alouette which John O'Brien had requested from Baldonnel on the other side of Ireland. It came down low across the water, went out and turned before coming in low, a second and third time. Then it went into a low hover in a rocky area close to the shore. From the side of the helicopter a man came down on a winch into the water and grabbed something. He then started shouting at the lifeboat. The water was shallow. Below was a rock-shelf. Thick seaweed, nine or ten feet long, made it almost impossible for the crew to see a way through. They knew that if their propeller hit a rock it could put the engine out of action. When the boat got within five or ten yards, Whitie tore off his shoes, dived in, swam to the man in the water and caught hold of something. It was Nick.*

The man on the winch was hoisted back into the helicopter and Denis O'Hara manoeuvred still closer. Whitie, a particularly strong swimmer, got himself and Nick next to the boat. What happened next is described only by Martin. Nick's body had become entangled in a fishing line. At the end of the line was a strengthened section made of wire, which was known as a 'trace'. Thinking it was a booby-trap, Whitie shouted, 'Bomb!'

Denis O'Hara pushed the throttle. Sean and Martin were holding onto Whitie. Nick's body was weighing Whitie down. To Martin it felt like 'a tug of war'. The boat and men went one way. Nick's body went the other and fell back into the water. The boat circled around and Whitie jumped in a second time, this time joined by Martin. His uncle shouted at him to get back in the boat 'or you'll get tangled up in the wrack', as he called the seaweed. Martin obeyed but found clambering back over the inflatable tube a lot more difficult than expected. Back

---

* The man in the water on the end of the helicopter's winch was 23-year-old Michael Treacy. For weeks he had nightmares from which he would wake screaming and crying. Source: Michael Treacy interviewed for this book, 8 March 2004.

on board he was of more use. Whitie was holding Nick under the arms and Martin grabbed one of his legs. When he did so he was shocked to see a fishing hook stuck in the left thigh. Whitie gently raised Nick up and Sean took him in both arms. He told me:

> I brought him ever so gently down the side of the boat and laid him on the floor. I was shocked, deeply shocked to see this poor boy killed in this way. There was no blood . . . His body was intact apart from his lower left leg which was really in bad shape . . . The look on his face was as if he was asleep . . . a very, very peaceful look . . . An awful feeling came over me when I took all this in. Whitie got into the boat and Denis O'Hara got sick and he couldn't look.

When Whitie said, 'Cover the boy up', the crew put their jackets over him. Martin told me:

> As we were racing in at high speed I could see the trace all wrapped around him, and the hook in his leg. I thought it must be hurting him. I couldn't take on board he was actually dead. I remember quite vividly the speed we were going. There was a bit of turbulence and a couple of times I fell on top of your brother and the jackets covering him kept blowing off. I could see his hair blowing in the wind. Whitie kept covering his head up so no one could see.

In Mullaghmore they were met by a 'vast' crowd. Martin told me, 'I have never seen so many press in all my life.' He stood back from the lifeboat and watched as a reporter came up and started to ask questions. Whitie grabbed his notebook and ripped it, saying, 'No names!' When they walked into the Beach Hotel, the proprietors offered them blankets, tea and sandwiches but they had no appetite.

An ambulance was waiting for Nick's body. It had come from Ballyshannon, four miles north of Bundoran. The lifeboat's crew did what they could to shield his body from view as a gurney was carried through the shallow water and out towards them, keeping the press at bay. Sean would never forget trying to get Nick's body out of the boat without further damaging his injured legs. 'It was hard, very, very hard,' he said. 'As gentle as can be in the world, we managed to get the remains of your brother onto the stretcher and into the ambulance.'

As Sean was talking to me, John produced a photograph of the scene. I stared and stared, and picked out the people until I could identify almost everyone. It was as terrible a photograph as I had ever seen, but it also gave me what I wanted: a sense of being there, made all the more intense for having one of the people in the photo talking me through it.

I had seen the photograph once before. In 1999 I had been given a video tape of a documentary made for German television about the attack. I curled up beside Isabella on our sofa and watched. My knowledge of German was limited but it was enough for me to get the gist of what was being said. It was nothing unexpected. Suddenly my world caved in as, without any warning, there on the screen was a distant photograph of Nick's body being lifted from a lifeboat. I stopped and rewound the tape, unable to believe what I had seen. After the shock subsided, I fell to pieces and sobbed my eyes out. I was angry and resentful that I had never known of this photograph; but I was also pleased to have seen it with my own eyes and know that his limp little body had looked much as if he had been asleep. Now I was seeing the same photograph again but this time I was prepared and receiving the context I needed to make sense of it.

Later that afternoon the crew had taken the lifeboat back to Bundoran and put it in its shed. Martin told me, 'The town was quiet but I saw a man with a bottle dancing in the street, saying, "The old bastard is dead."' When Whitie told Martin, 'Come on, we're going for a swim', he replied, 'What on earth do I want to swim for?' 'To wash the death off you,' he said. The teenager and his uncle swam out into the surf.

Later I wrote in my journal:

Listening to Martin made me feel a little nearer to the moment of recovering Nick's body. These details were known to someone, and until now that someone had not been me. Now that I had gathered the detail, its power had gone away. The unknown detail was horrendous, whereas the known detail merely shocking. And

I felt soothed to have gathered it up, had my shock and moved on, feeling as if a device that had the potential to blow up in my mind had been defused.

Martin wept two or three times in the couple of hours we spoke, with sobs and apologies each time. When it came time to leave, we chatted right up to the last minute. I talked of my parents, and his eyes lit up and he grinned from ear to ear. As he left, it occurred to me that he seemed much happier than when we met, and I remembered how often I had felt lighter, by talking to others about what was locked up inside me.[4]

Sean's anguish after the rescue only became worse:

We went to the inshore rescue meeting the following week and there was nothing discussed about it. Nobody thanked about the efforts that were made. There was no recognition of the great work to launch the boat . . . to be ignored afterwards was very hurtful . . . and I said, 'Bye bye, boys.' I left the lifeboat. A rescue was a rescue to me, no matter who it was. Whitie would have been a local republican sympathiser, but it didn't matter to Whitie. There was no politics in this. The man done everything he could that day, he nearly burst his heart trying to get that little boy out of the water.

By the time I said goodbye to Sean and John at Finner Camp, I was exhausted. I drove back to my Sligo hotel. With so much going on in my head, I did not feel like sleeping. I sat up late into the night writing for long stretches in my journal:

I felt a huge relief to look into Sean's eyes as he told me how they had found Nick's body, and handed it over to the ambulance. He cared deeply. He had tears in his eyes when he told me how he felt, looking at Nicky's body. He had done me a great service in being part of the crew who had to perform this grim task, and for describing it with such clarity just the way I wanted it – un-sanitised, un-sensationalised, just as it was with the details as they were. We estimated the time of finding his body at between 1pm and 1:30pm. Knowing this, and yesterday finding my hospital notes, showing that I arrived at the hospital at 1pm, makes the jigsaw fit together so painfully tightly, but helps me get close to Nick, close to his death, close to that time when we parted without a goodbye.[5]

Visiting Sligo Hospital with Amanda in January 2004, we stood in the mortuary and I later recorded:

A simple room with curtained windows and red carpet and white marble altar, it was until that moment one of the few rooms that Nick had ever been into that I had not. In that respect I felt close to him but strangely the room didn't otherwise unlock any great emotion for me, other than a general sadness . . . After about 10 minutes of silent thought I gave Amanda a prolonged hug and squeeze and heard from her the little noises, swallows and sniffs that accompany tears.

We laughed, darkly, at the hum of the refrigerators next door where the mortuary's bodies are stored. Nicky's remains were recovered from Mullaghmore, a place where the noise of breaking waves and whirling gulls filled the air, and taken to Mersham churchyard in Kent, where the bleating of sheep dominated. But in between, such natural beauty was largely absent and this room, functional as it was, conveyed nothing of the natural order or sense of eternity that would have connected me to feeling Nicky's spirit.[6]

Briefly I glimpsed into the adjoining room where the bodies of Nick, Paul and my grandparents had been laid out and examined by Ireland's State Pathologist, Professor John Harbison.

An identical twin once wrote about holding his brother's body:

I raised him to an almost upright position to embrace him. He was heavy. His back was wet, the only indication of the life just ended. I laid him down and took his right hand and placed it on my cheek and temple, uncurling his fingers with my hand. Our hands were exactly the same size, our fingernails identical. I kissed his hand and said his name aloud softly, over and over again and wept quietly, feeling myself shrivel and weaken. The twins were gone. I was alone.[7]

The account horrified and fascinated me, and I wished I could have had such a moment with Nick but knew this was impossible. Reading the *Irish Times* one morning I came across an article about the retirement of John Harbison as State Pathologist. 'He suddenly seems very contactable whereas until I read that article he had seemed a figure from 1979 and very far removed,' I wrote in my journal.[8] When I later called his office, he immediately said he would help in any way he could and invited me to visit him in Dublin. I took up his offer.

On Thursday morning I went straight from the airport to his office housed in temporary portacabins at the Fire Brigade Training School. He came out dressed in tweeds and a tie, warm and interested, even indulgent in the care and gentleness he showed as he settled me in his office. He had just handed over his responsibilities to a new State Pathologist and was helping with the transition after almost forty years in the job. While I hung my coat he adjusted an electric heater and pulled onto his desk a vast and bulging red folder with 'Mountbatten' written in large handwriting across its front. We spoke about generalities at first but my eye kept going to the folder. It made me tense with fear and excitement. I knew I needed to do this but I was frightened. I felt as if a door was being held open for me to go back to the Sligo Mortuary of 1979 and to carry out one fundamental, terrible but necessary act: to see Nicky one last time.

Last month with Amanda I had got a sense of the place but it hadn't been somewhere that spoke to me. I had felt that I was in the right place but the trail was cold. I had looked at the door that led to the white-tiled room beyond where post mortem examinations were carried out. I could see through a small gap in the doors but didn't go through them as the mortuary was in use that day. Instead I had stayed in what the hospital called the 'Chapel Of Rest'. Now, sitting in Dr Harbison's office, I was about to be taken through those doors and into the night of August 27th 1979.

Dr Harbison endeared himself to me very quickly. I had heard that he was a very strong and energetic character. He was Lecturer in Medical Jurisprudence at Trinity College, Dublin and I expected him to be rather over-bearing. But in the four hours we spent together he listened to every question in full and with the greatest of patience before proceeding with his answers.[9]

I had been found in the water face down; why, I asked Dr Harbison, had I not drowned? He suggested several possible factors: First, a function of the body, known as glottic spasm, constricts the airway when fluid enters it, even in an unconscious state. Second: if I had inhaled a small amount of salt water it might have been survivable, whereas the same amount of freshwater might have killed me.* Third, at the moment of detonation, my lungs might have been filled with air having just breathed in and this might have made me float to the surface and be visible to the rescuers. Possibly Nick had just breathed out giving him less buoyancy and resulting in his body not coming to the surface. Hearing this made me realise that my survival might perhaps have been more a matter of chance than I had ever realised. It might even have come down to the heads-I-lived, tails-I-died chance that I had just inhaled when the bomb blew up. My journal continues:

Dr Harbison opened up the sealed file with a pair of scissors explaining he hadn't seen its contents since the inquest in 1980. He had been relieved to find it hadn't been thrown out during the move from his former office. After much searching he had found the file at home.

Immediately a photograph tumbled out, face up. It was Grandpapa. I felt like I had been hit by a dart that had sped out

* John Harbison explained the reason. The salinity of sea water is greater than that of body tissue. Therefore salt water does not transfer across the lung-lining and into the blood as quickly as fresh water because the transfer requires a process called osmosis. For this to occur efficiently, a positive salt 'gradient' (a difference in the levels of salt) is needed across the dividing surface. With fresh water this gradient exists. The result is the transfer of mass from the water into the cells of the body. This causes the cells to swell up and break apart releasing potassium into the body's tissues and causing death.

of the folder six feet away. But I didn't flinch, at least I think I didn't. 'Oh dear, that's not very nice,' said Dr Harbison, gathering the photo up and putting it back in the file . . . Deep down I felt I wanted to go on but I wasn't sure. I needed to work gently uphill for however long it took, listening to Dr Harbison read and explain his post mortem reports before I took a decision on whether to look at the photographs.

I had first obtained the reports some months before and had felt a strange relief, in addition to the obvious pain, in reading them. I had shown them to Mum who had had a similar feeling in reading them. We had both laughed later in sharing our belief that Grandpapa would have been absolutely delighted at his report. It spoke about how he was in remarkably good condition for a 79-year-old. Heart: fit and healthy with only moderate hardening of the arteries. Arteries leading to the brain: very good condition. Teeth: excellent condition and demonstrating very high quality dentistry.

In reading the post mortem reports I had been aware of how many of the terms were beyond my layman's understanding. I didn't have any context or previous experience of such documents nor could I judge which injuries would have been fatal and which survivable.

Slowly Dr Harbison took me through the reports until we got to Nick's. It listed many injuries but his trunk was 'remarkably free of injury'. He had received damage to his brain, lungs and kidneys and had a broken spleen. He had been knocked unconscious instantly and died very soon after. I wrote in my journal:

Dr Harbison was answering my questions with care, expertise, patience and honesty but I knew that one last step remained: the photographs. I was tense, preparing to look at the photographs of my beloved 14-year-old identical twin. I would of course have declined had it not been for the aching pain I had felt for 24 years at never having had a last look at Nicky. I had never seen him dying or dead. And by the time I reached his grave 7 days after his funeral my child's mind had hung in blank incomprehension.

I had wondered if he really was in that grave at all. I had wondered what his remains looked like. Those questions had been in my head for 24 years. Now I had the chance to come face to face one last time.

For some seconds I looked at the first photo. I could feel myself digesting the information coming off the photograph. It was a process that absorbed me. Then I lowered my eyes to Nicky's chest and quite unexpectedly the steely calm left me and a stirring feeling welled up from somewhere low in my chest. For a second or two my eyes got blurry with tears. I blinked and my mind took over again, my stirring feeling left, and I was able to say very quietly, 'That's the jumper Nanny knitted.' I hadn't thought of that jumper since I last saw Nicky. It had completely gone from my mind. Now I looked at the photograph, the thing that knocked me sideways was not the state of his body; I had prepared myself for that. It was the knitting of Nanny in whose woollen V-neck he had been killed. She had been like a second mother. For the last couple of years she had stopped coming to Classiebawn with us, staying instead at home in Mersham. In 1979 she was 87 and she wrote on hearing that Nicky was dead that her heart had broken. In Professor Harbison's office I just had not expected to have Nanny there with me, but I looked at that lovingly knitted little V-neck, whose individual strands of wool were so clearly caught by the Garda photographer's camera, and it wasn't Nicky's body that jolted me, for it was utterly lifeless and painless; what jolted me was the sudden reminder of the living pain that Nanny went through for the last years of her long life. She died five years later.

I moved my eyes to Nicky's face and looked into his eyes . . . I stared and felt my brain absorbing the information like a dry sponge. I didn't break down, scream, hurl the pack of photographs at the wall and throw myself on the floor. I felt gentle and still . . . I was prepared (although it wasn't till now that I knew this for sure) to look at his physical remains and study them for what they were: the housing that his spirit had resided in. His wonderful, unique life force had gone forever. The flesh, blood, bone and hair left behind were his but he wasn't in them. I needed to see his body because, among other reasons, I had felt unbalanced after his death by not being able to look at his wounds, and be as intimate with his body in death as I had been in life. After seeing his body, I had thought I would feel more balanced in this respect; and I had been right. Today I feel another wound has healed.

For years I had been unable entirely to rid my mind of the agonising thought that perhaps if Nick had been pulled quickly into a boat he might have lived. This had been introduced by the January 1980 press coverage of the inquests into the deaths which had stated that my grandfather and Nick had been knocked unconscious by the bomb and, unable to save themselves, had drowned. When John Harbison finished reading me his post mortem report, I asked if Nick might have survived if he had been lifted into the boat alongside me. He delved into the report again and looked at the notes he had jotted as he had worked on Nicky's body. The immediacy of the evidence was in no doubt; one of the pages, relating to my grandfather's autopsy, had dried blood on it. After a careful review, he told me that there was no single injury he could see that guaranteed Nick's death, but when he looked at the photographs he changed his opinion. They betrayed in an instant what the text did not: the sheer brute force of the blast on his head. After one look he said, 'No, he was not going to survive. This degree of head injury implies massive damage to the brain.'[10] In an instant a nagging doubt evaporated, after decades in my mind: Nick had not been left to die in the water. I felt huge relief pass through me.

I was pleased that my family had never seen the bodies; they had neither needed nor wanted to. However, for some entirely irrational reason I had always thought it sad that Nick's body had been identified only by a Garda. Now I was pleased that at least one member of the family had seen his sweet face and diminutive body in their last appearance. I later realised that there had existed in my mind, even if subconsciously, a feeling that I had somehow abandoned Nick in this final duty. That trace of unreasoned and unreasonable emotion now disappeared.

Sitting in Professor Harbison's portacabin, staring at the photographs of Nick, tears had not come but I knew they would. At a quarter to midnight that evening in my Dublin hotel room, I finished my paper-work and walked into the bathroom. I was squeezing toothpaste onto my brush when I looked into the mirror and saw my face for the first time since seeing Nick's in the photographs. We were still identical and I broke down utterly. It was exactly the release I needed.

If my children ever suffer bereavement when still young, I will urge them, once they are ready, actively to mourn. If it is what they want, I will encourage them to grapple with the trauma in close-up and slow motion and from every angle they desire until the box of un-resolved grief unlocks for them. This is not a prescription for a good recovery, and for some people it might be the opposite of what they need. But for me it provided more than therapy; it was liberation.

27

PEACE

In March 2004 I opened the *Irish Independent* and was amazed to read these remarks by the Irish Justice Minister: 'No true republican could have looked through binoculars at the children on a boat in Mullaghmore before deliberately blowing them to pieces; and no true republican could publicly lie and lie again about his involvement with those matters . . .'[1] He was campaigning for an election at the time* and he went on to say that the Provisional IRA movement had 'stolen and abused the language of republicanism to justify a savage, anti-democratic, crime-ridden, and shameful campaign . . . The truth is that the Provisionals are the embodiment of all that is anti-republican. Their ideology, methods and values would have disgusted the founders of our State.'[2]

I was struck by what he said because it helped me resolve an inner conflict. On the one hand, I felt very attracted to the Irish way of life and recognised that a large part of that way of life was rooted in republicanism. On the other hand, I was repelled by republicanism's dominant force, the IRA. That the minister saw the IRA as 'anti-republican' brought home to me that republicanism meant different things to different people.

I took no particular pleasure in seeing the party of Gerry Adams and

---

* Sinn Féin were running a strong campaign in the lead-up to the Republic's elections.

Martin McGuinness being given a hard time. They had been prime movers in bringing IRA violence to an end and they seemed to have been doing valuable political work since then. I agreed with one commentator who told me in 2003, 'Sinn Féin are getting a huge following from other Catholics not because anyone wants to return to violence but because they have a clearer voice in the debate. They say what has to be said and they are very good at it. They have demonstrated they can change and that is fantastic.'[3] It seemed a lasting peace was much more likely with them at the heart of the process; and peace without surrender was the overriding imperative. This pragmatism had been a hallmark of my grandfather's career. He had succeeded repeatedly in wooing the power of nationalist movements, then harnessing it within a democratic process. This had often necessitated overcoming and overruling objections to dealing with anti-British movements, even violent ones. I felt sure he would have wanted the republican movement represented at the peace negotiations and beyond, even if it included men who had authorised his assassination.

Following the peace agreement of 1998, the IRA had slowly responded to demands that it should address itself to the community on which it had preyed. In July 2002 many felt a milestone had been reached when the IRA issued an apology for the deaths and injuries among civilians. They had killed 642 of them.

> While it was not our intention to injure or kill non-combatants, the reality is that . . . on a number of . . . occasions, that was the consequence of our actions . . . We offer our sincere apologies and condolences to their families . . . We also acknowledge the grief and pain of their relatives . . . We remain totally committed to the peace process and to dealing with the challenges and difficulties which this presents. This includes the acceptance of past mistakes and of the hurt and pain we have caused to others.[4]

At the time it seemed like another of the tiny steps in the right direction; what mattered to me was that the bombs and bullets had stopped. By then one in four of Northern Ireland's population had been caught up in an explosion and over eighteen thousand people had been charged with terrorism offences.[5]

On Thursday, 28 July 2005, the IRA declared an end to its violence. *The Irish Times* wrote: 'by any standards the political achievement of Gerry Adams, Martin McGuinness and their allies in dismantling an undefeated terrorist organisation from the inside is colossal.'[6] But some IRA supporters felt the terms for which they finally settled were not very different from what had been on offer three decades earlier. One asked, 'Why could we not have avoided the long war . . .? Why did so many people have to die to bring us back round to accepting what we rejected in 1974 and called everybody else bastards for accepting?'[7] It was too late; by then the IRA had killed 1,778 people,* making it 'by far the most lethal agent in the conflict'.[8] Its own death toll was 293. In Belfast in 2004 I was told that some of the IRA with long memories were asking: 'Is this what it was all for? So Martin McGuiness can fly business class?'

The peace occasionally faltered and even temporarily stalled but time and again it was revived and slowly began to take on a feeling of permanence. When violence stubbornly continued to rise to the surface of everyday life in Northern Ireland, few people found it surprising. The conditions which caused the Troubles had arisen over centuries; it was unrealistic to expect them to disappear overnight. But these occurrences were the exceptions, and the environment seemed to have changed radically. Some attributed this to increasing prosperity and the emergence of a multicultural society; others pointed to long-overdue political reforms.

Not everyone welcomed peace. One report[9] by a Catholic community group in west Belfast said many residents felt the quality of life worsened in the decade following the peace agreement.† The report's

---

* The number killed by the IRA amounted to 48.5 per cent of those killed in the Troubles. The largest single category of IRA victims was civilians, of which they killed 642. Next was British forces, of which they killed 456.

† The withdrawal of the IRA from certain streets left some residents feeling exposed; one said, 'People were scared to do drug dealing but they are not now.' The report stated that 66 per cent of households surveyed in one area had reported stress despite the benefits brought by peace, and concluded 'it's a self-perpetuating cycle of mental ill-health' stemming from the Troubles.

author stated: 'There has been a very profound community loss. A lot of its identity was based around resistance to the state and with peace that has been lost . . . Social relations were very strong, even if for negative reasons, and in that sense, some do miss the Troubles.'[10]

The power-sharing assembly produced scenes of old and bitter enemies working together and apparently enjoying themselves enormously. The Democratic Unionist and Sinn Féin politicians Ian Paisley and Martin McGuinness, respectively First Minister and Deputy First Minister, were photographed laughing together so often that they became known as the 'Chuckle Brothers'. Meanwhile the international community, aware of the dramatic changes brought about by the peace process, were quick to invite the protagonists to help in other conflicts. In July 2008 Martin McGuinness accepted the invitation of an American philanthropist to attend a summit in Baghdad aimed at bringing together warring factions in post-war Iraq.

Only when I got to know John Maxwell in 2003 did I realise how much I would like to visit Paul's grave. Four months later I went to Enniskillen to meet John at the town's Breandrum cemetery. It contained both Protestant and Catholic graves. As he led me in, he said, 'Enniskillen has always been a fairly well-integrated town, religious-wise', but I was still struck by a sense of apartheid as we turned a corner and headed into the Protestant area. Paul's grave had a dark grey, almost black headstone. The lettering on it was gold and had been recently touched up. It looked as good as new. But the passing of the years was evident; the ground had subsided on one side causing the headstone to lean very slightly. On it was inscribed:

IN EVER LOVING MEMORY OF
PAUL MAXWELL, AGED 15 YEARS,
ONLY SON OF JOHN AND MARY
WHO DIED ALONGSIDE
EARL MOUNTBATTEN OF BURMA
ON BOARD SHADOW V ON 27TH AUGUST 1979

Inscribed above was:

For Lycidas is dead, dead ere his prime,
Young Lycidas, and hath not left his peer:
Who would not sing for Lycidas? He knew
Himself to sing, and build the lofty rhyme.
He must not float upon his watery bier
Unwept, and welter to the parching wind,
Without the meed of some melodious tear.

Milton[11]

I had brought some flowers with me and, as I knelt to arrange them, Paul's last words to me on *Shadow V* filled my head: 'Tim, what's the time?' John and I had been talking quietly by the grave but now my words stuck in my throat. I got up and gave him a long hug.

The Troubles affected John in many ways. Some of the youngsters he taught died in the violence; friends were at the 1987 Remembrance Day service in Enniskillen when the IRA blew it up. He told me, 'It was terrible to see the effect it had on some people ... It eats them up inside ... it's like a disease ... You can't say very much to them; they have had a big loss; you understand their loss; and it's highly complex.' But one thought had always been in his mind: 'I'll have to do something to try and bring the two communities together.' He remembered his own education in Enniskillen. 'I never met Catholic boys as friends until I was in my last year at school and we got together in a sort of peer group. But in other places like parts of Belfast, you never mixed with the opposite tribe even at that age.'[12] He was the driving force behind setting up an integrated school for Catholics and Protestants in Enniskillen. Opening in 1989, at first it had struggled to survive, but when later it received government funding its future was assured. John found the project very therapeutic. It seemed to me to be a highly pragmatic response to the divisions in Ireland and I asked him if integrated schooling was now well established nationally. I was shocked when he told me that 95 per cent of schools in Ireland were still segregated.

My repeated visits to Ireland washed away regret which had lingered after Nick's death. A big part of this was that I had not had any conscious experience of the moment when we were parted. After my visits I found it easier to live in the moment, a perception heightened when I read of a Zen commentator who had said that 'the two principal bars to living in the present are regrets about the past and fear for the future'. The quotation rang true. I had now dispelled the regret and linked to that came a release from a fear. During my therapy some years before, I had come to recognise that at a subconscious level I was leading my life fearful of a sudden, unspecified separation. Now that my emotional experience of Nick's death was becoming more complete, his death seemed resolved. As a result I was losing my anxiety, albeit largely subconscious, about possible future separations. When my father was dying in 2005, I felt thoroughly prepared for the pain of being parted from him. When he died, I was able to benefit from the sort of deep and active mourning largely unavailable to me as a boy; I felt this was a dividend from the time and energy I had invested in going back to Ireland. There were to be many other dividends that revealed themselves to me slowly over months and years. One day I was putting diesel in my car when I noticed something odd: the smell was having no effect on me. For twenty-four years it had given me flashbacks to being in the Wood-Martins' boat, freezing cold and covered in diesel. I am now free from that symptom and very grateful for it.

Over the years I had allowed myself to gain the impression that Nick's spirit was somehow trapped at Classiebawn. My visits allowed me to realise that the place had not held him, it had held my mind. Through my return trips I was freeing myself mentally and now at last I was starting to enjoy the place again. I wrote in my journal in January 2004:

> I feel much more relaxed to be here than on my first trips in August and October last year. Then I was transfixed by the prospect of the emotional bungee jumps ahead. Those trips had unleashed a maelstrom inside me and made me incapable of touching business or personal matters other than the sole, all-invading issue of the bomb. Its negative, awful grip on my psyche has withered by my coming here and confronting it all.[13]

After a year of repeated visits, I made a final trip with Isabella and our three children, Amber and Milo having gained a brother, Ludovic, the year before. We settled in a hotel in Westport for a week, taking the children boating, riding and catching crabs from the harbour wall. We went to see my Brabourne grandmother's former home, Westport House, and our distant cousins who now live there. At the end of our stay we visited Classiebawn.

> I had told the children all about it and the first thing we did was speed up through the tower and onto the roof. From there we went down to the beach and in the warmest of Irish sunshine ran wild on the vast empty sands, alone except for three horses and their riders. We talked to them. Like most four-year-old girls, Amber was thrilled, especially when the last of them obliged by turning at the end of the beach and galloping back past us in a dazzling display of the freedom offered by this rugged coast. Isabella sat with Ludo while I joined Amber and Milo in their running and splashing, laughter and screams. We were happy and care-free.
>
> We gave the children boiled eggs, toast and corn-on-the cob in Classiebawn, said goodbye to Hugh and Caroline and returned to Westport. With the children snoring in the adjoining room we showered, ate and drank and watched the Athens Olympics, both feeling on top of the world.
>
> At 5:30 this afternoon I put Isabella and the children on a plane back to London. Her eyes filled with tears as we kissed goodbye. I walked away feeling my tummy turning. Later she left a message saying the last 5 days have been the most fantastic of her life. I guessed why. On this holiday I had spent more time than ever as a hands-on Daddy to the children. She, like me, sensed that the shadows of my past were lifting.[14]

I drove on alone to Sligo for my final visit. The next day was the twenty-fifth anniversary of the attack. I rang a friend who updated me on local news and told me the *Sligo Weekender* was marking the anniversary with a twelve-page colour supplement. Stopping for petrol on the way to Mullaghmore next day, I bought a copy. Inside was the picture of Nick's body being wheeled from the lifeboat to an ambulance. I wrote in my journal:

How lonely it looked. Here were Nicky's remains being wheeled away by strangers. It is totally illogical but I wish someone he knew and loved had been there to take him to hospital and then home. I wish I could have done that. I wish I could do it today.

I started as I do on any 'big' day with a cooked breakfast, a fortification against the day ahead. When I parked on the north side of Mullaghmore Head the sea was dark and rough and a cold wind was blowing – nothing like the day of the bomb. Every now and then the sun came from between the clouds in intense bursts and I settled for a few minutes in a hollow from where I could look across the sea at the castle, as captivatingly beautiful as ever.

In Mullaghmore, protected from the wind and now in warm sunshine, I walked along the harbour walls and then set off along the beach in shirtsleeves, Classiebawn in the background behind me, the beach fully revealed by the low tide. As I hopped across streams carrying recent rainwater into the sea I felt supremely happy to have reached the year's summit. Later I sat in the car with the door open and devoured a bar of chocolate which had melted in the sun. It was a pleasure to be alive, minute by minute. I chatted to a mother who was trying to coax her daughter onto the beach. Everyone there and in the village seemed to be enjoying the sudden improvement in the weather that had arrived just in time for the weekend. I walked back into the harbour where a TV news crew were in action. As I passed I heard the reporter say into the camera, 'Another generation is here now who would know of 1979 mainly through history.' I didn't stop.

I drove out of the village and suddenly saw something that made me pull over: flowers at the gates of Classiebawn. I got out and found there were 16 bouquets. Among them were lilies of the type we had often had in the castle in my childhood. Beside them were a photo of the family, some newspaper articles and messages. One said: 'With the remembrance and affection of the people of Mullaghmore.' I was so pleased not to have driven away without seeing these. A minute later I had decided to go back one last time to Mullaghmore Head. I parked and walked over the grassy, craggy field that led to the sheer cliff, overlooking the spot where *Shadow V* had blown up. No one was there. I had no idea what I would do at the edge but on reaching it I suddenly found myself saying the Lord's Prayer: 'Our Father, who art in heaven . . .' At this spot, on this day, the words seemed perfect. 'Forgive us our trespasses, as we forgive those who trespass against us . . .'

I stared out to sea then turned for Sligo Airport, happy to be headed for home and family. In the air I saw the coastline running towards Lisadell. The Gore-Booths had finally sold it a few months earlier. Its contents had been auctioned and scattered to the four winds. Beyond Lissadell lay Classiebawn but I did not strain my eyes looking for it as once I would have. I glanced down and noticed the Irish landscape had all but disappeared beneath a bright layer of cloud.[15]

In 1979 I came away from Ireland with an understanding of the country and its people which was that of an innocent fourteen-year-old. I did not ask difficult questions and this helped me get along happily, largely untouched by suspicion, fear and hate. My return to Ireland equipped me with a far greater understanding of the situation in which I had been immersed and an equally greater understanding of my own feelings. I gained a firm basis for the forgiveness which had crept over me in the intervening years. Perhaps the most difficult question was how I felt about Thomas McMahon. At the end of the year I accepted at least this: that if I had been born into a republican stronghold, lived my life as dictated by conditions in Northern Ireland, and been educated through the events of the 1960s and 1970s, my life might well have turned out the way Thomas McMahon's did. In this respect I felt ultimately inalienable even from him.

In May 2006 I took my mother back to Classiebawn. Until then she had stayed away, primarily because my father had never felt it would be entirely safe. He had died the previous year, and eight months later she hopped on a plane with me and we spent two days exploring together, her first visit in twenty-six years. We wandered along the harbour wall in Mullaghmore, my mother holding my arm. She was now stooped with age but her mind was sharp. Pointing to a building facing the harbour, she said, 'That was Hannan's Hotel, where we first stayed.' I listened to her stories of their early married life, and gathered her a little closer on my arm.

She enjoyed the visit as much as I did, and, despite the occasional tears, took it easily in her stride. My favourite moment came as we said goodbye after seeing Dick and Elizabeth Wood-Martin. My mother had shaken hands with Elizabeth, but when I kissed Elizabeth goodbye my mother returned and gave her a kiss as well. As I watched, I suddenly saw a flash of tenderness between these two resilient women. Both were mothers; one had saved the child of the other.

The next summer, my extended family debated where to spend a week's holiday together. I suggested Delphi in County Mayo. When my mother said she liked the idea, her children and grandchildren quickly concurred. We stayed in the lodge and fished, sailed, beach-combed, swam and walked the hills in glorious sunshine. Then one evening we made a plan to return to Classiebawn as a family for the first time since 1979. Next morning, with my mother in the lead car, we set off in a winding convoy of three generations, siblings and spouses, in-laws and cousins, hampers and dogs. We picnicked on the beach and then drove up to the castle. Little groups of family split off and went their different ways. The younger generation talked about the unexpected quirkiness of what they found. My brothers-in-law were seeing it for the first time and spoke of the majesty of the landscape.

Outside I saw Joanna standing and staring at the flat, calm sea. I walked over and put an arm around her shoulder. Without turning she said through quiet tears, 'I feel like Moses standing on Sinai and looking at the promised land. Except that I know we can never go there. Even if we could it would not be the same.' I realised then how my visits had changed me. When I was a boy, Dr Moran had written: 'Soon in the future when all this trouble will be over I hope you can enjoy this lovely part of the world which God put here for us all to enjoy.' Standing beside my sister I now knew that time had come.

Having been reunited with Tony Heenan in November 2003, I wrote in my journal:

Today in Sligo, 24 years after the murders, I sense that Thomas McMahon's moral vacuum has been defeated. The bloodbath he engineered failed to turn me to hatred. Instead I left Ireland feeling a love which I projected primarily onto one man: Tony Heenan. He has wit, humour and above all, compassion. He cares. And my heart sings because I recognise that on August 27th 1979 Heenan defeated McMahon and I am the proof.[16]

Churchill was allegedly told by a man, 'If I had not been a German I would have wanted to be an Englishman', to which he replied, 'If I had not been an Englishman, I too would have wanted to be an Englishman.' If I were to be reborn and God asked me how I would like to come back, I would say English. But if there were no positions available I would be sorely tempted to choose Irish. And if God said, 'Would you like to return as your brother Heenan or your brother McMahon?' I would be forced to say, 'You choose for me, Father.' He would make the right choice. Wouldn't he?

28

WORDS WITH NICK

In October 2003 I had known exactly what I needed to do next: spend some time alone in Classiebawn. Hugh Tunney was away but he had invited me to go to the empty castle at any time I wanted. My journal for Wednesday 8 October 2003 reads:

> Today I had an hour that was the hardest and best, perhaps, of any hour in my life. As I drove to Classiebawn from Sligo it was blowing a gale. With the clouds only a few hundred feet from the ground and visibility much reduced in the rain, there was no sign of Benbulben as I drove past and no sign of Inishmurray when I reached Classiebawn. I got to the castle at about ten and opened the gates – code 3333, Grandpapa's old Romsey phone number. I went in by the back door and passing the kitchen I had a flash-back of bringing in the catch from *Shadow V* in a yellow plastic tub filled with mackerel, pollock, crabs and lobsters. I walked to the sink and there were the scales in which I had weighed the fish as a child. Closing my eyes, I could hear the clatter of Mrs Kennedy's implements and detect her oncoming bad humour. I expected her son Paddy Joe, always in a hurry, to come charging in with a box of provisions from the beaten-up old van, a relic from before I was born.
>
> Walking up the stairs I noticed the great shark rods were gone

from the wall, and the racks that held them. In the drawing room I lit a fire which soon became a furnace. The matchbox holder on the mantelpiece was the one we had left there in 1979. From the fireplace came the roar of the wind, the Atlantic fury funnelled from above, funnelled from 1979, breaching the chimney and berating the grate. I was in a room I hadn't been able to find in 24 years, a room with the smells, sounds, feel and atmosphere of boyhood. My senses told me I had arrived as close to 1979 as to make almost no difference. If I closed my eyes the 1979 drinks trolley appeared in the corner of the room. I imagined Peter would come in at any moment to check who was back from the morning's activities and how close we were to being ready for lunch.

I had in my pocket a compact disc I had made for this moment. It was a copy of *Hot Hits 6*, the scratched and warped vinyl disc I had found in the castle earlier that year. Now I crossed the room to a CD player in the corner and inserted it into the machine.

As the music played I closed my eyes and a connection to childhood opened. I could picture the card table that had often stood near the fire, a half-completed hand of Canasta on its green baize top. I looked out of the windows and saw only ghostly stratus over the shoreline. The castle was cocooned in the storm and I was cocooned in mine. The great rollers smashing against the point were coming right in through the windows over me and I swayed as 1979 closed in all around me, tight and snug, a perfect and irresistible fit. When will Dad be back from golf at Bundoran? Are the riding party visible yet, headed back along the beach, tiny commas on the vast page of sand? They must be wet through by now and galloping for home, surely? I must turn the music down for Grandpapa next door.

Each song had long since been lost to my mind's recall yet now hearing them again I realised they were being summoned from a place far within and every word was familiar. Some of the lyrics jabbed and taunted me:

So the drums went Boom . . .
And the music stopped and we stood still
And a few were saved and the people said
'Amen'[1]

As the music poured over me it acted like straps tightening over my rib cage, convulsing me into the type of crying I had not done since a tiny child and which would have been loud enough to be heard in far-off rooms. I knew I was in no danger of being heard. Inside a double-glazed granite castle at the top of a hill on the edge of the Atlantic in an autumn storm, I would not disturb a soul.

I sat on the floor near the fire where Nick and I had crawled as infants and walked as children and played together Dover Patrol, Computer Battleships, Attack, Risk, Monopoly, and Connect 4. My eyes dripped with tears and my breathing became staggered as my thoughts started to dance in and out of 1979. The castle was empty but its rooms were charged and its passageways open. I said 'Nicky?' and then started to scratch out words on a pad of paper.

I just said 'Nicky?' for the first time since 1979. It was very quiet. 'Nicky? Nick! Nick?' Louder now. If he was on the stairs, or the landing above, he'd have heard. 'Where are you?' (Much quieter, knowing he can't hear.)

'I can't believe you're alive. I <u>knew</u> you were alive. Why didn't you let me know, why didn't you tell me? Show me your hand. Does it hurt?* What happened to you in the water? I was so stunned in the boat that picked me up. I couldn't work out what was wrong with me. They say I tried to get out of the boat. Maybe my subconscious was trying to tell them the only way it knew how, that I didn't want to be separated from you, if they wanted to take me they must also be sure they had you.

Come here, I want to hug you, not just with my arms, I want to put all four limbs around you and squeeze. You haven't changed a bit; take that anorak off! I saw a photo of you, dead. But you looked like you

---

* Bizarrely, it was not until five months later that I learned that Nick had suffered shrapnel wounds on the back of his right hand.

were alive, no harm visible. Who was carrying you though? I'm sorry I don't know, I'll ask. Do you think I haven't done very well? It's taken twenty-four years to get here. I've gone on the only way I knew how. I would have done better with you to help me, I'm sure . . .

How long have you got? Mum's OK – she never really stops thinking about you. Dad's psyche is so different, he talks about you and I can tell it's the hardest thing in his life.

What else? I've done just what you would have done. You would have loved being a grown-up. But I'm glad you didn't have to go through some of the shit.

Do you come here often? Can I come back? Have you been able to see me since then? I love you. You're more vivid today than any time in the last twenty-four years. I expect you'll be just as vivid if I live to die old. Cheer up, I may die tomorrow. Oh, before you go: I love you, love you, miss you. I'd choose to come back again as a twin, if I could have you again. I won't see you again, will I? Will I? Nick?

The monologue proved to be the turning point in my trips to Ireland. Slowly I recovered my state of mind and at 12:55pm I turned on my mobile phone and sent a text message to my lift, waiting in the village: 'Ready to roll'. It summed up how I felt about life. Finally I had said goodbye to Nick and let him go. I felt light and easy. Soon I found myself thinking back to the excitement I had felt in the harbour a couple of months earlier. Now it was clear to me what I had been anticipating, what I had subconsciously understood I was approaching. It was my final goodbye to Nick.

EPILOGUE

The bomb gave my mother a new name: she inherited her father's title and became Countess Mountbatten of Burma. Afterwards, wherever she went, people told her where they were at the moment they heard of the bomb. Many who listened to her talk gave her a squeeze of the hand, a smile or some other salute. They recognised in her the strength of a parent who had seen her child killed and whose response had been to redouble her work for others. They were moved by her ongoing love for the Irish and her complete lack of bitterness. They enjoyed her light touch, her lack of introspection and her humour.

Emerging from bandages and drugs in September 1979, I followed Tony Heenan's advice to take life 'one day at a time'. My parents' example guided me, as did that of my brothers and sisters. I found my parents largely unchanged by the bomb; they were the same strong, caring people. One change, however, was noticeable. They had reached adulthood and seen service in the Second World War as their parents had done in the First World War. But until the bomb they had not seen their children deeply tested. While my parents were incapacitated, my siblings stepped in and carried on. My parents' respect and gratitude for that was profound and they told them so. In the years that followed, my brothers, sisters, sister-in-law, aunt, uncle and cousins paid a price for what they endured in Ireland. They rebuilt their lives and took their places as well-rounded contributors to their own families and communities. That is their story, not mine.

In an obituary of my father, who died in 2005, my mother was quoted as having said: 'The past 25 years would have been far more difficult without my husband. In fact it would have been unbearably ghastly. We have been married a long time, but I dare say that if we had a spare lunch or dinner and had to pick one person, we'd still choose each other.'[1] I feel similarly towards my mother and siblings, aunt and cousins, not out of gratitude for their help, nor because of the bond of shared experience, but for the fun to be had with them.

After my trips to Ireland were complete, I found a surge of new energy. Isabella and I moved from London to the countryside. Soon we had two more daughters, Isla and Willa. The noise at home became tremendous but every mealtime now felt like a party with my closest friends.

Nick's grave is on the edge of Mersham, opposite our grandmother's. On her headstone are the words 'Reunited at last'; she had spent forty years as a widow. On Nick's headstone we put:

> He took his big candle
> and went into another room
> I cannot find;
> but I know he was here
> because of all the happiness
> he left behind.

APPENDIX:
FURTHER INFORMATION

Advice on issues raised in this book can be found at:

The Lone Twin Network
PO Box 5653
Birmingham
B29 7JY   www.lonetwinnetwork.org.uk

Twins and Multiple Births Association Bereavement Support Group
(Tamba BSG)
2 The Willows
Gardner Road
Guildford Surrey   +44 (0)1483 304442
GUI 4PG   www.tamba-bsg.org.uk

Twinless Twins Support Group, International
PO Box 980481
Ypsilanti
Michigan 48198   +1 888 205 8962
USA   www.twinlesstwins.org

The Multiple Births Foundation
Hammersmith House Level 4
Queen Charlotte's and Chelsea Hospital
Du Cane Road
London   +44 (0)20 8383 3519
WI2 OHS   www.multiplebirths.org.uk

The Compassionate Friends
(an organisation of bereaved parents and their families)
53 North Street
Bristol   0845 1232304
BS3 IEN   www.tcf.org.uk

Cruse Bereavement Care
PO Box 800   0844 477 9400
Richmond   Children and young people's
Surrey   helpline: 0808 808 1677
TW9 IRG   www.cruse.org.uk

Child Bereavement Charity
Aston House, High Street
West Wycombe
Buckinghamshire   +44 (0)1494 446648
HPI4 3AG   www.childbereavement.org.uk

ACKNOWLEDGEMENTS

I am completely indebted to my parents, brothers, sisters, aunt, and cousins for their role in the healing described in these pages, and the memories and documents only they could provide.

My foremost thanks go to Olga Edridge whose friendship, untiring support and editorial judgement helped shape this book from start to end, and transformed my experience of returning to Ireland. Whatever I write here would fail to capture the scale and depth of my gratitude.

I am immensely grateful to Helen Phelps who tirelessly researched this book. Her uncompromising standards and unfailing good humour proved to be a mainstay.

I must record my gratitude to June O'Brien among whose many tasks was the painstaking transcription of every interview; and Alex Barraki whose production skills kept us safe throughout.

Great thanks go to Caroline Gascoigne, publishing director at Hutchinson, whose sensitivity and skill made the editing of this book a joy. It would be remiss not to register my gratitude to her assistant Tess Callaway; to Hutchinson's managing editor Joanna Taylor, who also copy-edited the book, Hutchinson's director of publicity Emma Mitchell, and Vicki Robinson who created the index.

My thanks equally go to Jonathan Lloyd, my agent, and his colleagues at the Curtis Brown Group, especially Camilla Goslett; and to the late Giles Gordon.

Acknowledgements

I am most grateful to Peter Troughton and Philip Ziegler, the Trustees of the Broadlands Archives for their permission to reproduce from my grandfather's papers which are housed at Southampton University. Professor Chris Woolgar, Head of Special Collections at the University's Library, and senior archivist Karen Robson were unfailingly helpful and I thank them very much.

The people who agreed to give of their time, knowledge and care are too numerous to list individually but I cannot fail to single out some. Among them are Dick and Elizabeth Wood-Martin, Brian and Heather Best, Richard and Liz Wallace, Charlie and Kathy Pierce, Tony and Mary Heenan, James and Sacha Abercorn, Bobby Moorhead and most particularly Jamie and Sylvia Crathorne and David and Susie Dugdale.

John Maxwell, father of Paul, and Paul's mother Mary Hornsey were most helpful and I am indebted for their great understanding, and that of Paul's sisters, Lisa and Donna.

Among the others I would like to thank most sincerely are: Terry Baker; Cecil Barber; Philomena, Pat and John Barry; Susan Batten; Gill Bennett; Caroline Bentley; Ian Boyes; Sean Brennan; Professor Alan Browne; Diana Browne; the late Dr Elizabeth Bryan; Paul Burns; James Chambers; Margaret Connolly-Jones; Dr Dennis Coppel; John Courtney; Revd Sheila Cox; Patrick J. Davey; Edward Dawson; Sheilagh Densham-Paton; Catherine Doherty; Dr James Donovan; Dr Terence Dudeney; Elizabeth Duffy; Thomas Dunne; Stewart Eldon; Peter Emerson; Professor Richard English; Professor Roy Foster; Annie Foulds; Julie Fox; John Furlong; Bob Garratt; Dame Anne Griffiths; Kevin Henry; Mary Gantley; Maureen Gateley; Dr Donald Gibb; Sir Josslyn and Lady Gore-Booth; Robert and I. Christiane Graf; Michael Hampsey; Professor John Harbison; Toby Harnden; Chris Harper; the late James Hawthorne; Mrs Ron Heath (Betty); John Hennessy; Trevor Henry; Geoffrey Hornsey; Janie Ironside-Wood; Rachel Johnson; Dr Stewart Johnston; Patrick Jordan; Norman Kee; Michael Kelly; J. Christopher Durham Kenyon; Charles Kidd; Billy Kinlough; Peter S. Larkman ; Tosh Lavery; Claire Loftus; Rodney and Trudy Lomax; Mary Lowry; Jim Lucas; Bernard Lyden; May McGowan; Graham Mason; Marion Maxwell; Fionn McArthur; the late John McCann; Michael and Brid McCarthy; Pauric McCullagh; John McGerty; Peter and Grainne McHugh; Ray McHugh; Brian McLaurin; Hans-Rudiger Minow; John Moloney; Dr Desmond Moran; Michael Morland; W. James Morrison; Glen Morrison;

Fachtna Murphy; Kevin Mullins; Peter and Margaret Nicholson; John O'Brien; Dr Adrian O'Connell; Dr Brian O'Connor; Michael O'Connor; John O'Grady; Denis O'Hara; Richard M. Langworth; Malcolm Oldfield; Manfred, Inge and Nina Ottow; the late Professor J. Frank Pantridge; Jane Perkins; Dr Richard Porter; Sam Power; Nicholas Prins; Bob Pullin; Lord Puttnam (David); Colin Randall; David Reddaway; Juliet Roche; Shane Rodgers; Freda Rooney; Grace Ryan; Marshall Sandes; Martin Shelbourne; Amaro Silva; Yvonne Smith; Michael Sullivan; Mark Toher; Barbara Tolhurst; Michael Treacy; Tina Thomson; Hugh Tunney and Caroline Devine; William and Ruth Wilkinson; Lady Williams (Jane); the late Canon T. P. S. Wood; and Adam Woolfitt.

To anyone I have unwittingly omitted, I apologise.

I also thank the following organisations for their help: Ashford School; BBC Worldwide; Bank of England; Britannia Royal Naval College; British Airways Archive and Museum; British Library; Broadlands; Cabinet Office, London; Central Bank of Ireland; Central Statistics Office, Ireland; Centre for South Asian Studies, University of Cambridge; Centre for Kentish Studies, Maidstone; Churchill Centre; Churchill Museum and Cabinet War Rooms; Coldstream Guards; Department of Justice, Washington, DC; Derry City Council Harbour Museum; Fleet Air Arm Museum; Foreign and Commonwealth Office, London; An Garda Síochána; Grenadier Guards; Gordonstoun School; Imperial War Museum; Irish Courts Service; Irish Nursing Board; Irish Prison Service; Irish Times Archive; Lambeth Palace Library; Library of the Hellenic and Roman Societies; Linen Hall Library; London Transport Museum; Mary Evans Picture Library; Meteorological Office (National Meteorological Archive); Metropolitan Police Record Office; McGregor Industries; National Archives of Ireland; National Archives of the United Kingdom; National Library of Ireland; Nehru Memorial Museum and Library; Office of the Director of Public Prosecutions, Dublin; Order of St John; RAF Museum; RAF Northolt; Royal Victoria Hospital, Belfast; RTE Library; Sligo Coroner's Office; Sligo General Hospital; Sligo Reference Library; Sligo Champion; St. Patrick's Cathedral, Dublin; State Pathologist's Office, Dublin; UK Psychological Trauma Society; University of Southampton Library; Westminster Abbey Library and Muniments Room.

Text extracts

The majority of quotations in the text are acknowledged in the corresponding endnotes. In addition, grateful acknowledgement is made for permission to reproduce from the following:

Jung, C. G., *The Collected Works of C. G. Jung*, Vol. 10. © 1964 Bollingen, 1992 renewed. Reprinted by permission of Princeton University Press; diary of Grace Ryan reproduced with her kind permission; diary of India Hicks reproduced with her kind permission; diary and letters of 2nd Countess Mountbatten of Burma (Patricia) reproduced with her kind permission; letters, notes and photographs of 7th Lord Brabourne (John) reproduced by kind permission of 2nd Countess Mountbatten of Burma (Patricia); diary and letter from Lady Crathorne (Sylvia) to her sister Rachel reproduced with the kind permission of Sylvia Crathorne; extracts from *Mountbatten: the Official Biography* reproduced by kind permission of Philip Ziegler; extract from *Killing Rage* by Eamon Collins with Mick McGovern reproduced by kind permission of Granta Books; extracts from *Philip & Elizabeth: Portrait of a Marriage* by Gyles Brandreth, published by Century. Reprinted by permission of The Random House Group Ltd; extracts from *Blood-Dark Tracks - A Family History* reproduced by kind permission of Joseph O'Neill.

Photographs

Frontispiece: © 1979 The Hon. Philip Knatchbull.

Plates: 1 © 1966 Malcolm Aird/Robert Estall Agency; 2 © 1966 Malcolm Aird/Robert Estall Agency; 3 FKV Photo Services Ltd, London. Ref. 70/23; 4 FKV Photo Services Ltd, London. Ref. 70/31; 5 © Trustees of the Broadlands Archives; 6 © 1966 Malcolm Aird/Robert Estall Agency; 7 © 1976 the author; 8 © 1970 Adam Woolfitt; 9 © 1967 James Crathorne; 10 By 7th Lord Brabourne. © the author; 11 By 7th Lord Brabourne. © the author; 12 © 1966 Malcolm Aird/Robert Estall Agency; 13 By 7th Lord Brabourne. © the author; 14 © 1966 Malcolm Aird/Robert Estall Agency; 15 By 7th Lord Brabourne. Reproduced by permission of 2nd Countess Mountbatten of Burma; 16 By 7th Lord Brabourne. Reproduced by permission of 2nd Countess Mountbatten of Burma; 17 By 7th Lord Brabourne. Reproduced by permission of 2nd Countess Mountbatten of Burma; 18 By 7th Lord Brabourne. Reproduced by permission of 2nd Countess Mountbatten of Burma; 19 © 1979 Robert Graf; 20 © 1979 Press Association Images; 21 © 1979 Champion Publications; 22 © 1979 Champion Publications; 23 © 1979 Press Association Images; 24 © 1979 Press Association Images; 25 © 1979 James Crathorne; 26 © 1979 Champion Publications; 27 © 1979 *Irish Times*; 28 © 1988 Maxwell Photography; 29 © 1979 An Garda Síochána; 30 © 1979 Mirrorpix; 31 © 1979 Katrina Thomson; 32 © 1979 Press Association Images; 33 © 2003 Olga Edridge; 34 © 1979 Champion Publications; 35 © 2004 the author.

NOTES

Preface

1 Revd. Professor Peter J. Gomes, Memorial Church, Harvard University, Cambridge, Massachusetts.
2 Richard English, 'Coming to Terms with the Past: Northern Ireland', *History Today*, vol. 54/7, London, 2004.
3 Iris Murdoch, *The Nice and the Good*, London, Chatto and Windus, 1968, p. 179. Reprinted by permission of The Random House Group Ltd.

Prologue

1 Philip Ziegler, *Mountbatten: The Official Biography*, (London: Collins), 1985, p. 700.

Chapter 1 – Twins

1 Diary of 2nd Countess Mountbatten of Burma (Patricia), 23 April 1974.
2 The Hon. Nicholas Knatchbull to 1st Earl Mountbatten of Burma, 2 May 1974.
3 Diary of 2nd Countess Mountbatten of Burma (Patricia), 28 April 1974.

4 John Kempe to 7th Lord and Lady Brabourne (John and Patricia), 8 September 1979, Brabourne Papers, Mersham.

5 Peter S. Larkman, Gordonstoun School reports, summer term 1979, Brabourne Papers, Mersham.

6 Michael Mavor, Gordonstoun School report, summer term 1979, Brabourne Papers, Mersham.

Chapter 2 – Family

1 1st Earl Mountbatten of Burma to 2nd Countess Mountbatten of Burma (Patricia), 31 December 1953, Brabourne Papers, Mersham, quoted by Philip Ziegler, *Mountbatten: The Official Biography*, (London: Collins), 1985, pp. 573–74.

2 1st Earl Mountbatten of Burma to the author, 28 February 1972.

3 1st Earl Mountbatten of Burma to the author, 15 March 1972.

4 1st Earl Mountbatten of Burma to 1st Countess Mountbatten, 14 February 1941, Broadlands Archives, reference: S142, quoted by Philip Ziegler, *Mountbatten: The Official Biography*, (London: Collins), 1985, p. 575.

5 Janet Morgan, *Edwina Mountbatten, A Life of Her Own*, (London: HarperCollins), 1991, p. 321.

6 Janet Morgan, *Edwina Mountbatten, A Life of Her Own*, (London: HarperCollins), 1991, p. 433.

7 Janet Morgan, *Edwina Mountbatten,A Life of Her Own*, (London: HarperCollins), 1991, p. 433.

8 Janet Morgan, *Edwina Mountbatten, A Life of Her Own*, (London: HarperCollins), 1991, p. 433.

9 Janet Morgan, *Edwina Mountbatten, A Life of Her Own*, (London: HarperCollins), 1991, p. 459.

10 Iris Portal, 'Song at Seventy', c.1975, p. 105. The unpublished manuscript is at the Centre for South Asian Studies, Cambridge, England. Reproduced by courtesy of Lady Williams (Jane) and Mrs James Batten (Susan).

11 Diary of Lady Brabourne (Doreen), 7 March 1939, Brabourne Papers, Mersham.

12 Iris Portal, 'Song at Seventy', c.1975, p. 7. Reproduced by courtesy of Lady Williams (Jane) and Mrs James Batten (Susan).

13 *Chicago Tribune*, quoted by Gyles Brandreth, *Philip & Elizabeth: Portrait of a Marriage*, (London: Century), 2004, p. 55.

14 The Hon. Nicholas Knatchbull to 1st Earl Mountbatten of Burma, 21 June 1979.

15 1st Earl Mountbatten of Burma to the Hon. Nicholas Knatchbull, 25 June 1979.

Chapter 3 – Classiebawn

1 Janet Morgan, *Edwina Mountbatten: A Life of Her Own*, (London: HarperCollins), 1991, p. 321.

2 2nd Countess Mountbatten of Burma (Patricia) to 1st Earl Mountbatten of Burma, 12 September 1971, Broadlands Archives, reference: S26, quoted by Philip Ziegler, *Mountbatten: The Official Biography*, (London: Collins), 1985, p. 697.

3 Michael Kelly, interviewed for this book, 22 August 2007.

4 John Barry to the author, 27 November 2006.

5 Elizabeth Wood-Martin, interviewed by the author, 7 October 2003.

6 Author to 1st Earl Mountbatten of Burma, 4 September 1973.

7 1st Earl Mountbatten of Burma to Captain Richard Hermon, 25 January 1960, Broadlands Archives, reference: MB1/N36.

8 Posthumous BBC radio broadcast, c. August 1979.

9 1st Earl Mountbatten of Burma to Stewart Scheftel, 13 April 1964. Broadlands Archives, reference: MB1/N17.

10 1st Earl Mountbatten of Burma to Sir Arthur Galsworthy, British Ambassador to Dublin, 17 March 1975, Broadlands Archives, reference: Classiebawn BR/Add/1/3.

11 1st Earl Mountbatten of Burma to Liam Cosgrave TD, Taoiseach, 17 March 1975, Broadlands Archives, reference: Classiebawn BR/Add/1/3.

12 Liam Cosgrave, Taoiseach, to 1st Earl Mountbatten of Burma, 4 April 1975, National Archives of Ireland, Department of the Taoiseach, 2005/151/1508. Reproduced with permission.

13 Minutes of Classiebawn Estate Meeting, 25 August 1975, Broadlands Archives.

14 Quoted by Philip Ziegler, *Mountbatten: The Official Biography*, (London: Collins), 1985, p. 697.

Chapter 4 – Edge of Troubles

1 1st Earl Mountbatten of Burma to Donal O'Sullivan, Irish Ambassador to London, 17 July 1972, Broadlands Archives, reference: Classiebawn BR/Add/1/1.

2 Joe McGowan, *In the Shadow of Benbulben*, Dublin, 1993, p. 111.

3 Joe McGowan, *Sligo Weekender* supplement, 24 August 2004, p. 6.

4 Richard English, *Armed Struggle: The History of the IRA*, (London: Pan Books), 2003, p. 379.

5 1st Earl Mountbatten of Burma to Lord Grey of Naunton, 19 August 1971, Broadlands Archives, reference: MB1/N37.

6 1st Earl Mountbatten of Burma to Arthur P. Hockaday, Cabinet Office, 26 May 1972, Broadlands Archives, reference: Classiebawn BR/Add/1/1.

7 Arthur P. Hockaday, Cabinet Office, to 1st Earl Mountbatten of Burma, 4 July 1972, Broadlands Archives, reference: Classiebawn BR/Add/3/3. Reproduced under licence.

8 Arthur P. Hockaday, Cabinet Office, to 1st Earl Mountbatten of Burma, 17 July 1972. Broadlands Archives, reference: Classiebawn BR/Add/1/1. Reproduced under licence.

9 Tour Diaries of 1st Earl Mountbatten of Burma, 13 July 1972, cited by Philip Ziegler in *Mountbatten: The Official Biography*, (London: Collins), 1985, p. 697.

10 1st Earl Mountbatten of Burma to Lord Zuckerman (Solly), 24 July 1972, Broadlands Archives, reference: Classiebawn BR/Add/3/3.

11 Diary of 2nd Countess Mountbatten of Burma (Patricia), 24 August 1972.

12 Sir Robert Mark, Metropolitan Police Commissioner, to 1st Earl Mountbatten of Burma, 7 June 1974, Broadlands Archives, reference: Classiebawn BR/Add/3/4. Reproduced by courtesy of the Metropolitan Police Authority.

13 Sir Robert Mark, Metropolitan Police Commissioner, to 1st Earl Mountbatten of Burma, 12 June 1974, Broadlands Archives, reference: Classiebawn BR/Add/3/4. Reproduced by courtesy of the Metropolitan Police Authority.

14 Sir Arthur Galsworthy, British Ambassador to Dublin, to Foreign and Commonwealth Office, London, 25 June 1974, Broadlands Archives, reference: Classiebawn BR/Add/3/4.

15 G. W. Harding, Republic of Ireland Department, Foreign and Commonwealth Office, to John Barratt, Private Secretary to 1st Earl Mountbatten of Burma, 26 June 1974.

16 1st Earl Mountbatten of Burma to Sir Arthur Galsworthy, British Ambassador to Dublin, 11 July 1974, Broadlands Archives, reference: Classiebawn BR/Add/3/4.

17 1st Earl Mountbatten of Burma to Sir Robert Mark, Metropolitan Police Commissioner, 19 July 1974, Broadlands Archives, reference: Classiebawn BR/Add/3/4.

18 *Evening Press*, Dublin, 12 August 1974.

19 1st Earl Mountbatten of Burma to Sir Robert Mark, Metropolitan Police Commissioner, 11 July 1974, Broadlands Archives, reference: BR/Add/3/4.

20 *Irish Press*, Dublin, 14 August 1974.

21 1st Earl Mountbatten of Burma to Sir Arthur Galsworthy, British Ambassador to Dublin, 26 June 1975, Broadlands Archives, reference: Classiebawn BR/Add/1/3.

22 Aideen Gore-Booth to 1st Earl Mountbatten of Burma, 6 June 1975, Broadlands Archives, reference: Classiebawn BR/Add/1/3. Reproduced by courtesy of Sir Josslyn Gore-Booth, 9th Baronet.

23 John Hennessy, retired Garda Sergeant, Cliffoney, interviewed by the author, 22 January 2004.

24 1st Earl Mountbatten of Burma to Sir Robert Mark, Metropolitan Police Commissioner, and Sir Arthur Galsworthy, British Ambassador to Dublin, 14 June 1976, Broadlands Archives, reference: Classiebawn BR/Add/1/3.

25 1st Earl Mountbatten of Burma to Sir Arthur Galsworthy, British Ambassador to Dublin, 14 June 1976, Broadlands Archives, reference: Classiebawn BR/Add/1/3.

26 Diary of 2nd Countess Mountbatten of Burma (Patricia), 8 August 1976.

27 Fionn McArthur, interviewed for this book, 14 April 2004.

28 Diary of 2nd Countess Mountbatten of Burma (Patricia), 4 August 1978.

29 Diary of 1st Earl Mountbatten of Burma, 5 August 1978.

30 Charles H. Browne to Commander H. B. Webb (Ben), Private Secretary to 1st Earl Mountbatten, 10 August 1965, Broadlands Archives, reference: Classiebawn BR/Add/2/6. Reproduced by courtesy of Patricia Millard.

31 *Irish Independent*, Dublin, 30 August 1979.

32 1st Earl Mountbatten of Burma to Aideen Gore-Booth, 2 July 1979, Broadlands Archives, reference: Classiebawn MB1/N37.

33 Sir David McNee, Metropolitan Police Commissioner, to 1st Earl Mountbatten of Burma, 10 July 1979, Broadlands Archives, reference: Classiebawn BR/Add/3/4. Reproduced by courtesy of the Metropolitan Police Authority.

34 W. Robin Haydon, British Ambassador to Dublin, to 1st Earl Mountbatten of Burma, 17 July 1979.

35 8th Lord Brabourne (Norton), interviewed by the author, 6 February 2004.

36 Diary of 2nd Countess Mountbatten of Burma (Patricia), 16 August 1979.

37 Diary of 2nd Countess Mountbatten of Burma (Patricia), 20 August 1979.

38 Quoted in Brian Hoey, *Mountbatten: The Private Story*, (London: Sidgwick & Jackson), 1994, p. 15.

39 Diary of 2nd Countess Mountbatten of Burma (Patricia), 25 August 1979.

40 Aideen Gore-Booth to 1st Earl Mountbatten of Burma, 27 February 1978, Broadlands Archives, reference: Classiebawn BR/Add/3/4. Reproduced by courtesy of Sir Josslyn Gore-Booth, 9th Baronet.

41 Unpublished memoir of Aideen Gore-Booth, c.1992, section 249. Reproduced by courtesy of Sir Josslyn Gore-Booth, 9th Baronet.

Chapter 5 – Bomb

1 Hugh Tunney, interviewed by the author, 23 August 2003.

2 Grace Ryan, interviewed for this book, 29 March 2004.

3 Gyles Brandreth, *Philip & Elizabeth: Portrait of a Marriage*, (London: Century), 2004, pp. 153–54.

4 Juliet Berridge, formerly Juliet Roche, interviewed for this book, 24 October 2007.

5 James Lohan, retired Garda, interviewed for this book, 26 November 2003.

6 Evidence of Garda James Lohan, Trial, Day 2, morning, questions 54 and 58.

7 Evidence of Garda James Lohan, Trial, Day 2, question 58.

8 Evidence of Garda James Lohan, Trial, Day 2, question 58.

9 John Maxwell, interviewed by Denzil McDaniel for *The Impartial Reporter*, Enniskillen, 26 August 2004.

10 7th Lord Brabourne (John), 'August 27th 1979: An Account of the Events immediately following the Explosion of the Bomb', December 1979, Brabourne Papers, Mersham.

11 William Wilkinson, interviewed by the author, 5 December 2003. The following quotations from William Wilkinson are taken from this interview.

12 Account of Garda Kevin Mullins, 28 August 1979, confirmed in an interview for this book, 27 November 2003.

13 7th Lord Brabourne (John), 'August 27th 1979: An Account of the Events immediately following the Explosion of the Bomb', December 1979, Brabourne Papers, Mersham.

14 Diary of 2nd Countess Mountbatten of Burma (Patricia) for 27 August 1979, written 24 September 1979.

15 Evidence of Garda John Geraghty, Trial, Day 2, morning, question 124.

Chapter 6 – Rescue

1 Siobhán Burgess, 30 August 1979, confirmed in an interview for this book, 11 July 2009.

2 William Wilkinson, interviewed by the author, 5 December 2003. The following quotations from William Wilkinson are taken from this interview.

3 Charles Pierce, interviewed by the author, 12 January 2004.

4 Kathryn Pierce interviewed by the author, 12 January 2004. The following quotations from Kathryn Pierce are taken from this interview.

5 7th Lord Brabourne (John), written account of 8 September 1979.

6 7th Lord Brabourne (John), 'August 27th 1979: An Account of the Events immediately following the Explosion of the Bomb', December 1979, Brabourne Papers, Mersham. The following quotations from 7th Lord Brabourne are taken from this account.

7 Glen Morrison, interviewed for this book, 1 November 2005.

8 W. James Morrison, interviewed for this book, 3 and 5 November 2005.

9 Edward Dawson, interviewed by the author, 12 March 2004.

10 Elizabeth Wood-Martin, interviewed by the author, 25 August 2003.

11 Account of Elizabeth Wood-Martin, 28 August 1979, confirmed in an interview by the author, 25 August 2003.

12 Richard Wood-Martin, interviewed by the author, 7 November 2003.

13 Elizabeth Wood-Martin, interviewed by the author, 7 November 2003. The following quotations from Elizabeth Wood-Martin are taken from this interview.

14 Account of Richard Wood-Martin, 28 August 1979, confirmed in an interview by the author, 25 August 2003.

15 John Maxwell, interviewed by the author, 12 November 2003. The following quotations from John Maxwell are taken from this interview.

16 Elizabeth Wood-Martin, interviewed by the author, 25 August 2003. The following quotation from Elizabeth Wood-Martin is taken from this interview.

17 Richard Wood-Martin, interviewed by the author, 25 August 2003. The following quotation from Richard Wood-Martin is taken from this interview.

18 Elizabeth Duffy, interviewed by the author, 22 June 2004. The following quotation is taken from this interview.

19 The Hon. Philip Knatchbull, interviewed by the author, 2 January 2004.

20 Lady Crathorne (Sylvia), interviewed by the author, 18 December 2003. The quotation was in notes written by Lady Crathorne at Classiebawn, 5 September 1979.

21 Account of Manfred Ottow, 3 September 1979, confirmed in an interview for this book, 20 June 2008.

22 Commander William (Gus) Mulligan, 28 August 1979.

23 Robert Graf, interviewed by the author, 25 August 2004.

24 Richard Wallace, interviewed by the author, 2 December 2003. The following quotations from Richard Wallace are taken from this interview.

25 Brian Best, interviewed by the author, 3 December 2003. The following quotations from Brian Best are taken from this interview.

26 Diary of 2nd Countess Mountbatten of Burma (Patricia) for 27 August 1979, written 24 September 1979.

27 Account of Peter McHugh, 28 August 1979, confirmed in an interview for this book, 14 November 2003.

28 Michael Hampsey, interviewed for this book, 19 June 2008.

29 Edward Dawson, interviewed by the author, 12 March 2004. The following quotations from Edward Dawson are taken from this interview.

30 Rodney Lomax, interviewed by the author, 12 November 2003.

31 Trudy Lomax, interviewed by the author, 12 November 2003.

32 Hugh Tunney, interviewed by the author, 23 August 2003.

33 Diary of Grace Ryan, 27 August 1979.

34 Rachel Johnson, interviewed for this book, 8 January 2004.

35 Dr Terence Dudeney, interviewed for this book, 8 January 2008.

36 Professor Alan Browne, interviewed for this book, 27 April 2004.

37 Cecil Barber, interviewed for this book, 12 November 2003.

38 Grainne McInerney, interviewed for this book, 15 February 2008.

39 Account of Grainne McInerney, 5 September 1979, confirmed in an interview for this book, 15 February 2008.

40 Evidence of Garda James Lohan, Trial, Day 2, question 62.

41 Terry Baker interviewed by the author, 8 October 2003. The following quotations from Terry Baker are taken from this interview.

42 *Daily Mail*, London, 28 August 1979.

43 Inge Ottow, interviewed for this book, 20 June 2008.

44 Manfred Ottow, interviewed for this book, 24 June 2008.

45 Inge Ottow, interviewed for this book, 20 June 2008.

Chapter 7 – Have a Nice Day

1 James Orr, Equerry to HRH The Duke of Edinburgh (Prince Philip), to 7th Lord Brabourne (John), 5 September 1979. Brabourne Papers, Mersham. Reproduced by courtesy of Geoffrey Orr.
2 Diary of India Hicks, 27 August 1979.
3 Diary of India Hicks, 27 August 1979.
4 Diary of India Hicks, 27 August 1979.
5 Metropolitan Police Special Branch, memorandum, 27 August 1979.
6 The Hon. Philip Knatchbull, interviewed by the author, 2 January 2004.
7 Lady Joanna Knatchbull, interviewed by the author, 4 April 2008. The following quotations from Lady Joanna Knatchbull are taken from this interview.
8 J. Frank Pantridge, *An Unquiet Life*, (Hillsborough, Northern Ireland: Pantridge Foundation), 1995, p. 75.
9 Diary of Grace Ryan, 27 August 1979.
10 Kevin Henry, interviewed by the author, 9 October 2003.
11 John Maxwell, interviewed by the author, 12 November 2003.
12 Professor Frank Pantridge, interviewed for this book, 19 December 2003.

Chapter 8 – Hospital

1 Dr Anthony (Tony) Heenan, interviewed by the author, 9 November 2003. The following quotations from Dr Heenan are taken from this interview.
2 Diary of 2nd Countess Mountbatten of Burma (Patricia) for 27 August 1979, written 24 September 1979.
3 Report by Dr Denis Boland, 26 September 1979. The following quotations from Dr Boland are taken from this report. Reproduced by courtesy of Sligo General Hospital.
4 Lady Crathorne (Sylvia), interviewed by the author, 18 December 2003. The quotation from an unidentified nurse was in notes written by Lady Crathorne at Classiebawn, 5 September 1979.
5 7th Lord Brabourne (John), 'August 27th 1979: An Account of the Events immediately following the Explosion of the Bomb', December 1979, Brabourne Papers, Mersham.

6 Mary Cox (formerly Mary Lowry), interviewed by the author, 21 January 2004. The following quotations from Mary Cox are taken from this interview.

7 Lady Pamela Hicks, interviewed by the author, 9 December 2003. The following quotations from Lady Pamela Hicks are taken from this interview.

8 Mary McGoldrick (formerly Mary Gantley), interviewed for this book, 23 March 2004.

9 Report by Dr Denis Boland, 26 September 1979. Reproduced by courtesy of Sligo General Hospital.

10 5th Duke of Abercorn (James), interviewed by the author, 20 November 2003.

11 Unpublished account of David Hicks, 19 September 1979, reproduced by courtesy of Ashley Hicks. The following quotations from David Hicks are taken from this account.

12 Statement of Detective Garda John P. Reynolds (Jack), 10 September 1979.

13 Dr Stewart Johnston, interviewed by the author, 31 March 2004.

14 Dr Stewart Johnston, interviewed by the author, 31 March 2004.

15 J. Frank Pantridge, An Unquiet Life, (Hillsborough, Northern Ireland: Pantridge Foundation), 1995, p. 75.

16 Diary of Grace Ryan, 27 August 1979.

17 Posthumous BBC Radio broadcast, c. August 1979.

18 Peter Nicholson, interviewed by the author, 7 October 2003.

19 Diary of Grace Ryan, 28 August 1979.

20 Diary of 2nd Countess Mountbatten of Burma (Patricia) for 27 August 1979, written 24 September 1979.

21 2nd Countess Mountbatten of Burma (Patricia), quoted in Alf McCreary, Tried By Fire: Finding Hope Out of Suffering in Northern Ireland, Basingstoke, Hampshire, 1986.

22 Chicago Tribune, 29 August 1979, quoting New York Times news source.

23 The Hon. Michael-John Knatchbull (Joe), interviewed by the author, 11 March 2004. The following quotations from Michael-John Knatchbull are taken from this interview.

24 Lady Joanna Knatchbull, interviewed by the author, 4 April 2008.

The following quotations from Joanna Knatchbull are taken from this interview.

25 The Hon. Michael-John Knatchbull (Joe), interviewed for this book, 11 March 2004. The following quotations from Michael-John Knatchbull are taken from this interview.

26 India Hicks to 7th Lord Brabourne (John), 26 May 2005. Reproduced by courtesy of India Hicks.

27 J. Christopher Durham Kenyon, interviewed by the author, 23 September 2004.

28 Dr Brian O'Connor, interviewed for this book, 13 May 2004.

29 India Hicks to 7th Lord Brabourne (John), 26 May 2005. Reproduced by courtesy of India Hicks.

30 7th Lord Brabourne (John), interviewed by the author, 3 October 2003. The following quotations from 7th Lord Brabourne are taken from this interview.

31 *Sligo Champion*, 7 September 1979.

32 Telegram from HRH The Prince of Wales (Prince Charles) to the author, 28 August 1979.

33 7th Lord Brabourne (John), interviewed by the author, 29 October 2003.

34 Diary of 2nd Countess Mountbatten (Patricia) for 30 August 1979, written 24 September 1979.

35 Lady Crathorne (Sylvia), interviewed by the author, 18 December 2003. The quotation was in notes written by Lady Crathorne at Classiebawn, 5 September 1979.

36 Unnamed member of the Dáil, quoted in *Sunday World*, Dublin, 2 September 1979.

37 Lady Crathorne (Sylvia), interviewed by the author, 18 December 2003. The quotation was in notes written by Lady Crathorne at Classiebawn, 5 September 1979.

38 Jack Lynch, quoted in *Daily Mirror*, 1 September 1979.

39 The Hon. Mrs David Dugdale (Susie), interviewed by the author, 17 December 2003.

Chapter 9 – Friends from England

1 7th Lord Braboune (John), interviewed by the author, 2 October 2004.

2 Lady Crathorne (Sylvia), interviewed by the author, 18 December 2003. The quotation was in notes written by Lady Crathorne at Classiebawn, 5 September 1979.

3 Lady Crathorne (Sylvia) to her sister Rachel, 18 September 1979.

4 Lady Crathorne (Sylvia) to her sister Rachel, 18 September 1979. The following quotation from Lady Crathorne is taken from this correspondence.

5 The Hon. Mrs David Dugdale (Susie), interviewed by the author, 17 December 2003.

6 Lady Crathorne (Sylvia) to her sister Rachel, 18 September 1979.

7 7th Lord Brabourne (John), interviewed by the author, 3 October 2003.

8 Lady Joanna Knatchbull to 7th Lord Brabourne (John), 2 September 1979, Brabourne Papers, Mersham.

9 2nd Lord Crathorne (Jamie), interviewed by the author, 18 December 2003.

10 7th Lord Brabourne (John), interviewed by the author, 3 February 2004.

11 Diary of 2nd Countess Mountbatten of Burma (Patricia) for 30 August 1979, written 24 September 1979.

Chapter 10 – Funerals

1 Robert H. V. Moorhead, interviewed by the author, 16 February 2004.

2 Robert H. V. Moorhead to 7th Lord Brabourne (John), 1 September 1979.

3 Robert H. V. Moorhead, interviewed by the author, 16 February 2004. The following quotations from Robert Moorhead are taken from this interview.

4 8th Lord Brabourne (Norton), interviewed by the author, 6 February 2004.

5 7th Lord Brabourne (John) to Dr Donald Coggan, Archbishop of Canterbury, 2 September 1979, Brabourne Papers, Mersham.

6 Diary of India Hicks for 4 September 1979.

7 Sir Charles H. W. Troughton (Dick) to 7th Lord and Lady Brabourne (John and Patricia), 8 September 1979, Brabourne Papers, Mersham.

The following quotations from Sir Charles H. W. Troughton are taken from this correspondence.

8 *Evening Herald*, Dublin, 5 September 1979.

9 Lady Crathorne (Sylvia) to her sister Rachel, 18 September 1979. The following quotations from Lady Crathorne are taken from this correspondence.

10 Lady Pamela Hicks to the author, 26 May 2009.

11 Robert H. V. Moorhead to 7th Lord and Lady Brabourne (John and Patricia), 6 September 1979. The following quotations from Robert Moorhead are taken from this correspondence.

12 The Holy Bible (King James), Epistle of Paul the Apostle to the Romans, Chapter 8, verses 31–39.

13 Address by Donald Coggan, Archbishop of Canterbury, 6 September 1979. Reproduced by courtesy of the trustees of Lambeth Palace Library.

14 'Jerusalem', words by William Blake, music by Sir Charles Hubert Parry.

15 Helen E. Bowden, letters to 7th Lord and Lady Brabourne (John and Patricia), 31 August 1979, Brabourne Papers, Mersham.

16 From A. A. Milne, *The House at Pooh Corner*, London, 1928 © the trustees of Pooh Properties. Published by Egmont UK Ltd and used with permission.

Chapter 11 – Leaving Ireland

1 Lady Joanna Knatchbull, interviewed by the author, 4 April 2008.

2 Robert H. V. Moorhead to 7th Lord and Lady Brabourne (John and Patricia), 6 September 1979. Reproduced by courtesy of Robert Moorhead.

3 Diary of 2nd Lord Crathorne (Jamie), 7 September 1979. Reproduced by courtesy of Jamie Crathorne.

4 Lady Crathorne (Sylvia) to her sister Rachel, 18 September 1979.

5 Lady Joanna Knatchbull, interviewed by the author, 4 April 2008.

6 Diary of 2nd Countess Mountbatten of Burma (Patricia), written 24 September 1979.

7 2nd Countess Mountbatten of Burma (Patricia), interviewed by the author, 3 February 2004.

8 Lady Crathorne (Sylvia) to her sister Rachel, 18 September 1979.

9 7th Lord Brabourne (John) to Mr and Mrs Maxwell (John and Mary), 9 September 1979, Brabourne Papers, Mersham.

10 Dr Anthony Heenan (Tony), interviewed by the author, 9 November 2003.

11 Peter Mullaney to 2nd Countess Mountbatten of Burma (Patricia), 26 September 1979, Brabourne Papers, Mersham. Reproduced by courtesy of Annie Kate Mullaney.

12 Teresa Daly to 2nd Countess Mountbatten of Burma (Patricia), 18 September 1979, Brabourne Papers, Mersham.

13 Rodney Lomax, interviewed by the author, 22 January 2004.

14 John Barry to the author, 27 November 2006. Reproduced by courtesy of John Barry.

15 Diary of 2nd Countess Mountbatten of Burma (Patricia) for 10 September 1979, written 24 September 1979.

16 Mary Cox (formerly Mary Lowry), interviewed by the author, 21 January 2004.

Chapter 12 – London

1 Lady Joanna Knatchbull, interviewed by the author, 4 April 2008.

2 Diary of 2nd Countess Mountbatten of Burma (Patricia), written 24 September 1979.

3 W. E. Henley, 'Invictus', in *Other Men's Flowers*, selected and annotated by Field Marshall Lord Wavell (A. P. Wavell), London, 1944.

4 Diary of 2nd Countess Mountbatten of Burma (Patricia), written 24 September 1979.

5 *Irish Times*, Dublin, 21 September 1979.

6 David Niven to 7th Lord Brabourne (John), 7 September 1979, Brabourne Papers, Mersham.

7 Diary of 2nd Countess Mountbatten of Burma (Patricia), written 24 September 1979. The following quotations from the 2nd Countess Mountbatten of Burma are taken from this diary entry.

8 Michael B. Mavor, 12 September 1979, The Gordonstoun Flag Service, Gordonstoun Record 1980, p. 15.

9 Saul Diskin, *The End of the Twins: A Memoir of Losing a Brother*, (New York: The Overlook Press), 2001, p. 247.

Chapter 13 – Friends in Scotland

1 Sir Charles H. W. Troughton (Dick) to 2nd Countess Mountbatten of Burma (Patricia), 20 September 1979, Brabourne Papers, Mersham. Reproduced by courtesy of Peter Troughton.
2 Lady Joanna Knatchbull to 7th Lord and Lady Brabourne (John and Patricia), 21 September 1979, Brabourne Papers, Mersham.
3 Sir Charles H. W. Troughton (Dick) to 7th Lord Brabourne (John), 23 September 1979, Brabourne Papers, Mersham. Reproduced by courtesy of Peter Troughton.
4 Diary of 2nd Countess Mountbatten of Burma (Patricia), 13 October 1979.

Chapter 14 – Home and Away

1 Diary of 2nd Countess Mountbatten of Burma (Patricia), 9 October 1979.
2 Piers McGillycuddy to the author, 27 September 1979. Reproduced by courtesy of Piers McGillycuddy.
3 Mahin Kooros to the author, 3 October 1979. Reproduced by courtesy of Mahin Kooros.
4 Diary of 2nd Countess Mountbatten of Burma (Patricia), 12 October 1979.
5 7th Lord Brabourne (John), October 1979, Brabourne Papers, Mersham.
6 Diary of 2nd Countess Mountbatten of Burma (Patricia), 17 October 1979.
7 Diary of 2nd Countess Mountbatten of Burma (Patricia), 20 October 1979.
8 *Sunday People*, London, 22 October 1979.
9 Lord Annan (Noël) to 2nd Countess Mountbatten of Burma (Patricia), 24 October 1979, Brabourne Papers, Mersham. Reproduced by courtesy of Juliet Annan.
10 Diary of 2nd Countess Mountbatten of Burma (Patricia), 29 October 1979.
11 Diary of 2nd Countess Mountbatten of Burma (Patricia), 29 October 1979.
12 Diary of 2nd Countess Mountbatten of Burma (Patricia), 29 October 1979.

13 David Niven to the author, 8 November 1979.

14 Diary of 2nd Countess Mountbatten of Burma (Patricia), 5 November 1979.

15 Diary of 2nd Countess Mountbatten of Burma (Patricia), 6 November 1979.

16 Sheilagh Densham-Paton to 7th Lord Brabourne (John), 27 October 1979, Brabourne Papers, Mersham. Reproduced by courtesy of Sheilagh Densham-Paton.

17 Miss 'Mungie' Mungeam, secretary to the chairman, British Red Cross Society, London, to 2nd Countess Mountbatten of Burma (Patricia), 16 November 1979, Brabourne Papers, Marsham. Reproduced by courtesy of the British Red Cross.

18 Paul Burns to 7th Lord Brabourne (John), 17 November 1979, Brabourne Papers, Mersham. Reproduced by courtesy of Paul Burns.

19 Diary of 2nd Countess Mountbatten of Burma (Patricia), 19 November 1979.

20 Diary of 2nd Countess Mountbatten of Burma (Patricia), 19 November 1979.

21 Diary of 2nd Countess Mountbatten of Burma (Patricia), 18 November 1979.

22 Obituary of Norris McWhirter, *Daily Telegraph*, 21 April 2004.

23 Norris McWhirter to 7th Lord and Lady Brabourne (John and Patricia), 25 November 1979, Brabourne Papers, Mersham.

24 Diary of 2nd Countess Mountbatten of Burma (Patricia), 7 December 1979.

25 Michael Mavor, Gordonstoun School report, autumn term 1979, Brabourne Papers, Mersham.

26 Peter S. Larkman, Gordonstoun School report, autumn term 1979, Brabourne Papers, Mersham.

Chapter 15 – Steps of St Paul's

1 Diary of 2nd Countess Mountbatten of Burma (Patricia), 20 December 1979.

2 Diary of 2nd Countess Mountbatten of Burma (Patricia), 20 December 1979. The following quotations from the 2nd Countess Mountbatten of Burma are also taken from her diary.

3 Address by HRH The Prince of Wales (Prince Charles), St Paul's Cathedral, London, 20 December 1979.

4 Mary Hornsey (formerly Mary Maxwell) to the author, 3 May 2005.

5 7th Lord Hornsey Lady Brabourne (John and Patricia), interviewed by the author, 3 October 2003.

6 Diary of 2nd Countess Mountbatten of Burma (Patricia), 23 December 1979.

7 Chris Harper, manager of the Eriff Fishery 1977–1980, interviewed for this book, 28 May 2008.

8 W. Desmond McEvoy to 7th Lord Brabourne (John), 18 September 1979, Brabourne Papers, Mersham. Reproduced by courtesy of David McEvoy.

9 Bill Lange to 7th Lord Brabourne (John), 16 October 1979, Brabourne Papers, Mersham.

10 Marchioness of Hartingdon (Amanda), later Duchess of Devonshire, to 7th Lord Brabourne (John), 8 September 1979, Brabourne Papers, Mersham. Reproduced by courtesy of the Duchess of Devonshire.

11 Letter from Pat Ryan, published by the *Sunday Independent*, Dublin, 11 April 2004.

Chapter 16 – New Decade

1 Robert. H. V. Moorhead to 7th Lord Brabourne (John), 1 September 1979, Brabourne Papers, Mersham.

2 Statement released by Dr Desmond Moran, Sligo, 8 January 1980.

3 Dr Desmond Moran to Lady Pamela Hicks, 22 January 1980. Reproduced by courtesy of Dr Moran.

4 Norris McWhirter to 7th Lord and Lady Brabourne (John and Patricia), 25 November 1979.

5 Diary of 2nd Countess Mountbatten of Burma (Patricia), 13 August 1980.

6 Diary of 2nd Countess Mountbatten of Burma (Patricia), 24 August 1980.

7 Diary of 2nd Countess Mountbatten of Burma (Patricia), 27 August 1980.

8 *Sligo Journal*, 9 May 1981.

Chapter 17 – Lone Twin

1 Julia Orange, 'Plight of the Single Twin', *The Times*, London, 1 May 1989.
2 Julia Orange, 'Plight of the Single Twin', *The Times*, London, 1 May 1989.
3 Best man's speech by David Loftus at the author's wedding, 11 July 1998.
4 Quoted by Cassandra Jardine, *Daily Telegraph*, London, 3 February 1997.
5 Brian James, 'Was Mountbatten betrayed?', *The Times*, London, 25 August 1989.
6 4th Marquess of Milford Haven (George) to *The Times*, London, 9 November 1994.
7 Author to *The Times*, London, 10 November 1994.
8 Ronan Fanning, 'What really mattered is that he came at all', *Sunday Independent*, Dublin, 4 June 1995.
9 Mícheál Mac Donncha to *Irish Times*, Dublin, 7 June 1995.

Chapter 18 – The Sound of the Bomb

1 *Sunday Times*, London, 26 January 1997.
2 Author to Richard and Elizabeth Wood-Martin, 30 March 2000.

Chapter 19 – Castle Revisited

1 Author's journal, 15 August 2003.
2 Charles H. Browne to 7th Lord Brabourne and Lady Brabourne (John and Patricia), 7 May 1982, Brabourne Papers. Reproduced by courtesy of Patricia Millard.
3 Lady Pamela Hicks interviewed by the author, 9 December 2003.
4 Caroline Devine, interviewed by the author, 23 August 2003.
5 Author's journal, 14 August 2003.
6 Author's journal, 15 August 2003. The following quotation is also taken from this journal entry.
7 Hugh Tunney interviewed by the author, 23 August 2003. The following quotations from Hugh Tunney are taken from this interview.
8 Author's journal, 25 August 2003.

Chapter 20 – Village Revisited

1 Author's journal, 25 August 2003.
2 Author's journal, 25 August 2003.
3 Elizabeth Wood-Martin, interviewed by the author, 25 August 2003.
4 Author to Richard and Elizabeth Wood-Martin, 5 September 2003.
5 Author's journal, 7 October 2003.
6 Rachel Johnson, interviewed for this book, 8 January 2004.
7 Mary Hornsey (formerly Mary Maxwell), interviewed by the author, 4 December 2003.
8 Author's journal, 12 November 2003.
9 John Maxwell, interviewed by the author, 12 November 2003. The following quotations from John Maxwell are taken from this interview.
10 Author's journal, 12 November 2003.
11 Author's journal, 10 October 2003.
12 Unpublished memoir of Aideen Gore-Booth, c.1992, pp. 75–76. Reproduced by courtesy of Sir Josslyn Gore-Booth, 9th Baronet.
13 James Nelson, *Sligo Weekender*, 24 August 2004.
14 Mary Cox (formerly Mary Lowry), interviewed by the author, 21 January 2004.
15 Derek Hill to 2nd Countess Mountbatten of Burma (Patricia), 1 September 1979, Brabourne Papers, Mersham.
16 Professor Alan Browne to 7th Lord Brabourne (John), 30 August 1979, Brabourne Papers, Mersham.
17 Author's journal, 26 August 2004.
18 Robert Graf, interviewed by the author, 25 August 2004.
19 Joe McGowan, *Sligo Weekender* anniversary supplement, 24 August 2004, p. 6.
20 Written account of Aideen Gore-Booth, 1 September 1979.
21 Liam Carey to author, 16 December 2004.
22 *Blütiger Montag* by Minow-Films for WDR, broadcast by ARD in Germany, 12 November 1998, and broadcast by TG4 in Ireland as *Séideán Staire: Bloody Monday, Lord Mountbatten and the IRA*, 1 May 2007.
23 Notes taken by 7th Lord Brabourne (John) during telephone

conversation with Mr Hans-Rudiger Minow, producer of *Blütiger Montag*, c.1998, Brabourne Papers, Mersham.

24 Aideen Gore-Booth, 'People who helped after disaster of Shadow V', 1979. Brabourne Papers, Mersham.

25 Lady Pamela Hicks to the author, 25 May 2009.

26 *Western Journal*, 7 September 1979.

27 Elizabeth Duffy, interviewed for this book, 26 November 2003.

28 *Donegal Democrat*, 15 July 1983.

29 Author's journal, 25 January 2004.

30 Author's journal, 26 January 2004.

Chapter 21 – Rescue Revisited

1 Author's journal, 3 December 2003. The following quotation also comes from the author's journal.

2 Brian Best, interviewed by the author, 3 December 2003.

3 Richard Wallace, interviewed by the author, 2 December 2003.

4 Richard Wallace to 7th Lord Brabourne (John), 9 December 1979, Brabourne Papers, Mersham. Reproduced by courtesy of Richard Wallace.

5 Charles Pierce to the author, 11 November 2003.

6 Kathryn Pierce, interviewed by the author, 12 January 2004. The following quotations from Kathryn Pierce are taken from this interview.

7 Charles Pierce, interviewed by the author, 12 January 2004.

8 Author to Charles and Kathryn Pierce, 14 January 2004.

9 Author's journal, 5 December 2003.

10 William Wilkinson, interviewed by the author, 5 December 2003.

11 Elizabeth Duffy, interviewed by the author, 22 June 2004. The following quotations from Elizabeth Duffy are taken from this interview.

12 I. Christiane Graf, interviewed by the author, 25 August 2004. The following quotations from I. Christiane Graf are taken from this interview.

13 Author's journal, 18 December 2003.

14 2nd Lord and Lady Crathorne (Jamie and Sylvia), interviewed by the author, 18 December 2003.

Chapter 22 – Hospital Revisited

1 Mary Cox (formerly Mary Lowry), interviewed by the author, 21 January 2004.
2 Dr Anthony (Tony) Heenan, interviewed by the author, 9 November 2003. The following quotations from Dr Heenan are taken from this interview.
3 Author's journal, 10 November 2003.
4 Unpublished obituary of Lady Brabourne (Doreen), by Cecil Gould, sent by Iris Portal to 7th Lord Brabourne (John), 22 December 1979, Brabourne Papers, Mersham.
5 Author's journal, 11 November 2003. The following quotations are taken from this journal entry.
6 Lady Joanna Knatchbull, interviewed by the author, 4 April 2008. The following quotations from Lady Joanna Knatchbull are taken from this interview.
7 Dr Anthony (Tony) Heenan, interviewed by the author, 9 November 2003. The following quotations from Dr Heenan are taken from this interview.

Chapter 23 – Trial: The People versus Thomas McMahon and Francis McGirl

1 Superintendent Patrick O'Connell, High Court, Dublin, 5 September 1979.
2 *Irish Times*, 6 November 1979.
3 Evidence of Detective Sergeant Thomas Dunne, Trial, Day 2, afternoon, question 3a.
4 Evidence of Detective Garda John P. Reynolds (Jack), Trial, Day 3, morning, question 41.
5 Evidence of J. Dermot Mullooly, Trial, Day 3, morning, question 142.
6 Evidence of J. Dermot Mullooly, Trial, Day 3, morning, question 203.
7 Judgment, Trial, Day 14.
8 Evidence of Dr Dieter Gross, Trial, Day 12, afternoon, question 285.
9 Evidence of Detective Sergeant Michael Niland, Trial, Day 5, morning, question 153.
10 Evidence of Kevin Murray, Trial, Day 1, morning, question 301.

11 Evidence of Sergeant Vincent Fanning, Day 2, morning, question 175.
12 Evidence of Garda John Geraghty, Trial, Day 2, morning, question 118.
13 Evidence of Rodney Lomax, Trial, Day 3, afternoon, question 127a.
14 Evidence of Francis McGirl, Trial, Day 2, afternoon, question 182.
15 Evidence of Francis McGirl, Trial, Day 2, afternoon, questions 157a and 156a.
16 Evidence of Francis McGirl, Trial, Day 2, afternoon, questions 237a and 215a.
17 Evidence of Francis McGirl, Trial, Day 2, afternoon, question 207a.
18 Evidence of Francis McGirl, Trial, Day 2, afternoon, question 194a.
19 Evidence of Sergeant Vincent Fanning, Trial, Day 2, morning, question 188.
20 Evidence of Sergeant Vincent Fanning, Trial, Day 2, morning, question 198.
21 Chief Justice Liam Hamilton, Trial, Day 2, morning, question 384.
22 Evidence of Detective Sergeant John McGerty, Trial, Day 2, afternoon, question 83a.
23 Evidence of Detective Inspector Michael Canavan, Trial, Day 2, afternoon, question 61a.
24 Evidence of Francis McGirl, Trial, Day 2, afternoon, question 150a.

Chapter 24 – Garda Revisited

1 Nina Ottow, interviewed for this book, 23 June 2008.
2 Superintendent Philip McMahon, quoted in *Evening Herald*, Dublin, 28 August 2004.
3 Written account of Shane Rodgers, 30 August 1979, confirmed in an interview for this book, 2 April 2004.
4 Rodney Lomax, interviewed by the author, 22 January 2004.
5 Brigadier J. M. Glover (Defence Intelligence staff), 'Northern Ireland: Future Terrorist Trends', November 1978.
6 John Hennessy, interviewed by the author, 22 January 2004.
7 Lady Pamela Hicks, interviewed by the author, 9 December 2003.
8 Evidence of Detective Garda Kevin Henry, Trial, Day 1, afternoon, questions 40 and 42.

9 John Maxwell, interviewed by the author, 12 November 2003. The following quotations from John Maxwell are taken from this interview.

10 John Courtney, interviewed by the author, 20 January 2004.

11 Fionn McArthur, interviewed for this book, 14 April 2004.

12 1st Earl Mountbatten of Burma to 'Ted', 4 September 1978.

13 1st Earl Mountbatten of Burma to Aideen Gore-Booth, 1 September 1978, Broadlands Archives.

14 Aideen Gore-Booth to 1st Earl Mountbatten of Burma, 14 February 1979, Broadlands Archives. Reproduced by courtesy of Sir Josslyn Gore-Booth, 9th Baronet.

15 British Embassy in Dublin, 18 April 1979.

16 W. Robin Haydon, British Ambassador to Ireland, 24 July 1979.

17 Republic of Ireland Department, Foreign and Commonwealth Office, London, 2 August 1979.

18 John Courtney, interviewed by the author, 20 January 2004.

19 Paul Potts, *Daily Telegraph*, London, 11 January 1980.

20 Paul Potts, *Daily Telegraph*, London, 11 January 1980.

21 Dr James Donovan, interviewed by the author, 20 January 2004. The following quotations from Dr Donovan are taken from this interview.

22 Patrick Jordan, interviewed by the author, 19 March 2004.

Chapter 25 – IRA

1 Arthur P. Hockaday, Cabinet Office, to 1st Earl Mountbatten of Burma, 17 July 1972, Broadlands Archives. Reproduced under licence.

2 Garda, interviewed by the author, 13 November 2003. Name withheld.

3 Report released by the National Archives of Ireland, 28 December 2007, National Archives of Ireland, Department of Foreign Affairs, London Embassy, 2007/58/5. Reproduced with permission.

4 Paul Potts, *Daily Telegraph*, London, 11 January 1980.

5 Detective Inspector Michael Canavan, Trial, Day 2, afternoon, question 102a.

6 John Courtney, interviewed by the author, 20 January 2004.

7 Toby Harnden, interviewed for this book, 4 August 2008.

8 Richard English, Professor of Politics at Queen's University, Belfast, interviewed for this book, 31 July 2008.

9 Eamon Collins with Mick McGovern, *Killing Rage*, (London: Granta Books), 1997, p. 101.

10 Joseph O'Neill, *Blood-Dark Track – A Family History*, (London: Granta Books), 2000, p. 240.

11 Jack Kenealy and Liam Kelly, *Daily Mirror*, London, 24 November 1979.

12 Toby Harnden, '*Bandit Country': The IRA & South Armagh*, (London: Hodder & Stoughton), 1999, pp. 202–3.

13 Richard English, *Armed Struggle: The History of the IRA*, (London: Pan Books), 2004, p.344.

14 Peig Lynch, quoted by Joseph O'Neill, *Blood-Dark Track – A Family History*, (London: Granta Books), 2000, p. 291.

15 Catherine McCartney, talking about the 2005 murder of her brother Robert McCartney, *Taking a Stand*, BBC Radio 4, 20 January 2009.

16 Front page of *Daily Mail*, London, 24 November 1979.

17 Interview with prison officer on 8 August 2007. Name withheld.

18 *Irish Independent*, 8 August 1998.

19 Quoted in *The Sunday Times*, London, 26 January 1997.

20 *Daily Telegraph*, London, 5 April 1999.

21 Richard English, Professor of Politics at Queen's University, Belfast, interviewed for this book, 2 April 2008.

22 Tom Brady, *Irish Independent*, 29 September 2006.

23 John Courtney, interviewed by the author, 20 January 2004.

24 Obituary of Francis McGirl by Owen Carron, former Sinn Fein MP for Fermanagh and South Tyrone, *Leitrim Observer*, 22 March 1995.

25 Colin Randall, former senior reporter for *Daily Telegraph* who attended the funeral of Francis McGirl, interviewed for this book, 24 June 2005.

26 Colin Randall, *Daily Telegraph*, London, 18 March 1995.

27 *An Phoblacht/Republican News*, Dublin, 5 January 1980.

28 Toby Harnden, '*Bandit Country': The IRA & South Armagh*, (London: Hodder & Stoughton), 1999, pp. 202–3.

29 Patrick, quoted by his son, Nicky Campbell, *Blue-eyed Son: The Story of an Adoption*, (London: Pan Books), 2004.

30 Pat Thompson, quoted in Toby Harnden, '*Bandit Country': The IRA*

& *South Armagh*, (London: Hodder & Stoughton), 1999, p. 204.

31 Joseph O'Neill, *Blood-Dark Track – A Family History*, (London: Granta Books), 2000, p. 297.

32 Gerry Adams, interviewed by Erik Amfitheatrof, *Time* magazine, 19 November 1979.

33 Introduction by academic to Martin McGuinness's lecture, 'Ireland: Prospects for Peace', Institute of Politics, Harvard University, 14 November 1997.

34 John Hume, Social Democratic and Labour Party annual conference, Belfast, 1988.

35 Un-named IRA representative, *Irish Times*, Dublin, 1 September 1979.

36 *An Phoblacht/Republican News*, Dublin, 1 September 1979.

37 Joseph O'Neill, *Blood-Dark Track – A Family History*, (London: Granta Books), 2000, p. 133.

Chapter 26 – Face to Face

1 John O'Brien, interviewed by the author, 11 November 2003. The following quotations from John O'Brien are taken from this interview.

2 Sean Brennan, interviewed by the author, 11 November 2003. The following quotations from Sean Brennan are taken from this interview.

3 Martin Shelbourne, interviewed by the author, 21 December 2004. The following quotations from Martin Shelbourne are taken from this interview.

4 Author's journal, 21 December 2004.

5 Author's journal, 11 November 2003.

6 Author's journal, 29 January 2004.

7 Saul Diskin, *The End of the Twins: A Memoir of Losing a Brother*, (New York: The Overlook Press), 2001, p. 270.

8 Author's journal, 26 March 2004.

9 Author's journal, 18 March 2004. The following quotations from the author's journal are taken from this entry.

10 Professor John Harbison, interviewed by the author, 18 March 2004.

Chapter 27 – Peace

1 Michael McDowell, Minister for Justice, Equality and Law Reform,

address to the Progressive Democrats, Dublin, 12 March 2004, quoted in *Irish Independent*, Dublin, 13 March 2004.

2 Michael McDowell, Minister for Justice Equality and Law Reform, address to the Progressive Democrats, Dublin, 12 March 2004, quoted in *Irish Independent*, Dublin, 13 March 2004.

3 James Hawthorne, Controller of BBC Northern Ireland 1978–1987, interviewed by the author, 3 December 2003.

4 *An Phoblacht /Republican News*, Dublin, 16 July 2002.

5 Richard English, *Armed Struggle: The History of the IRA*, (London: Pan Books), 2004, p. 381.

6 Fintan O'Toole, *Irish Times*, 2 August 2005.

7 Anthony McIntyre, quoted in Richard English, *Armed Struggle: The History of the IRA*, (London: Pan Books), 2004, p. 319.

8 Richard English, *Armed Struggle: The History of the IRA*, (London: Pan Books), 2004, p. 378.

9 Dr David Connolly, University of York, 'At a Post-Conflict Juncture: An assessment of mental health and developmental needs in Whiterock, West Belfast', Belfast, 2007.

10 Dr David Connolly, University of York, quoted in *The Times*, London, 6 September 2007.

11 From *Lycidas*, a lament by John Milton (1608–74) for a friend drowned while crossing the Irish Sea from Chester in 1637.

12 John Maxwell, interviewed by the author, 12 November 2003.

13 Author's journal, 21 January 2004.

14 Author's journal, 24 August 2004.

15 Author's journal, 26 August 2004.

16 Author's journal, 29 November 2003.

Chapter 28 – Peace

1 From 'Banner Man' by Blue Mink; lyrics reproduced by courtesy of Cauliflower Music Ltd.

Epilogue

1 Obituary of 7th Lord Brabourne (John), London, *Daily Telegraph*, London, 24 September 2005.

BIBLIOGRAPHY

Abercorn, Sacha, *Feather from the Firebird* (Kilcar, Ireland: Summer Palace Press), 2003.

Amant, Virgine, *Yeats' Landscapes: Travels with WB Yeats* (London: Caxton Editions), 2000.

An Crann *The Tree* (collected work), *Bear in Mind, Stories of the Troubles* (Belfast: Lagan Press), 2000.

Brandreth, Gyles, *Philip & Elizabeth: Portrait of a Marriage* (London: Century), 2004.

Broad, Richard, Taylor Downing, Caroline Elliston, Isobel Hinshelwood, Annie Kossoff, Sarah Manwaring-Wright, Ian Stuttard, Adrian Wood, *The Troubles: The background to the question of Northern Ireland* (London: Thames Television Ltd/Macdonald Futura), 1980.

Campbell, Nicky, *Blue-eyed Son: The Story of an Adoption*, (London: Pan Books), 2004.

Chambers, James, *Palmerston: 'The People's Darling'* (London: John Murray), 2004.

Collins, Eamon, *Killing Rage* (London: Granta Books), 1997.

Coogan, Tim Pat, *The Troubles* (London: Arrow Books), 1996.

Cummins, Barry, *Unsolved* (Dublin: Gill & Macmillan), 2007.

Didion, Joan, *The Year of Magical Thinking* (New York: Alfred A. Knopf), 2006.

Diskin, Saul, *The End of the Twins: A Memoir of Losing a Brother* (Woodstock, New York: The Overlook Press), 2001.

Ellis, Walter, *The Beginning of the End* (Edinburgh: Mainstream Publishing), 2006.

Emberdove Ltd, *Mountbatten: Eighty Years in Pictures* (London: Macmillan), 1979.

English, Richard, *Armed Struggle: The History of the IRA* (London: Pan Books), 2004.

English, Richard, 'Coming to Terms with the Past: Northern Ireland', *History Today*, vol.54/7, London, 2004.

Ewart-Biggs, Jane, *Pay, Pack and Follow – Memoirs* (London: Weidenfeld and Nicolson), 1984.

Foster, R. F., *The Oxford Illustrated History of Ireland* (Oxford University Press), 2000.

Foster, R. F., *Modern Ireland 1600–1972* (London: Penguin Books), 1989.

Foster, R. F., *The Irish Story: Telling tales and making it up in Ireland* (Oxford University), 2003.

Harnden, Toby, *'Bandit Country': The IRA & South Armagh* (London: Hodder & Stoughton), 2000.

Hoey, Brian, *Mountbatten: The Private Story* (London: Sidgwick & Jackson), 1994.

Hough, Richard, *Mountbatten: Hero of Our Time* (London: Pan Books), 1981.

Hewitt, John, *The Selected John Hewitt* (Belfast: Blackstaff Press), 1991.

James, Dermot, *The Gore-Booths of Lissadell* (Dublin: The Woodfield Press), 2004.

Jenkins, Roy, *Churchill* (London: Macmillan), 2001.

Kee, Robert, *Ireland: A History* (London: Abacus), 2003.

Lewis, C. S., *A Grief Observed* (London: Faber and Faber), 1966.

McGowan, Joe, *In the Shadow of Benbulben* (Aeolus Publications), 1993.

McGowan, Joe, *Inishmurray: Island Voices* (Aeolus Publications), 2004.

Mallie, Eamonn and McKittrick, David, *The Fight for Peace* (London: Heinemann), 1997.

McKittrick, David, Seamus Kelters, Brian Feeney, Chris Thornton and David McVea, *Lost Lives* (Edinburgh: Mainstream Publishing), 2004.

Moloney, Ed, *A Secret History of the IRA* (London: Penguin Books), 2003.

Morgan, Janet, *Edwina Mountbatten: A Life of Her Own* (London: HarperCollins), 1991.

Mountbatten, Pamela, *India Remembered* (London: Pavilion), 2007.

O'Callaghan, Sean, *The Informer* (London: Corgi), 1999.

O'Connor, Niamh, *Cracking Crime* (Dublin: The O'Brien Press), 2001.

O'Neill, Joseph, *Blood-Dark Track – A Family History* (London: Granta Books), 2000.

Pantridge, J. Frank, *An Unquiet Life* (Hillsborough, Northern Ireland: Pantridge Foundation), 1995.

Powell, Jonathan, *Great Hatred, Little Room: Making Peace in Northern Ireland* (London: The Bodley Head), 2008.

Reddy, Tom, *Murder Will Out* (Dublin: Gill and Macmillan), 1990.

Woodward, Joan, *The Lone Twin: Understanding Twin Bereavement and Loss* (London: Free Association Press), 1998.

Yeats, W. B., *The Collected Poems of W. B. Yeats* (Ware, Hertfordshire: Wordsworth Editions), 2000.

Ziegler, Philip, *From Shore to Shore: The Diaries of Earl Mountbatten of Burma, 1953–1979* (London: Collins), 1989.

Ziegler, Philip, *Mountbatten: The Official Biography* (London: Collins), 1985.

INDEX